I0003345

BOCP - QUICK REFERENCE STUDY GUIDE

930 Questions - Business Objects Certified Professional for Crystal Reports

by
Antonia Iroko

AuthorHouse™ UK Ltd.
500 Avebury Boulevard
Central Milton Keynes, MK9 2BE
www.authorhouse.co.uk
Phone: 08001974150

First published by AuthorHouse 1/07/2008

ISBN: 978-1-4343-2059-9 (sc)

Printed in the United States of America
Bloomington, Indiana

This book is printed on acid-free paper.

Acknowledgements

My appreciation goes to all those who supported me, both friends and family from the beginning to the end of writing this study guide and the E-books over the last three years. I would especially like to thank Ade Adeoshun for proof reading my work and extracting all my images, thank you very much, a special thanks also goes to Bijith Amat, Philip Gevaux and Fumilayo Dipeolu for proof reading several chapters and to my all other colleagues and friends who volunteered to proof read my book taking time out of their busy schedules, but most importantly I would like to thank God. A special thanks goes to my mum for all her encouragement and support, thank you Mum

Credits

Author
Antonia Iroko

Technical Reviewer
Ade Adeoshun
Philip Gevaux

Proof Readers:
Fumilayo Dipeolu
Bijith Amat

Trademark Acknowledgements

Limits of Liability and Disclaimer of Warranty

Summary of Contents

Contents

Introduction

Welcome to BOCP 900 plus Practice Questions for Crystal Reports. Each chapter covers questions on the various sections of Crystal Reports utilization, functionality and development.

Crystal Reports is an advanced reporting software package, which provides users with exceptional reporting functionalities. Crystal Reports provides outstanding reporting functionalities, which is utilized by many companies to achieve their reporting requirements. The study guide questions will test the reader's knowledge of the functionalities within Crystal Reports and how these functions can be applied to various aspects of reporting to achieve specific goals.

Who Should Use This Book

The study guide questions are aimed at Crystal Reports Designers and Developers preparing for the certification exams (BOCP), it also acts a knowledgebase for Beginners to Advanced users. Readers are advised to use this study guide in conjunction with hands-on-practice and classroom based courses, this will give readers a greater insight into the functionalities of Crystal Reports.

Topics Covered in This Book

There are 17 chapters in this book, which include a total of 930 questions. The chapters are organized as follows:

Chapter 1 Report Settings and Options: In this chapter questions relating to report settings are covered, this consists of subject matter relating to Report Options and Options settings which can be applied to reports prior to creation or during the report development stage. This chapter consists of **71 questions**. At the end of this chapter the user will have been tested on the following report settings: Layout, Database, Format Editor, Reporting, Fields, Dependency Checker and Field settings.

Chapter 2 Creating a Datasource: In this chapter questions relating to the creation of data sources are covered. Creating a data source is the first stage of report development and must be implemented before designing a report. There are several datasource connections available including an ODBC or DSN connection. The main sample databases used to derive questions for this section are Microsoft Access and Microsoft SQL Server. This chapter consists of **17 questions**.
Chapter 3 The Database Expert: Questions in this chapter relate to the utilization of the Database Expert to create links between database tables, subject matter covered in this chapter includes links and joins types, setting a database location, mapping fields and creating new data sources. There are **67 questions** in this chapter.

Chapter 4 Creating and Working with Formulas: This chapter covers questions on the Functions and Operators of within the Formula Workshop. Areas covered include date formulas, number formulas, variables, arrays, strings, financial functions, processing reports and report alerts. There are a total of **213 questions** in this chapter.

Chapter 5 Report Formatting: Questions in this chapter cover the following topics: the Section Expert, Highlighting Expert, Format Painter, Format Editor and report design format. There are **83 questions** in this chapter.

Chapter 6 Using the Select Expert: Consists of **36 questions** based on the functionalities which exist within the Select Expert for record and group selection.

Chapter 7 Creating Parameters: This chapter covers questions on the application and utilization of parameters. This includes parameter types and settings. This chapter will also test your knowledge of creating and using Dynamic and Static parameters. There are **38 questions** in this chapter.

Chapter 8 Creating Report Groups: This chapter covers questions on report group creation, dynamic group creation and group sorting. There are **38 questions** in this chapter.

Chapter 9 Creating Charts: This chapter covers questions on chart creating, chart types and chart type selection for specific data types. There are **44 questions** in this chapter.

Chapter 10 Creating Cross-Tab: This chapter covers questions on Cross-Tabs and its utilization to present data in a tabular format. There are **26 questions** in this chapter.

Chapter 11 Creating Custom Functions: This chapter covers questions on creating Custom Functions; areas covered include the utilization of Custom Functions via the Extractor and Editor. There are **34 questions** in this chapter.

Chapter 12 Previewing and Exporting Reports: This chapter covers questions on the following topics, report previewing, saving and exporting options. There are **35 questions** in this chapter.

Chapter 13 Creating Subreports: This chapter covers questions on Subreports, covering linked and unlinked Subreports, On-Demand Subreports and the integration of variables within Subreports. There are **43 questions** in this chapter.

Chapter 14 Using the Repository: This chapter covers questions on the Repository and its functionality in conjunction with SQL Commands and Custom Functions. There are **29 questions** in this chapter.

Chapter 15 Business Views: This chapter covers questions on Business Views and their logical data structural formation. Business Views present data in a logical business format giving users the flexibility to create reports from various datasources; you will gain knowledge of creating Business Views and arranging data fields into a logical business formats for reporting. There are **108 questions** in this chapter.

Chapter 16 Report Management: This chapter covers questions on the Field Explorer, Report Explorer, Workbench, Dependency Checker and Publishing a Report to Business Objects Enterprise. There are **29 questions** in this chapter

Chapter 17 Building Reports: This chapter is a bonus chapter which includes basic report creation lessons. There are **19 questions** covered in this section.

Structure of Study Guide Questions

All study guide questions are multiple-choice questions; answers are either single or multiple. Questions which require multiple answers will be indicated with ***(Multiple Answers)*** after the question. Some questions have been created using sample data; readers can create their own sample data which can be used to create similar scenarios when utilizing hands-on-practice while answering study guide questions.

Software Version

Crystal Reports XI R_2

Exam Required to Obtain Certification

Business Objects Certified Professional for Crystal Reports consists of two exams, RDCR201 and RDCR301. The certification exam pass criteria is outlined in the table below, refer to the Business Objects website for up to date exam requirements: http://www.businessobjects.com/services/training/certification.asp

Exam	Number of Questions in Exam	Completion Time	Pass Mark
RDCR201	45	90	65
RDCR301	40	80	70

Exam Syllabus

Each exam certification covers the following topics. Please refer to the Business Objects website for regular exam content updates:
http://www.businessobjects.com/services/training/certification.asp

RDCR201

Topics	Competencies Covered
Create a Basic Report	➢ Connect To A Data Sources ➢ Add Tables Within The Database Expert ➢ The Design Environment ➢ Working With Objects ➢ Previewing And Saving A Report ➢ Record Selection ➢ Data Organization
Format a Report	➢ Format Objects ➢ Adding Graphical Elements ➢ Insert Fields ➢ Section Formatting ➢ Chart Creation ➢ Creating Report Templates
Formulas	➢ Create Formula ➢ Functions And Operators ➢ Control Structures ➢ Variables ➢ Arrays
Manage Reports	➢ Exporting A Report ➢ Workbench ➢ Repository
Creating an Advanced Report	➢ Creating Parameters ➢ Dynamic Cascading Prompts ➢ Cross-Tabs ➢ Running Total ➢ Report Alerts ➢ TopN

RDCR301

Topics	Competencies Covered
Report Processing Techniques	➢ Understanding Of Multi-Pass Report Process ➢ Database Expert ➢ Links And Joins ➢ Configuring Datasources ➢ Update Reports With Database Changes ➢ Data Processing On Server ➢ Report Validation
Using Subreports	➢ Definition Of A Subreport ➢ Unlinked Subreports ➢ Linked Subreports ➢ On-Demand Reports ➢ Using Shared Variables Within Subreports ➢ Using Shared Array Values Within Subreports ➢ Link Un-linkable Data
Create complex formulas	➢ Evaluation Time Function ➢ Dynamic Arrays ➢ Print State Function ➢ Loop Control Structures And Arrays ➢ Custom Functions ➢ Hyperlink Reports

Booking Your Exam

Pearson VUE is the Authorized Testing Agency for booking the BOCP exams. Exams can be booked via http://www.vue.com/

Chapter 1 - Report Settings and Options

Creating a new report involves the application of appropriate settings for the type of report being created. This section covers questions on the range of report types available when creating a new report and the standard functions of each report type. You will also be tested on report settings using Report Options, Options Tab, Document Properties and Summary Information.

Key Areas:

- **Report Options**
- **Options**
- **Report Creation Wizard**
- **Working With the Document Properties**
- **Setting Report Options and Options**
- **The Design Environment**

Q1: Which type of database is the sample database that installs with Crystal Reports?

A. Paradox DB
B. SQL Server
C. Oracle
D. Microsoft Access
E. Sybase

Q2: When you select File – New and Standard Report. Which one of following dialog boxes will appear?

A. Database Expert Wizard

B. File Expert Wizard

C. Report Creation Wizard

D. SQL Database Creation Wizard

E. Standard Report Creation Wizard Dialog box

Q3. Which of the following options will appear when you select File – New from the Menu Bar? *(Multiple Answers)*

A. Standard Report

B. Blank Report

C. Cross –Tab Report

D. Mailing Label Report

E. OLAP Cube Report

F. Subreport

G. Main Report

Q4: You select File – New and Blank Report. Which one of following dialog boxes will appear?

A. Database Expert
B. File Expert
C. Report Creation Wizard
D. SQL Database
E. Standard Report Creation Wizard

Q5: You select File – New – and Cross-Tab Report. Which of following dialog boxes will appear?

A. Database Expert
B. File Expert
C. Report Creation Wizard
D. SQL Database
E. Cross-Tab Report Creation Wizard

Q6: You select File – New and Mailing labels Report. Which of following dialog boxes will appear?

A. Database Expert
B. File Expert
C. Report Creation Wizard
D. SQL Database
E. Mailing labels Report Creation Wizard

Q7: You are creating a Standard Report. Which of the following are located under the Available Data Sources? *(Multiple Answers)*

A. Current Connections
B. Favorites
C. History
D. Create New Connection
E. Repository

Q8: You have created a connection to the database and selected two tables from the Available Data Sources using the arrow (>). Which section will the tables appear under?

A. Available Tables

B. Tables Select

C. Selected Data Tables

D. Selected Tables

E. Table Wizard

Q9: You have selected one table from the Available Data Sources and clicked next. Which of the following sections will appear within the Standard Report Creation Wizard dialog box?

A. The Links section

B. Available Fields and Fields to Display

C. Available Data Sources

D. Available Files

E. Grouping

Q10: You have selected two tables from the Available Data Sources. Which of the following sections will appear when you click next?

A. Available Fields and Fields to Display

B. Available Data Sources

C. Available Files

D. Grouping

E. Link

Q11: Which one of the following cannot be performed within the Standard Report Creation Wizard?

A. Select Data Sources

B. Select Tables

C. Select Fields

D. Summarize fields

E. Insert Subreport

F. TopN

G. Bottom

H. Charts

I. Filter Fields

J. Select Template

Q12: Which of the following can be performed within the Standard Report Creation Wizard? *(Multiple Answers)*

A. Create Links
B. Filter Fields
C. Create Groups
D. Sort fields
E. Select Report Template

Q13: Which of the following can be performed within the Mailing labels Report Creation Wizard? *(Multiple Answers)*

A. Linking
B. Selection of Tables
C. Selection of Fields
D. Filtering
E. Select Mailing Label Types

Q14: You are creating a Mailing Label report. Which of the following are adjustments that can be made to the labels? *(Multiple Answers)*

A. Label Size
B. Label Structure
C. Page Margins
D. Printing Direction
E. Gaps between Labels
F. Gaps between Stamps

Q15: Which of the following Printing Directions are available under the printing direction section of the Mailing Labels Report Creation Wizard. ? *(Multiple Answers)*

A. Across Then Down
B. Down Then Up
C. Up Then Down
D. Down Then Across

Q16: Which of the following margins can be adjusted under the Page Margins section of the Mailing Labels Report Creation Wizard. ? *(Multiple Answers)*

A. Top
B. Left
C. Right
D. Bottom
E. Forward
F. Backward

Q17: Which of the following settings are available when setting the gaps between Labels? *(Multiple Answers)*

A. Horizontal
B. Vertical
C. Bilateral
D. Unilateral

Q18: Your have created a report with an alert and each time you refresh the report the alert report dialog box appears, how can you turn off the dialog box?

A. Select File – Report Options and uncheck Display Alerts on Refresh
B. Select File – Report Options and check Display Alerts on Refresh
C. Select Reports –Alerts and uncheck Display Alerts on Refresh
D. Select Reports –Alerts and check Display Alerts on Refresh

Q19: You drill-down within your report and notice the header does not appear on the next page, what can you do?

A. Select File – Format Options and check Show All Headers On Drill Down
B. Right-click the Details Section and select Section Expert and check Show All Headers On Drill Down
C. Select Report - Group Expert and check Show All Headers On Drill Down
D. Select File – Report Options and check Show All Headers On Drill Down

Q20: How would you avoid null values from appearing on all reports created via your desktop? *(Multiple Answers)*

A. Choose Report | Options | Reporting Tab and check Convert Database NULL Values to Default
B. Choose Format | Options | Reporting Tab and check Convert Database NULL Values to Default
C. Choose View | Options | Reporting Tab and check Convert Database NULL Values to Default
D. Choose Report | Reporting Options | Reporting Tab and check Convert Database NULL Values to Default
E. Choose File | Options | Reporting Tab and check Convert Database NULL Values to Default
F. Choose File | Options | Reporting Tab and check Convert Other NULL Values To Default

Q21: Which of the following Advanced Options can be set within the Options section of the Database Tab? *(Multiple Answers)*

A. Use indexes or Server speed
B. Perform Grouping on server
C. Database Server is Case Insensitive
D. Select Distinct Data for browsing
E. Reset the data source
F. Perform Query Asynchronously
G. Verify On First Refresh
H. Verify Stored Procedures On First Refresh
I. Verify When Database Driver Upgraded
J. Automatic Smart Linking

Q22: You have just opened a report and you notice there is no Group Tree. Which of the following should be implemented to retrieve the Group Tree?

A. Edit – Group – and tick the Create Group Tree from the drop-down menu
B. File – Report Options – and check the Create Group Tree checkbox
C. View – Group – and tick the Create Group Tree from the drop-down menu
D. Report– Group – and tick the Create Group Tree from the drop-down menu

Q23: Which of the following options can you set within the Options section of the Database Tab? *(Multiple Answers)*

A. Perform query asynchronously
B. Verify first refresh
C. Reset the data source
D. Verify stored procedure on first refresh
E. Verify when Database driver upgraded

Q24: You have created a report, which you have saved with data, however, each time you open the report, the report opens with no data. How can you rectify this problem?

A. Choose File | reporting options | select the reporting tab and uncheck the box with Discard Saved Data When Loading Reports
B. Choose database | options | select the reporting tab and uncheck the box with Discard Saved Data When Loading Reports
C. Choose format | options | select the reporting tab and uncheck the box with Discard Saved Data When Loading Reports
D. Choose report | options | select the reporting tab and uncheck the box with Discard Saved Data When Loading Reports
E. Choose File | options | select the reporting tab and uncheck the box with Discard Saved Data On Open

Q25: You want to turn the 'perform grouping on server' option ON for all reports. Which of the following applies?

A. Choose File \ Report Options \ and check the Perform Grouping On Server checkbox
B. Choose File \ Options \ Database Tab \and check the Perform Grouping On Server checkbox
C. Choose File \ Edit\ Options \ and check the Perform Grouping On Server checkbox
D. Choose File \ Database\ Options \ and check the Perform Grouping On Server checkbox
E. Choose Database \Perform Grouping On Server

Q26: Which of the following settings apply to both Design View and Preview? *(Multiple Answers)*

A. Rulers and Guidelines
B. Tool Tips and Section Names
C. Tool Tips and Grid
D. Short Section Names and Show Hidden Sections
E. Section Names
F. Show Hidden Sections and Page Breaks in Wide Pages

Q27: You have opened a report in preview mode, and you notice the section names, i.e. Group Header #1 is displayed as 'GH 1' and the Details Section is displayed as 'D'. Which one of the following will retrieve the names?

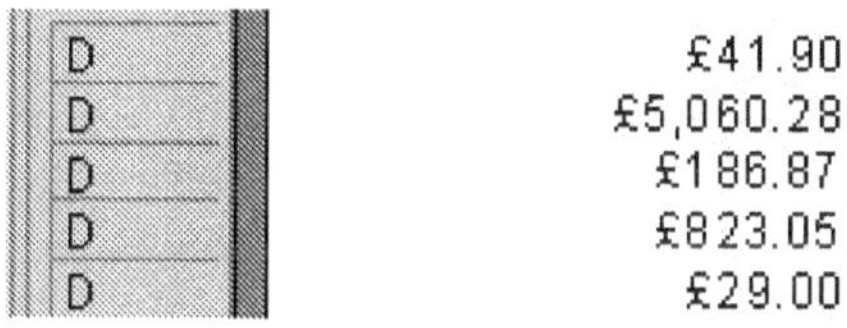

D £41.90
D £5,060.28
D £186.87
D £823.05
D £29.00

£41.90
£5,060.28
£186.87
£823.05
£29.00

A. File – Options –Layout Tab –Preview Section and Short Section Names
B. File – Options –Layout Tab –Preview Section and check Section Names
C. File – Report Options –Layout Tab –Preview Section and Short Section Names
D. File – Report Options –Layout Tab –Preview Section and check Section Names

Q28: You are in Preview Mode and you notice a Grid behind your text, you would like to remove these. Which of the following apply?

A. Select View and uncheck Grids
B. Select Report and uncheck Grids
C. Select File and uncheck Grids
D. Select File, Options, Layout Tab, under Preview uncheck Grid
E. Select File, Report Options, Layout Tab, under Preview uncheck Grid

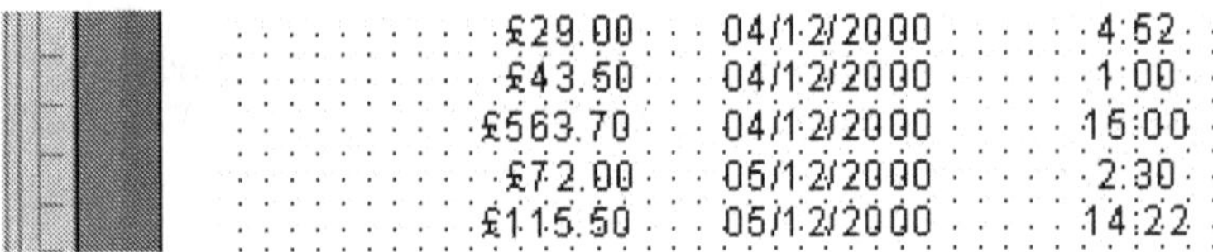

Q29: Which of the following settings allows the user to set default setting for all reports created on their desktop?

A. Report Options
B. Options

Q30: Which of the following will retrieve a descriptive name for report sections in design mode?

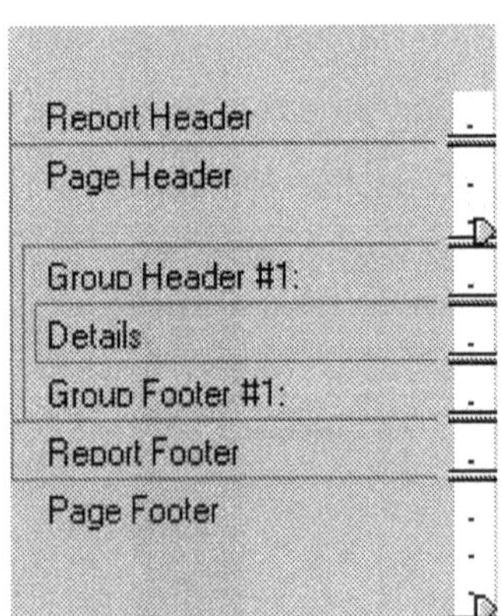

A. File – Report Options –Layout Tab - Design View section and check Short Section Names
B. File – Report Options – Layout Tab - Design View section and check Section Names
C. File – Options – Layout Tab - Design View section and check Short Section Names
D. File – Options – Layout Tab - Design View section and check Section Names

Q31: Which of the following settings is unique to the Design View only?

A. Rulers and Guidelines
B. Tool Tips and Section Names
C. Tool Tips and Grid
D. Short Section Names and Show Hidden Sections
E. Section Names
F. Show Hidden Sections and Page Breaks in Wide Pages

Q32: Which of the following settings is unique to the Preview only? *(Multiple Answers)*

A. Rulers and Guidelines
B. Tool Tips and Section Names
C. Tool Tips and Grid
D. Short Section Names and Show Hidden Sections
E. Section Names
F. Show Hidden Sections
G. Page Breaks in Wide Pages

Q33: Which of the following settings allows the user to set default settings for the current report only?

A. Report Options
B. Options

Q34: You notice fields placed in the Details sections in design mode appears as XXXXX when previewed and not as logical field names. Which of the following must be implemented to rectify this?

A. Choose File | Report Options | under Field Options turn on the show field names check box in the field options section of the Layout tab
B. Choose File | Options | Layout tab |under Field Options section check the Show Field Names checkbox
C. Choose File | Options | Layout Tab| under Field Options turn on the show field names check box in the field options section of the Layout tab
D. Choose File |Report Options | under Field Options turn off the show field names check box in the field options section of the Layout tab

Page Header	Amount Paid	Discount	Date
Group Header #1:	XXXXXXXXXXXXXXXXXXXXXXXXXXXXXXXXXXXXXXXXX		
Details	(£55,555.56)	01/03/1999	13:23
Group Footer #1:			

Q35: You do not want the field headings of text placed in the Details Section to appear. What should you do?

A. Choose Format | Options | Layout Tab | uncheck Insert Detail Field headings
B. Choose File | Options | Layout Tab | uncheck Insert Detail Field headings within the Field options section
C. Choose Report | Options | Layout Tab | uncheck Insert Detail Field headings
D. Choose View | Options | Layout Tab | uncheck Insert Detail Field headings

Q36: When you insert a group, the group name does not appear on the report. Which of the following should you change to prevent this from happening?

A. Select File – Report Options – Layout Tab – and check the Insert Group Name with Group checkbox
B. Select File – Options – Layout Tab – and check the Insert Group Name with Group checkbox
C. Select File – Report Options – Reporting Tab – and check the Insert Group Name with Group checkbox
D. Select File – Options – Reporting Tab – and check the Insert Group Name with Group checkbox

Q37: Each time you open the finance report, it opens as a 46% page size, and you want it to appear as a 100% page size. Which of the following apply?

A. File – Options – Change Preview Page Starts with Fit Page to Full Size
B. File – Options – Layout Tab and check Pages Start with Full Size (100%)
C. File – Report Options – Change Preview Page Starts with Fit Page to Full Width
D. File – Options – Change Preview Page Starts with Fit Page to Full Width

Q38: You notice that your database driver is CASE sensitive, what should you do to change it? *(Multiple Answers)*

A. From the Menu Bar, select File | options | Database Tab | and check the database server is case-insensitive
B. From the Menu Bar, select File | report options and check the database server is case-insensitive
C. Database Expert - Right-click Database Connection – Report Options and uncheck database server is case-insensitive
D. Database Expert - Right-click Database Connection – Database Link Options and uncheck database server is case-insensitive

Q39: You want to view only tables owned by Antonia when creating any reports. Which of the following apply? *(Multiple Answers)*

A. Select File, Report Options, Database Tab, under the Data Explorer section enter Antoni% under Owner LIKE: (%,_)
B. Select File, Options, Database Tab, under the Data Explorer section enter Antoni% under Owner LIKE: (%,_)
C. Select Database, Database Expert from the Menu Bar within your connection, right-click tables, select options from the drop-down menu, under the Data Explorer section enter Antoni% under Owner LIKE: (%,_)
D. Select Report, Database Expert from the Menu Bar within your connection, right-click tables, select options from the drop-down menu, under the Data Explorer section enter Antoni% under Owner LIKE: (%,_)

Q40: You have applied a Tool Tip to your report, however each time you place the cursor over the text, in preview mode, the tool-tip does not appear. Which of the following will resolve the issue?

A. File –Report Options –Layout Tab – and check the Tool Tips check box under preview
B. View –Layout Tab – and check the Tool Tips check box under preview
C. Format –Options –Layout Tab – and check the Tool Tips check box under preview
D. File –Options –Layout Tab – and check the Tool Tips check box under preview

Q41: There are several tables in the database that you are creating your reports from. You are currently working with tables from the Finance department. Which start with Fin_. You want to see only these tables when creating any report. *(Multiple Answers)*

A. Select File, Report Options, Database Tab, under the Data Explorer section enter Antoni% under Table name LIKE: (%,_)
B. Select File, Options, Database Tab, under the Data Explorer section enter Antoni% under Table name LIKE: (%,_)
C. Select Database, Database Expert from the Menu Bar within your connection, right-click tables, select options from the drop-down menu, under the Data Explorer section enter Antoni% under Table name LIKE: (%,_)
D. Select Report, Database Expert from the Menu Bar within your connection, right-click tables, select options from the drop-down menu, under the Data Explorer section enter Antoni% under Table name LIKE: (%,_)

Q42: You want to ensure all stored procedure used for report creation are being verified. What should you do?

A. Choose File \ Options within the Advanced Options check the verify stored procedure on 1st refresh
B. Choose File \ Report Expert within the Advanced Options check the verify stored procedure on 1st refresh
C. Choose View \ Report Options within the Advanced Options check the verify stored procedure on 1st refresh
D. Choose File \ Options\Database Tab\ Advanced Options\ check the verify stored procedure on First refresh

Q43: You want to view only the System Tables within the Database Expert, What should you do?

A. Right click the database from the Database Expert select options from the drop-down menu, within the Data Explorer section, uncheck table, Stored Procedures, Synonyms and views and check the System Tables' checkbox.
B. Right click the database from the SQL Expert Data Explorer select options, from the drop-down menu, uncheck table, Stored Procedures, Synonyms and views and check the systems tables checkbox
C. Right click the database from the Database Expert Data Explorer select report options, from the drop-down menu, uncheck table, Stored Procedures, Synonyms and views and check the System Tables' checkbox.
D. Right click the database from the SQL Expert Data Explorer select report options, from the drop-down menu, uncheck table, Stored Procedures, Synonyms and views and check the systems tables checkbox

Q44: You want to list tables and fields by name, as they appear in the database. Which of the following methods should you implement?

A. Select File, Report Options, and Database Tab, then select Show Name
B. Select File, Smart Tag Options, and Database Tab, then select Show Name
C. Select File – Options – Database Tab – under the Tables and Fields section, select the Show Name Button
D. Select File, Report Expert Options, and Database Tab, then select Show Name

Q45: Which of the following field data types can be set within the Options Fields Tab? *(Multiple Answers)*

A. String
B. Number
C. Text
D. Field
E. Currency
F. Date
G. Time
H. Date and Time
I. Boolean

Q46: Which of the following Report-Checking Options are available via the Dependency Checker Options Tab? *(Multiple Answers)*

A. Compile statistics
B. Compile Formulas
C. Compile Custom Functions
D. Validate Files
E. Validate Report
F. Validate Hyperlinks URLs
G. Verify Database
H. Compile SQL Expressions

Q47: Which of the following Multi-Report Checking Options are available via the Dependency Checker Options Tab ? *(Multiple Answers)*

A. Check Files
B. Check Repository Custom Functions
C. Check Repository objects (text and bitmap)
D. Check reports part Hyperlinks
E. Check sub files which are imported
F. Check Subreports which are re-imported on open
G. Check Subreports which are re-imported on close

Q48: You have hidden the details section in your report. However, in the design view, this section still shows, with a grey section behind it. How do you completely hide this section in the design view?

A. From the Section Expert, select detail section and tick hide drill-down OK
B. From the Select Expert, select detail section and tick hide drill-down OK
C. Select File | Options | select the Layout Tab and uncheck Show Hidden Sections
D. From the report expert, select detail section and tick hide drill-down OK
E. Select File | Options | select the Layout Tab and check Show Hidden Sections

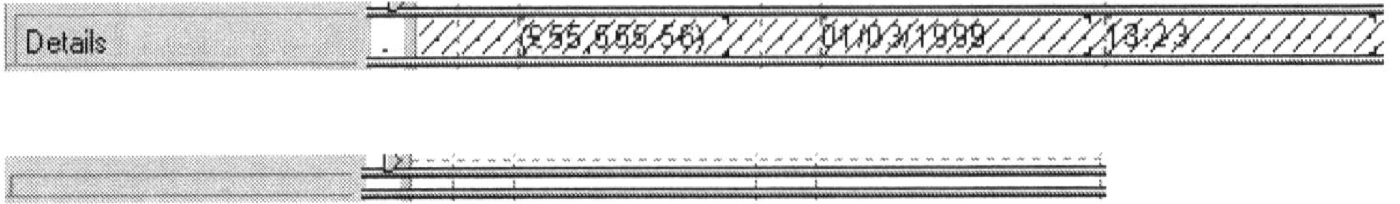

Q49: You are in Preview Mode and you notice the Guidelines, Rulers, ToolTips, Section Names and Page Breaks appear, what can you do to remove these?

A. Select View and uncheck guidelines, Rulers, ToolTips, section names and page breaks appear
B. Select Report and uncheck guidelines, Rulers, ToolTips, section names and page breaks appear
C. Select File and uncheck guidelines, Rulers, ToolTips, section names and page breaks appear
D. Select File, Options, Layout Tab, under Preview uncheck guidelines, Rulers, ToolTips, section names and page breaks appear
E. Select File, Report Options, Layout Tab, under Preview uncheck guidelines, Rulers, ToolTips, section names and page breaks appear

Q50: You have received several calls from users who cannot see the Stored Procedures in the database, when trying to create reports via the ODBC data source connection, what check should the users implement? *(Multiple Answers)*

A. Select File – Options – Database Tab – from the Data Explorer section – check the Stored Procedure checkbox
B. Right-click the field within the Database Expert and select options from the drop-down list and check the show Stored Procedures checkbox
C. Right-click View Expert within the Database Expert and select options from the drop-down list and check the show Stored Procedures checkbox
D. Right-click the database within the Database Expert, select options from the drop-down list and check the show Stored Procedures checkbox under Data Explorer

Q51: You notice the tool tip appears each time you place the cursor over a field in your report, you want to turn off the Tool Tip. Which of the following apply?

A. File – Options – Layout Tab – uncheck Tool Tips checkbox in the preview section
B. File – Options – Reporting Tab – check Tool Tips checkbox in the preview section
C. File – Report Options – Reporting Tab – check Tool Tips checkbox in the preview section
D. File – Options – Formula Editor Tab – check Tool Tips checkbox in the preview section

Q52: When creating a formula, the comments appear as green (Default Setting) how can you customize the color?

A. File, Report Options, Formula Editor tab, highlight comment under color element section and change foreground to required color
B. File, Report Options, Formula Editor tab, highlight comment under the Default Formula Languages section and change foreground to required color
C. File, Options, Formula Editor tab, highlight comment under the color element section and change foreground to required color
D. File, Options, Formula Editor tab, highlight comment under the Default Formula Languages section and change foreground to required color

Q53: Which option settings apply to all reports created via the desktop they are set on?

A. Report Options
B. Options
C. File Options
D. Report Settings

Q54: Which of the following formula elements can you change? *(Multiple Answers)*

A. Comment
B. Text Selection
C. Formula
D. Custom Function
E. Report Data Type
F. Keyword
G. Text

Q55: Where can you set the Grid size for your reports?
A. File – Options – Fields Tab – under the Grid options section, set Grid Size
B. File – Options – Layout Tab – under the Grid options section, Grid Size
C. File – Options – Font Tab – under the Grid options section, Grid Size
D. File – Options – Reporting Tab – under the Grid options section, Grid Size

Q56: You want to ensure all fields are set to the same font size within your report. Which of the following applies?

A. File – Report Options – Fields Tab, select field type tab within the field format section and format field type as required
B. File – Options – Font Tab and format field types as required
C. Report -Options – Fields Tab, select field type tab and format field type as required
D. Database – Report Options – Fields Tab, select field type tab and format field type as required

Q57: Where can you switch on the 'perform grouping on server' option? *(Multiple Answers)*

A. Choose database from the Menu Bar and select perform grouping on server
B. Choose File | Report Options | check the Perform Grouping On Server checkbox
C. Choose File | Options | select the Database Tab and check the Perform Grouping On Server checkbox
D. Choose File | Report | check the Perform Grouping On Server checkbox

Q58: You want to ensure that each time the main report is opened the Subreport is re-imported. What should you do?

A. Select |File| report options| reporting TAB| check the re-import Subreport when opening reports.
B. Select |File| Edit options | reporting TAB | check the re-import Subreport when opening reports.
C. Select |Database options | reporting TAB | check the re-import Subreport when opening reports.
D. File | Options | Reporting TAB and check the re-import Subreport on Open.

Q59: You want to add the following information to your report: Author, Title, Keywords, Title, Subject, and Comments. Which of the following apply?

A. File | Report Options | as Enter details required
B. File | Options |as Enter details required
C. Report | Report Options |as Enter details required
D. File | Summary Info | as Enter details required

Q60: You have added tables to your report via the Database Expert. The tables are not linked automatically. Which of the following will activate automatic linking?

A. File - Report Options – check the Automatic Link checkbox
B. File – Options – Check the Automatic Link checkbox
C. File –Report Options – Database Tab – Advanced Options and check the Automatic Smart Linking checkbox
D. File –Options – Database Tab – Advanced Options sections and check the Automatic Smart Linking checkbox

Q61: You want to check the following attributes: the total time taken to edit a report; the last person to save the report; the revision number; last printed; created; and saved. Where can this information be found?

A. File |Summary Info | Summary Tab
B. File | Summary Info | Info Tab
C. File | Summary Info | Statistics Tab
D. File |Summary Info | Edit Tab

Q62: You have created a template report, which you want to make available via the template directory. Which of the following apply?

A. Choose Report | Summary Info | Check the Save Preview Picture checkbox
B. Choose File | Summary Info | Check the Save Preview Picture checkbox
C. Choose File | Report Options | Summary Info | Check the Save Preview Picture checkbox
D. Choose File | Options | Check the Save Preview Picture checkbox

Q63: You do not want the Group Tree to appear in any report created via your desktop. Which of the following apply?

A. File – Options – Fields Tab – uncheck Display Group Tree
B. File – Report Options – Fields Tab – uncheck Display Group Tree
C. File – Options – Layout Tab – uncheck Display Group Tree
D. File – Report Options – Layout Tab – uncheck Display Group Tree
E. File – Options – Layout Tab – check Display Group Tree

Q64: The tables in the Field Explorer appear as follows:

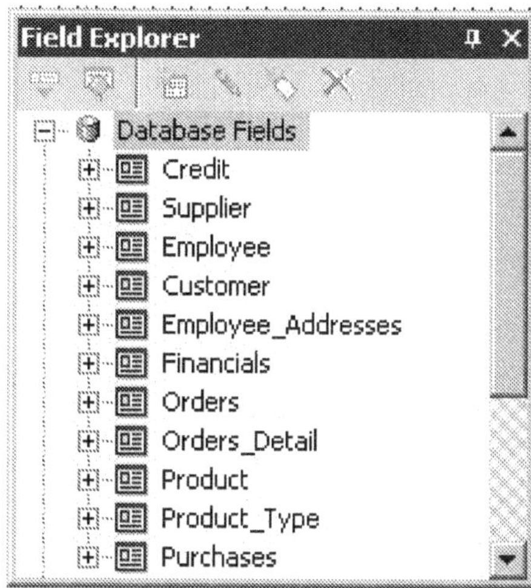

You want to arrange tables in alphabetical order. Which of the following apply? *(Multiple Answers)*

A. File - Report Options - and check the Sort Tables Alphabetically checkbox

B. File – Options – Database Tab- and check the Sort Tables Alphabetically checkbox

C. Database – Database Expert - Right-click the database and select options from the drop-down list and check the Sort Tables Alphabetically checkbox

D. File - Options - and check the Sort Tables Alphabetically checkbox

Q65. You want to prevent users from modifying the sales report you have created. Which of the following apply?

A. Select File – Options and check the Save Lock Report Design checkbox, enter new password and confirm password and click OK – OK

B. Select File – Report Options and check the Save Lock Report Design checkbox, enter new password and confirm password and click OK – OK

C. Select Report – Report Options and check the Save Lock Report Design checkbox, enter new password and confirm password and click OK – OK

D. Select Database – Report Options and check the Save Lock Report Design checkbox, enter new password and confirm password and click OK – OK

Q66. Using Save As can modify a locked report?

A. True

B. False

Q67: You want to unlock your report giving report designers permission to change the report design. How would you unlock the report?

A. Select File – Options –and uncheck the Save Lock Report Design, you will be prompted for a New Password, enter your password, Confirm Password and click ok
B. Select Report – Report Options –and tick the Save Lock Report Design, you will be prompted for a New Password, enter your password, Confirm Password and click ok
C. Select File – Report Options –and uncheck the Save Lock Report Design, you will be prompted your Password, enter your password and click ok and save
D. Select Report - Options –and tick the Save Lock Report Design, you will be prompted for a New Password, enter your password, Confirm Password and click ok

Q68: You have checked the following checkboxes 'Perform Grouping on Server' and 'Use Indexes Or Server For Speed' within the Report Options section. Which of the following will be automatically greyed out?

A. Database Server is Case-Insensitive
B. Perform Query Asynchronously
C. Convert Other NULL Values to Default
D. Convert Database NULL Values to Default

Q69: You try to format fields within your report, all formatting options are greyed out and you cannot move any fields within your report. Which of the following Report Options has been set?

A. Save Lock Report Design
B. Read-only

Q70: You want your report to be saved after every two minutes. Which of the following settings apply?

A. File – Report Options - check the Autosave Reports After checkbox and enter 2 minutes
B. File – Options - check the Autosave Reports After checkbox and enter 2 minutes
C. File – Options - Reporting Tab - and check the Autosave Reports After checkbox and enter 2 minutes
D. File – Report Options - Reporting Tab and check the Autosave Reports After checkbox and enter 2 minutes

Q71: You want to ensure all Repository based objects within your reports are updated when the report is opened. Which of the following settings apply?

A. File – Report Options - under Enterprise Settings check the Update Enterprise Report Properties on Save
B. File - Options - under Enterprise Settings check the Update Enterprise Report Properties on Save
C. File – Options - Database Tab - under Enterprise Settings check the Update Enterprise Report Properties on Save
D. File – Options - Reporting Tab - under Enterprise Settings check the Update Connected Repository Objects on Open checkbox

Chapter 2 -Creating a Datasource

Chapter 2 covers questions on setting up a data source connection; this is the starting point when creating a report.

Key Areas:

- **New Connnection**
- **Administrative Tools**
- **Database Drivers**
- **ODBC**
- **DSN**

Q1. The Business Objects Enterprise Administrator has provided you with the details of the ODBC connection on the server, i.e. name of connection, database name, user name and password; you want to configure an ODBC locally for report design and future deployment, (system used is Windows XP) which of the following apply?

A. Start – Control Panel – Administrative Tools - click the data sources ODBC connection icon, select the System DSN Tab and click configure, enter the ODBC name provided, a description of your choice and the name of the database and click next, enter your authentication details and click next, a drop list of all available databases will appear, select the required database and click next and next and test data source

B. Start – Control Panel – Administrative Tools - click the data sources ODBC connection icon, select the User DSN tab and click configure, enter the ODBC name provided, a description of your choice and the name of the database and click next, enter your authentication details and click next, a drop list of all available databases will appear, select the required database and click next and next and test data source

C. Start – Control Panel – Administrative Tools - click the data sources ODBC connection icon, select the DSN tab and click configure, enter the ODBC name provided, a description of your choice and the name of the database and click next, enter your authentication details and click next, a drop list of all available databases will appear, select the required database and click next and next and test data source

D. Start – Control Panel – Administrative Tools - click the data sources ODBC connection icon, select the Report DSN tab and click configure, enter the ODBC name provided, a description of your choice and the name of the database and click next, enter your authentication details and click next, a drop list of all available databases will appear, select the required database and click next and next and test data source

Q2. You want to check the current version of the SQL Server ODBC driver. Which of the following apply?

A. Start – Control Panel – Administrative Tools - click the data sources ODBC connection icon, select the tracing tab and scroll down to the required name
B. Start – Control Panel – Administrative Tools - click the data sources ODBC connection icon, select the drivers tab and scroll down to the required name
C. Start – Control Panel – Administrative Tools - click the data sources ODBC connection icon, select the System DSN drivers tab and scroll down to the required name
D. Start – Control Panel – Administrative Tools - click the data sources ODBC connection icon, select the User DSN drivers tab and scroll down to the required name

Q3. What are direct Database Drivers?

A. A driver provided by Crystal
B. A driver for indirect access to Crystal
C. The driver provided by the vendor to establish Connectivity between Crystal and the vendors database
D. None of the above

Q4. You want to connect to a direct database driver, what should you do?

A. Create New Connection via the Database Expert, click more data sources and select the database required
B. Create New Connection via the view Expert, click more data sources and select the database required
C. Create New Connection via the File Expert, click more data sources and select the database required
D. Create New Connection via the Data Explorer, click more data sources and select the database required

Q5. A DSN file has been created. Which of the following information will it contain? *(Multiple Answers)*

A. Driver
B. Uid
C. Database
D. Wsid
E. App
F. Server
G. Description

Q6. Direct Database Drivers are provided for which of the following? *(Multiple Answers)*

A. ACT! 3.0, Informix
B. Btrieve, Field Definitions
C. COM Data, Java Data
D. Sybase, JDCB (JNDI)

Q7. You are creating a new connection. Which of the following connections are available within the Database Expert? *(Multiple Answers)*

A. ODBC
B. OLAP
C. OLE DB
D. Oracle Server
E. Outlook Exchange
F. Sybase
G. XML

Q8. You have tried to connect to Sybase via the direct database driver and you receive the message 'no items found', what could the issue be?

A. You do not have access to the database
B. You need to reinstall the database
C. You have not installed the appropriate database client software on your PC to establish connectivity
D. You need to reinstall Crystal

Q9. What does ODBC stand for?

A. Open Data Connection
B. Open Database Connectivity
C. OLAP Database Connectivity
D. Ordinary Database Connectivity

Q10. Which of the following are OLE DB providers? *(Multiple Answers)*

A. Microsoft ISAM 1.1 OLE DB Provider
B. Microsoft OLE DB Provider for DTS Packages
C. Microsoft OLE DB Provider for OLAP Services
D. Microsoft for Oracle
E. Microsoft OLE DB Provider for Sybase
F. Microsoft for SQL Server

Q11. You want to create a connection to Microsoft SQL Server via an OLE DB. Which of the following apply?

A. Within the Database Expert select OLE DB, enter the details for the server, user ID, password and database and click next, property values can be edited if required and click next
B. Within the Database Expert select DB, enter the details for the server, user ID, password and database and click next, property values can be edited if required and click next
C. Within the Database Expert select the Microsoft SQL Server, enter the details for the server, user ID, password and database and click next, property values can be edited if required and click next
D. Within the Database Expert – create new connection – select OLE DB, select Microsoft OLE DB Provider for SQL Server and click next, enter the details for the server, user ID, password and database and click next, property values can be edited if required and click next

Q12. The Business Objects Enterprise Administrator has provided you with the name of the ODBC on the server, you want to create an ODBC connection, which will enable you to publish and schedule reports via Business Objects Enterprise. Which of the following should you use?

A. System DSN
B. User DSN
C. File DSN
D. Drivers

Q13. You have been informed that the name of the database has changed, you want to amend your ODBC connection to reflect this change what should you do?

A. A new ODBC connection is required
B. Once an ODBC connection is created, it cannot be amended, it must be deleted
C. Within the ODBC Data Source Administrator, highlight your ODBC Connection and click the configure button, enter or select the new server name
D. None of the above

Q14. You want to create an ODBC connection to a Microsoft Access Database. Which of the following apply?

A. Within the ODBC Data Source Administrator, select the DSN tab and click the Add button, select the Microsoft Access Driver from the driver list and click finish, within the OBDC Microsoft Access Setup dialog box select enter the Data source Name and description and click the select button to select the database
B. Within the ODBC Data Source Administrator, select the SND tab and click the Add button, select the Microsoft Access Driver from the driver list and click finish, within the OBDC Microsoft Access Setup dialog box select enter the Data source Name and description and click the select button to select the database
C. Within the ODBC Data Source Administrator, select the Access tab and click the Add button, select the Microsoft Access Driver from the driver list and click finish, within the OBDC Microsoft Access Setup dialog box select enter the Data source Name and description and click the select button to select the database
D. Within the ODBC Data Source Administrator, select the System DSN tab and click the Add button, select the Microsoft Access Driver from the driver list and click finish, within the OBDC Microsoft Access Setup dialog box select enter the Data source Name and description and click the select button to select the database

Q15. What is the definition of a Silent Connection?

A. A Silent Connection works on the premise that all information has been provided and attempts to connect
B. Silent Connect PROMPTS for login information
C. Silent Connect attempts to connect on after information has been provided

Q16. Which if the following are connection types? *(Multiple Answers)*

A. Silent Connect
B. Simple Connect
C. Drive connect

Q17. Which of the following are the three are connection types generally used?

A. ODBC/OLE DB/Direct DB drivers
B. ODBC/OLEE/SIMPLE ACCESS
C. NONE OF THE ABOVE

Chapter 3 - The Database Expert

The Database is the central point for report creation; this chapter will test your knowledge of the Database Expert, Connectivity, and Links, resetting the Data Source location and mapping fields.

Key Areas:

- ❑ **New Connnection**
- ❑ **Database Expert**
- ❑ **Connect To A Data Sources**
- ❑ **Add Tables Within The Database Expert**
- ❑ **Table Links and Joins**

Q1: Which section of Crystal Reports is used to link tables?

A. Database Expert Links Tab

B. Database Expert report table tab

C. Database Data link table tab

D. Database data table Links Tab

Q2: You want to view the database properties. Which of the following apply?

A. Right-click the table within the Database Expert (Links Tab) and select properties from the dropdown menu

B. Right-click the database connection within the Database Expert (Data Tab) and select properties from the dropdown menu

C. Right-click the database connection within the Database Expert (Database Tab) and select properties from the dropdown menu

D. Right-click the table within the Database Expert (Linking Tab) and select properties from the dropdown menu

Q3: Which of the following are Database Expert connectivity options? *(Multiple Answers)*

A. Current Connections

B. Repository based SQL Command

C. Historical data sources

D. Create New Connection

E. Customized Favorites

Q4: How can you add your current database connection to your favorites folder?

A. From the Menu Bar select file and save as into the favorites folder
B. From the Database Expert, drag and drop the database into the folder
C. Right-click the database within the Current Connections and select the add to favorites
D. From the Database Expert, select file and save as into the favorites folder

Q5: You have just refreshed a report and would like to check the current database connection. Which of the following apply?

A. File- Database - Current Location
B. Report - Database Expert - Current Location
C. Database - Database Expert - Current Connections
D. View - Database - Database Expert - Current Connections

Q6: You are connected to a SQL Server database via an ODBC connection. Which of the following database properties can you view within the Database Expert? *(Multiple Answers)*

A. User ID
B. Password
C. Database
D. Database Type
E. Data Source Name
F. DSN Default Properties
G. File Name
H. Field Count

Q7: You want to remove a database from the favourite's folder, what should you do?

A. Delete the favorites folder from the view expert and delete the database from the favorites folder
B. Expand the Favorites folder - Right-click the database and select delete favorite
C. Delete the favorites folder from the visual expert and delete the database from the favorites folder
D. Highlight database within the Database Expert and press the delete button on your keyboard

Q8: Which of the following best describes the connection method to a Data source via an ODBC?

A. File, New, Blank Report, the Database Connection dialog box will appear, expand the Create New Connection and the cross beside the ODBC connection, double click the Make New Connection and select the Data source Name and click Next, enter your password and user is and click Finish, select the cross beside the tables and select the required tables using the > arrow to put reports in the selected tables section, click the Links Table and create the appropriate links
B. File, New, Blank Report, the Database Expert dialog box will appear, expand the Create New Connection within Available Data Sources and the cross beside the ODBC connection, double click the Make New Connection and select the Data source name and click Next, enter your password and user id and click Finish, select the required tables using the > arrow to put reports in the selected tables section, click the Links Table and create the appropriate links
C. File, New, Blank Report, the Database Files dialog box will appear, expand the Create New Connection and the cross beside the ODBC connection, double click the Make New Connection and select the Data source Name and click Next, enter your password and user is and click Finish, select the cross beside the tables and select the required tables using the > arrow to put reports in the selected tables section, click the Links Table and create the appropriate links

Q9: Which of the following applies to the Datasource Location functionality? *(Multiple Answers)*

A. Used to set a new database location
B. Automatically changes the database location
C. Changes the database drivers to the new database source chosen

Q10: You have opened an existing report and you want to add an additional table, how would you select your data source?

A. Choose the report expert from the database menu and select create new connection
B. Choose the file expert from the database menu and select create new connection
C. Choose the formula expert from the database menu and select create new connection
D. Choose the format expert from the database menu and select create new connection
E. Choose Database Expert from the database menu and select create new connection

Q11: You want to point the sales report database to a new location via the ODBC connection. Which of the following apply?

A. From the Menu Bar select database - set database location - highlight the table in the Current Data Source section of the Set Datasource Location dialog box, in the Replace With section expand Create New Connection, expand ODBC (RDO) and Double Click Make New Connection, select New ODBC connection, enter user id and password, expand Tables within the new connection, highlight table and click the update button
B. From the Menu Bar select File - database - set database location - highlight the table in the Current Data Source section of the Set Datasource Location dialog box, in the Replace With section click the cross beside Create New Connection, click the cross beside ODBC (RDO) and Double Click Make New Connection, select New ODBC connection, enter user id and password, expand Tables within the new connection, highlight table and click the update button
C. From the Menu Bar select View -database - set database location - highlight the table in the Current Data Source section of the Set Datasource Location dialog box, in the Replace With section click the cross beside Create New Connection, click the cross beside ODBC (RDO) and Double Click Make New Connection, select New ODBC connection, enter user id and password, expand Tables within the new connection, highlight table and click the update button
D. From the Menu Bar select Report -database - set database location - highlight the table in the Current Data Source section of the Set Datasource Location dialog box, in the Replace With section click the cross beside Create New Connection, click the cross beside ODBC (RDO) and Double Click Make New Connection, select New ODBC connection, enter user id and password, expand Tables within the new connection, highlight table and click the update button

Q12: In the Field Explorer you notice the field names are not listed alphabetically, what should you do to create an alphabetical field name list?

A. Right-click the database from the File expert and select option from the drop-down menu, under list table and description, select the button for both.
B. Right-click the database from the view expert and select option from the drop-down menu, under list table and description, select the button for both.
C. Right-click the database from the report expert and select option from the drop-down menu, under list table and description, select the button for both.
D. Right-click the database from the Database Expert and select option from the drop-down menu, under the tables and field section check the sort fields alphabetically.
E. Right-click the database from the SQL expert and select option from the drop-down menu, under list table and description, select the button for both.

Q13: You have set your report to a new location, the region_name field, which you have not used in the current report, has been deleted from the new datasource and the EmployeeID field which you have used has been renamed as WorkerID, how would you proceed?

A. The Map Fields dialog box will appear, in the unmapped fields section the Region_Code and employeeID will appear, uncheck the Match Type checkbox and highlight the employeeID in the report fields section and the WorkerID in the new datasource section and click the map button.
B. Choose - report - set location - highlight the current database in the current datasource section and highlight the new datasource in the replace with section and click the update button, the mapping dialogue box will appear, highlight the employeeID in the unmapped section and the worker_id in the mapped section and click on the map button, this will create a map of the employeeID as Worker_ID
C. Choose - File - set location - highlight the current database in the current datasource section and highlight the new datasource in the replace with section and click the update button, the mapping dialogue box will appear, highlight the employeeID in the unmapped section and the worker_id in the mapped section and click on the map button, this will create a map of the employeeID as Worker_ID
D. Choose - view - set location - highlight the current database in the current datasource section and highlight the new datasource in the replace with section and click the update button, the mapping dialogue box will appear, highlight the employeeID in the unmapped section and the worker_id in the mapped section

and click on the map button, this will create a map of the employeeID as Worker_ID

Q14: Which of the following activates the Map field dialog? *(Multiple Answers)*

A. A field name has changed
B. A field name no longer exist
C. A field data type has changed
D. A field contains more data

Q15: How do you ensure your report is picking up the latest version of the database?

A. Refresh Report
B. Close and open report
C. Preview Report
D. Verify database

Q16: You want to view the SQL coding generated by your report. Which of the following apply?

A. Choose File - Show SQL Query
B. Choose View - Show SQL Query
C. Choose Database - Database Expert -Show SQL Query
D. Choose Database - Show SQL Query
E. Choose Report - Show SQL Query

Q17: You can edit the SQL generated by your report from within the Show SQL Query dialog box?

A. True
B. False

Q18: You want to disconnect one of the two data sources you are connected to. Which of the following apply? *(Multiple Answers)*

A. Select Database from the Menu Bar and select Disconnect Database, from the Data Explorer, select the Database and click log off
B. Select Database from the Menu Bar and select disengage, from the Data Explorer, select the Database and click log off
C. Select Database from the Menu Bar and select End Session, from the Data Explorer, select the Database and click log off
D. From the Field Explorer, highlight the database and select Log on or off Server, from the Data Explorer highlight database and click log off and close
E. Select Database from the Menu Bar and select Log on or off Server, from the Data Explorer highlight database and click log off and close

Q19: The Links Tab within the Database Expert provides you with which of the following?

A. Current tables, links and indexes, Auto Arrange only
B. Current tables, links and indexes, Auto Arrange, Auto-link, Order links only
C. Current tables select for report creation, their links and indexes, Auto Arrange, Auto-link, Order links, clear links only
D. Current tables used for report creation, links and index legend, Auto Arrange, Auto-link Order links, clear links, delete links and link options
E. Current tables, links and indexes, Auto Arrange, Auto-link, Order links, clear links, delete links and link options, update link

Q20: Which of the following are methods of Auto-Links? *(Multiple Answers)*

A. By Key
B. By Name
C. By Field
D. By Data Type

Q21: The Database Expert Links Tab only appears if two or more tables are selected for report design?

A. True
B. False

Q22: You want to change the join type between two tables. Which methods apply? *(Multiple Answers)*

A. From the Database Expert Links Tab, double click the link between the two tables and change the join type
B. From the Database Expert Links Tab, right-click the link between the two tables and choose link options from the drop down menu and change the join type
C. Within the Database Expert Links Tab, highlight the link between the two tables and click link options button
D. From the toolbar select link type select tables, right-click table and select link

Q23: You right click the link between two tables in the Database Expert. Which of the following Link Options will be available? *(Multiple Answers)*

A. Delete Link
B. Reconnect Link
C. Remove all Link
D. Reverse Link

Q24: Which of the following removes all links created between tables in the Database Expert?

A. Override Linking
B. Revert Linking
C. Clear Links
D. Remove All Links
E. Delete Links

Q25: You try to link two tables together based on a field with different data types. Which of the following error messages will be displayed?

A. Database is unreadable
B. You do not have permission to the database
C. You do not have permission to create this link
D. Data types are not compatible

Q26: Which of the following buttons allows the Designer to activate the processing order for links?

A. Arrange Links
B. Order Links
C. Auto Arrange Links
D. Smart Linking

Q27: Within the Database Expert you try to create Smart Linking by key, the link cannot be created. Which of the following could be the possible cause? *(Multiple Answers)*

A. Not supported by Database Driver
B. Database not connected
C. Driver Not Installed
D. Key relationships are not present

Q28: Which of the following is an essential aspect of database creation?

A. Schema relation Analysis
B. Normalization
C. Optimization relationship join
D. Concept Analysis

Q29: Which of the following link types are available in the Database Expert Link Tab? *(Multiple Answers)*

A. (=) link
B. [<] link
C. [<=] link
D. [! =] link
E. [=!] link
F. [>!]
G. [>] link
H. [>=] link

Q30: A client_id link has been created between the client table and the purchase table; you want to extract all client purchases. Which link type should you apply?

A. (=) link

B. [>] link

C. [>=] link

D. [<] link

E. [<=] link

F. [! =] link

Q31: You want to return records from the left table matching records from the right table every time the joining field in the left table is less than or equal to the joining field in the right table. Which one of the following links should you use?

A. (=) link

B. [>] link

C. [>=] link

D. [<] link

E. [<=] link

F. [! =] link

Q32: You want to return all combination of records from both tables where the joining fields are not equal. Which one of the following links should you use?

A. (=) link

B. [>] link

C. [>=] link

D. [<] link

E. [<=] link

F. [! =] link

Q33: You want to return records from the left table matching records from the right table every time the joining field in the left table is greater than or equal to the joining field in the right table. Which one of the following links should you use?

A. (=) link

B. [>] link

C. [>=] link

D. [<] link

E. [<=] link

F. [! =] link

Q34: You want to extract a comparison between Managers in the Finance Department and Managers in the Sales Department, you want to make sure Managers in the Finance Department are not earning more than Managers in the Sales Department; you have created a link based on the remuneration field. Which link type will you use?

A. (=) link
B. [>] link
C. [>=] link
D. [<] link
E. [<=] link
F. [! =] link

Q35: You want to return records from the left table matching records from the right table every time the joining field in the left table is less than the joining field in the right table. Which one of the following links should you use?

A. (=) link
B. [>] link
C. [>=] link
D. [<] link
E. [<=] link
F. [! =] link

Join Type

SAMPLE TABLES

Link both tables on location

ExamNo	Center Location
RDCR201	Harrow
RDCR301	BlackWard
RDCR400	Beeston

CRYSTAL_EXAM_CENTERS

CandNo	Cand Location
CR1033	Purley
CR1099	BlackWard
CR5667	Beeston

CANDIDATE_LOC

Fig 3

Q36: Which of the following join types will produce the results as illustrated in the table below?

ExamNo	Center Location	CandNo	Cand Location
RDCR201	Harrow	NULL	NULL
RDCR301	BlackWard	CR1099	BlackWard
RDCR400	Beeston	CR5667	Beeston

A. Right Outer Join
B. Full Join
C. Left Outer Join
D. Inner Join

Q37: Which of the following join types will produce the results as illustrated in the table below?

ExamNo	Center Location	CandNo	Cand Location
RDCR301	BlackWard	CR1099	BlackWard
RDCR400	Beeston	CR5667	Beeston

A. Right Outer Join
B. Full Join
C. Inner Join
D. Left Outer Join

Q38: You want to show all records in the CANDIDATE_LOC table that are unmatched to the records in the CRYSTAL_EXAM_CENTERS. Which of the following will you use?

A. Full Outer Join
B. Left Outer Join
C. Right Outer Join
D. Inner Join

Q39: Using the tables in *Fig 3*, you link both tables on location and you have created a Left Outer Join between the tables. What will the result of this join be?

A. Will include records in the right table (CRYSTAL_EXAM_CENTERS) that are unmatched with rows in the left table (CANDIDATE_LOC)
B. Will include records in the left table (CRYSTAL_EXAM_CENTERS)
C. Will include records in the right table (CANDIDATE_LOC)
D. Will include records in the left table (CRYSTAL_EXAM_CENTERS) that are unmatched with rows in the right table (CANDIDATE_LOC)

Q40: Which of the following are join types in Crystal Reports?

A. Inner join, Left Outer Join, Right Outer Join, Full Outer Join, Equal Link
B. Inner join, Left Outer Join, Right Outer Join, Full Outer Join
C. Full Inner Join, Left Outer Join
D. Full Inner Join, Full Left Outer Join, Full Right Join

SAMPLE TABLES

You link both tables on location

ExamNo	Center Location
RDCR201	Harrow
RDCR301	BlackWard
RDCR400	Beeston

CRYSTAL_EXAM_CENTERS

CandNo	Cand Location
CR1033	Purley
CR1099	BlackWard
CR5667	Beeston

CANDIDATE_LOC

Q41: You want to extract data for all centers with registered candidates and those centers with no registered candidates. Which join type should you apply?

A. Inner Join
B. Left Outer Join,
C. Right Outer Join,
D. Full Outer Join

Q42: You want to find out all exams centre locations that have registered candidates excluding those that have not. Which of the following should be used?

A. Full Outer Join
B. Inner Join
C. Left Outer Join
D. Right Outer Join

Q43: Which of the following join types will produce the results as illustrated in the table below?

A. Right Outer Join
B. Full Join
C. Left Outer Join
D. Inner Join

ExamNo	Center Location	CandNo	Cand Location
NULL	NULL	CR1033	Purley
RDCR301	BlackWard	CR1099	BlackWard
RDCR400	Beeston	CR5667	Beeston

SAMPLE TABLES

You link both tables on location

ExamNo	Center Location
RDCR201	Harrow
RDCR301	BlackWard
RDCR400	Beeston

CRYSTAL_EXAM_CENTERS

CandNo	Cand Location
CR1033	Purley
CR1099	BlackWard
CR5667	Beeston

CANDIDATE_LOC

Q44: Which of the following join types will produce the results as illustrated in the table below?

A. Right Outer Join
B. Full Join
C. Left Outer Join
D. Inner Join

ExamNo	Center Location	CandNo	Cand Location
NULL	NULL	CR1033	Purley
RDCR301	BlackWard	CR1099	BlackWard
RDCR400	Beeston	CR5667	Beeston
RDCR201	Harrow	NULL	NULL

Q45: Which of the following are the Enforced Join types available via the Database Expert?
(Multiple Answers)

A. Enforced but Not
B. Not Enforced
C. Enforced From
D. Enforced To
E. Enforced Both

Q46: Which Enforced Join type is the default option?

A. Enforced but Not
B. Not Enforced
C. Enforced From
D. Enforced To
E. Enforced Both

Q47: Which of the following links is enforced only when necessary?

A. Enforced but Not
B. Enforced From
C. Enforced To
D. Enforced Both
E. Not Enforced

SAMPLE TABLES

You link both tables on location

ExamNo	Center Location
RDCR201	Harrow
RDCR301	BlackWard
RDCR400	Beeston

CRYSTAL_EXAM_CENTERS

CandNo	Cand Location
CR1033	Purley
CR1099	BlackWard
CR5667	Beeston

CANDIDATE_LOC

Q48: You have created a link from the CRYSTAL_EXAM_CENTERS table to the CANDIDATE_LOC table, you select records from the CANDIDATE_LOC table and not from the CANDIDATE_LOC table, and the select statement still includes records from the CRYSTAL_EXAM_CENTERS table. Which of the following link options apply?

A. Enforced but Not
B. Not Enforced
C. Enforced From
D. Enforced To
E. Enforced Both

Q49: You have created a link from the CRYSTAL_EXAM_CENTERS table to the CANDIDATE_LOC table and you select records from the CRYSTAL_EXAM_CENTERS table but not from the CANDIDATE_LOC table. The select statement still includes records from both tables. Which of the following link options apply?

A. Enforced but Not
B. Not Enforced
C. Enforced From
D. Enforced To
E. Enforced Both

Q50: Which of the following reporting criteria work effectively with a server based grouping method? *(Multiple Answers)*

A. Reports with groups

B. Specified groups ONLY

C. Reports with sort applied

D. Reports with hidden sections

E. TopN, Bottom, Average, Distinct Count, Sample Variance, Max, Min based reports

F. Summary Group Header or Group Footer based reports

G. Summaries not based on Group Header or Group Footer

Q51: You want to perform grouping on the server and use indexes or server for speed which of the following apply? *(Multiple Answers)*

A. Choose File - Report Options and check the use indexes or server for speed and check the Perform Grouping On Server checkbox

B. Choose File - Report and check the use indexes or server for speed and check the Perform Grouping On Server checkbox

C. Choose File - Report expert Options and check the use indexes or server for speed and check the Perform Grouping On Server checkbox

D. Choose Database - Database Expert - Right-click the database and select Options from the drop-down menu and check the use indexes or server for speed and check the Perform Grouping On Server checkbox

Q52: What are the benefits of using the 'perform grouping on server' option? *(Multiple Answers)*

A. Memory processing improvements

B. Transfer improvements

C. Connection time improvements

D. Improves processing speed

Q53: Which of the following will improve report-processing performance? *(Multiple Answers)*

A. Use indexes to link tables

B. Use indexes or server for Speed

C. Try to avoid the use of data type conversion

D. Use constant expressions

E. Use SQL expressions

Q54: Which of the following refer to server based grouping? *(Multiple Answers)*

A. The performance of reporting
B. Aggregate calculation based on Group Headers
C. No aggregate calculations
D. The performance of aggregate sectioning
E. Aggregate calculation on Group Footers of records
F. TopN calculations
G. Bottom calculations

Q55: Which of the following are advantages of using ODBC? *(Multiple Answers)*

A. Flexibility
B. Changes can be implemented to use the same ODBC connection to connect to different databases
C. None of the above

Q56: What are the five layers used to access ODBC data sources

A. Crystal Report layer \ ODBC translation layer | ODBC layer | dbms TRANSLATION LAYER | Database layer
B. Crystal Report layer \ ODBC translation layer | ODBC Format| dbms TRANSLATION LAYER | Database layer
C. Crystal Report layer \ ODBB translation layer | ODBC layer | dbms TRANSLATION LAYER | Database layer
D. Crystal Report layer \ ODBB translation layer | ODBC layer | dbbms TRANSLATION LAYER | Database layer

Q57: One of the advantages of using ODBC connections is its flexibility to access a wide range of data from one section.

A. True
B. False

Q58: You want to connect to a client/server database. What are the three general usable methods of connection?

A. ODBC/OLEE/SIMPLE ACCESS
B. NONE OF THE ABOVE
C. ODBC ONLY
D. ODBC/OLE DB/Direct DB drivers

Q59: Which of the following are database connectivity technologies? *(Multiple Answers)*

A. ODBC
B. Access database
C. OLE DB
D. SQL Database

Q60: Describe an OLE database connection

A. OLE DB enables the communication between the reporting system and SQL Server
B. OLE DB enables the communication between the reporting system and Microsoft Access
C. OLE DB enables the communication between the reporting system and Microsoft Excel
D. OLE DB enables the communication between the reporting system and DBMS

Q61: To set up an ODBC datasource you must have the ODBC data driver installed on your machine.

A. True
B. False

Q62: The database password has changed; you need to reconfigure the password via the ODBC driver to re-establish connection to your report. Which of the following apply? (Windows Environment)?

A. From the Program Files, double-click Administrative Tools - Data Sources (ODBC) datasource, select the systems tab, highlight the data source to be changed and click the configure button, click next, enter the new password, click next, next again and click the test the datasource button, then click OK.

B. Select All Programs – Connect To - double-click Administrative Tools - Data Sources (ODBC) datasource, select the systems tab, highlight the data source to be changed and click the configure button, click next, enter the new password, click next, next again and click the test the datasource button, then click OK.

C. From the Program Files, double-click Administrative Tools – Services - systems tab, highlight the data source to be changed and click the configure button, click next, enter the new password, click next, next again and click the test the datasource button, then click OK.

D. From the control panel, double-click Administrative Tools, - Data Sources (ODBC) datasource, select the systems tab, highlight the data source to be changed and click the configure button, click next, enter the new password, click next, next again and click the test the datasource button, then click OK.

Q63: You want to set up an ODBC data source for Microsoft SQL Server, what should you do?

A. From the Control Panel double click the ODBC datasource icon, select the Systems Tab, click Add, select the ODBC Driver, select Microsoft SQL ServerDriver (*.mdb), click finish, enter the datasource name and description in the box that appears and click the select button to select the database, click ok, your ODBC connection will now appear in the Database Expert when creating a Crystal Report.
B. From the Control Panel double click Administrative Tools – select the ODBC datasource icon, select the Systems Tab, click Add, select the ODBC Driver, select Microsoft SQL ServerDriver, click finish, enter the datasource name and description in the box that appears and click the select button to select the Server you would like to connect to, click ok, enter the authenticity of the login ID, change the default database and click NEXT and finish, your ODBC connection will now appear in the Database Expert when creating a Crystal Report.
C. From the Control Panel double click the ODBC datasource icon, select the Systems Tab, click Add, select the ODBC Driver, select Microsoft SQL ServerDriver (*.mddb), click finish, enter the datasource name and description in the box that appears and click the select button to select the database, click ok, your ODBC connection will now appear in the Database Expert when creating a Crystal Report.
D. From the Control Panel double click the ODBC datasource icon, select the Systems Tab, click Add, select the ODBC Driver, select Microsoft SQL ServerDriver (*.mdbb), click finish, enter the datasource name and description in the box that appears and click the select button to select the database, click ok, your ODBC connection will now appear in the Database Expert when creating a Crystal Report.

Q64: You want to set up an ODBC data source for Microsoft Access. Which of the methods would you employ?

A. From the Control Panel double click the ODBC datasource icon, select the Systems Tab, click Add, select the ODBC Driver, select Microsoft Access Driver (*.mcdb), click finish, enter the datasource name and description in the box that appears and click the select button to select the database, click ok, your ODBC connection will now appear in the Database Expert when creating a Crystal Report.
B. From the Control Panel double click the ODBC datasource icon, select the Systems Tab, click Add, select the ODBC Driver, select Microsoft Access Driver (*.mdb), click finish, enter the datasource name and description in the box that appears and click the select button to select the database, click ok, your ODBC connection will now appear in the Database Expert when creating a Crystal Report.
C. From the Control Panel double click the ODBC datasource icon, select the Systems Tab, click Add, select the ODBC Driver, select Microsoft Access Driver (*.mddb), click finish, enter the datasource name and description in the box that appears and click the select button to select the database, click ok, your ODBC connection will now appear in the Database Expert when creating a Crystal Report.
D. From the Control Panel double click the ODBC datasource icon, select the Systems Tab, click Add, select the ODBC Driver, select Microsoft Access Driver (*.mdbb), click finish, enter the datasource name and description in the box that appears and click the select button to select the database, click ok, your ODBC connection will now appear in the Database Expert when creating a Crystal Report.

Q65: You want to connect to a SQL Server via an OLE connection. Which of the following methods would you employ?

A. From the Database Expert, Select the Create New Connection, select ODBC (ADO), from the OLE DB (ADO) dialog box select Microsoft OLE DB Provider for SQL Server and click Next, enter the server, user ID, password and database and click next, the Advanced Information dialog box will appear, add or remove properties if required and click finish
B. From the Database Expert, Select the Create New Connection, select OLE DB file (DSN), from the OLE DB (ADO) dialog box select Microsoft OLE DB Provider for SQL Server and click Next, enter the server, user ID, password and database and click next, the Advanced Information dialog box will appear, add or remove properties if required and click finish
C. From the Database Expert, Select the Create New Connection, select OLE DB (ADO), from the OLE DB (ADO) dialog box select Microsoft OLE DB Provider for SQL Server and click Next, enter the server, user ID, password and database and click next, the Advanced Information dialog box will appear, add or remove properties if required and click finish
D. From the Database Expert, Select the Create New Connection, select OLE DB file (DSN), from the OLE DB (DOA) dialog box select Microsoft OLE DB Provider for SQL Server and click Next, enter the server, user ID, password and database and click next, the Advanced Information dialog box will appear, add or remove properties if required and click finish

Q66. You want to change the location of your database this can be done within the Field Explorer, by right-clicking the Database Fields and selecting Set Datasource Location

A. True
B. False

Q67. You want to arrange tables in the Field Explorer in alphabetical order. Which of the following apply?

A. Right-click the Database Fields within the Field Explorer and select Sort Tables
B. Right-click the Database Fields within the Field Explorer and select Sort Tables Alphabetically
C. Right-click the Database Fields within the Field Explorer and select asc or desc Tables
D. Right-click the Database Fields within the Field Explorer and select Table Sort

Chapter 4 - Creating and Working with Formulas

This chapter covers formula creation within Crystal Reports. Question will cover the creation of arrays, date calculations, nested formulas, control structures and number formulas. You will also be tested on formula error detection and modification and the use of Functions and Operators within the Formula Workshop.

Key Areas

- ❑ **Create Formula**
- ❑ **Functions And Operators**
- ❑ **Control Structures**
- ❑ **Variables**
- ❑ **Arrays**
- ❑ **String Formulas**
- ❑ **Numbers Formulas**
- ❑ **Date Calculations**
- ❑ **Financial Functions**
- ❑ **Working With Null Values**
- ❑ **SQL Expressions**
- ❑ **Control Structures**
- ❑ **Processing A Report**
- ❑ **Creating Report Alerts**

Q1. Which of the following languages can be used to create formulas in Crystal Reports?
(Multiple Answers)

A. Crystal syntax

B. Visual Basic

C. Basic Syntax

D. PL SQL

Q2. Identify the Parentheses Operator in the following formula?

WhilePrintingRecords;
NumberVar Total_Score; Total_Score:= tonumber({Sample_Exam_Results___2005.SCORE})

A. :=

B. =

C. NumberVar

D. Total_Score

Q3. Formulas cannot be used as groups

A. True

B. False

Q4. You are creating a formula within the Crystal Formula Editor, and would like to choose from a list of possible formula functions. What must you do to produce this list?

A. Ctrl-space
B. Alt F9
C. Ctrl Alt F8
D. F8
E. F1

Q5. Within which of the following sections can you rename a formula? *(Multiple Answers)*

A. Function Workshop
B. Operators Workshop
C. Field Explorer - Formula Fields – Select Formula – Press (F2) to Rename or Right-click and select Rename from the drop-down menu
D. Within the Formula Workshop– Select Formula – Press (F2) to Rename or Right-click and select Rename from the drop-down menu

Q6. Which of the following statements are true? *(Multiple Answers)*

A. .(period) separates the table name from the field name
B. {} surrounds the database fields, formula names and parameter fields
C. ' 'separates the table name from the field name whilst using a database field
D. \\ Denotes a statement
E. ( ) Denotes a statement

Q7. Which of the following are true in relation to commenting report formulas? *(Multiple Answers)*

A. Explains formula functionality
B. // Denotes a comment in Crystal
C. \\ Denotes a comment in Crystal
D. Can be used to deciphers the syntax used
E. Can be used to provide information for future programming changes

Q8. You have created a report and would like to insert a new formula. What should you do?

A. Choose Report | Field Explorer | right click the formula fields and select New, enter formula name, this should bring you to the Formula Workshop -Formula Editor
B. Choose View | Field Explorer | right click the formula fields and select New, enter formula name, this should bring you to the Formula Workshop -Formula Editor
C. Choose Database | Field Explorer | right click the formula fields and select New, enter formula name, this should bring you to the Formula Workshop - Formula Editor
D. Choose Format | Field Explorer | right click the formula fields and select New, enter formula name, this should bring you to the Formula Workshop - Formula Editor

Q9. Which of the following is used to separate multiple arguments in functions?

A. ;
B. :
C. :=
D. ?
E. ,

Q10. What does the following formula represent when it appears in the report footer: - Sum({Orders.Order Amount})

A. A sum of sales by Group Header
B. Grand Total for entire report
C. A sum of sales by Page Header
D. A sum of sales by Group Footer

Σ Report Area:Sum of Orders.Order Amount

Q11. Which of the following is used for Basic Syntax commenting?

A. // Denotes a comment in Basic Syntax
B. \\ Denotes a comment in Basic Syntax
C. 'Denotes a comment in Basic Syntax
D. Denotes a comment in Basic Syntax
E. _Denotes a comment in Basic Syntax

Q12. You have created a formula. Which of the following signs precedes the formula?

A. $
B. //
C. :
D. ?
E. @

Q13. Your formula contains multiple statements. Which of the following must you use to separate the statements?

A. //
B. :
C. :=
D. ?
E. ,
F. ;

WhilePrintingRecords
NumberVar Total_Score
Total_Score:= tonumber({Sample_Exam_Results_2005.SCORE}) Total_Score

Q14. Which of the following would you include when commenting your formulas? *(Multiple Answers)*

A. Brief explanation of the formula
B. Explanation of function
C. Explanation of database structure
D. Field used and why
E. Definition of variable

Q15. Which of the following statements are true? *(Multiple Answers)*

A. A local variable is not visible in a Subreport
B. A local variable in one formula cannot be accessed in another formula
C. You can access the value of a local variable in one formula from a different formula
D. You can share a local variable with a Subreport
E. You can access the value of a Global Variable in one formula from a different formula
F. A Global Variable declared in one formula can be accessed by another formula
G. A Global Variable cannot be seen in a Subreport
H. You can pass a Shared variable from a Subreport to the Main report
I. You can pass a Shared variable from a from a Main report to a Subreport

Q16. Formulas cannot be used within alerts

A. True
B. False

Q17. Which of the following can be declared as variables within Crystal Reports? *(Multiple Answers)*

A. CurrencyVar
B. TimeVar
C. TextVar
D. DateTimeVar
E. NumberVar
F. BooleanVar
G. StringVar
H. DateVar
I. DataVar

Q18. Which one of the following keys will activate HELP?

A. F2
B. F1
C. F3
D. F4

Date Functions and Formulas

Q1. You want to convert the value below to a date time format. Which script will you use? 4/10/2005 *(Multiple Answers)*

A. #4/10/2005#
B. #4/10/2005
C. 4/10/2005##
D. ##4/10/2005##
E. CDateTime(4/10/2005)

Q2. You want to extract the day from the events date. Which of the following apply?

A. DatePart ('dd',{Events.EventsDate} ,1)
B. DatePart ({Events.EventsDate},'d')
C. DatePart ({Events.EventsDate},'dd')
D. DatePart ('d', {Events.EventsDate})

Q3. Which of the following will display the Current Date and Time? *(Multiple Answers)*

A. CurrentDate + "" + CurrentTime

B. PrintDate + "" + PrintTime

C. CurrentDateTime

D. CurrentDate + CurrentTime

E. PrintDate + PrintTime

Q4. Which of the following can you specify within a DateDiff Formula? *(Multiple Answers)*

A. IntervalType

B. Type

C. LastDayofWeek

D. BeginDate for Interval Calculation

E. EndDate for Interval Calculation

Q5. What does the following formula represent?

Sum({Sales.sales.Amount},{Sales.SaleDate}, "monthly")

A. A sum of sales by Sales Rep Group Header

B. Sales amount subtotal ordered by monthly date group

C. A sum of sales by Group Footer

D. Grand Total for entire report

Q6. What will the following return?
#07:07#

A. 7.7.00am

B. 7.7am

C. 07:07:00am

D. 7;7am

Q7. You want to highlight all sales made on Wednesday as 'Required' and all others as 'Not Required'. Using the Sales Date which of one the following apply?

A. if DayOfWeek ({Orders.SalesDate}) = 'Wednesday' then 'Required' else 'Not Required'

B. if WeekdayName({Orders.SalesDate}) = 'Wednesday' then 'Required' else 'Not Required'

C. if WeekdayName (DayOfWeek ({Orders.SalesDate})) = 'Wednesday' then 'Required' else 'Not Required'

D. if WeekdayName (DayOfWeek ({Orders.SalesDate})) = crWednesday then 'Required' else 'Not Required'

Q8. What will the following formula return Date({Order.Despatch}) – Date({Order. RequestDate})? *(Multiple Answers)*

A. Number of days between Dates

B. Converts datetime to date

C. Date

D. String

Q9. How would you convert a string field type which contains date information? *(Multiple Answers)*

A. DateValue

B. Cdate

C. CurDate

D. Dval

Q10. You want to create a formula to determine how many days are required before an order is due. Which of the following apply?

A. "Order Number " + text({Orders.Order ID}) + " is required in " + text({Orders.Required Date} - {Orders.Order Date}) + "days"

B. "Order Number " + totext({Orders.Order ID}) + " is required in " + totext({Orders.Required Date} - {Orders.Order Date}) "days"

C. "Order Number " + tonumber({Orders.Order ID}) + " is required in " + todate({Orders.Required Date} - {Orders.Order Date}) + "days"

D. "Order Number " + totext({Orders.Order ID}) + " is required in " + totext(round(tonumber({Orders.Required Date} - {Orders.Order Date})),0) + "days"

Q11. Your company is conducting a competition. The rules are based on the day of purchase. All customers who purchased a product on Monday will be eligible for a 50% discount on their next purchase. Which of the following apply?

A. if day({Orders.OrderDate}) = crMon then 'Customer is eligible for 50% discount on next Purchase'
B. if day({Orders.OrderDate}) = crMonday then 'Customer is eligible for 50% discount on next Purchase'
C. if day({Orders.OrderDate}) = Monday then 'Customer is eligible for 50% discount on next Purchase'
D. if day({Orders.OrderDate}) = Mon then 'Customer is eligible for 50% discount on next Purchase'

Q12. The Events Date and Time are held in separate fields and you want to display them together. Which of the following apply? *(Multiple Answers)*

A. DateTimeTime({Events.Date},{Events.Time})
B. TimeDate({Events.Date},{Events.Time})
C. DateTimeValue ({Events.Date},{Events.Time})
D. DateTime ({Events.Date},{Events.Time})
E. ToText(DateValue({Events.Date})) + "" + Totext(Time({Events.Date}))

Q13. What does the DateDiff function return?

A. Number of data dates between dates
B. Number of digits between dates
C. Extracts number of Days, Months, Weeks, Years, Hours, Seconds between two specified dates
D. Converts Date to Datetime

Q14. Which of the following are intervals that can be used within the DateDiff function? *(Multiple Answers)*

A. yyyy
B. q
C. m
D. y
E. d
F. w
G. ww
H. h
I. n
J. s

Q15. You have received a request to produce a report which highlights the previous month deliveries; (for this example the current month is December) these are deliveries made in November of the present year, and those delivered in the past seven days. If none of these deliveries fall within this category then display the delivery date only. Which of the following formulas apply? *(Multiple Answers)*

A. if ({Delivery.DeliveryDate})in LastFullMonth then 'Last Months Orders' else if Month({Delivery.DeliveryDate})= 11 and Year({Delivery.DeliveryDate})= year(CurrentDate) then 'Current Year November Orders' else if {Orders.ShippedDate} in Last7Days then 'Orders Made in the Last Seven Days' else Totext({Orders.ShippedDate})
B. if ({Delivery.DeliveryDate})in LastFullMonth then 'Last Months Orders' else if Month({Delivery.DeliveryDate})= 11 and Year({Delivery.DeliveryDate})= year(CurrentDate) then 'Current Year November Orders' else if {Orders.ShippedDate} in Last7Days then 'Orders Made in the Last Seven Days' else ({Orders.ShippedDate})
C. if ({Delivery.DeliveryDate})in LastFullMonth then 'Last Months Orders' else if Month({Delivery.DeliveryDate})= 11 and Year({Delivery.DeliveryDate})= (CurrentDate) then 'Current Year November Orders' else if {Orders.ShippedDate} in Last7Days then 'Orders Made in the Last Seven Days' else ({Orders.ShippedDate})
D. if ({Delivery.DeliveryDate}) = LastFullMonth then 'Last Months Orders' else if Month({Delivery.DeliveryDate})= 11 and Year({Delivery.DeliveryDate})= year(CurrentDate) then 'Current Year November Orders' else if {Orders.ShippedDate} = Last7Days then 'Orders Made in the Last Seven Days' else Totext({Orders.ShippedDate})

E. if month({Delivery.DeliveryDate})= Month(CurrentDate) - 1 then 'Last Months Orders' else if Month({Delivery.DeliveryDate})= 11 and Year({Delivery.DeliveryDate})= year(CurrentDate) then 'Current Year November Orders' else if {Orders.ShippedDate} = Last7Days then 'Orders Made in the Last Seven Days' else Totext({Orders.ShippedDate})

Q16. You want to find the number of days between the Order Date and the Dispatch Date. Which of the following formulas apply?

A. dateserial("d", {Order. Order Date}, {Order. Dispatch Date})
B. datepart("d", {Order. Order Date}, {Order. Dispatch Date})
C. datemart("d", {Order. Order Date}, {Order. Dispatch Date})
D. datediff("d", {Order. Order Date}, {Order. Dispatch Date})

Working with Numbers

Q1. You want your report to return a random number. Which of the following functions will achieve this?

A. Sgn
B. Abs()
C. Random
D. Exp
E. Rnd
F. Truncate

Q2. Which of the following will produce 50.00 when applied to a result field containing 49.30?

A. Round({result},0)

B. RoundUp({result},0)

C. Rnd

D. Rnd({result},0)

Q3. You multiple a number field by a currency field. What will the result be?

A. Number field
B. Text Field
C. Currency Field
D. An error message will ensue

Q4. You receive an error message, which reads "The remaining text does not appear to be part of the formula", when you check the following formula.
CostList.UnitCost} * { CostList.Quantity}. Which of the following will rectify this error?

A. CostList.UnitCost * { CostList.Quantity}
B. CostList.UnitCost} * { CostList.Quantity}
C. {CostList.UnitCost} * CostList.Quantity}
D. {CostList.UnitCost} * { CostList.Quantity}

Q5. Which of the following will produce 64?

A. 4^3 (Exponentiation)
B. Sgn(3 to 4)
C. Abs(3)~3
D. Mod(3,3,2)

Q6. Which of the following will produce 17.40 when applied to a result field containing 17.45?

A. Truncate({result},1)
B. Round({result},0)
C. RoundUp({result},1)
D. Rnd
E. Rnd({result},0)

Q7. You have created the following formula.

{Cost.TotalCost} / {Cost.UnitCost}

You receive the following error message :- 'Can't divide by zero'
What should you do to rectify the problem?

A. Multiple the {Cost.TotalCost} * {Cost.UnitCost}
B. Multiple the {Cost.TotalCost} * {Cost.UnitCost} * -1
C. If {Cost.TotalCost} = 0 then 0 else {Cost.TotalCost} / {Cost.UnitCost}
D. If {Cost.UnitCost} = 0 then 0 else {Cost.TotalCost} / {Cost.UnitCost}

Q8. Which of the following will produce the total amount of sales per representative?

A. Sum(Sales.SaleRep},{Sales.sales.Amount})

B. Sum({Sales.SaleRep},{Sales.sales.Amount})

C. Sum({Sales.sales.Amount},{Sales.SaleRep})

D. Sum({Sales.sales.Amount} & + "" +&{Sales.SaleRep})

Q9. You have created the following formula. You receive the error message 'Can't divide by zero'. What should you do to rectify the problem?

If {Client.ClientID} = "DRP" Then {Cost.TotalCost} / {Cost.UnitCost}

A. Multiple the {Cost.TotalCost} * {Cost.UnitCost}

B. Multiple the {Cost.TotalCost} * {Cost.UnitCost} * -1

C. If {Cost.TotalCost} = 0 then 0 else {Cost.TotalCost} / {Cost.UnitCost}

Q10. You have created the following formula and receive the error message 'The remaining text does not appear to be part of the formula'. How can you rectify this problem?

NumberVar TotalOrdSum: =Count ({Command.Client Order Amount})
If {Command.Client ID} = 501 Then
TotalOrdSum: = Count ({Command.Client Order Amount})
else 0

A. NumberVar TotalOrdSum: =Count ({Command.Client Order Amount}) If {Command.Client ID} = 501 Then TotalOrdSum: = Count ({Command.Client Order Amount}) 0

B. NumberVar TotalOrdSum:=Count({Command.Client Order Amount}) if {Command.Client ID} = 501 Then TotalOrdSum:= Count({Command.Client Order Amount});

C. NumberVar TotalOrdSum:= Count({Command.Client Order Amount}); if {Command.Client ID} = 501 Then TotalOrdSum:= Count({Command.Client Order Amount}) else 0

D. NumberVar TotalOrdSum:=Count({Command.Client Order Amount}) if {Command.Client ID} = 501 Then TotalOrdSum:= Count({Command.Client Order Amount}) Else NOT 501

Q11. Which of the following will convert (777.300) to 777?

A. Sgn
B. Abs()
C. Int
D. Truncate

Q12. You want to convert the exam cost field {Exam.ExamCost} to a currency. Which of the following is a currency converter formula syntax? *(Multiple Answers)*

A. ${Exam.ExamCost}
B. CCur({Exam.ExamCost})
C. CStr({Exam.ExamCost})
D. CDbl({Exam.ExamCost})
E. DB({Exam.ExamCost})

Q13. Which of the following Crystal functions will give you 631? When applied to: 1244 and 1875

A. PopulationStdDev()
B. StdDev
C. Variance
D. MakeArray

Q14. Which of the following converts a fractional dollar price to a decimal price?

A. DollarFR
B. DollarFFR
C. DollarDDE
D. DollarDE

Q15. You apply a summary (Sum Grand Total to the Total figures below). Which of the following results will be produced?

Record Number	Total
1	1
2	1
3	1
4	0
5	0
6	0
7	0
8	0
9	0
10	0
11	0
12	0

A. 3

B. 9

C. 12

D. 10

Q16. You apply a summary (Distinct Count to the data below). Which of the following results will be produced?

Record Number	Total
1	1
2	1
3	1
4	0
5	0
6	0
7	0
8	0
9	0
10	0
11	0
12	0

A. 3

B. 9

C. 12

D. 2

E. 10

Q17. You apply a summary (Count to the data below). Which of the following results will be produced?

Record Number	Total
1	1
2	1
3	1
4	0
5	0
6	0
7	0
8	0
9	0
10	0
11	0
12	0

A. 3

B. 9

C. 12

D. 2

E. 10

Q18. A request has been made to highlight the discounts that will be assigned to clients based on their orders. For orders less than or equal to 40, a 5% discount will be awarded, between 41 and 80, 10% and 81 and over, 15%. Which of the following formulas apply?

A. if count({Order_Details.Quantity}) = 40 then 'Eligible for 5% Discount' else if count({Order_Details.Quantity}) <= 41 and count({Order_Details.Quantity})<= 80 then 'Eligible for 10% Discount' else if count({Order_Details.Quantity}) = 81 then 'Eligible for 15% Discount'

B. if count({Order_Details.Quantity}) <= 41 then 'Eligible for 5% Discount' Else if count({Order_Details.Quantity}) >= 41 and count({Order_Details.Quantity})<= 80 then 'Eligible for 10% Discount' else if count({Order_Details.Quantity}) >= 81 then 'Eligible for 15% Discount'

C. if count({Order_Details.Quantity}) >= 40 then 'Eligible for 5% Discount' Else if count({Order_Details.Quantity}) >= 41 and count({Order_Details.Quantity})<= 80 then 'Eligible for 10% Discount' Else if count({Order_Details.Quantity}) >= 81 then 'Eligible for 15% Discount'

D. if count({Order_Details.Quantity}) <= 40 then 'Eligible for 5% Discount' Else if count({Order_Details.Quantity}) >= 41 and count({Order_Details.Quantity})<= 80 then 'Eligible for 10% Discount' Else if count({Order_Details.Quantity}) >= 81 then 'Eligible for 15% Discount'

Q19. Due to data entry errors the delivery_days field contains characters, you want to extract only fields which contain numbers. Which of the following will extract fields which contain numbers only?

A. If Numeric({dispatch.deliverydays}) then {dispatch.deliverydays})

B. If ToNumber({dispatch.deliverydays}) then {dispatch.deliverydays})

C. If IsNumeric({dispatch.deliverydays}) then {dispatch.deliverydays})

D. If IsNumber({dispatch.deliverydays}) then {dispatch.deliverydays})

Working With Strings

Q1. How would you concatenate the following string fields?

Client.Client.Title
Client.Client.FName
Client.Client.LName

A. Client.Client.Title & "Client.Client.FName" & "Client.Client.LName"

B. Client.Client.Title & " " & Client.Client.FName & " " & Client.Client.Lname

C. "Client.Client.Title" & "Client.Client.FName" & "Client.Client.LName"

D. "Client.Client.Title" *"Client.Client.FName" *"Client.Client.LName"

Q2. You want to extract the first letter of the Client's first name to produce the following: - Mrs A. Thompson, using the following fields

Client.Client.Title
Client.Client.FName
Client.Client.LName

A. Client.Client.Title & " " & Client.Client.Fname =[1] & "." Client.Client.Lname

B. Client.Client.Title & " " & Client.Client.Fname=1 & "." Client.Client.Lname

C. Client.Client.Title & " " & Client.Client.Fname .1 & "." Client.Client.LName

D. Client.Client.Title & " " & Client.Client.Fname [1] & "." Client.Client.Lname

E. Client.Client.Title & " " & Client.Client.Fname [1] & "."& Client.Client.LName

Q3. Which of the following is a Subscript formula? *(Multiple Answers)*

A. {Client.FullName} [5 to 8]

B. {Client.FullName} (5 to 8)

C. {Client.FullName} {5 to 8}

D. {Client.FullName} '5 to 8'

Q4. You want to display 1678 as one thousand six hundred and seventy eight. Which of the following apply?

A. ToNumber(1678,0)
B. ToWords(1678,0)
C. ToNumbers(1678,0)
D. ToWord(1678,0)
E. ToText(1678,0)

Q5. Data in the surname field has been entered in capital letters, and you want to display the surname field on your report in lowercase letters, however the First letter of the surname must be displayed as a capital letter. Which of the following will achieve this aim?

A. ProperCase({Surname})
B. lowercase({Surname})
C. lowercase(uppercase({Surname}))
D. Proper({Surname})

Q6. You receive the following error message when the following variables are declared "The remaining text does not appear to be part of the formula". Which of the following will rectify the problem?

```
CurrencyVar SaleAmount;
StringVar RecvName
DateTimeVar DispatchDate;
```

A. CurrencyVar SaleAmount StringVar RecvName; DateTimeVar DispatchDate;
B. CurrencyVar SaleAmount StringVar RecvName DateTimeVar DispatchDate
C. CurrencyVar SaleAmount; StringVar RecvName; DateTimeVar DispatchDate ;
D. CurrencyVar SaleAmount: StringVar RecvName; DateTimeVar DispatchDate ;

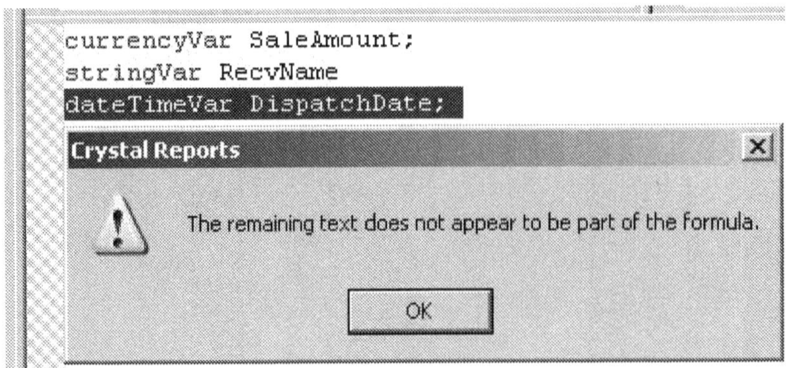

Q7. Data in the firstname field has been entered with spaces, and you want to eliminate these spaces and display the firstname on the report. Which of the following apply?

A. Truncate({firstname})

B. Truncate({firstname},1)

C. Trun({firstname})

D. Trim({firstname})

Q8. You created a formula as follows
" Thank You for buying £ " + {Client. Sales} + " in goods last month."
You receive the following error message : 'A string is required here'. What should you do to rectify the problem?

A. " Thank You for buying £ " + ({Client. Sales})+ " in goods last month."

B. " Thank You for buying £ " + Client. Sales + " in goods last month."

C. " Thank You for buying £ " + {Client. Sales} + " in goods last month.

D. Thank You for buying £ " + {Client. Sales} + " in goods last month."

E. " Thank You for buying £ " + ToText({Client. Sales}) + " in goods last month."

Q9. If a clients_id begins with LON then display' London based clients', otherwise display 'other cities'. Which of the following formulas will produce the result required? *(Multiple Answers)*

A. if {Orders.CustomerID} startswith "LON" then "London based clients" else "other cities"

B. if {Orders.CustomerID} like "LON" then "London based clients" else "other cities"

C. if {Orders.CustomerID} is "LON" then "London based clients" else "other cities"

D. if {Orders.CustomerID} is like %LON then "London based clients" else "other cities"

E. IIF ({Orders.CustomerID} Startswith 'LON', ' London based clients,' other cities ')

F. Switch ({Orders.CustomerID} Startswith 'LON', "London based clients", NOT ({Orders.CustomerID}Startswith 'LON'), " other cities ")

Q10 The title, firstname and last name, are held in different fields. You want to display all three in the same formula, putting a dot between the title and first name, lastname, and you also want the city to appear in brackets beside the lastname and in uppercase. Which of the following formulas will achieve this? *(Multiple Answers)*

Example: Ms.Antonia.Iroko (LONDON)

A. {Clients.Title} + "." + {Clients.FirstName} + " " + {Clients.LastName} + " (" + uppercase({Clients.City})+ ") "
B. {Clients.Title} + "." + {Clients.FirstName} + " " + {Clients.LastName} + " (" + upcase({Clients.City})+ ") "
C. {Clients.Title} + "." + {Clients.FirstName} + " " + {Clients.LastName} + " (" + uppercase({Clients.City})+ ") " +
D. {Clients.Title} & "." & {Clients.FirstName} & "." & {Clients.LastName} & " (" & uppercase({Clients.City}) & ") "
E. {Clients.Title} & "." & {Clients.FirstName} & "." & {Clients.LastName} & " (" & ucase({Clients.City}) & ") "

Q11. Which of the following is a Boolean formula?

A. if ({customer.region}) = 'al' then true else false
B. If {@Submit hours} = 0 then "Submitted on Time" else If {@Submit hours} = 1 then "Submitted in 1 Hour" else "Submitted in " + ToText({@Submit hours}, 0) + "hours"
C. ToText ({@1000s formula},2,',',':')
D. Create the following formula: distinctCount({Client.ClientID},{Client.Country}) and place it in the details section

Q12. Which of the following will convert a datetime datatype to a string? *(Multiple Answers)*

A. Cstr()
B. ToText()
C. ToWord()
D. C()

Q13. What will be the result of the following formula?

"30" & "40" & "5"

A. 75
B. Syntax Not recognized
C. 30405

Q14. CStr applied to 289.81 will return which of the following?

A. Two hundred and eighty nine hundred and eight one
B. 289
C. Converts 289.81 to a string
D. 290

Q15. You have been asked to change the following formula to a CASE statement. Which of the following is correct?

if {Dispatch.DispatchDays} = 0 then "Dispatched Same Day" else if {Dispatch.DispatchDays} = 1 then "Dispatched in 1 Day" else "Dispatched in " + ToText({Dispatch.DispatchDays}, 0) + "Days"

A. Select {Dispatch.DispatchDays} CASE 0: "Dispatched On Time" CASE 1: "Dispatched in 1 Day" Default: "Dispatched in " + ToText({Dispatch.DispatchDays} , 0) + "Days"

B. Select {Dispatch.DispatchDays} CASE: "Dispatched On Time" CASE : "Dispatched in 1 Day" Default: "Dispatched in " + ToText({Dispatch.DispatchDays} , 0) + "Days"
C. Select {Dispatch.DispatchDays} CASE 0 "Dispatched On Time" CASE 1 "Dispatched in 1 Day" Default: "Dispatched in " + ToText({Dispatch.DispatchDays} , 0) + "Days"
D. Select {Dispatch.DispatchDays} CASE 0: "Dispatched On Time" CASE 1: "Dispatched in 1 Day" Default: "Dispatched in " + ({Dispatch.DispatchDays} , 0) + "Days"

Q16. Within the Formula Workshop - Formula Editor. Which of the following can be accessed? *(Multiple Answers)*

A. Functions
B. Operators
C. Reports Fields
D. Database Tables and Fields

Q17. You want to present a report which displays the maximum number of each product purchased, and the Client who purchased the product, your report contains a group based on product name. Which of the following formulas will give you the results required?

A. 'The Maximum quantity of' + " " + ({Products.ProductName}) + " " + 'ordered by' + " " + {Clients.ClientID} + " " + 'is' + " " + totext(Maxi ({Order_Details.Quantity}, {Products.ProductName}))

B. 'The Maximum quantity of' + " " + ({Products.ProductName}) + " " + 'ordered by' + " " + {Clients.ClientID} + " " + 'is' + " " + totext(Maximum ({Order_Details.Quantity}, {Products.ProductName}))

C. 'The Maximum quantity of' + " " + ({Products.ProductName}) + " " + 'ordered by' + " " + {Clients.ClientID} + " " + 'is' + " " + totext(Max ({Order_Details.Quantity}, {Products.ProductName}))

D. 'The Maximum quantity of' + " " + ({Products.ProductName}) + " " + 'ordered by' + " " + {Clients.ClientID} + " " + 'is' + " " + Maximum ({Order_Details.Quantity}, {Products.ProductName})

Q18. Which function has been applied to the 'firstname' string that will produce the results below?

FIRSTNAME	RESULT
Antonia	65.00
Mary	78.00
Lance	76.00
John	74.00

A. StrCmp()

B. Filter()

C. AscW()

D. Ascci()

E. Space()

Q19. Which of the following functions has been applied to 'Client_id' to produce the result?

CLIENT_ID	RESULT
1	I
2	11
3	111
6	VI

A. Convert()

B. Tonumber()

C. Roman()

D. Totext()

Q20. You want to extract the first four letters of the town field. Which of the following formulas will produce the correct result? *(Multiple Answers)*

A. {Client. Town}[4]

B. {Client. Town}[1 TO 4]

C. {Client. Town}[1&2&3&4]

D. Left ({Client. Town}, 1,4)

E. Left ({Client. Town}, 4)

F. Mid ({Client. Town}, 1,4)

G. TrimLeft ({Client. Town}, 1,4)

Q21. You have created the following formula to establish the time span for student's assignment submissions. The formula produces the following error message "a string is required here". How do you rectify this error?

if {@Submit days} = 0 then "Submitted on Time" else {@Submit days}

A. if ({@Submit days}) = 0 then "Submitted on Time" else ({@Submit days})

B. if (({@Submit days}) = 0 then "Submitted on Time" else ({@Submit days}))

C. if ToText ({@Submit days}) = 0 then "Submitted on Time" else ({@Submit days})

D. if ({@Submit days}) = 0 then "Submitted on Time" else ToText({@Submit days} , 0)

Q22. You have been informed of a data inputting error made by one of your staff. A number has been entered between characters in the firstname field. Which of the following formulas will highlight the data error entry?

A. if Roman({Client.FirstName}) then 'Data Input Error'else {Client.FirstName}

B. if not NumericText ({Client.FirstName}) then 'Data Input Error'else {Client.FirstName}

C. if ProperCase ({Client.FirstName}) then 'Data Input Error'else {Client.FirstName}

D. if Val({Client.FirstName}) then 'Data Input Error'else {Client.FirstName}

Q23. Old student registration codes started with a prefix of their country, e.g. UK users will have a code of UK9883003, and US users with a prefix of US9883002. The length of the string old code was nine and has now changed to seven. New codes will only contain the digits. You now want to display only digits without the prefix? *(Multiple Answers)*

A. if length({@reg_code})= 9 then mid({@reg_code},3,7) else {@reg_code}

B. right({@reg_code},7)

C. left({@reg_code},7)

D. mid({@reg_code},4,7)

Using Functions – Crystal Financial Functions

Q1. You have just sold your corporate bonds and would like to calculate the Accrued interest. Which of the following Crystal financial functions can be used to calculate the Accrued Interest for your bonds, which pays periodical interest?

A. AmorLINC
B. ACCRINT
C. AmorDEGRC
D. ACCRINTM
E. CoupNCD

Q2. You want to calculate the price per $200 face value of a security when the first period is odd. Which of the following functions can be used?

A. OddLYield
B. OddPrice
C. OddFPrice
D. OddFieldYield

Q3. Which of the following Crystal financial functions calculates the number of days from the settlement date to the next coupon date?

A. CoupDayBS
B. CoupDaysNC
C. CoupNCD
D. AmorDEGRC
E. ACCRINTM
F. CumlPRINC

Q4. Which of the following functions calculates the number of regular payments on a loan, or for an investment annuity?

A. NPER
B. XNPV
C. MIRR
D. CULM
E. IPMT
F. EFFEC
G. EFFECT

Q5. Which of the following functions calculates the interest rate for a fully invested security?

A. XIRR

B. XNPV

C. CUMIPMT

D. INTRATE

E. IPMT

F. EFFEC

G. EFFECT

Q6. Which of the following Crystal financial functions can be used to calculate Accrued Interest for a bond, which pays interest on maturity?

A. AmorLINC

B. ACCRINT

C. CoupNCD

D. AmorDEGRC

E. ACCRINTM

Q7. Your client procured bonds with a maturity date in the next five years. Which of the following functions will compute the interest payments between a given settlement date and maturity date?

A. COUPNUM

B. CoupDayBS

C. CoupDaysNC

D. CoupNCD

E. ACCRINTM

F. CumlPRINC

Q8. Which of the following Crystal Financial Function can be used to calculate the depreciation of an asset? *(Multiple Answers)*

A. AmorLINC

B. ACCRINT

C. AmorDEGRC

D. DISC

E. ACCRINTM

F. CoupNCD

Q9. Which of the following calculates the price on a discounted security?

A. PRICEMATV
B. PRICEMAT
C. PRICEDISC
D. PRICEMATT

Q10. Which of the following Crystal Financial Function calculates the number of days from a coupon's last payment date, to the settlement date?

A. CoupDayBS
B. ACCRINT
C. CoupNCD
D. AmorDEGRC
E. ACCRINTM
F. CumlPRINC

Q11. Which of the following Crystal Financial Functions calculates the number of days in the coupon period, including the settlement date?

A. CoupDayBS
B. CoupDays
C. CoupNCD
D. AmorDEGRC
E. ACCRINTM
F. CumlPRINC

Q12. You want to calculate the interest rate applicable to a loan. Which of the following functions apply?

A. RateDV
B. Rate
C. RateInt
D. Pricematv
E. Pricedisc

Q13. You want to calculate the yield value of a security when the first period is odd. Which of the following functions can be used?

A. OddPriceYield
B. OddFYield
C. OddLPrice
D. YieldPrice

Q14. Which of the following will calculate the price value of a security, where interest is paid upon maturity?

A. PRICEMATV
B. PRICEMAT
C. PRICEDISC
D. PRICEMATT

Q15. Which of the following Crystal Financial Function calculates the future value of a loan?

A. DISC
B. Ipmt
C. ISPMT
D. Nper
E. FV
F. CoupNCD

Q16. Which of the following calculates the next coupon date following a given settlement date?

A. DISC
B. Ipmt
C. ISPMT
D. CoupPCD
E. FV
F. CoupNCD

Q17. Which of the following calculates the internal rate of return?

A. IRR
B. IRTRN
C. IRRTRN
D. Nper
E. OddFYield

Q18. Your client has taken out a loan, and you want to calculate the cumulative interest paid. Which of the following apply?

A. DISC
B. DB
C. CUMPRINC
D. CUMIPMT
E. CULM
F. DDB

Q19. Your client has taken out a loan, and you want to calculate the cumulative principal paid. Which of the following apply?

A. DISC
B. DB
C. CUMPRINC
D. CUMIPMT
E. CULM
F. DDB

Q20. Which of the following converts a dollar decimal price to a fractional dollar price?

A. DollarFR
B. DollarFFR
C. DollarDDE
D. DollarDE

Q21. Given, its interest rate, the term, present value, and future value. Which of the following calculates a payment?

A. PMT

B. PPMT

C. CUMPRINC

D. CUMIPMT

E. CULM

F. DDB

Q22. Which of the following calculates fixed declining balance depreciation, for an asset?

A. DISC

B. DB

C. CUMPRINC

D. CUMIPMT

E. CULM

F. DDB

Q23. Which function calculates double-declining balance depreciation, for an asset?

A. DISC

B. DB

C. CUMPRINC

D. CUMIPMT

E. CULM

F. DDB

Q24. Which of the following functions calculates the principal portion of a payment?

A. PPmt

B. PMMT

C. PV

D. MPT

Q25. Which function calculates the discount rate for a security?

A. DISC
B. DB
C. CUMPRINC
D. CUMIPMT
E. CULM
F. DDB

Q26. Which function calculates the effective annual interest?

A. DISC
B. EFF
C. CUMIPMT
D. CULM
E. DDB
F. EFFEC
G. EFFECT

Q27. Which of the following functions is used to gauge the impact on a bonds price, when the bond yields changes?

A. MyieldBond
B. MDuration
C. MIRR
D. NPer

Q28. Which of the following functions calculates a Macaulay duration?

A. DUR
B. DURATION
C. DRR
D. DDDRR
E. DR

Q29. Which of the following functions calculates the internal rate of return, for an investment?

A. XIRR
B. EFF
C. CUMIPMT
D. CULM
E. DDB
F. EFFEC
G. EFFECT

Q30. Which of the following functions calculates the net present value, for an investment?

A. XIRR
B. XNPV
C. CUMIPMT
D. CULM
E. DDB
F. EFFEC
G. EFFECT

Q31. Which of the following functions calculates the present or future value of an annuity?

A. PVV
B. PPV
C. PPBB
D. PV

Q32. Which of the following functions calculates the interest portion of a payment?

A. XIRR
B. XNPV
C. CUMIPMT
D. CULM
E. IPMT
F. EFFEC
G. EFFECT

Q33. Which of the following functions calculates the nominal annual interest?

A. CoupDayBS
B. ISPMT
C. CoupNCD
D. Nominal
E. ACCRINTM
F. CumlPRINC

Q34. Which of the following functions calculates the modified internal rate of return implicit in a set of cash flows?

A. XIRR
B. XNPV
C. MIRR
D. CULM
E. IPMT
F. EFFEC
G. EFFECT

Q35. Which of the following functions calculates the straight-line interest portion of a payment?

A. ISPMT
B. XNPV
C. MIRR
D. CULM
E. IPMT
F. EFFEC
G. EFFECT

Q36. Which of the following functions calculates straight-line balance depreciation, for an asset?

A. ISPMT
B. SLN
C. MIRR
D. CULM
E. IPMT
F. EFFEC
G. EFFECT

Q37. Which of the following functions calculates the sum of the years digits depreciation, for an asset?

A. SYD
B. SLN
C. VDB
D. CULM
E. IPMT
F. EFFEC
G. EFFECT

Q38. Which of the following functions calculates declining balance depreciation, for an asset?

A. SYD
B. SLN
C. VDB
D. CULM
E. IPMT
F. EFFEC
G. EFFECT

Q39. Which of the following functions calculates a payment?

A. Pmt
B. PMMT
C. PV
D. MPT

Q40. Which of the following functions calculates the interest rate implied to a mortgage?

A. Rate
B. Yield
C. PV
D. Pmt

Q41. Which of the following functions calculates the future value of a completely invested coupon?

A. ISPMT
B. XNPV
C. MIRR
D. CULM
E. RECEIVED
F. EFFEC
G. EFFECT

Q42. Which of the following financial functions calculates the yield of a security, a discounted yield, and the yield of a security where interest is paid on maturity? *(Multiple Answers)*

A. OddPriceYield
B. OddFYield
C. YieldDisc
D. YieldMat
E. YieldPrice
F. Yield

Q43. Which of the following financial functions are utilized for Treasury bill calculations? *(Multiple Answers)*

A. TBILLEQ
B. TBILLPRICE
C. TBILLYIELD
D. TBILLYLD
E. TBILLPRC

Working With Null Values

First Name	Last Name	Exam ID	Score	Flag Nulls	Exam Date	Version
Anthony	Richard	RDCR200	77	77	05/06/2005	***Version XI***
Anthony	Richard	RDCR600	56	56	02/02/2005	***Version XI***
Anthony	Richard	RDCR500	50	50	09/07/2005	***Version XI***
Anthony	Richard	RDCR300			08/08/2005	***Version XI***
Anthony	Richard	RDCR400	89	89	08/01/2005	***Version XI***
Anthony	Richard	RDCR100	80	80	20/01/2005	***Version XI***
Micheal	Hanson	RDCR100	79	79	01/01/2005	***Version XI***
Metaer	Rogers	RDCR500	100	100	30/11/2005	***Version XI***
Metaer	Rogers	RDCR100	85	85	22/08/2005	***Version XI***
Metaer	Rogers	RDCR200	66	66	21/09/2005	***Version XI***
Metaer	Rogers	RDCR300	88	88	09/08/2005	***Version XI***
Christopher	Tailer	RDCR100			11/11/2005	***Version XI***
Edith	Miller	RDCR100	60	60	02/03/2005	***Version XI***
John	Johnson	RDCR100			21/01/2005	***Version XI***
John	Johnson	RDCR200	79	79	30/12/2005	***Version XI***
John	Johnson	RDCR500	79	79	09/09/2005	***Version XI***
John	Johnson	RDCR300	89	89	07/07/2005	***Version XI***
John	Johnson	RDCR400	90	90	07/05/2005	***Version XI***
John	Johnson	RDCR100	46	46	06/06/2005	***Version XI***
Antonia	Iroko	RDCR100	90	90	04/04/2005	***Version XI***

Q1. Based on the information above, you have created a formula to flag nulls which exist in the score field, however the formula does not seem to work. Which of the following could be the possible cause?

if isnull({Sample_Exam_Results___2005.SCORE}) then 'Error' else {Sample_Exam_Results___2005.SCORE}

A. The Convert Database NULL Values to Default checkbox is checked

B. The Convert Database NULL Values to Default checkbox is unchecked

C. The convert other Null Values to default checkbox is unchecked

D. The convert other Null Values to default checkbox is checked

Q2. Which of the following functions can be used to handle null values in a formula? *(Multiple Answers)*

A. NextIsNull

B. IsNull

C. PreviousIsNull

D. Null

Q3. Which of the following functions will flag the first null record?

A. IsNull
B. NextIsNull
C. PreviousIsNull
D. Previous

Q4. Which of the following Crystal functions will flag the last record?

A. IsNull
B. NextIsNull
C. PreviousIsNull
D. Next

Q5. You want to convert database values to default. What should you do?

A. Choose Database\ Options and check the Convert Database NULL Values to Default and convert other Null Values to default
B. Choose Report\ Report Options and check the Convert Database NULL Values to Default and convert other Null Values to default
C. Choose Report and check the Convert Database NULL Values to Default and convert other Null Values to default
D. Choose File\ Report Options and check the Convert Database NULL Values to Default

Q6. NextIsNull and PreviousIsNull cannot be used on databases that do not support Null Values

A. True
B. False

Q7. What is the definition of Null? *(Multiple Answers)*

A. Zero in database field
B. No value in database field
C. Empty String
D. Spaces in database field
E. None of the above

Q8. You count a null string field. It results in the following?

A. Zero
B. Length of zero
C. Null
D. Error

Working with Arrays

Q1. An additional certification exam code (RDCR500a) has been assigned to the current exam certification path. You want to add the new code to your existing codes. Which of the following methods will allow you to add the new code and display it in your report?

A. Local StringVar array ExamCodes := ["RDCR200a", "RDCR300a", "RDCR400a"];
Redim ExamCodes [4];
ExamCodes [4] := "RDCR500a";
join(ExamCodes,",")

B. Local StringVar array ExamCodes := ["RDCR200a", "RDCR300a", "RDCR400a"];
Redim Preserve ExamCodes [4];
ExamCodes [4] := "RDCR500a";
join(ExamCodes,",")

C. Local StringVar array ExamCodes := ["RDCR200a", "RDCR300a", "RDCR400a"];
Preserve ExamCodes [4];
ExamCodes [4] := "RDCR500a";
join(ExamCodes,",")

D. Local StringVar array ExamCodes := ["RDCR200a", "RDCR300a", "RDCR400a"];
Redim ExamCodes (4);
ExamCodes (4) := "RDCR500a";
join(ExamCodes,",")

E. Local StringVar array ExamCodes := ["RDCR200a", "RDCR300a", "RDCR400a"];
Redim ExamCodes (4);
ExamCodes (4) := "RDCR500a";
join(ExamCodes,",")

Q2. Arrays cannot be shared between a main report and a Subreport.

A. True
B. False

Q3. Which of the following is the Redim syntax in Crystal?

A. Redim X[n]
B. Redim x( )
C. Redim x { }
D. Redim x | |

Q4. Which of the following is the Redim syntax in Basic?

- Redim X[n]
- Redim x( )
- Redim x { }
- Redim x | |

Q5. What will the following function produce?

[({Retail.Amount *.6) , ({Retail.Amount *.6) , ({Retail.Amount *.75)]

A. Subscript
B. In Array
C. Make Array
D. Array
E. An error message

Q6. What will the following array return?

Sum([100,75,45,2])

A. 222
B. 100
C. 4
D. 0
E. NONE OF THE ABOVE

Q7. Which one of the following statements is true? *(Multiple Answers)*

A. Array subscripts start at 1 in Crystal.
B. Array subscripts start with 0, (default in VB).
C. Crystal does not support arrays with zero elements.
D. Crystal does not support arrays with 1 element.

Q8. Which of the following are not variable declarations in Crystal? *(Multiple Answers)*

A. BooleanVar

B. NumberVar

C. CurrencyVar

D. DateVar

E. RangeVar

F. ArrayVar

Q9. What are the data types in an array described as?

A. Array functionalities

B. Array Run

C. Array Formatting

D. Elements

Q10. Your arrays size exceeds 1000 elements. Which of the following arrays accommodates this?

A. Multiple arrays

B. Single Multiple arrays

C. Redim Arrays

D. Array Functions

Q11. What role does Redim Preserve play in arrays?

A. Changes the size of the array

B. Multiples the next array

C. Subtracts the array function

D. None of the above

E. All of the above

Q12. Arrays can be shared

A. True

B. False

Q13. Elements of an array can be changed

A. True

B. False

Q14. Values can be assigned to an array.

A. True

B. False

Q15. What does 'Redim' in an array stand for?

A. The size of which the array is incremented by

B. The volume of the array

C. The width of the array

D. The Length of the array

Q16. You want to retrieve the biggest subscript of an array. Which of the following should you use?

A. Ubound (x)

B. Redim x[n]

C. Redim Preserve x[n]

D. Preserve

Q17. What does preserve in an array do?

A. Elements in the array are maintained

B. Elements in the array are changed

C. Elements in the array are not duplicated

D. Elements in the array are duplicated

Q18. You have created the following formula. You have also placed the script below into the Select Expert. What will the code enact?

```
Formula
BooleanVar ResultArray;
StringVar array  arrayExamCode;
if {?Exam Code} = "ALL" then
arrayExamCode := {Exams.ExamCode}
else
arrayExamCode := {?Exam Code};
ResultArray := true;

Script
StringVar array  arrayExamCode;
{Exams.Exam Code} = arrayExamCode
```

A. Separates Parameter values

B. Sets all parameters to false

C. Sets all parameters to 'Y'

D. If Parameter prompt is set to All, return all records else return value entered

Q19. An additional certification exam code (RDCR500a) has been assigned to the current exam certification path. You want to replace the old codes with your new code. Which of the following methods will allow you to add the code and display it on your report?

A. Local StringVar array ExamCodes := ["RDCR200a", "RDCR300a"];
Redim ExamCodes [3];
ExamCodes [3] := "RDCR500a";
ExamCodes [3]

B. Local StringVar array ExamCodes := ["RDCR200a", "RDCR300a"];
Preserve Redim ExamCodes [3];
ExamCodes [3] := "RDCR500a";
ExamCodes [3]

C. Local StringVar array ExamCodes := ["RDCR200a", "RDCR300a"];
Redim Preserve ExamCodes [3];
ExamCodes [3] := "RDCR500a";
ExamCodes [3]

D. Local StringVar array ExamCodes := ["RDCR200a", "RDCR300a"];
Redim ExamCodes (3);
ExamCodes (3) := "RDCR500a";
ExamCodes (3)

Q20. Which of the following are Array Operators? *(Multiple Answers)*

A. Make Array

B. Subscript

C. In Array

D. Redim

E. Preserve

F. Preserve Rem

G. Redim Preserve

Q21. What is the element limit of array in Crystal Reports?

A. 10

B. 1000

C. 2000

D. 0

E. 1

Q22. Exams taken by candidates are placed in the same field, i.e. RDCR200, RDCR300, RDCR400. You want the individual exam codes to appear as separate elements. Which of the following will you use?

A. Share()

B. Split()

C. Separate()

D. Divide()

Q23. Student Exam Records are stored as illustrated in the table below, you want to create a formiula which will highlight all students who have completed the required three exams with a status of 'Certified' and 'Not Certified' for all others. Which one of the following formulas will produce the results required?

Results Table

Candidate Number	Exam 1 Of 3	Exam 2 Of 3	Exam 3 Of 3
1	Completed	Completed	Completed
2	Completed		
3			
4	Completed		Completed
5	Completed	Completed	Completed
6	Completed	Completed	Completed
7	Completed	Completed	Completed

A. Local StringVar Array BOCPArray; BOCPArray := [({Results Table.Exam 1 Of 3}), ({{Results Table.Exam 2 Of 3}),({{Results Table.Exam 3 Of 3})]; UBound (BOCPArray); if UBound (BOCPArray) = 3 then 'Certified' else 'Not Certified'

B. Local StringVar Array BOCPArray; MAKEArray := [({Results Table.Exam 1 Of 3}), ({{Results Table.Exam 2 Of 3}),({{Results Table.Exam 3 Of 3})]; UBound (BOCPArray); if UBound (BOCPArray) = 3 then 'Certified' else 'Not Certified'

C. Local StringVar PreserveArray BOCPArray; BOCPArray := [({Results Table.Exam 1 Of 3}), ({{Results Table.Exam 2 Of 3}),({{Results Table.Exam 3 Of 3})]; UBound (BOCPArray); if UBound (BOCPArray) = 3 then 'Certified' else 'Not Certified'

D. Local StringVar Array BOCPArray; BOCPArray := [({Results Table.Exam 1 Of 3}), ({{Results Table.Exam 2 Of 3}),({{Results Table.Exam 3 Of 3})]; UnBound (BOCPArray); if UnBound (BOCPArray) = 3 then 'Certified' else 'Not Certified'

Q24. Which of the following formulas will outline 'Early Deliveries or Lates deliveries given the date required and the date delivered

A. Global DateVar Array DeliveryStatusArray:= [Date({Orders.Required Date}), Date({Orders.Delivered})];
if DeliveryStatusArray[2] < DeliveryStatusArray[1]
then 'Early Delivery'
else 'Late Delivery'
B. Global DateVar Array DeliveryStatusArray:= [Date({Orders.Required Date}), Date({Orders.Delivered})];
if DeliveryStatusArray(2)< DeliveryStatusArray(1)
then 'Early Delivery'
else 'Late Delivery'
C. Global DateVar Array DeliveryStatusArray:= (Date({Orders.Required Date}), Date({Orders.Delivered}));
if DeliveryStatusArray[2] < DeliveryStatusArray[1]
then 'Early Delivery'
else 'Late Delivery'

Sql Expressions

Q1. How can you access the SQL Expression field?

A. Choose View | Field Explorer | Right-Click the SQL Expression fields and click new.
B. Choose file | Field Explorer | Right-Click the SQL Expression fields and click new.
C. Choose View | Report |Field Explorer | Right-Click the SQL Expression fields and click new.
D. Choose Database| Report |Field Explorer | Right-Click the SQL Expression fields and click new.

Q2. Which SQL Expression will display the Database name?

A. UserDB
B. Database()
C. Database{}
D. Database[]

Q3. You want to display the name of the database user on your report. Which of the following apply?

A. User()
B. UserDB
C. Database{}
D. Database[]

Q4. Which of the following are SQL Expression Functions? *(Multiple Answers)*

A. ASCII()
B. DIFFERENCE(,)
C. REPLACE(,,)
D. UCASE()
E. SPACE()

Q5. Which of the following is used to depict an SQL Expression name?

A. @
B. ~
C. #
D. ?
E. %

Q6. SQL Functions change in the SQL Expression Editor, depending on the type of database being used.

A. True
B. False

Q7. You have placed a SQL Expression field into your SQL language. What will appear?

A. SQL Expression Name
B. SQL Expression formula
C. It will not show in the SQL Query
D. Error message

Q8. You can use SQL expression fields within SQL Commands and Stored Procedures.

A. True
B. False

Q9. SQL Expressions improve performance of reports.

A. True
B. False

Q10. What are the basic requirements for using SQL Expression? *(Multiple Answers)*

A. SQL Database
B. ODBC Database
C. .dll extension file
D. .ora drivers required

Control Structures

Q1. Which of the following best describes a Control Structure? *(Multiple Answers)*

A. A formula
B. A process
C. None of the above
D. A statement which determines the order of execution of the other statements
E. The use of a formula to evaluate a process until a condition is encounter

Q2. Which of the following can be defined as a control structure? *(Multiple Answers)*

A. if WeekdayName (DayOfWeek ({Orders.SalesDate})) = 'Wednesday' then 'Required' else 'Not Required'
B. if ({Delivery.DeliveryDate})in LastFullMonth then 'Last Months Orders' else if Month({Delivery.DeliveryDate})= 11 and Year({Delivery.DeliveryDate})= year(CurrentDate) then 'Current Year November Orders' else if {Orders.ShippedDate} in Last7Days then 'Orders Made in the Last Seven Days' else Totext({Orders.ShippedDate})
C. ProperCase({Surname})
D. Select {Dispatch.DispatchDays} CASE 0: "Dispatched On Time" CASE 1: "Dispatched in 1 Day" Default: "Dispatched in " + ToText({Dispatch.DispatchDays} , 0) + "Days"

Q3. Which of the following statements is true in relation to a 'For Loop'?

A. The For Loop, is a counter variable
B. The For Loop, keeps track of how many times a variable is used in a program
C. The For Loop, is a specific piece of logic has been cycled though
D. The For Loop, uses a counter variable to determine how many times a particular part of logic has been rotated though

Q4. Which of these statements is true in relation to a 'While Do Loop'?

A. The While Do Loop evaluates a condition after each occurrence of the loop and stops if the condition is no longer true
B. The While Do Loop evaluates a condition during each occurrence of the loop and stops if the condition is no longer true
C. The While Do Loop halts when a condition defined is no longer true
D. The While Do Loop evaluates a condition and continues if the condition is no longer true

Q5. Which of the following statements apply to an 'Option Loop'? *(Multiple Answers)*

A. Denote the maximum number of loops
B. Used for loop counts over 100000
C. Used for loop counts over 10000
D. Used for loop counts over 10000000

Q6. Which of the following are control structures? *(Multiple Answers)*

A. do while
B. exit for
C. exit while
D. for := to step do
E. if then else
F. option loop
G. select case : default:
H. while do
I. while

Q7. Which of the following statements is true in relation to a 'For' loop?

A. The For Loop is a counter variable
B. The For Loop keeps track of how many times a variable is used in a program
C. The For Loop is a specific piece of logic has been cycled though
D. The For Loop uses a counter variable to trace of how many times a particular part of logic has been rotated though

Q8. Which of the following apply to a 'While Do' loop?

A. Assesses the condition and if the condition is reached it stops
B. Assesses the condition for a specified number only
C. Assesses the condition and if the condition is achieved it performs the application of the condition set in the do section of the code, the procedure is continued until the condition is no longer applicable
A. Loops through the value of a specified number of times?
D. None of the above

Q9. Which of the following apply to a 'For Loop'?

A. Loops through the values of a specified period?
B. Assesses the condition and if the condition is reached it stops
C. Assesses the condition for a specified number only
D. Assesses the condition and if the condition is achieved it performs the application of the condition set in the do section of the code, the procedure is continued until the condition is no longer applicable

Processing A Report

Q1. Which of the following are report processing stages, in Crystal Reports? *(Multiple Answers)*

A. Pass 1
B. Pass 2
C. Pre-Pass 1
D. Pre-Pass 2
E. Pre-Pass 3
F. Pass 4
G. Pass 3

Q2. You have used 'Total Page Count'. Which of the following stages will it be processed under?

A. Pre-Pass 1
B. Pre –pass 2
C. Pass 3
D. Pass 1
E. Pass 4
F. Pre-pass 3
G. Pass 4

Q3. Which of the following formulas is processed under the Pre-Pass 1 reporting stage?

A. If WeekdayName (DayOfWeek ({Orders.SalesDate})) = 'Wednesday' then 'Required' else 'Not Required'
B. 20 + 10
C. "Order Number " + totext ({Orders.Order ID}) + " is required in " + totext({Orders.Required Date} - {Orders.Order Date}) + "days"
D. WhilePrintingRecords; NumberVar array EHArray;Sum(EHArray [1 to 40])

Q4. Recurring formulas are processed under which of the following?

A. Pre-Pass 1
B. Pre –pass 2
C. Pass 3
D. Pass 1
E. Pass 4
F. Pre-pass 3
G. Pass 4

Q5. Constant formulas are processed under which of the following report processing stages?

A. Pre-Pass 1
B. Pre –pass 2
C. Pass 3
D. Pass 4
E. Pre-pass 3
F. Pass 4

Q6. A formula which falls within the BeforeReadingRecords category; is processed before records are read from the database.

A. True
B. False

Q7. Which of the following fall into the Pre-Pass 1 stage?

A. WhilePrintingRecords
B. WhileReadingRecords
C. BeforeReadingRecords
D. EvaluateAfter

Q8. Which of the following are processed under Pass 1?

A. WhilePrintingRecords
B. WhileReadingRecords
C. BeforeReadingRecords
D. EvaluateAfter

Q9. Which of the following report processing functions can be applied to the formula below?

If {Client.City} = 'London' then '20% Discount Applicable' else '5% % Discount Applicable'

A. EvaluateBefore
B. EvaluateAfter
C. BeforeReadingRecords
D. WhileReadingRecords

Q10. Which of the following report processing functions can be applied to the formula below?

If Sum({Sales.Amount},{Sales.Rep}) > 100000 then 'Top Sales Person'

A. WhilePrintingRecords
B. EvaluateAfter
C. BeforeReadingRecords
D. WhileReadingRecords

Q11. You have opened a report and used saved data to re-run the report. Which of the report processing stages will it be processed under?

A. Pass 1
B. Pass 2
C. Pre-Pass 1
D. Pre-Pass 4
E. Pre-Pass 2

Q12. Running Totals are processed under which of the following?

A. Pre-Pass 1
B. Pre –pass 2
C. Pass 3
D. Pass 1
E. Pass 4
F. Pre-pass 3
G. Pass 2

Q13. 'TopN' and 'Bottom' are processed under which of the following stages?

A. Pass 1
B. Pass 2
C. Pre-Pass 1
D. Pre-Pass 4
E. Pre-Pass 2

Q14. Which of the following are processed under Pass 2? *(Multiple Answers)*

A. Cross-Tabs
B. Subreports
C. Group Selection
D. Running Totals
E. WhilePrintingRecords
F. PrintTime
G. Grand Total Summary
H. OLAP Grids
I. Charts
J. On Demand

Q15. Which of the following are evaluation time functions? *(Multiple Answers)*

A. WhileReadingRecords
B. WhilePrintingRecords
C. EvaluateAfter ()
D. BeforeReadingRecords
E. AfterReadingRecords
F. DuringPrintingRecords

Q16. You have created a formula and you want this particular formula to be processed after the result of another formula has been retrieved. Which of the following should you use?

A. WhileReadingRecords
B. WhilePrintingRecords
C. EvaluateAfter ()
D. BeforeReadingRecords

Creating Report Alerts

Q1. You want to create an Alert. Which of the following must be completed for the Alert to work?

A. Choose Report |Select Alert, create or modify alerts, new, assign a name, you must enter a message, a condition and a name, before the alert will work
B. Choose Report |Select Alert |create or modify alerts | new | assign a name | you do not have to enter a message, but you must assign a condition and a name, before the alert will work
C. Choose Report |Select Alert | create or modify alerts| new | assign a name | you must enter a message, but a condition is not required, before the alert will work
D. Choose Report |Select Alert | create or modify alerts| new | assign a name | you must enter a message, not name required and no condition is required, before the alert will work

Q2. You want to display the Alert message in the Report Header. Which of the following formulas apply? *(Multiple Answers)*
Alert Name: PropertyAlert
Alert Message: 'There are properties within the Buyers purchasing requirements'

A. If IsAlertEnabled ("PropertyAlert") = true then AlertMessage("PropertyAlert")
B. If IsAlertTriggered ("PropertyAlert") = true then AlertMessage("PropertyAlert")
C. If AlertEnabled ("PropertyAlert") = true then AlertMessage("PropertyAlert")
D. If AlertTriggered ("PropertyAlert") = true then AlertMessage("PropertyAlert")

Q3. You want to delete the Property Alert. Which of the following apply?

A. Select Format from the menu – Alerts – Create or Modify Alerts, highlight the Alert required and click the Delete button
B. Select View from the menu – Alerts – Create or Modify Alerts, highlight the Alert required and click the Delete button
C. Select Report from the menu – Alerts – Create or Modify Alerts, highlight the Alert required and click the Delete button
D. Select File from the menu – Alerts – Create or Modify Alerts, highlight the Alert required and click the Delete button

Q4. You want to change the name of the Alert. Which of the following apply?

A. Select Format from the menu – Alerts – Create or Modify Alerts, highlight the Alert required and click Edit and modify name as required
B. Select View from the menu – Alerts – Create or Modify Alerts, highlight the Alert required and click Edit and modify name as required
C. Select Report from the menu – Alerts – Create or Modify Alerts, highlight the Alert required and click Edit and modify name as required
D. Select File from the menu – Alerts – Create or Modify Alerts, highlight the Alert required and click Edit and modify name as required

Q5. Which of the following will happen when you refresh a report with an Alert?

A. The Report Alert dialog box will appear, click the Alert button to view records applicable to the Alert condition
B. The Report Alert dialog box will appear, click the View button to view records applicable to the Alert condition
C. The Report Alert dialog box will appear, click the Records button to view records applicable to the Alert condition
D. The Report Alert dialog box will appear, click the View Records button to view records applicable to the Alert condition

Chapter 5 - Report Formatting

Chapter 5 consists of questions, which will test your knowledge of formatting the contents of a report. The Section Expert, Highlighting Expert, Format Painter and Format Editor will be covered.

Key areas

- **Format Objects**
- **Adding Graphical Elements**
- **Insert Fields**
- **Section Formatting**
- **Creating Report Templates**

Q1. You want to highlight (in Red) all sales that have fallen below or equal the 1000 minimum sales target set for each month. Your report is grouped by the order date and you have created a sum of total sales based on the order date. Which of the following apply? ***(Multiple Answers)***

A. From the Menu Bar select format – Format Field – select the font tab, click the formula box X+2 beside calculation and enter: if {Sales.SalesTotal} <= 1000 then Crred

B. From the Menu Bar select format – Format Field – select the font tab, click the formula box X+2 beside color and enter: if {Sales.SalesTotal} > 1000 then crrred

C. Select the Sum of Total Sales, from the Menu Bar select format – Format Field – select the font tab, click the formula box X+2 beside color and enter: if {Sales.SalesTotal} < 1000 then crrred

D. From the Menu Bar select format – Format Field – select the font tab, click the formula box X+2 beside color and enter: if {Sales.SalesTotal} < 1000 then red

E. Right-click the SalesTotal field and select Format Field – select the font tab, click the formula box X+2 beside color and enter: if {Sales.SalesTotal} <= 1000 then Crred

Q2. Which of the following are Date orders in the Format Editor? *(Multiple Answers)*

A. DDY

B. DMY

C. MDY

D. YMD

Q3. Which of the following has a floating currency applied and which one has a Fixed Currency option applied?

A.
£ 10,259.10
£ 1,142.13
£ 29.00
£ 43.50
£ 563.70

B.
£10,259.10
£1,142.13
£29.00
£43.50
£563.70

Q4. Which of the following Text Interpretations types are available via the Format Editor?
(Multiple Answers)

A. XML Text
B. HTML Text
C. RTF Text
D. TXT Text

Q5. You want to apply AM and PM to your time field, under which tab in the Format Editor would you find this function

A. Time
B. Date
C. Date and Time
D. Date only

Q6. You notice the AM and PM functions are greyed out. Which of the following could be the cause?

A. The 24 hour button is selected
B. The 12 hour button is selected
C. Use System Default Format is checked
D. Symbol position is not set

Q7. The comments field contains long text, you want to display all text on your report without compromising the number of fields you already have in your report. How can you ensure that all text in the comments field are displayed?

A. Tick the Can Grow checkbox from the Font Tab of the Format Editor
B. Tick the Can Grow checkbox from the Common Tab of the Format Editor
C. Tick the Can Grow checkbox from the Border Tab of the Format Editor
D. Tick the Can Grow checkbox from the Paragraph Tab of the Format Editor

Q8. You want to highlight all sales representatives who operate in London; the field must be displayed in Arial Black. Which of the following apply?

A. Select the City Field, from the Menu Bar select format – Format Field – select the font type tab, click the formula box X+2 beside calculation and enter: if {Rep.City} = 'London' then "Arial Black"

B. Select the City Field, from the Menu Bar select format – Format Field – select the font tab, click the formula box X+2 beside font and enter: if {Rep.City} = 'London' then "Arial Black"

C. Select the City Field, from the Menu Bar select format – Format Field – select the color tab, click the formula box X+2 beside font and enter: if {Rep.City} = 'London' then "Arial Black"

D. Select the City Field, from the Menu Bar select format – Format Field – select the font tab, click the formula box X+2 beside font and enter: if {Rep.City} is like 'Lon' then "Arial Black"

Q9. The text in your report appears as follows:

.Laguna Rd 743

Nobb Hill 215

Howard's End 25

Harfordshire Blvd 15

Covington Cross

Which setting will change it back to?

743 Laguna Rd.

215 Nobb Hill

25 Howard's End

15 Harfordshire Blvd

Covington Cross

A. Right-click the field and select Format Field, click the Paragraph Tab, under Reading order, set back to Right to Left from Left to Right

B. Right-click the field and select Format Field, click the Paragraph Tab, under Reading order, set back to Left to Right from Right to Left

C. Right-click the field and select Format Field, click the font tab, under Reading order, set back to Left to Right from Right to Left

D. Right-click the field and select Format Field, click the Common Tab, under Reading order, set back to Right to Left from Left to Right

10. Your text appears as follows: 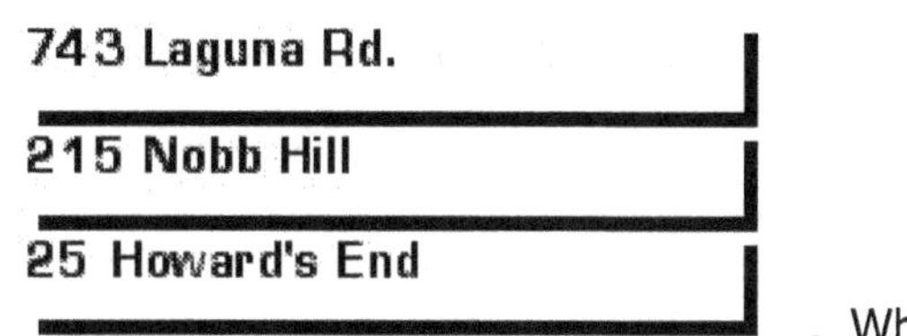

, Which of the following has been applied to the text?

A. Border Shadow
B. Tight Horizontal
C. Drop Shadow
D. Border background color

Q11. You want the currency symbol ($)to appear after the currency. Where can you implement this setting within the Format Editor?

A. Right-click field – Format Field – Format Editor -Number Tab – Customized - Currency Symbol Tab – check the Enable Currency Symbol and select the position required
B. Right-click field – Format Field – Format Editor -Currency Number Tab - Currency Symbol Tab and Position
C. Right-click field – Format Field – Format Editor -Currency Symbol Tab - Number Tab and Position
D. Right-click field – Format Field – Format Editor -Position Tab - Number Tab and Position

Q12. You want to provide users with the functionality to email sales representatives directly from your report. You have email addresses stored in the database table, which you have placed on the report. Which of the following methods apply?

A. Right-click the report and select Format Field, click the Format tab and select Current E-mail Field Value from the Hyperlink Type
B. Right-click the report and select Format Field, click the Report tab and select Current E-mail Field Value from the Hyperlink Type
C. Right-click the field and select Format Field, click the Hyperlink Tab and select Current E-mail Field Value as the Hyperlink Type
D. Right-click the report and select Format Field, click the Paragraph Tab and select Current E-mail Field Value from the Hyperlink Type

Q13. You want to apply a color to a field's text. Where can this be applied within the Format Editor?

A. Border Tab
B. Common Tab
C. Paragraph Tab
D. Hyperlink Tab
E. Font Tab

Q14. You want to apply conditional formatting to a report field, which of the following can you use?

A. Format Editor
B. Selection Expert
C. Group Expert
D. Group Section
E. Field Editor
F. Highlighting Expert

Q15. You are working with a date field that appears in the following date format (mmddyy). How would you change this to (ddmmyyyy)?

A. Right-click the field, select Format Field, click the Date and Time tab, click Customize, click the Date Tab, select the DMY button under order and in the format section set Month to 3, Day to 1 and Year to 1999 and click ok
B. Right-click the field, select Format Field, click the Date and Time tab, click Customize, click the Date Tab, select the DMY button under order and in the format section change Month to 03, Day to 01 and Year to 1999 and click ok
C. Right-click the field, select Format Field, click the Date and Time tab, click Customize, click the Date Tab, select the DMY button under order and in the format section change Month to 03, Day to 1 and Year to 1999 and click ok
D. Right-click the field, select Format Field, click the Date and Time tab, click Customize, click the Date Tab, select the DMY button under order and in the format section change Month to 03, Day to 01 and Year to 99 and click ok

Q16. You do not want users to move fields within the report. Which of the following apply?

A. Tick the Lock Position and Size checkbox from the Paragraph Tab of the Format Editor
B. Tick the Lock Position and Size checkbox from the Common Tab of the Format Editor
C. Tick the Lock Position and Size checkbox from the Border Tab of the Format Editor
D. Tick the Lock Position and Size checkbox from the Font Tab of the Format Editor
E. Tick the Read-Only Checkbox from the Common Tab of the Format Editor

Q17. Your Boolean formula displays a True or False result. You want to change it to Yes or No. Which of the following apply?

A. Right-click the field, select Format Field, click the Formula tab and select Yes or No from the Boolean Text drop down menu
B. Right-click the field, select Format Field, click the String tab and select Yes or No from the Boolean Text drop down menu
C. Right-click the field, select Format Field, click the Common Tab and select Yes or No from the Boolean Text drop down menu
D. Right-click the field, select Format Field, click the Boolean tab and select Yes or No from the Boolean Text drop down menu

Q18. You want to prevent an object from being formatted in your report. How can you achieve this? *(Multiple Answers)*

A. Right-click object and select Format Field, from the drop-down menu, select the Common Tab and place a tick in the read only check box
B. Highlight field, from the Menu Bar select format – Format Field, select the Common Tab and place a tick in the Lock Position and Size check box
C. Select object, right-click and select No format
D. Select object, right-click and select Format, Field type, Read Only
E. Highlight field, from the Menu Bar select format – Format Field, select the Common Tab and place a tick in the read only check box

Q19. You want to apply a 90-degree rotation to your text. What should you do?

A. Right-click the field, select Format Field, click the Common Tab, and under Text rotation select 90 degrees from the drop-down list.

B. Right-click the text, select Format Field, and click the Paragraph Tab, under Text rotation 90 degrees from the drop-down list.

C. Right-click the text, select Format Field, and click the format tab, under Text rotation and degrees 90 degrees from the drop-down list.

Examno	Examno
RDCR201	RDCR201
RDCR301	RDCR301
RDCR401	RDCR401
RDCR501	RDCR501

Q20. How would you suppress duplicate records?

A. Right-click the field, select Format Field, click the Paragraph Tab, and check the suppress If Duplicated checkbox

B. Right-click the field, select Format Field, click the Font tab, and check the suppress If Duplicated checkbox

C. Right-click the field, select Format Field, click the Common Tab, and check the suppress checkbox

D. Right-click the field, select Format Field, click the Common Tab, and check the Suppress Duplicated records only checkbox

E. Right-click the field, select Format Field, click the Common Tab, and check the Suppress If Duplicated checkbox

Q21. You want to create a borderline around your text. Which of the following apply?

A. Right-click the field, select Format Field, click the Paragraph Tab and apply a single line from the drop-down menu to the Left, Right, Bottom and Top section of the fields

B. Right-click the field, select Format Field, click the font tab and apply a single line from the drop-down menu to the Left, Right, Bottom and Top section of the fields

C. Right-click the field, select Format Field, click the Border Tab and apply a single line from the drop-down menu to the Left, Right, Bottom and Top section of the fields

D. Right-click the field, select Format Field, click the Common Tab and apply a single line from the drop-down menu to the Left, Right, Bottom and Top section of the fields

Q22. When a field is placed in the details section it appears as follows:

Red Pen
Silver Plated Pen
Silver Rim Pen

You notice the section around the text extends as far as the longest text in the field. You want to
limit this extension to individual text length

Red Pen
Silver Plated Pen
Silver Rim Pen

Which of the following should you apply?

A. Right-click the field, select Format Field, click the Paragraph Tab and check the Tight Vertical checkbox
B. Right-click the field, select Format Field, click the Border Tab and check the Tight Horizontal checkbox
C. Right-click the field, select Format Field, click the Paragraph Tab and check the Border Control checkbox
D. None of the above, this cannot be done

Q23. Your dates appear as follows:

14/12/2000
04/12/2000
09/12/2000
06/12/2000
03/12/2000

You want to change the format to appear as follows:. Which of the following apply?

14-12-2000
04-12-2000
09-12-2000
06-12-2000
03-12-2000
16-12-2000
12-12-2000

A. Right-click the field, select Format Field, click the Date and Time tab, click Customize, click the Date Tab, under separators, set first and second to –
B. Right-click the field, select Format Field, click the Date and Time tab, click Customize, click the Date Tab, under separators, set first and second to _
C. Right-click the field, select Format Field, click the Date and Time tab, click Customize, click the Time Tab, under separators, set first and second to -
D. Right-click the field, select Format Field, click the Date and Time tab, click Customize, click the Date Tab, under separators, set first and second to +

Q24. How would you apply a Tool Tip to a field?

A. Right-click the field, select Format Field, click the Paragraph Tab and enter the text in the Tool Tip Text space
B. Right-click the field, select Format Field, click the Border Tab and enter the text in the Tool Tip Text space
C. Right-click the field, select Format Field, click the string tab and enter the text in the Tool Tip Text space
D. Right-click the field, select Format Field, click the Common Tab and enter the text in the Tool Tip Text space

Q25. Which tab within the Format Editor allows you to set indentations, spacing, reading order and Text Interpretation?

A. Border Tab
B. Common Tab
C. Paragraph Tab
D. Hyperlink Tab
E. Font Tab

Q26. You want to set line spacing between your texts. Which of the following are line spacing types? *(Multiple Answers)*

A. Normal
B. Exact
C. Multiple
D. Single

Q27. You are writing a report for an overseas firm. The currency symbol required is as follows: ($). How would you apply this symbol to the currency field?

A. Right-click the field, select Format Field, click the Currency tab, and check the display currency symbol, click customize and select currency symbol tab, enter your symbol in the currency symbol section provided
B. Right-click the field, select Format Field, click the Monetary tab, and check the display currency symbol, click customize and select currency symbol tab, enter your symbol in the currency symbol section provided
C. Right-click the field, select Format Field, click the Finance tab, and check the display currency symbol, click customize and select currency symbol tab, enter your symbol in the currency symbol section provided

D. Right-click the field, select Format Field, click the Number tab, and check the display currency symbol, click customize and select currency symbol tab, enter your symbol in the currency symbol section

Q28. The text in the Details Section of your report appears as follows. What action can be taken to remove the line running through the text?

~~Successful~~

~~Successful~~

~~Successful~~

~~Successful~~

A. Right-click the field, select Format Field, click the font tab, under the Effects section uncheck the underline checkbox
B. Right-click the field, select Format Field, click the font tab, under the Effects section uncheck the strikeout checkbox
C. Right-click the field, select Format Field, click the font tab, under the Effects section uncheck the line checkbox
D. Right-click the field, select Format Field, click the font tab, under the Effects section uncheck the cross-out checkbox

Q29. Which of the following are formats available within the Hyperlink tab of the Format Editor? *(Multiple Answers)*

A. A Website On The Internet
B. A Current Website Field Value
C. A Hyperlink To An Email Address
D. A File
E. Current E-Mail Field Value

Q30. Which of the following are DHTML Viewer Only options within the Hyperlink Tab? *(Multiple Answers)*

A. You can create a Hyperlink to Another Report Object
B. Report Part Drill-Down
C. Email indentation
D. Map Email Hyperlink

Q31. Which of the following are Border Line style options available via the Format Editor?
(Multiple Answers)

A. None
B. Single
C. Double
D. Dashed
E. Dotted

Q32. What is the difference between Lock Position and Size, and the Read-only formats, within the Format Editor?

A. With the Lock Position and Size, you cannot move or resize the field it is applied to but you can format the field, with the Read-only format applied you cannot format or resize the field but it can be moved
B. With the Lock Position and Size, you can move, format the field or resize the field it is applied to but you cannot delete it, with the Read-only format applied you can only format or resize the field but it cannot be moved
C. With the Lock Position and Read-only format applied you cannot delete the field
D. With the Lock Position and Read-only format applied you cannot move the field

Q33. Which of the following are the indentation types that can be set within your report?
(Multiple Answers)

A. First Line
B. Second Line
C. Right
D. Left
E. Top
F. Bottom

Q34. You know the currency field contains numbers, however it appears as follows: on your report. Which of the following apply? *(Multiple Answers)*

$ #####
$ 29.00
$ #####
$ #####
$ 29.00
$ 43.50
$ #####

A. Expand Field
B. Allow Field Clipping is disabled
C. Allow Field Clipping is enabled
D. Check the Can Grow checkbox

Q35. Which of the following Tabs are available when formatting a section via the Section Expert? *(Multiple Answers)*

A. Common Tab
B. Border Tab
C. Paragraph Tab
D. Hyperlink Tab
E. Color Tab

Q36. What is the default design layout of a Blank Report?

A. Report Header|Page Header|Detail|Report Footer|Page Footer
B. Page Header| Report Header |Detail|Report Footer|Page Footer
C. Page Header| Report Header |Detail|Page Footer| Report Footer
D. Page Header| Detail| Report Header |Page Footer| Report Footer

Q37. You have created a report with one group and you want the detailed section to appear after a drill-down. What should you apply to the section?

A. Choose Report from the Menu Bar | select Section Expert | highlight the Details Section and check Free-From placement
B. Choose Report from the Menu Bar | select Section Expert | highlight the Details Section and check the Hide (Drill-Down OK) checkbox
C. Choose Report from the Menu Bar | select Section Expert | highlight the Details Section and check Suppress
D. Choose Report from the Menu Bar | select Section Expert | highlight the Details Section and check Keep Together

Q38. You want to resize the Details Section of your report to remove all spaces at the bottom. You right-click the grey area of the details section. What is the next step?

A. Select arrange lines
B. Size section
C. Fit section
D. Insert line

Q39. You have created a report with several groups; you want the contents of each group to appear within the allocated groups. Which of the following should be applied to the section?

A. New Page Before
B. Keep Together
C. Suppress Blank Sections
D. New Page After
E. Keep Group Together

Q40. You want to format a section of your report. What should you use?

A. Format Editor
B. Selection Expert
C. Group Expert
D. Group Section
E. Section Expert

Q41. You have created a report with two groups; you do not want the Details Section to appear upon drill-down. What should you apply to the section?

A. Free-From placement should be applied to the detail section
B. Hide should be applied to the details section
C. Suppress the details section
D. Keep Together should be applied to the details section

Q42. Your report contains groups which start on new pages, you would like the page number to start from 1 upon the beginning of every new group. What should you do?

A. From the Section Expert check the New Page After
B. From the Section Expert check the New Page Before
C. From the Section Expert check the Keep Together
D. From the Section Expert check the Print at bottom of page
E. From the Section Expert check the Reset Page No After checkbox

Q43. You perform a conditional suppress on a Group Header in the Section Expert. What will the color of the x+2 button be?

A. x+2 will be green

B. x+2 will be blue

C. x+2 will be red

D. x+2 will not change

Q44. You want to insert a second details section. Which of the following apply?

A. Right click the grey area of the Details Section and select insert section below

B. Right click the grey area of the Details Section and select format section and insert, delete, arrange lines and fit section.

C. Right click the grey area of the Details Section and you can select alignment, select insert, delete, arrange lines and fit section.

D. Right click the grey area of the Details Section and you can select Report format, select insert, delete, arrange lines and fit section.

Q45. Each time you view your report there are several blank sections. What should you do?

A. From the Section Expert Suppress Blank Section

B. From the Section Expert apply New Page After

C. From the Section Expert apply New Page Before

D. Refresh report and this should clear the blank section

Q46. You would like to place a watermark behind the data displayed in your report. Which section formatting function will allow you to apply this watermark?

A. This formatting method does not exist in Crystal Reports

B. Export the report to Excel and re import into Crystal

C. Underlay Section formatting

D. Print the report and scan the watermark in through Photoshop

E. Use Acrobat Reader

Q47. You have created a report with a group with its associated records displayed in the details section; you want the group and its contents to start on a new page. From the Section Expert select the Group and tick

A. Free-From placement
B. Reset Page Number
C. Keep Together
D. New Page Before

Q48. You have created a group and would like to format the Group with multiple columns. Which one of the following statements is true?

A. Format multiple columns can only be applied to the details section
B. Right click the group, select Section Expert from the pop-up menu and tick the checkbox, which read Format multiple columns
C. From the toolbar select report and Group Expert, select format multiple columns under the Group Header
D. From the toolbar select report and Section Expert, select format multiple columns under the Group Header

Q49. Which of the following provides access to the Section Expert? *(Multiple Answers)*

A. From the Menu Bar select Report –Section Expert
B. Select the Section Expert icon from the toolbar
C. Right-click the grey area of the section and select Section Expert from the drop-down menu
D. Choose format from the Menu Bar and select Section Expert.

Q50. You have created a report and would like to use the Highlighting Expert. What are the advantages of using the Highlighting Expert? (Multiple Answers)

A. Knowledge of Crystal or Basic Syntax is not required
B. The same format can be used for several fields
C. Formatting based on font style, color, border, background, and value can be applied to several fields
D. Fields can be formatted based on the results of other fields

Q51. You have three fields in your report and you want to change (Field1) and (Field2) to reflect the same formatting as (Field 3). What can you use to achieve this?

A. Format Painter
B. Highlighting Expert
C. Format Ruler
D. Format Page
E. Report Options

Q52. Using the Highlighting Expert, you want the client_id to be assigned the color red if the client city equals 'London'. Which of the following apply?

A. Right-click client_id and select Highlighting Expert from the drop-down menu, select New, in the Item Editor section select Value of city is equal to 'London' then Font color = red and click ok
B. Right-click client_id and select Highlighting Expert from the drop-down menu, select New, in the Item Editor section select Value of client_id is equal to 'London' then Font color = red and click ok
C. Right-click client_id and select Highlighting Formatter from the drop-down menu, select New, in the Item Editor section select Value of city is equal to 'London' then Font color = red and click ok
D. Right-click client_id and select Highlighting Section from the drop-down menu, select New, in the Item Editor section select Value of city is equal to 'London' then Font color = red and click ok

Q53. You have applied a format to the client_id field using the Highlighting Expert. You want to add additional formatting to the same field, where client_id will equal Blue if Country is USA. Which of the following apply?

A. Right-click client_id and select Highlighting Expert from the drop-down menu, click New, in the Item Editor section select Value of client_id is equal to 'USA' then Font color = blue and click ok
B. Right-click client_id and select Highlighting Formatter from the drop-down menu, click New, in the Item Editor section select Value of country is equal to 'USA' then Font color = blue and click ok
C. Right-click client_id and select Highlighting Expert from the drop-down menu, click New, in the Item Editor section select Value of country is equal to 'USA' then Font color = blue and click ok

D. Additional Formatting cannot be applied to a field which has already been formatted using the Highlighting Expert

Q54. What does the Format Painter allow you to do?

A. Format Painter allows you to delete objects.
B. Format Painter allows you to copy formatting from one field to another, by Right-clicking the field you want use and selecting Format Painter and clicking the field you want to apply the formatting to
C. Format Painter allows you to copy text only, by Right-clicking the field you want use and selecting Format Painter and clicking the field you want to apply the formatting to
D. Format Painter allows you to copy numbers only, by Right-clicking the field you want use and selecting Format Painter and clicking the field you want to apply the formatting to
E. Highlight changes

Q55. You have placed an Object in the Report Header area. This object will print once at the beginning of the report.

A. True
B. False

Q56. You have created a report template and you now want to apply all the necessary formatting to this template without connecting to a data source. What function within Crystal can you use to create this template?

A. Create Template Detail
B. Create a Template Field Object
C. Create Report | Template Details
D. Template Layout Function with data source set to Log off model

Q57. Where do the sample templates reside by default?

A. \Program Files\Business Objects\Crystal Reports 11.5\en\Templates
B. \Program Files\Crystal Reports 11\Templates
C. \Program Files\Business Objects\Sample\Crystal Reports 11\Templates
D. \Program Files\Business Objects\Sample Reports\Crystal Reports 11\Templates

Q58. You want to apply the sales template to the sales report you have just created. How would you do this? ***(Multiple Answers)***

A. Choose Report | Template Expert | from the Template Expert box select the template required and apply to the current report
B. Click the Template Expert icon and select the sales template and click ok
C. Choose Format | Template Expert | from the Template Expert box select the template required and apply to the current report
D. Choose View | Template Expert | from the Template Expert box select the template required and apply to the current report

Q59. You have created a report, which you have saved to the templates folder as a Sales template. You now want to apply the template to the report but notice it does not appear in the available templates list. Which of the following will rectify this problem?

A. Verify the database connection
B. Press F5 within the available templates section
C. Open the report from the templates folder – select file, Summary Info and enter a title
D. Press F5 within windows explorer

Q60. How would you create a report using an existing template?

A. Select Report - from the Standard Report Creation Wizard choose the tables - create links – choose fields to display – group by – apply summaries and filters if required and select a template from the available templates and click finish
B. Select Template - from the Standard Report Creation Wizard choose the tables - create links – choose fields to display – group by – apply summaries and filters if required and select a template from the available templates and click finish
C. Select Format - from the Standard Report Creation Wizard choose the tables - create links – choose fields to display – group by – apply summaries and filters if required and select a template from the available templates and click finish
D. Select New – Using the Report Creation Wizard select Standard Report choose the tables - create links – choose fields to display – group by – apply summaries and filters if required and select a template from the available templates and click finish

Q61. You have selected the Europe Sales Template; however a Preview Picture does not appear. How can you rectify this?

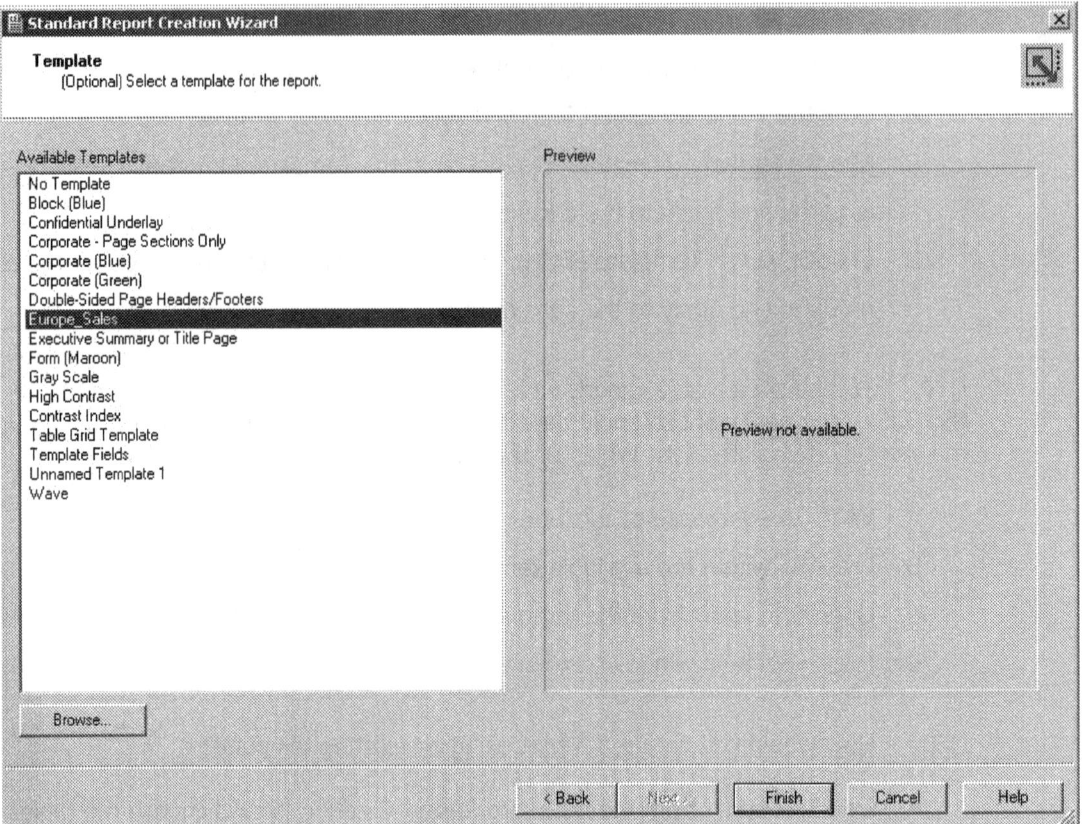

A. Verify the database connection
B. Press F5 within the available templates section
C. Open the report from the templates folder – select file, Summary Info and check the Save Preview Picture checkbox
D. Press F5 within windows explorer

Q62. You have changed your mind about the template, that you previously removed. Which of the following methods will allow you to reapply the template?

A. Choose File | Template Expert | select template to be applied and click the 'reapply previous template' radio button and click OK
B. Choose View | Template Expert | select template to be applied and click the 'Re-Apply Last Template' radio button and click OK
C. Choose Format | Template Expert | select template to be applied and click the 'Re-Apply Last Template' radio button and click OK
D. Choose Report | Template Expert | and click the 'Re-Apply Last Template' radio button and click OK

Q63. You want to remove the template, which you applied to your report. What should you do?

A. Choose File | Template Expert | select template to be applied and click the 'Undo the current template' radio button and click OK

B. Choose Report | Template Expert | and click the 'Undo the current template' radio button and click OK

C. Choose View | Template Expert | select template to be applied and click the 'Undo the current template' radio button and click OK

D. Choose Format | Template Expert | select template to be applied and click the 'Undo the current template' radio button and click OK

Q64. You want to undo the report template applied to a report; however the undo button is greyed out. What could be the possible reason? *(Multiple Answers)*

A. The report was initially created using a template, hence it cannot be removed

B. You have closed the report down and reopened it

C. You have not refreshed the report

D. None of the above

Q65. You want to specify the type of data, which should appear within your template field. Which of the following must you implement?

A. Right-Click the Template field and select edit template, replace the space(10) with the database field type

B. Right-Click the Template field and select edit template, replace the space(110) with the database field type

C. Right-Click the Template field and select edit template, replace the space(11) with the database field type

D. From the Field Explorer Right-Click the Template field and select edit template, replace the space(10) with the database field type

Q66. You have created a report and want to format the report to insert a blank line after every 7th record in the detail section. Which of the following formulas should you apply?

A. Insert a detail section b, Remainder (RecordNumber) <> 0 should be added to the detail section b of the report, under the Section Expert and under the Common Tab and suppress x+2 section

B. Insert an additional detail section (detail section b), place the following formula Remainder (RecordNumber, 7) <> 0 in detail section b of the report, under the Section Expert select the Common Tab and click on the suppress x+2 section

C. Insert a detail section b, Remainder (RecordNo = 7) <> 0 should be added to the detail section b of the report, under the Section Expert and under the Common Tab and suppress x+2 section

D. Insert a detail section b, Remainder (RecordNumber) = 7 should be added to the detail section b of the report, under the Section Expert and under the Common Tab and suppress x+2 section

Q67. You want to create a report template without a data source. Which of the following methods apply?

A. Select File - New - Blank Report, select a data source from the Database Expert, click the ok button and insert a Template Field Object, format the template field object accordingly

B. Select Report – Report Template, do not select a data source from the Database Expert, click the cancel button and insert a Template Field Object, format the template field object accordingly

C. Select Report – Report Template, select a data source from the Database Expert, click the ok button and insert a Template Field Object, format the template field object accordingly

D. Select File - New - Blank Report, do not select a data source from the Database Expert, click the cancel button and insert a Template Field Object, format the template field object accordingly

Q68. You want to add a title to a report. Which of the following should you use?

A. Insert - Text Object and enter title

B. Report - Text Object and enter title

C. Text - Text Object and enter title

D. View - Text Object and enter title

Q69. You want to increase the height and width of a Text Object. Which of the following apply?

A. Right-click the Text Object, from the dropdown menu select Grid, enter the Height and Width required
B. Right-click the Text Object, from the dropdown menu select Size and Position, enter the Height and Width required
C. Right-click the Text Object, from the dropdown menu select X and Y, enter the Height and Width required
D. Right-click the Text Object, from the dropdown menu select Height and Width, enter required size

Q70. You want to insert an Acrobat Reader file into your current report. What procedure should you follow?

A. This function does not exist
B. Select File – insert – Acrobat Reader file – locate file and click ok
C. Select Insert – File - – locate file and click ok
D. Select Insert – OLE Object – Highlight Adobe Acrobat Document - select Create from File, browse to locate the file

Q71. Which of the following can be inserted into a report? *(Multiple Answers)*

A. Cross-Tab
B. Text Object
C. File Object
D. OLAP Grid, Pictures, Map
E. Subreport
F. OLE Object, Box
G. Line, Chart

Q72. You want to add the company logo to a report. Which of the following apply?

A. Select Insert - Picture, from the dialog box locate the logo and click OK, place the logo in a required section of your report
B. Select Insert - Object, from the dialog box locate the logo and click OK, place the logo in a required section of your report
C. Select View - Insert - Picture from the toolbar, locate the logo and click OK, place the logo in your report
D. Select Report - Insert - Picture from the toolbar, locate the logo and click OK, place the logo in your report

Q73. Which of the following appear under OLE Object insertion? *(Multiple Answers)*

A. Adobe Acrobat Document
B. Adobe Photoshop image
C. Bitmap image
D. Media Clip
E. Microsoft Excel Chart

Q74. You have grouped your report by Exam Number and you want to add the text 'Exam Number' beside the database field within the group. Which of the following apply?

A. Select Insert Text Object, places the Text Object in the group, enter Exam Number, drag the group into the Text Object after the Exam Number:
B. Select Insert Text Box, insert Text Box in the group, enter Exam Number, drag the group into the Text Box after the Exam Number:
C. Select Insert Object, insert object in the group, enter Exam Number, drag the group into the object after the Exam Number:
D. Select Insert Textbook Object, insert Textbook object in the group, enter Exam Number, drag the group into the Textbook object after the Exam Number:

Q75. You want to align all fields in the details section. Which method applies?

A. Right-click the grey area of the details (b) section and select Align Tops
B. Right-click the grey area of the details (b) section and select Align all objects
C. Right-click the grey area of the details (b) section and select 'Select All Section Objects, Right-click highlighted fields and select Align- Tops or as required
D. Right-click the grey area of the details (b) section and select Tops

Q76. You want to set all fields in the Details Section to the same size. Which method applies?

A. Right-click the grey area of the details (b) section and select Same Size
B. Right-click the grey area of the details (b) section and select section Same Size
C. Right-click the grey area of the details (b) section and select Align Same Size
D. Right-click the grey area of the details (b) section and select 'Select All Section Objects, Right-click highlighted fields and select Size – Same Size

Q77. You want to apply a background color to a field's text. Where can this be applied within the Format Editor?

A. Border Tab
B. Common Tab
C. Paragraph Tab
D. Hyperlink Tab
E. Font Tab

Q78. You want to insert a section below your existing Group Header #1. Which of the following methods apply? *(Multiple Answers)*

A. Select Format – Section Expert – highlight Group Header #1 and select Insert
B. Select File – Section Expert – highlight Group Header #1 and select Insert
C. Select Report – Section Expert – highlight Group Header #1 and select Insert
D. Right-click the grey section of GroupHeader#1 and select Insert Section below

Q79. You have two sections within your report GroupHeader#1a and GroupHeader#1b. You want to combine both sections together. Which of the following apply? *(Multiple Answers)*

A. Select Report – Section Expert – highlight Group Header #1a and select merge
B. Right-click the grey section of GroupHeader#1a and select merge section below
C. Select File – Section Expert – highlight Group Header #1a and select merge
D. Right-click the grey section of GroupHeader#1b and select merge section below

Q80. How would you resize the details section of your report?

A. You can double space the report by right-clicking the Details Section and select double spacing from the pop-up menu
B. You can double space the report by right-clicking the Details Section and select space and a half
C. Place the cursor on the bottom line of the detail section, the cursor will display two lines with an up and down arrow, pull down or up according to your requirements

Q81. Which one of the following can be used to set dynamic locations for graphics?

A. Dynamic Graphic Location
B. Active Graphic Location
C. ActiveX Graphic Location
D. XML Graphic Location

Q82. Dynamic Graphic Location Conditional formatting can be applied to a Blob Field?

A. True
B. False

Q83. Where can Allow ~Field Clipping be activated?

A. Within the Format Editor – Border Tab – Click Customize – Number Tab and Check the Allow Field Clipping checkbox
B. Within the Format Editor – Number Tab – Click Customize – Number Tab and Check the Allow Field Clipping checkbox
C. Within the Format Editor – Currency Tab – Click Customize – Number Tab and Check the Allow Field Clipping checkbox
D. Within the Format Editor – Common Tab – Click Customize – Number Tab and Check the Allow Field Clipping checkbox

Chapter 6 - Using the Select Expert

This Chapter will test your knowledge of using the Select Expert in conjunction with the Record Group Selection and the Group Selection. Questions will also relate to the TopN and Bottom functions within Crystal Reports.

Key areas

- **Filtering Report Data**
- **Group Selection**
- **Record Selection**
- **Formula Editor**

Q1: You want to create a report for the top 5 sales return per country. Which of the following must you implement?

A. Insert a group based on the country field and a summary sum of sales based on the group created, from the Menu Bar select report and group expert and select top 5 based on the sum created.

B. Insert a group based on the country field and a summary sum of sales based on the group created, from the Menu Bar select report and record sort expert and select top 5 based on the sum created.

C. Insert a group based on the country field and a summary sum of sales based on the group created, from the Menu Bar select report and Group Sort Expert and select top 5 based on the sum created.

D. Insert a group based on the country field and a summary sum of sales based on the group created, from the Menu Bar select report and Section Expert and select TopN where N is 5 based on the sum of sales created.

Q2: You want to design a report based on a specific date range. Which of the following would you use from within the Select Expert?

A. Is Between

B. Is in Range

C. Is greater than or equal

D. Is < =

Q3: You have received an urgent request to filter the sales report to show sales records in the months April, May and June of the current year. Which of the following methods will enable you to achieve this without creating a complex formula?

A. From the Menu select Report| Select Expert| and select New| select the Date field from the Choose Field Dialog box and click ok| select 'is in the period' | select Calendar1stQuarter
B. From the Menu select Report| Select Expert| and select New| select the Date field from the Choose Field Dialog box and click ok| select 'is in the period' | select Calendar1stQtr
C. From the Menu select Report| Select Expert| and select New| select the Date field from the Choose Field Dialog box and click ok| select 'is in the period' | select Calendar2ndQtr
D. From the Menu select Report| Select Expert| and select New| select the Date field from the Choose Field Dialog box and click ok| select 'is in the period' | select Calendar2stQuarter

Q4: You select a string field within the Select Expert and leave the 'Is Equal' section Blank. Which of the following will occur?

A. {TableName.FieldName} = ""
B. An error message will be produced
C. {TableName.FieldName} <> ""
D. {TableName.FieldName} ""

Q5: From the Select Expert, you are presented with a choice of record filtering operations. 'Is One Of ' has been selected, this will allow

A. Only two items to be specified
B. Numeric values only
C. Discrete values only
D. Multiple value selection

Q6: You want to extract data for the current month only. Which of the following Select Expert options apply? *(Multiple Answers)*

A. Is One Of
B. Between
C. MonthToDate
D. Is greater than

Q7: You have created a sales report and would like to extract data for the First Quarter of the Calendar Year. What is the best method to follow?

A. Right-click the date field, | from the drop down menu select format field and apply your formula for the Calendar1stQtr.
B. Choose Report | Section Expert | apply Calendar1stQtr
C. Highlight the date field, choose report | Select Expert | from the drop down menu select is in period | Calendar1stQtr.
D. Choose File | options and apply the Calendar1stQtr formula

Q8: Which two are not valid date functions within the Select Expert? *(Multiple Answers)*

A. Last8Days
B. Last7Days
C. Last4WeeksToSat
D. Last4WeeksToSun
E. LastFullMonth
F. LastFullWeek
G. All DatesToToday

Q9: The 'Is like' operation will only work with a string

A. True
B. False

Q10: You have created a report and would like to extract records that contain the partial letters"RDCR" from the EXAM_ID field. Which of the following apply?

A. {Exams.Exam_ID} Startswith 'RDCR'
B. {Exams.Exam_ID} Is between
C. {Exams.Exam_ID} like "* RDCR*"
D. {Exams.Exam_ID} Is equal to 'RDCR'

Q11: You do not specify a value in the 'Is equal' section of the Select Expert, this will produce an error message

A. True
B. False

Q12: You have created a sales report and would like to extract data for the current year. Select the two options which apply? *(Multiple Answers)*

A. Right-click the date field, | from the drop down menu select format field and apply your formula for the YearToDate.
B. Choose Report | Section Expert | apply YearToDate
C. Highlight the date field, choose Report | Select Expert | from the drop down menu select 'is in the period' | select YearToDate.
D. Year({TableName.SalesDate}) = Year(CurrentDate)
E. Choose File | options and apply the YearToDate formula

Q13: You have created a sales report and would like to extract data based on the Sales Date for the previous complete week. What is the best method to follow?

A. Week({Sales.Sales Date}) in Week – 1
B. {Sales.Sales Date} in LastFullWeek
C. {Sales.Sales Date} in LastFullWeek – 7
D. {Sales.Sales Date} in LastFullWeek + 7

Q14: Which of the following are not valid date options when using the Select Expert Tool 'Is In The Period'? *(Multiple Answers)*

A. WeekToDateFromMonday
B. WeekToDateFromToday
C. WeekToDateFromSun
D. WeekToDateFromSat
E. MonthToDate
F. YearToDate

Q15: Which one of the following is not available for a Date Format in the Select Expert when using 'Is In The Period' ?

A. DatesToYesterday
B. AllDatesFromToday
C. AllDatesFromTomorrow
D. Aged0To30Days
E. Aged31To60Days
F. Aged61To90Days
G. Aged0To31Days

Q16: You have received an urgent request to filter the sales report to show sales records in the last three months of the current year. Which of the following methods will enable you to achieve this without creating a complex formula?

A. From the Menu select Report| Select Expert| and select New| select the Date field from the Choose Field Dialog box and click ok| select 'is in the period' | select Calendar1stQuarter
B. From the Menu select Report| Select Expert| and select New| select the Date field from the Choose Field Dialog box and click ok| select 'is in the period' | select Calendar4thQtr
C. From the Menu select Report| Select Expert| and select New| select the Date field from the Choose Field Dialog box and click ok| select 'is in the period' | select Month4thQuarter
D. From the Menu select Report| Select Expert| and select New| select the Date field from the Choose Field Dialog box and click ok| select 'is in the period' | select Calendar2stQuarter

Q17: You have created a report and would like to extract records where client names begin with 'An' and 'Sm'. Which of the following must you use?

A. Is equal to
B. Is One Of
C. Is Between
D. Starts with
E. Like '**'
F. Left({Client.ClientName},2) in ["An","Sm"]

Q18: From the Select Expert, you are presented with a choice of record filtering operations. Is Any Value has been selected, this will

A. Eliminate any other selection criteria you have applied to the report
B. Produce an error message
C. Only work if you leave the section blank
D. Include all records

Q19: What is the Default option within the Select Expert?

A. Is equal to
B. Is Any Value
C. Is in
D. Is Like

Q20: You want to type in a formula directly into Records Selection Formula Editor. Which of the following apply?

A. Report – Select Expert – Formula – Show Formula – Formula Editor
B. View – Select Expert – Formula – Show Formula – Formula Editor
C. Format – Select Expert – Formula – Show Formula – Formula Editor
D. Edit – Select Expert – Formula – Show Formula – Formula Editor

Q21: You want to extract the following data. Which of the following will apply? *(Multiple Answers)*

Merchandise Type Name = Suitcase and
Merchandise Class = Travel and
Quantity Purchased is less than or equal to 2 and
Year Ordered is in the Current Year

A. {Merchandise_Type.Merchandise Type Name} = "Suitcase" and {Merchandise.Merchandise Class} = "Travel" and {Orders_Info.Quantity} <= 2 and {Orders.Required Date} in YearToDate
B. {Merchandise.Merchandise Type Name} = "Suitcase" and {Merchandise.Merchandise Class} = "Travel" and {Orders_Info.Quantity} <= 2 and Year({Orders.Required Date}) = Year(CurrentDate)
C. {Merchandise.Merchandise Type Name} = "Suitcase" and {Merchandise.Merchandise Class} = "Travel" and {Orders_Info.Quantity} in 0 to 2 and Year({Orders.Required Date}) = Year(CurrentDate)
D. {Merchandise.Merchandise Type Name} = "Suitcase" and {Merchandise.Merchandise Class} = "Travel" and {Orders_Info.Quantity} < 2 and Year({Orders.Required Date}) = Year(CurrentDate)

Q22: You have created a report and would like to add a Group Selection criteria. Which two apply? *(Multiple Answers)*

A. From the Select Expert, click the Show Formula >>>, click the Group Selection radio button, select formula editor and enter your criteria
B. From the Select Expert, click the Record Selection radio button, select formula editor and enter your criteria
C. From the Select Expert, click the records tab, select formula editor and enter your criteria
D. From the select Section Expert, click the Group Selection radio button, select formula editor and enter your criteria
E. Select Report - Selection Formulas and select Group from the dropdown menu and apply criteria

Q23: You have created a sort order on the following fields {Exam.ExamName} and { Exam.ExamCity} and would like to reverse the order. You can reverse the order of the fields from the Record Sort Expert by selecting Report – Record Sort Expert and using the arrow to sort the fields

A. True

B. False

Q24: Which of the following are Select Expert options? *(Multiple Answers)*

A. Record Selection

B. Group Selection

C. Group Sort Selection

D. Record Sort Selection

Q25: You enter the following selection criteria in the Select Expert. Where can you view the full code generated by your selection?

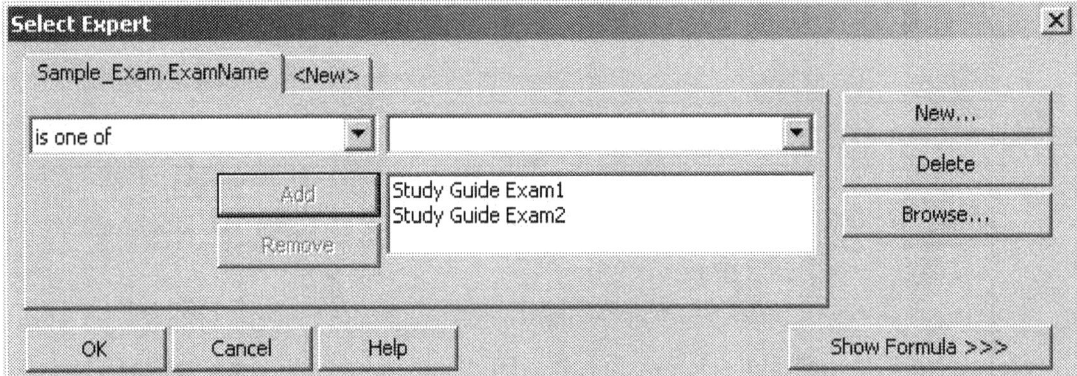

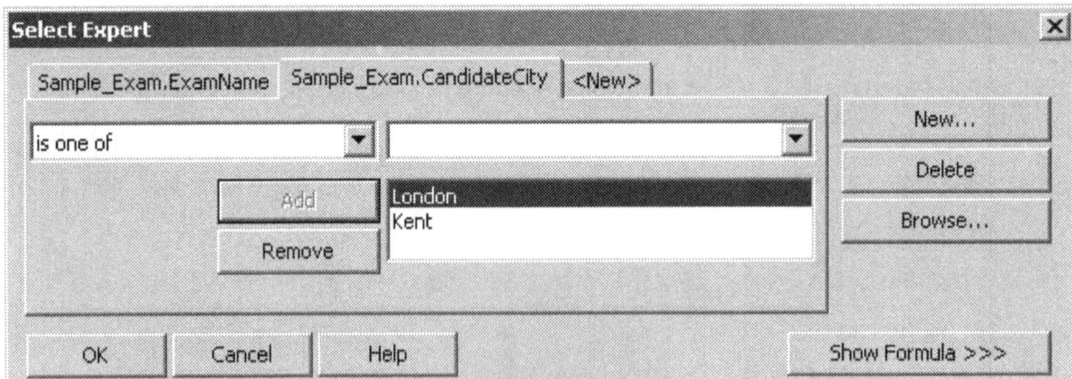

A. Click Show Formula – Formula Workshop

B. Click Show Formula – Formula Editor

C. Click Show Formula – Formula Browser

D. Click Show Formula – Formula Editor

Q26. You apply the following formula within the Select Expert section of your report. Which of the following records will appear?

{Sample_Exam_Candidate.CITY} = "Essex" or ({@score is number} in 50 to 60)

Record No.	City	Country	Score	Exam ID
1	Birmingham	England	0	RDCR700
2	London	England	80	RDCR100
3	London	England	90	RDCR100
4	London	England	85	RDCR100
5	London	England	46	RDCR100
6	Kent	England	70	RDCR100
7	Essex	England	60	RDCR100
8	Coventry	England	79	RDCR100
9	London	England	79	RDCR200
10	London	England	66	RDCR200
11	London	England	77	RDCR200
12	London	England	88	RDCR300
13	London	England	90	RDCR300
14	London	England	89	RDCR300
15	London	England	90	RDCR400
16	London	England	89	RDCR400
17	London	England	79	RDCR500
18	London	England	50	RDCR500
19	London	England	100	RDCR500
20	London	England	56	RDCR600

A. 7,18,21

B. 7,16,5

C. 7,18,20

D. 10,4,13,15

E. 3,7,8,10

Q27. You apply the following formula to the Select Expert section of your report. Which of the following records will appear?

({Sample_Exam_Candidate.CITY} = "London" and {Sample_Exam.ExamID} = "RDCR500") or ({@score is number} in 10 to 50)

Record No.	City	Country	Score	Exam ID
1	Birmingham	England	0	RDCR700
2	London	England	80	RDCR100
3	London	England	90	RDCR100
4	London	England	85	RDCR100
5	London	England	46	RDCR100
6	Kent	England	70	RDCR100
7	Essex	England	60	RDCR100
8	Coventry	England	79	RDCR100
9	London	England	79	RDCR200
10	London	England	66	RDCR200
11	London	England	77	RDCR200
12	London	England	88	RDCR300
13	London	England	90	RDCR300
14	London	England	89	RDCR300
15	London	England	90	RDCR400
16	London	England	89	RDCR400
17	London	England	79	RDCR500
18	London	England	50	RDCR500
19	London	England	100	RDCR500
20	London	England	56	RDCR600

A. 5,9,18,19

B. 2,6,8,19

C. 1,2,3,4

D. 18,19

Q28. The current date is the 13th of June 2006, you apply the following formula within the Select Expert. Which of the following records will be returned?

{Orders.Order Date} in WeekToDateFromSun

Record No	Merchandise Name	Price	Product Class	Order Date
1	Bronze Plated Pen	£764.85	Collectable Pens	30/06/2006
2	Bronze Plated Pen	£764.85	Collectable Pens	24/06/2006
3	Bronze Plated Pen	£764.85	Collectable Pens	13/06/2006
4	Bronze Plated Pen	£764.85	Collectable Pens	12/06/2006
5	Bronze Plated Pen	£764.85	Collectable Pens	10/06/2006
6	Bronze Plated Pen	£764.85	Collectable Pens	06/06/2006
7	Bronze Plated Pen	£764.85	Collectable Pens	26/06/2006
8	Bronze Plated Pen	£764.85	Collectable Pens	15/06/2006
9	Bronze Plated Pen	£764.85	Collectable Pens	06/06/2006
10	Bronze Plated Pen	£764.85	Collectable Pens	14/06/2006
11	Bronze Plated Pen	£764.85	Collectable Pens	03/06/2006
12	Bronze Plated Pen	£764.85	Collectable Pens	02/06/2006
13	Bronze Plated Pen	£764.85	Collectable Pens	26/06/2006
14	Bronze Plated Pen	£764.85	Collectable Pens	21/06/2006
15	Bronze Plated Pen	£764.85	Collectable Pens	28/06/2006
16	Bronze Plated Pen	£764.85	Collectable Pens	06/06/2006
17	Bronze Plated Pen	£764.85	Collectable Pens	22/06/2006
18	Bronze Plated Pen	£764.85	Collectable Pens	06/06/2006
19	Bronze Plated Pen	£764.85	Collectable Pens	13/06/2006

A. 1,2,3

B. 2,5,4, 19

C. 1,3

D. 2

E. 3,4,19

Q29. The current date is the 13th of June 2006, you apply the following formula within the Select Expert. Which of the following records will NOT be returned?

{Orders.Order Date} in AllDatesToToday

Blue Pen

No	Client Name	Order No	Merch No	Unit Price	Quantity	Cost	Order Date
1	Examhints	1570	2208	£53.90	3	£161.70	25/04/2006
2	Books and Books	1755	2209	£53.90	3	£161.70	21/06/2006
3	Folks Books	1557	2215	£53.90	1	£53.90	22/04/2006
4	Books and Books	1769	2212	£53.90	3	£161.70	25/06/2006

Green Pen

No.	Client Name	Order No	Merch No	Unit Price	Quantity	Cost	Order Date
5	Iroko Books	1537	1101	£14.50	3	£43.50	17/04/2006
6	Ink Only	3170	1104	£14.50	2	£29.00	26/06/2006
7	Great Stone	2985	1102	£14.50	2	£29.00	29/04/2006
8	Great Stone	1487	1104	£14.50	3	£43.50	05/04/2006
9	Iroko Books	2884	1104	£14.50	3	£43.50	03/04/2006
10	Stationary Gallore	1488	1105	£14.50	3	£43.50	05/04/2006
11	Great Stone	1666	1104	£14.50	3	£43.50	01/06/2006

A. 2,3,4

B. 2,4,6

C. 1,4,6

D. 6,11,10

Q30. Formulas can be created via the Select Expert

A. True

B. False

Q31. A Record Selection can be applied via the Standard Report Creation Wizard

A. True

B. False

Q32. The Record Selection criteria applied within the Select Expert will appear in which of the following sections of the SQL statement when viewing the Show SQL Query within Crystal Reports?

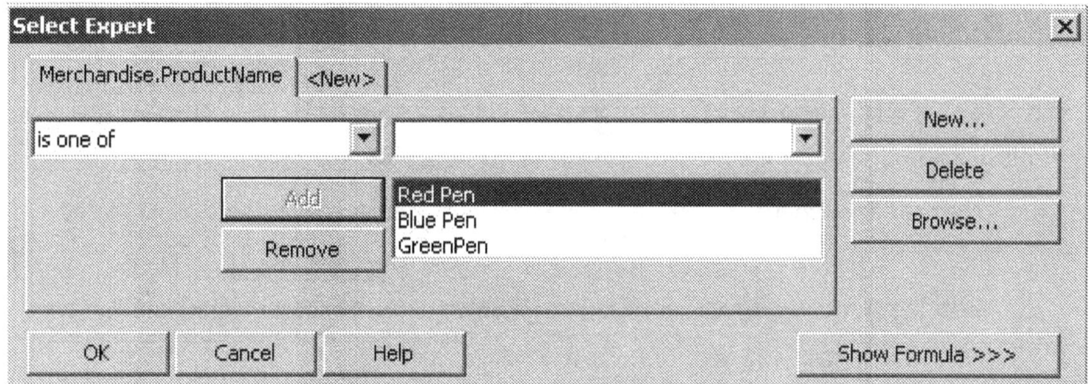

A. Select
B. Where
C. Order by
D. Group By

Q33. Your report is grouped by Exam_id which displays RDCR201, RDCR301 AND RDCR401, you have set the Select Expert Group Selection to One Of RDCR301 AND RDCR401. Which of the following statements are true? *(Multiple Answers)*

A. The report will only display data for RDCR301 AND RDCR401
B. Exams RDCR201, RDCR301 AND RDCR401 will still appear in the Group Tree
C. Exams RDCR201, RDCR301 AND RDCR401 will still appear in the Group Tree but there will be no data for RDCR201 in the report
D. Exam RDCR201 will not still appear in the Group Tree
E. There will be no data for RDCR201 in the report

Q34. A user has raised a query regarding the none retrieval of information when the Select Expert is used, the user entered field name is equal to 'iroko' in the Select Expert Record Selection of the report, the report has been refreshed however data is not being returned, you have queried the database and data for 'Iroko' exist. Which of the following could explain the problem?

A. The user did not verify the report before refreshing it
B. The user did not verify the database before refreshing the report
C. The user should enter startwith iroko rather than equals iroko
D. The Database Is Case Sensitive, the user should go into File- Report Options and check the Database Server Is Case-Insensitive

Q35. You have selected the following merchandise types: - "Ball Point Pen" and "Bronze Rim Pen"; you want to amend the Record Selection created within the Select Expert to add the "Gold Plated Pen". Which of the following methods apply? *(Multiple Answers)*

A. From the Menu Bar select Report – Select Expert – select the merchandise_type tab and from the drop-down menu beside Is One Of select Gold Plated Pen
B. From the Menu Bar select Report – Select Expert – Show Formula – Formula Editor, within the Formula Editor amend the formula to include the Gold Plated Pen {Merchandise.Product Name} in ["Ball Point Pen", "Bronze Rim Pen", "Gold Plated Pen"]
C. From the Menu Bar select Select Expert – Select Expert Expert – select the merchandise_type tab and from the drop-down menu beside Is One Of select Gold Plated Pen
D. From the Menu Bar select Select Expert – Show Formula – Formula Editor, within the Formula Editor amend the formula to include the Gold Plated Pen {Merchandise.Product Name} in ["Ball Point Pen", "Bronze Rim Pen", "Gold Plated Pen"]

Q36: You select a number field within the Select Expert and leave the 'Is Equal' section Blank. Which of the following will occur?

A. {TableName.FieldName} = ""
B. An error message will be produced
C. The OK button will be greyed out
D. {TableName.FieldName} ""

Chapter 7 - Creating Parameters

The Chapter covers questions on the application of parameters, parameter settings and types.

Key areas

- **Static Parameters**
- **Dynamic Paramaters**
- **Edit Mask**
- **Picklist Poupulation**

Sample Data

ID	Report Number
1	A1234
2	RDCR001
3	RDCR003
4	RDSSS0
5	PACE
6	TACE
7	SAECR2001
8	SAECR3001
9	BEOJ4001
10	BEOH5001
11	AE
12	33
13	8900
14	1
15	RIBE1
16	BOJCTS09
17	BOJCTS10
19	1900000
20	4000000
21	EAR1
22	Ear 6
23	Pac 56
24	907760

Fig 7.0

Q1: Which of the above named report ID's in fig 7.0 will appear when "AAAA" is placed in the Edit Mask? *(Multiple Answers)*

A. 5

B. 6

C. 13

D. 24

Q2: Which one of the report ID's in fig 7.0will appear when "aaaaaa" is placed in the Edit Mask?

A. 1

B. 2

C. 3

D. 4

Q3: Which one of the report ID's in fig 7.0 will appear when "######" is placed in the Edit Mask?

A. 7

B. 24

C. 8

D. 9

Q4: Which of the following report ID's in fig 7.0will appear when "????" is placed in the Edit Mask? *(Multiple Answers)*

A. 5

B. 6

C. 11

D. 10

Q5: Which one of the report ID's in fig 7.0will appear when "0" is placed in the Edit Mask?

A. 24

B. 22

C. 9

D. 14

Q6: Which of the report ID's in fig 7.0 will appear when "&&&&&&&" is placed in the Edit Mask? *(Multiple Answers)*

A. 2

B. 3

C. 19

D. 20

E. 25

Q7: The Edit Mask function is only available when setting a report parameter for one of the following data types. Which one is applicable?

A. Date
B. Currency
C. DateTime
D. String
E. Boolean
F. Time
G. Number

Q8: Which of the following has been placed in the Edit Mask to produce the following?

Enter a Value:

••••••••••••••

A. >
B. <
C. *******
D. Password
E. Security
F. ;

Q9: You have created a parameter. Which of the following signs precedes the parameter?

A. $
B. //
C. :
D. ?
E. @
F. %

Q10: Which of the following can be used to populate the parameter list with default values?
(Multiple Answers)

A. Append all database value
B. Enter default values manually
C. Import a pick list
D. Populated from another report

Q11: You want to be prompted with the parameter description. Which of the following settings apply?

A. Prompt With Description = True
B. Prompt With Description Only = True
C. Prompt With Description = False
D. Prompt With Description Only = False

Q12: The Parameter Default Values, in the sales report, do not contain the value you require to run the report. In addition, you cannot enter a value and must select one of the default values. Which of the following should be implemented?

A. Set Allow Multiple Values To True
B. Set Discrete Values To True
C. Set Customize Values To True
D. Set Allow Custom Values To True

Q13: You want users to be able to enter more than one value in the parameter dialog box when prompted. Which of the following apply?

A. Uncheck the Allow Multiple Values in the edit parameter field
B. Click the range values radio button
C. Check the Allow Multiple values
D. Set Allow Multiple Values to true
E. Click the discrete and range values radio button

Q14: Users of your report are required to enter a begin date, and end date, for the financial report. Which of following parameter options apply?

A. Allow discrete values
B. Allow multiple values
C. Allow range values
D. Allow custom values
E. Min Length
F. Max Length

Q15: Which of the following are mandatory to ensure that a parameter works? *(Multiple Answers)*

A. Parameter Name
B. Static or Dynamic Parameter
C. Prompting Text
D. Value Type
E. Allow Multiple Values
F. Default Value
G. Description of default values

Q16: Which if the following parameters can be displayed on the report, without further formula coding?

A. Range
B. Discrete
C. Multiple values
D. Custom Values

Q17: You have opened an exiting report and clicked the Refresh button. You are prompted to Use Current Parameter Values, or Prompt For New Parameter Values. You choose the latter. Which of the following apply?

A. The report will refresh immediately form the database
B. A new set of parameters values will be required after which the report will refresh directly from the database
C. The report will produce a database error message
D. The report will use the previous parameter values entered to refresh the report

Q18: You want to prevent users from entering sales values less than 2000, or greater than 100000, when running the sales report. Which of the following apply?

A. In the options settings section of the edit parameter dialog box set the Min value to 2001 and the Max value to 100000
B. In the options settings section of the edit parameter dialog box set the Min value to 2001 and the Max value to 99999
C. In the options settings section of the edit parameter dialog box set the Min Value to 2000 and the Max Value to 100000
D. In the options settings section of the edit parameter dialog box set the Min value to 2002 and the Max value to 99999

Q19: How are parameters integrated in reports? *(Multiple Answers)*

A. Select Expert
B. Group Selection
C. Record Selection
D. Report Busting indexes

Q20: Parameters can be used for grouping.

A. True
B. False

Q21: Parameter fields can be dragged and dropped from the Field Explorer, onto the report.

A. False
B. True

Q22: Which of the following allows the Report Designer to set customized parameter selections and restrictions?

A. Edit Mask
B. Min And Max Values
C. Allow Custom Values Set To False
D. Max Length And Min Length

Q23: You have created a parameter named Archive Numbers. You want to query the history table to retrieve archive numbers between 201 and 204. The parameter type is a Number. From the Select Expert you select the field archive_ number equals, and look for the parameter in the drop down list. The parameter does not appear in the drop down list. Which of the following reasons apply?

A. The data types of the parameter and the database field are different
B. You have not set Allow Multiple Values to true
C. You have not set allow range vales to true
D. You have not set allow discrete vales to true

Q24: You have created a Range Parameter that would be applied to the archive number within the Select Expert. Which of the following will allow you to integrate the parameter within the report?

A. {archive.number} in {?ArchiveNumber}
B. {archive.number} = {?ArchiveNumber}
C. {archive.number} in {?ArchiveNumber}to {?ArchiveNumber}
D. not ({archive.number} in [{?ArchiveNumber}])

Q25: You have created a Range Parameter, which you have applied to the archive number. When refreshing the report, you enter a range between 200 and 300. You uncheck the 'include this value' checkbox for the start range, which you have set as 200, and uncheck the include value checkbox for the 'end range', which you have set as 300. Which of the following is true?

A. Values over 200 will be included (plus 200 itself), and values up to 300 will be included
B. Values over and including 200 will be included and values up 300 but not 300 will be included
C. Values over 200 will be included (but not 200 itself), and values up to 300 will be included (but not 300 itself)
D. Values over 200 will be included (but not 200 itself), and values up to 300 will be included

Q26: You have specified a range for your parameter, with a start value of 10000, and an end value of 12999. You tick the no lower value checkbox for the start range. Which of the following values will appear? *(Multiple Answers)*

A	10
B	12888
C	10601
D	14909
E	10000

Q27: You have created a Static Parameter based on the company name with default values which you have populated from the database table. A company name has been added to the database however it is not showing in the pick list. Which of the following apply?

A. Static Parameters must be updated by selecting Action – and Append all database values
B. The report must be refreshed to pick up the list
C. The report was saved with data and therefore needs to be refreshed to include new figures in the pick list
D. The pick list will be updated after several refreshes

Q28: Which of the following can be used to display a Multiple Parameter?

A. Financial Function
B. Control Structure
C. Array functions
D. Range operators

Q29: You have created a Parameter and formula with the same name. The formula will fail to run due to a naming conflict

A. True
B. False

Q30: You want to create a Parameter which shows the user only the candidates associated with a particular Exam_ID. Which of the following apply?

A. Right-click the parameter within the Field Explorer and select New, enter the name and select the parameter type, for the list of values section select dynamic, enter the prompting group text, select a new data source, click insert and select Exam_ID from the table list, click the parameters section to select Parameter Exam_ID, insert the candidate's last name under the Exam_ID following the same procedure and click the parameter name, apply parameters to the Select Expert.
B. Right-click the parameter within the Field Explorer and select New, enter the name and select the parameter type, for the list of values section select static, enter the prompting group text, select a new data source, click insert and select Exam_ID from the table list, click the parameters section to select Parameter Exam_ID, insert the candidate's last name under the Exam_ID following the same procedure and click the parameter name, apply parameters to the Select Expert.
C. Right-click the parameter within the Field Explorer and select New, enter the name and select the parameter type, for the list of values section select static, enter the prompting group text, select a existing data source, click insert and select Exam_ID from the table list, click the parameters section to select Parameter Exam_ID, insert the candidate's last name under the Exam_ID following the same procedure and click the parameter name, apply parameters to the Select Expert.
D. Right-click the parameter within the Field Explorer and select New, enter the name and select the parameter type, for the list of values section select dynamic, enter the prompting group text, select a existing data source, click insert and select Exam_ID from the table list, click the parameters section to select Parameter Exam_ID, insert

the candidate's last name under the Exam_ID following the same procedure and click the parameter name, apply parameters to the Select Expert.

Q31: You refresh your report using the Use Current Parameter Values. Which of the following apply?

A. The report will refresh immediately form the database
B. You will be prompted for a new set of parameter values after which the report will refresh directly from the database
C. The report will produce a database error message
D. The report will use the previous parameter values entered to refresh the report

Q32: Which of the following options are available under 'Actions' within the parameter' dialog box? *(Multiple Answers)*

A. Append all database values
B. Export
C. Import
D. Clear

Q33: You want to set the order in which parameters appear in Business Objects Enterprise. Which of the following apply?

A. Right-click the parameter fields and select Order and change the parameter order using the arrows
B. Highlight one parameter field and use the arrow to move the parameter to the required position
C. Right-click the parameter fields and select Set Parameter Order and change the parameter order using the arrows

Q34: You have created two Static Parameters based on then Exam_ID and Candidate Name, you want to be prompted for the Exam_ID first and the Candidate Name second, how would you implement this format?

A. Highlight the parameter and press the arrow on your keyboard
B. Right-click the parameter and select set parameter order, use the arrow to achieve the order required
C. Integrate parameter within the Select Expert in the order required
D. This cannot be done once the parameters have been created

Q35: What is the difference between a Static and Dynamic Parameter? *(Multiple Answers)*

A. A Static Parameter's picklist is not directly linked to the database and must be updated manually
B. A Dynamic Parameter's picklist is directly linked to the database field and is up to date with current field values
C. A Dynamic Parameter consists of one or more parameters, hence giving the user the option to select only the values applicable to the initial value selected
D. A Static Parameter consists of one or more parameters, hence giving the user the option to select only values applicable the initial value selected

Q36. You have created and integrated a Static Parameter based on the exam_id field, when the report is refreshed there are no values present in the picklist. Which of the following should be used to populate the list?

A. Append all database values
B. Attach database fields
C. Insert database fields
D. Add database fields

Q37. Which of the following formulas will give the user the option to select all parameter values from a picklist when prompted or a specific value?
In this case the field name is {Clients.City} and the parameter is {?SelectClientCity}

A. In the Select Expert enter : {?SelectClientCity} ='All' or {Clients.City} = {?SelectClientCity})
B. In the Select Expert enter : {?SelectClientCity} ='' or {Clients.City} {?SelectClientCity})
C. In the Select Expert enter : {?SelectClientCity} ={Clients.City} or {Clients.City} ={?SelectClientCity})

Q38. You want to create a manual date parameter using the subscription date which will allow report users to enter dates manually with using the calendar. Which of the following formulas will work?

A. Create a Starts and End Date parameter using a string as the datatype, enter a default value of 'All' in both parameters. Create the following formula using the Subscription Date:
(@SubDate}

mid(totext({SubscriptionDate }),7,4) + "" +mid(totext({SubscriptionDate }),4,2) + "" + mid(totext({SubscriptionDate }),1,2) Enter the following formula in the Select Expert

{?StartDate} to {?EndDate} = 'All' or (@SubDate}in mid({?StartDate},7,4) + "" +

mid({?StartDate},4,2) + "" + mid({?StartDate},1,2) to mid({?EndDate},7,4) + "" +

mid({?EndDate},4,2) + "" + mid({?EndDate},1,2)

B. Create a Starts and End Date parameter using a string as the datatype, enter a default value of 'All' in both parameters. Create the following formula using the Subscription Date: (@SubDate}

Cdate(SubscriptionDate) Enter the following formula in the Select Expert

{?StartDate} to {?EndDate} = 'All' or (@SubDate}in mid({?StartDate},7,4) + "" +

mid({?StartDate},4,2) + "" + mid({?StartDate},1,2) to mid({?EndDate},7,4) + "" +

mid({?EndDate},4,2) + "" + mid({?EndDate},1,2)

Chapter 8 – Creating Groups

The following chapter covers questions on Groups and how they can be customized.

Key areas

- ❑ **Dynamic Groups**
- ❑ **Speicfied Order**
- ❑ **Group Tree**
- ❑ **Group Formatting**

Q1: You want to customize your group which of the following apply?

A. Right-click the group and select Change Group, from the drop-down menu select in Specified Order, in the Name Group section enter the name of your first specified group and click new, from the Define Named Group dialog box, select Is One Of from the dropdown list and add the data applicable to the first specified group and click ok, click the Others tab and select Put All Others Together With The Name you specify and click ok

B. Right-click the group and select Section Expert, from the drop-down menu select in Specified Order, in the Name Group section, enter the name of your first specified group and click new, from the Define Named Group dialog box, select Is One Of from the dropdown list and add the data applicable to the first specified group and click ok, click the Others tab and select Put All Others Together With The Name you specify and click ok

C. Right-click the group and select Group Section from the drop-down menu select in Specified Order, in the Name Group section, enter the name of your first specified group and click new, from the Define Named Group dialog box, select Is One Of from the dropdown list and add the data applicable to the first specified group and click ok, click the Others tab and select Put All Others Together With The Name you specify and click ok

D. Right-click the group and select group, from the drop-down menu select in Specified Order, in the Name Group section, enter the name of your first specified group and click new, from the Define Named Group dialog box, select Is One Of from the dropdown list and add the data applicable to the first specified group and click ok, click the Others tab and select Put All Others Together With The Name you specify and click ok

Q2: When you format a group name field, the changes are not reflected in the Group Tree.

A. True

B. False

Q3: You have grouped your report by the order date. Your Group Tree appears as illustrated in the diagram 1 below. You want to change the group to a monthly format as illustrated in the diagram 2. Which of the following apply?

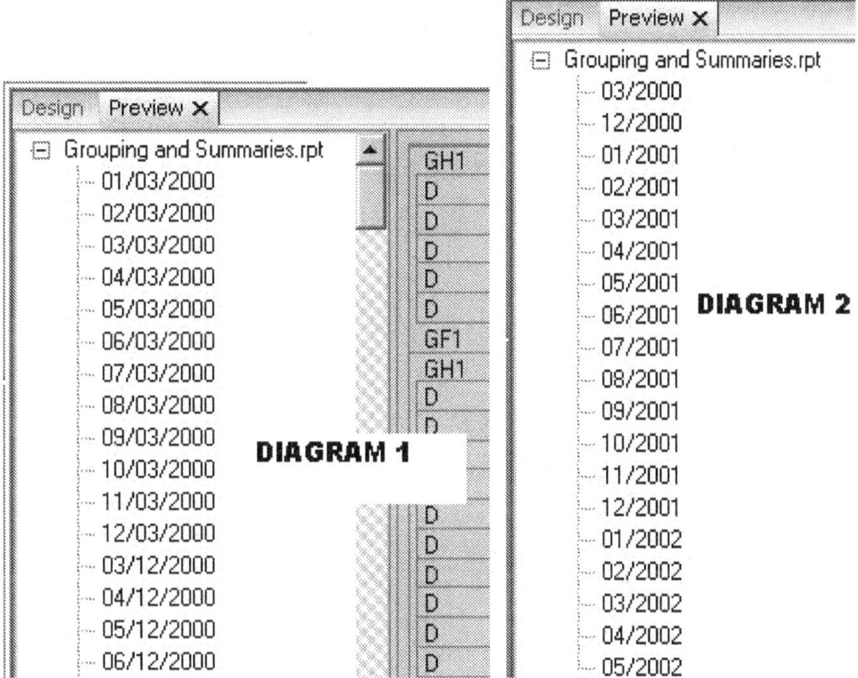

A. Right-click the Order Date group and select Section Expert, under 'The Section Will Be Printed' select for each month

B. Right-click the Order Date group and select group section, under 'The Section Will Be Printed' select for each month

C. Right-click the Order Date group and select group, under 'The Section Will Be Printed' select for each month

D. Right-click the Order Date group and select Change Group, under 'The Section Will Be Printed' select For Each Month

Q4: Which of the following are options available under the Change Group section, when applying a change to a date group? *(Multiple Answers)*

A. For each day, For each quarter

B. For each Month, For each half year

C. For each record

D. For each two weeks

E. For each half month

F. For AM/PM,

G. For each MM\DD\YYYY

H. For each Week

Q5: You want to prevent your group from breaking over several pages. What should you do?

A. Right-click the grey section of the group, select Change Group, select the Options Tab, and check the Keep Group Together checkbox

B. Select database, check the Keep Group Together checkbox

C. Select report, check the Keep Group Together checkbox

D. Select Format, check the Keep Group Together checkbox

Q6: Your date group spills over more than one page, however the heading for the group does not appear on the second page. What can you do to ensure the group title appears on each page?

A. Select database, check the Keep Group Together checkbox

B. Select report, check the Keep Group Together checkbox

C. Right-click the grey section of the group, select Change Group, select the Options Tab, and check the Repeat Group Header On Each Page

D. Select Format, check the Repeat Group Header On Each Page

Q7: Which of the following statements are true? *(Multiple Answers)*

A. The Group Sort Expert will be greyed out unless a group summary has already been created on the report.

B. The Group Tree will appear irrespective of the creation of a group

C. The Group Sort Expert will work, without a group

D. Grouping your report enables the Group Tree

Q8: You want to create a Dynamic Group based on options 1 to 3 below. Which of the following apply?

1. Exam City
2. Exam Center
3. Exam Score

A. if GroupName ({Exam.Exam Center}) = "Exam Center" then {Exam. Center } else if GroupName ({Exam.Exam City}) = "City" then {Exam. City } else if GroupName ({Exam.Exam Score}) = Exam Score then {Exam.Exam Score}
B. Create a parameter (Group Type) and enter options 1 to 3 in the picklist, create a formula as follows: if {? Group Type} = "Exam Center" then {Exam. Center } else if {? Group Type} = "City" then {Exam.City } else if {? Group Type} = "Exam Score" then {Exam. Score }, insert the formula as the group, Insert a candidate summary count based on the group
C. Create a parameter (Group Type) and enter options 1 to 3 in the picklist, insert the parameter as the group within the report, then create a formula as follows: if {? Group Type} = "Exam Center" then {Exam. Center } else if {? Group Type} = "City" then {Exam.City } else if {? Group Type} = "Exam Score" then {Exam. Score }, Insert a summary count based on the group
D. This cannot be done dynamic groups do not work within Crystal Reports

Q9: You have designed a report, which contains a chart. You can drill down into the chart to view data subsets. What sort has been applied to the chart?

A. Group Sort
B. Report Sort
C. Detail Sort
D. Header Sort

Q10: You want to add a group to your report. Which of the following can achieve this?

A. Choose Insert | Group | select group field and click ok
B. Choose Format | Group | select group field and click ok
C. Choose Report | Group Expert | select group field and click arrow and ok
D. Choose Edit | Group | select group field and click ok

Q11: You have inserted a section below the details section, the section name will be renamed as which of the following?

A. Details i, Details ii

B. Details a, Details b

C. Details Aa, Details Bb

Q12: Using the following Sales information in the diagram below:

Product Name	Sales for Month July
Ball Point Pen	£5000.00
Blue Pen	£90.00
Bronze Plated Pen	£3824.25
Bronze Rim Pen	£2159.4
Diamond Pen	£6000
Fountain Pen	£203.4
Gold Plated Pen	£7500
Gold Rim Pen	£548.7
Green Pen	£72.5
Red Pen	£99
Silver Plated Pen	£3298.5
Silver Rim Pen	£8000
Yellow Pen	£35.4

You have created a summary of product sales for the month of July, and would like to display the top three product sales for this month. Which of the following apply?

A. Select Format – Group Sort Expert – for this Group Sort select 'TopN' based on the sales summary for July and where N is 3 and click OK

B. Select Insert – Group Sort Expert – for this Group Sort select 'TopN' based on the sales summary for July and where N is 3 and click OK

C. Select Report –Record Sort Expert – for this Group Sort select 'TopN' based on the sales summary for July and where N is 3 and click OK

D. Select Report – Group Sort Expert – for this Group Sort select 'TopN' based on the sales summary for July and where N is 3 and click OK

Q13: You have created a summary of product sales for the Month of July which displays the top three product sales for this month. You want all other sales to be grouped under the title 'Other Sales'. Which of the following apply?

A. Select Format – Group Sort Expert –and check the include others with the name 'Others Sales for this period' and click OK
B. Select Report – Group Sort Expert – and check the include others with the name 'Others Sales for this period' and click OK
C. Select Insert – Group Sort Expert – and check the include others with the name 'Others Sales for this period' and click OK
D. Select Report –Record Sort Expert –and check the include others with the name 'Others Sales for this period' and click OK

Q14: By checking the 'include ties' in the Group Sort Expert. Which of the following will happen?

A. It will include individual fields whose summarized values are equal.
B. It will include Report Headers whose summarized values are equal.
C. It will include groups whose summarized values are equal.
D. It will include individual formulas whose summarized values are equal.

Q15: Which of the following statements can be used to add a summary to your report? *(Multiple Answers)*

A. Choose Insert | Summary | Choose type of calculation (sum, average, maximum, minimum) select the summary location, by group or by grand total and click OK
B. Insert Group Summary | Choose type of calculation (sum, average, maximum, minimum) select the summary location, by group or by grand total and click OK
C. Insert Group | Choose type of calculation (sum, average, maximum, minimum) select the summary location, by group or by grand total and click OK
D. Right-click field to summarize | Choose type of calculation (sum, average, maximum, minimum) select insert summary, select the summary location, by group or by grand total and click OK

Q16: You have created a group, and the group records spill over to the next page, which also include records from another group. What can you do to ensure this does not happen?

A. Use Repeating Headers
B. Use RepeatingFooters
C. Use RepeatedGroupHeaders
D. Use Keep Together

Q17: Which of the following is not available in the Group Sort Expert? *(Multiple Answers)*

A. No sort
B. Bottom totals
C. All
D. Top N
E. Bottom N
F. Top Percentage
G. Bottom Percentage
H. Top totals

Q18: You have created an Ascending Sort Order on a field which contains both numeric and text data. Which one is true?

A. The string fields will appear before the numbers field
B. You cannot perform a sort on a numeric field
C. You can perform a sort on the Text Object
D. The numbers will appear before the string fields

Q19: You add a group to a report. This action will produce a Group Header and a Group Footer.

A. True
B. False

Q20: Which of the following cannot be implemented through the Change Group Options? *(Multiple Answers)*

A. Ascending or Descending
B. Specified
C. Original
D. Keep Group Together
E. Repeat Group Header On Each New Page
F. Format Group Expert
G. Sum Group

Q21: You have created a report with two groups. Column headings appear in the Preview Tab above the first group, but with no corresponding records in the Details Section. Which of the following must you apply to rectify the problem? *(Multiple Answers)*

A. Create a second Details Section (Detail b) and move the column headings into it
B. Swap Detail b and Detail a so that the column headings are on top of the detail section that contains database fields.
C. Hide the Group Header along with the detail section
D. Select the Text Objects that comprise the column headings. Using the Format Editor, choose the suppress if duplicated formatting option

Q22: You have excluded sales which do not fall into the Top 3 sales category, however they still appear in the grand total. Which of the following methods will resolve this?

With others included

Product Name	Sales for Month July
Silver Rim Pen	£8000
Gold Plated Pen	£7500
Diamond Pen	£6000
Other Sales for this Period	£15,331.15
	£36,831.15

With others excluded

Product Name	Sales for Month July
Silver Rim Pen	£8000
Gold Plated Pen	£7500
Diamond Pen	£6000
	£36,831.15

A. Verify the database and the Grand Total will change to reflect the TopN sales figure
B. Create a running total based on the sales amount and place it in the report footer
C. Select View and Field Explorer - Right-click Running Total and select New, enter running total name, and summarize sales amount with a summary type of sum and click ok
D. None of the above

Q23: Summaries based on the Group Footer can be used in the alert creation process.

A. True

B. False

Q24: You have inserted a group into your sales report which you would now like to delete. What should you do?

A. Choose Format | Delete Group
B. Right-click the grey section of the group and select delete group from the drop-down menu
C. Choose Report | Delete Group
D. From the Section Expert, Delete Group
E. Select Edit and delete group

Q25: You have created a report with a group based on City, and you want users to have the functionality to drill down from a City of their choice to view the customers associated with that City. What should you do? *(Multiple Answers)*

A. Right-click the grey area of the detail section and select Hide (Drill-Down OK), when you double-click the group the Details Section will appear.
B. From the toolbar, select Report | Section Expert | highlight the Details Section and check the hide ((Drill-Down OK), when the user double-clicks the group the Details Section will appear.
C. Right-click the grey area of the Details Section and select suppress, when you double-click the group the Details Section will appear.
D. Right-click the grey area of the detail section and select do not show section, when you double-click the group the Details Section will appear.
E. Right-click the grey area of the Group and select do not show section, when you double-click the group the Details Section will appear.
F. Right-click the grey area of the detail section and select hide ((Drill-Down OK) from the drop-down list

Q26: You have created a sales report and would like to see the 'Client. Name' records appearing in an ascending order. What should you do?

A. Choose Report | Select Expert from the pull-down menu, or click the record sort expert button from the toolbar, from the available fields section, select Client name field and use the arrow > to place it into the sort-fields on your right, click the radio button under sort direction (Ascending)

B. Choose Report | Section Expert | Record Sort Expert from the pull-down menu, or click the record sort expert button from the toolbar, from the available fields section, select Client name field and use the arrow > to place it into the sort-fields on your right, click the radio button under sort direction (Ascending)

C. Choose Report | Record Sort Expert | from the pull-down menu, or click the record sort expert button from the toolbar, from the available fields section, select {Client. name} field and use the arrow > to place it into the sort-fields on your right, click the radio button under sort direction (Ascending)

D. Right-click field, select format field | Common Tab, Ascending

Q27: You want to create a summary report based on the number of clients per city. Which of the following will enable you to create the summary report?

A. Select file new and Blank Report , select the data source required and select the client table, click finish, from the insert group dialog box select Client_id as the group and click OK, drag the client_id field from the Field Explorer into the Details Section of the report and right-click the field and insert summary, select distinct count under calculate this summary and for the summary location, select the City group and click OK, hide the detail section and preview

B. Select file new and Blank Report from the Menu Bar, the Database Expert will appear, select the data source required and select the client table, click finish, from the detail section select insert from the Menu Bar a select group, from the insert group dialog box select city as the group and click OK, drag the client_id field from the Field Explorer into the Details Section of the report and right-click the field and insert summary, under calculate this summary select distinct count and for the summary location, select the City group and click OK, hide the detail section and preview

C. Select file new and Blank Report from the Menu Bar, the Database Expert will appear, select the data source required and select the client table, click finish, from the detail section select insert from the Menu Bar a select group, from the insert group dialog box select city as the group, drag the client_id field from the Field Explorer into the Details Section of the report and right-click the field and insert summary, select sum under calculate this summary and for the summary location, select the City group and click OK, hide the detail section and preview

D. Select file new and Blank Report from the Menu Bar, the Database Expert will appear, select the data source required and select the client table, click finish, and click OK, drag the client_id field from the Field Explorer into the Details Section of the report and right-click the field and insert summary, select distinct count under calculate this summary and for the summary location, and click OK, Suppress the detail section and preview

Q28: You have created a report with one group, and you do no want the Details Section to appear when the user double clicks the group. What should you apply to the details section?

A. Choose Report from the Menu Bar | select selection expert | highlight the Details Section and check Suppress

B. Choose Report from the Menu Bar | select Section Expert | highlight the Details Section and check the Hide (Drill-Down OK) checkbox

C. Choose Report from the Menu Bar | select Section Expert | highlight the Details Section and check Suppress

D. Choose Report from the Menu Bar | select Section Expert | highlight the Details Section and check Keep Together

Q29: You have created a report and would like to add a Group Selection criterion. What should you do?

A. From the Select Expert, click the Show Formula >>>, click the Group Selection radio button, select formula editor and enter your criteria

B. From the Select Expert, click the record selection radio button, select formula editor and enter your criteria

C. From the Select Expert, click the records tab, select formula editor and enter your criteria

D. From the select Section Expert, click the Group Selection radio button, select formula editor and enter your criteria

Q30: You have created a formula which outlines early and late deliveries. You have also created a group based on this formula, and want to highlight all Group Header backgrounds in red, if delivery is late. Which of the following apply?

A. Right-click grey section of group and select - Select Expert, select the color tab and click the background color formula box and enter the following formula if {@DeliveryStatus} = 'Late Delivery' then Crred else CrNoColor
B. Right-click grey section of group and select Section Expert, select the Common Tab and click the background color formula box and enter the following formula if {@DeliveryStatus} = 'Late Delivery' then Crred else CrNoColor
C. Right-click grey section of group and select Section Expert, select the color tab and click the background color formula box and enter the following formula if {@DeliveryStatus} = 'Late Delivery' then Crred else CrNoColor
D. Right-click grey section of group and select Section Expert, select the Font tab and click the background color formula box and enter the following formula if {@DeliveryStatus} = 'Late Delivery' then Crred else CrNoColor

Q31: You want to establish the percentage of orders by clients for the month of July. Which of the following apply? *(Multiple Answers)*

A. Create the following formula and place it in the client Group Header Sum ({Merchandise.Cost}) % Sum ({Merchandise.Cost}, { Merchandise. Merchandise Name})
B. Sum ({Merchandise.Cost}, { Merchandise. Merchandise Name}) %
C. Check the Show As Percentage of checkbox when inserting a summary
D. Create the following formula and place it in the client Group Header Sum ({Merchandise.Cost}, { Merchandise. Merchandise Name}) % Sum ({Merchandise.Cost})

Q32: You have drilled-down several levels within a report. Which of the following are true? *(Multiple Answers)*

A. Only the material appearing in the current tab will export
B. You can print all material in the report after drill-down
C. You cannot export drill-down information
D. Only the material appearing in the current tab will print

Q33: A request had been made for a report, the report should be group specific, the report must display only departments with over 15 staff in it; the report contains a department field and a distinct count of department staff and is grouped by department. Which of the following will achieve this result?

A. Create a distinct count of staff based on the department group, from the toolbar select Report and Select Expert and click the Show Formula button, and also check the Group Selection Button, and click on the Formula Editor, this will open up the Formula Workshop - Group Selection Formula Editor, enter the formula below based on the group summary created, DistinctCount ({Department.Staff}, { Department.Department}) > 15, save and close and click OK

B. Create a distinct count of staff based on the department group, from the toolbar select Report and Select Expert and click the Show Formula button, and also check the Group Selection Button, and click on the Formula Editor, this will open up the Formula Workshop - Group Selection Formula Editor, enter the formula below based on the group summary created, Count ({Department.Staff}, { Department.Department}) > 15, save and close and click OK

C. Create a distinct count of staff based on the department group, from the toolbar select Report and Select Expert and click the Show Formula button, and also check the Group Selection Button, and click on the Formula Editor, this will open up the Formula Workshop - Group Selection Formula Editor, enter the formula below based on the group summary created, DistinctCount ({Department.Staff}, { Department.Department}) >= 15, save and close and click OK

D. Create a distinct count of staff based on the department group, from the toolbar select Report and Select Expert and click the Show Formula button, and also check the Group Selection Button, and click on the Formula Editor, this will open up the Formula Workshop - Group Selection Formula Editor, enter the formula below based on the group summary created, DistinctCount ({Department.Staff}, { Department.Department}) <= 15, save and close and click OK

Q34. You have created a report which contains a date group, the date field used to create the group contains a Null field, you created a formula to display the word 'Blank' instead of displaying a Null field in the Group Tree, the word 'Blank' is not appearing in the Group Tree, what could the problem be?

A. Convert Database NULL Values to Default is checked

B. Convert Database NULL Values to Default is unchecked

Q35. Grouped data spills over onto the next page of your report. You want to highlight this information with the group title: Group Name (Continued from previous page). Which of the following will achieve this?

A. Create the following formula and place it in Group Header #2: if InRepeatedGroupHeader = true then {Sales_3.Region} + " (.......Continued from previous page)"
B. if InRepeatedGroupHeader = False then {Sales_3.Region} + " (.......Continued from previous page)"
C. Create the following formula and place it in Group Header #2: if InRepeatedGroupHeader = yes then {Sales_3.Region} + " (.......Continued from previous page)"
D. Create the following formula and place it in Group Header #2: if InRepeatedGroupHeader = no then {Sales_3.Region} + " (.......Continued from previous page)"

Q36. You have created a report with two group summaries, Group Header #1 is based on Continent Sales and Group Header #2 which the user will drill-down into is based on Regional Sales, when the user drills-down from continent sales into regional sales, Group Header #1 still appears at the top, you only want to see the sales information for regional sales. How can you implement this?

A. Within the Section Expert apply the following conditional formula by clicking the suppress conditional button for Group Header #2 (Region Group) and entering the following condition DrillDownGroupLevel = 1
B. Within the Section Expert apply the following conditional formula by clicking the suppress conditional button for Group Header #1 (Continent Group) and entering the following condition DrillDownGroupLevel <> 0
C. Within the Section Expert apply the following conditional formula by clicking the suppress conditional button for Group Header #2 (Region Group) and entering the following condition DrillDownGroupLevel <1
D. Within the Section Expert apply the following conditional formula by clicking the suppress conditional button for Group Header #1 (Continent Group) and entering the following condition DrillDownGroupLevel = 1

Q37. Given the following report information, you want to suppress regional information for Colorado and New Hampshire, including the header information and the footer information, and the title. Which of the following apply? (Multiple Answers)

Section				
RH	**SALES REPORT**			
GH1a	**Arkansas**			
GH1b	**States**	**Industry**	**Software**	**No of Sales**
D	Arkansas	Trading	Report Presx 8	9
D	Arkansas	Accounting	Crystal Reports XI	2
GH1a	**Colorado**			
GH1b	**States**	**Industry**	**Software**	**No of Sales**
D	Colorado	Banking	VisioPlus Reporting	4
D	Colorado	Manufacturing	Reporting Active	2
D	Colorado	Accounting	Crystal Reports 8.5	20
GH1a	**Iowa**			
GH1b	**States**	**Industry**	**Software**	**No of Sales**
D	Iowa	Accounting	Crystal Reports 10	40
GH1a	**New Hampshire**			
GH1b	**States**	**Industry**	**Software**	**No of Sales**
D	New Hampshire	Accounting	Crystal Reports 9	30

A. Right-click the Details Section and select the Section Expert, apply the following condition to the suppress condition button {Sales. Region} in ['Colorado', 'New Hampshire'];follow the same procedure for the Group Header and Footer

B. Right-click the Details Section and select the Section Expert, apply the following condition to the suppress condition button GroupNumber in [2,4] ;follow the same procedure for the Group Header and Footer

C. Right-click the Details Section and select the Section Expert, apply the following condition to the suppress condition button GroupNumber in [1,4] ;follow the same procedure for the Group Header and Footer

D. Right-click the Details Section and select the Section Expert, apply the following condition to the suppress condition button GroupNumber in [1,3] ;follow the same procedure for the Group Header and Footer

Q38. You want to view the restriction based on the groups within your report which of the following apply?

A. Create a formula within your report and enter GroupSelection

B. Create a formula within your report and enter GroupSelect

C. Create a formula within your report and enter RecordSelection

D. Create a formula within your report and enter RecordSelect

Chapter 9 - Creating a Chart

Chapter 9: The graphical representation of data involves the use of Charts. The selection of the Chart Type will depend highly on the type of data being displayed. Line Charts can be used for statistical presentations and pie Charts for geographical presentation of data. Questions in this chapter cover the various Chart Types available within Crystal Reports and the additional functionality present for further graphical manipulation.

Key areas

- **Chart Types**
- **Chart Selection**
- **Format Chart**
- **Chart Setttings**

Q1. Which of the following data categories can be used to create a Chart? *(Multiple Answers)*

A. Group Summaries and Subtotals

B. Data in the details section

C. Data within an existing Cross-Tab

D. Formulas with Evaluation Time Functions (WhilePrintingRecords)

E. Formulas with Shared variables or variables

F. Running Totals

G. OLAP data

Q2. Which of the following statements are untrue about Charts? *(Multiple Answers)*

A. Charts cannot be created from Running Totals

B. Charts cannot be created from Cross-Tabs

C. Charts cannot be deleted once created

D. Charts can only be created when summaries exists within the report

Q3. You place your Chart in the Report Header. What will the Chart represent?

A. All report data

B. Group Data only

C. Group Header data only

D. Group Footer data only

Q4. Given the data below, a request has been made to create a bar Chart. Which of the following Chart Types will be most appropriate?

Candidate Count	County	Month	Year	Result%	RDCR201	RDCR301
20	London	April	2006	80		
10	Merseyside	April	2006	80		50
12	Essex	April	2006	80	7	
16	Dublin	April	2006	60		89
90	Coventry	April	2006	70		90
34	London	August	2006	50	3	78
2	Merseyside	August	2006	70	50	10
4	Essex	August	2006	70		
53	Dublin	August	2006	70	70	
23	Coventry	August	2006	70		1
11	Kent	August	2006	20	50	10
10	Northampton	August	2006	60		

A. Percent bar Chart
B. Stacked
C. Stacked bar Chart
D. Side by side bar Chart

Q5. How do you save your existing Chart as a template?

A. Right-click the Chart and select Chart Expert, within the Data Tab select save as template, assign a name and save the Chart within the user defined folder
B. Right-click the Chart and select save as template, assign a name and save the Chart within the user defined folder
C. Right-click the Chart and select Chart Expert, within the template tab select save as template, assign a name and save the Chart within the user defined folder
D. Right-click the Chart and select save as template, assign a name and save the Chart within the user defined folder
E. None of the above, Charts cannot be saved as templates

Q6. Which of the following are Chart Types within the Chart Expert? *(Multiple Answers)*

A. Bar, Line, Area
B. Numeric Axis, Gauge, Gantt
C. Pie, Doughnut, 3D Riser
D. Pie, Doughnut, 2D Riser
E. XY Scatter, Stock, Radar, Bubble
F. Y Scatter, OLAP
G. Funnel, Histogram

Q7. You have entered data that is not compatible with the Chart Type selected. What will happen?

A. The OK button will be greyed out

B. An Exit Chart Expert dialog box will appear

C. Return to Chart Expert will be displayed

D. The Chart Expert will automatically choose the most appropriate Chart Type

Q8. You want to launch the Chart Expert. What should you do?

A. Choose Report, insert Chart, select the Chart Type, select the Data Tab for data type and Chart (group, advance, OLAP, or Cross-Tab) and text tab for titles

B. Choose insert Chart, a Chart placeholder will automatically appear, place this Chart in the required section, the Chart Expert will appear, select the Chart Type, data, axes and other customized settings

C. Choose Section Expert, insert Chart, select the Chart Type, select the Data Tab for data type and Chart (group, advance, OLAP, or Cross-Tab) and text tab for titles

D. Choose Report Expert, insert Chart, select the Chart Type, select the Data Tab for data type and Chart (group, advance, OLAP, or Cross-Tab) and text tab for titles

Q9. Within the Chart Expert, which of the following tabs are available? *(Multiple Answers)*

A. Type, Color Highlight, Data, Options

B. Axes, Text, Legend

C. Options, Highlight Expert

D. General, Templates, Data Grid, Selected Item

E. Axes, Text

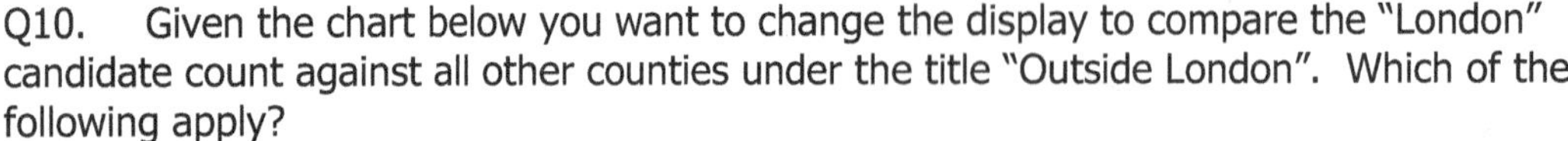

Q10. Given the chart below you want to change the display to compare the "London" candidate count against all other counties under the title "Outside London". Which of the following apply?

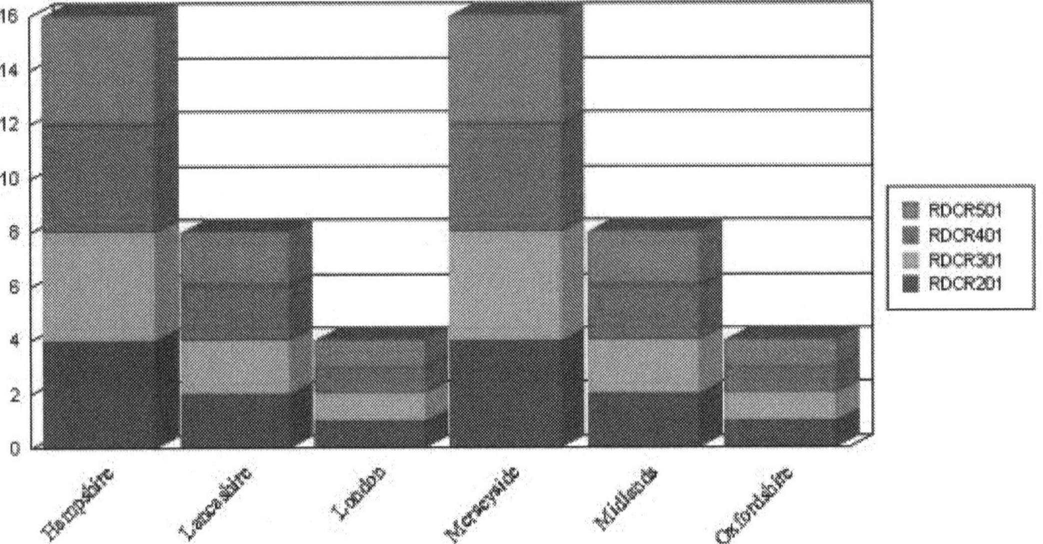

A. Right-click Chart and select Chart Expert, select the Data Tab and highlight the county field in the On Change of section, click the order button and select Specified Order from the Common Tab and click the Specified Order tab, select London from the Named Group, click the others tab, in the section named put all others together with the name 'Outside London'

B. Right-click Chart and select Chart Expert, select the Text tab and highlight the county field in the On Change of section, click the order button and select Specified Order from the Common Tab and, click the Specified Order tab and select London from the Named Group, click the others tab, in the section named put all others together with the name 'Outside London'

C. Right-click Chart and select Chart Expert, select the Group tab and highlight the county field in the On Change of section, click the order button and select Specified Order from the Common Tab and, click the Specified Order tab and select London from the Named Group, click the others tab, in the section named put all others together with the name 'Outside London'

D. Right-click Chart and select Chart Expert, select the Options Tab and highlight the county field in the On Change of section, click the order button and select Specified Order from the Common Tab and, click the Specified Order tab and select London from the Named Group, click the others tab, in the section named put all others together with the name 'Outside London'

Q11. The Advanced Layout Chart can be used to create a Chart where groups do not exist in the reports or where data does not exist in the Details Section of the report

A. True

B. False

Q12. You have created a Chart as displayed below. You want to change the order of the counties as follows: London, Midlands, Lancashire, and Merseyside. Which method is applicable?

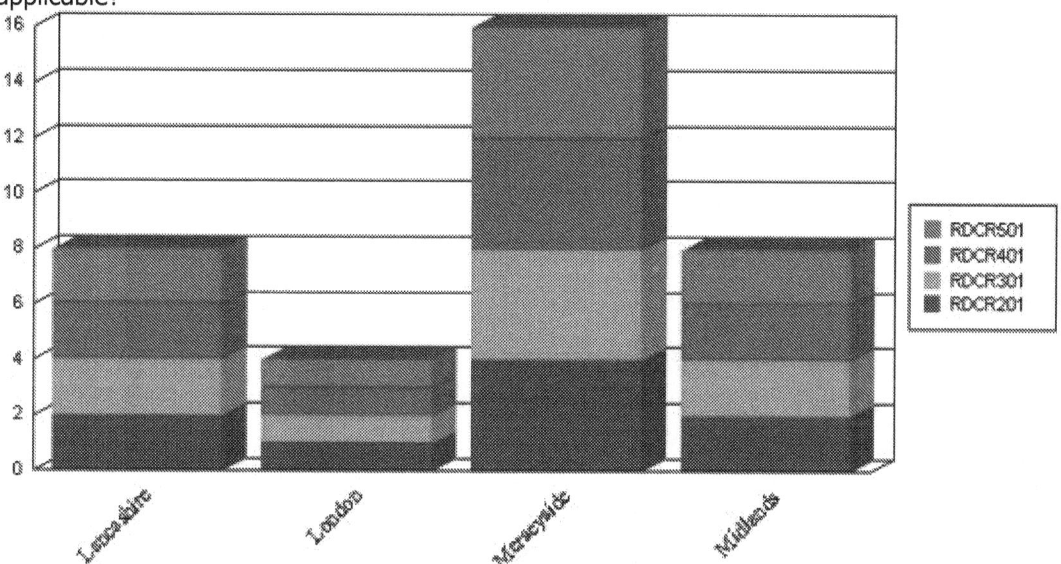

A. Right-click Chart and select Chart Expert, select the Specified Data Tab and highlight the county field in the On Change of section, click the order button and select Specified Order from the Common Tab and, click the Specified Order tab and select London, Midlands, Lancashire, Merseyside from the Named Group and click ok

B. Right-click Chart and select Chart Expert, select the Group Data Tab and highlight the county field in the On Change of section, click the order button and select Specified Order from the Common Tab and, click the Specified Order tab and select London, Midlands, Lancashire, Merseyside from the Named Group and click ok

C. Right-click Chart and select Chart Expert, select the Data Tab and highlight the county field in the On Change of section, click the order button, select Specified Order from the Common Tab, click the Specified Order tab and select London, Midlands, Lancashire, Merseyside from the Named Group and click ok

D. Right-click Chart and select Chart Expert, select the Options Tab and highlight the county field in the On Change of section, click the order button and select Specified Order from the Common Tab and, click the Specified Order tab and select London, Midlands, Lancashire, Merseyside from the Named Group and click ok

Q13. Which of the following are Chart Expert Data Layout Types? *(Multiple Answers)*

A. Advanced

B. Group

C. Cross-Tab

D. OLAP

Q14. You want to load a stored template into your existing Chart. Which of the following apply?

A. Right-click the Chart and select Chart Expert, and Load Template, select the required template from the categories section and click ok

B. Right-click the Chart and select Load Template, select the required template from the categories section and click ok

C. Right-click the Chart and select Chart options and Load Template, select the required template from the categories section and click ok

D. Right-click the Chart and select Template, select the required template from the categories section and click ok

Q15. You want to display the top 5 product sales within your advanced Chart. Which of the following apply?

A. Select Report from the Menu Bar and select Group Sort Expert and select Top N based on sum product sales where N equals 5 and click ok

B. Right-click Chart and select Chart Expert, select the Text tab and highlight the county field in the On Change of section, click the Top N button and select Top N based on sum product sales where N equals 5 and click ok

C. Select Report from the Menu Bar and select record sort expert and select Top N based on sum product sales where N equals 5 and click ok

D. Right-click Chart and select Chart Expert, select the Data Tab and highlight the Product field in the On Change of section of the Chart Expert, click the Top N button and select Top N based on sum of product sales where N equals 5 and click ok

Q16. You want to change the color of a bar within your Chart. Which of the following apply?

A. Right-click the Chart and select Chart Expert and format series riser, choose the required color from the Foreground color
B. Right-click the bar and select format series riser and choose the required color from the fore ground color
C. Right-click the Chart and select format Chart Expert and choose the required color from the fore ground color
D. Right-click the Chart and select format bar and choose the required color from the fore ground color

Q17. You have double-clicked a Chart to drill-down, but nothing happens. Which one of the following reasons could be the cause?

A. You have placed the Chart in the details section
B. The Chart contains a formula
C. The Chart is based on a running total
D. The Chart is an advanced Chart and therefore cannot be drilled-down into

Q18. Within which of the following Chart Expert sections do you select the data for your Chart?

A. Type
B. Fields
C. Axes
D. Data Options
E. Data

Q19. Within your report you have groups and summaries. Which Chart layout type will be most appropriate?

A. Advanced Chart
B. Group Chart
C. OLAP Chart
D. Cross Tab Chart

Q20. You want to change your Chart to a horizontal display. What should you do?

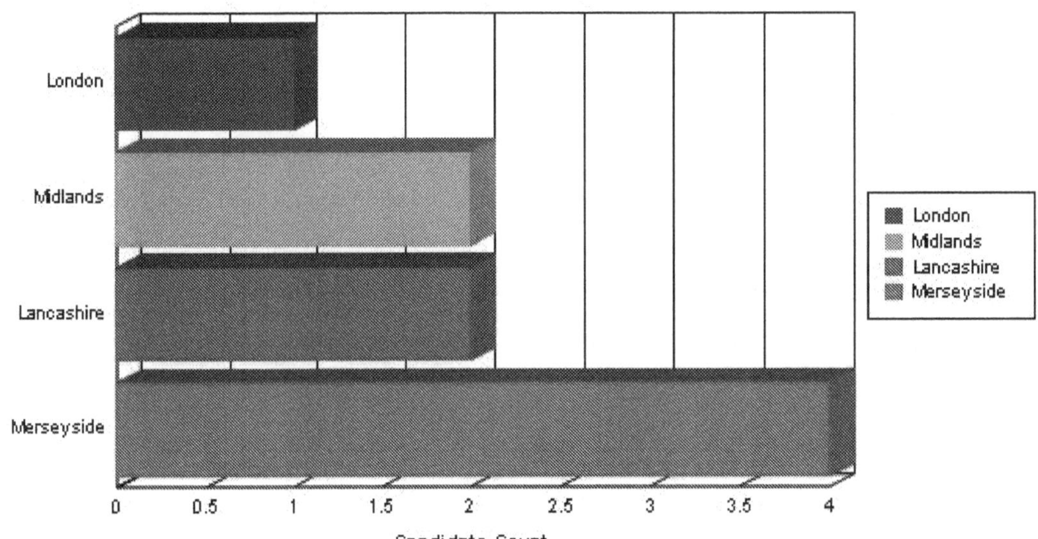

A. Right-click the Chart and select Chart options, from the appearance tab select Horizontal
B. Right-click the Chart and select Chart Expert, from the Type tab select Horizontal
C. Right-click the Chart and select Rotate Chart, from the drop-down menu select Horizontal
D. Right-click the Chart and format Chart Expert, from the Common Tab select Horizontal

Q21. Drill-down Charts are only applicable when a group and summaries exist within the report.

A. True
B. False

Q22. Your pie Chart appears as follows. You want to add depth to the Chart to appear as illustrated in fig 2. Which of the following apply?

A. Right-click the Chart and select Chart Expert, from the Axes tab select Use depth effect

B. Right-click the Chart and select Chart Expert, from the Depth tab select Use depth effect

C. Right-click the Chart and select Chart Expert, from the Type tab select Use depth effect

D. Right-click the Chart and select Chart Expert, from the Text tab select Use depth effect

Candidate Count per County

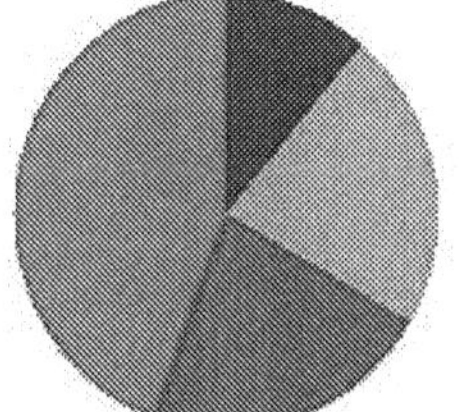

London 11.1%
Midlands 22.2%
Lancashire 22.2%
Merseyside 44.4%
Total: 100.0%

Candidate Count per County

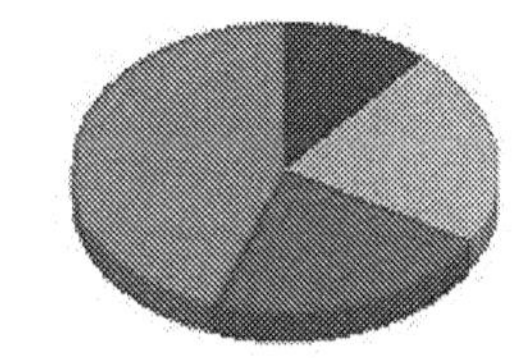

London 11.1%
Midlands 22.2%
Lancashire 22.2%
Merseyside 44.4%
Total: 100.0%

Q23. You can see the result of your Chart in preview mode.

A. True

B. False

Q24. Your Chart appears in black and white as illustrated below. Which of the following settings has been applied?

Candidate Count per County

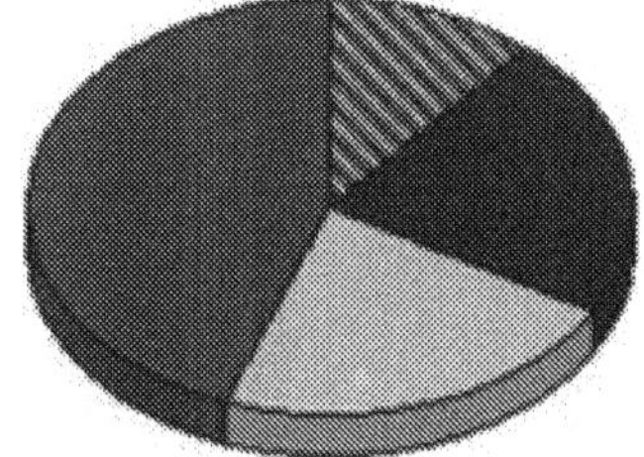

London 11.1%
Midlands 22.2%
Lancashire 22.2%
Merseyside 44.4%
Total: 100.0%

A. Chart Expert – Color –Chart Color: Black and White

B. Chart Expert – Color Highlights –Chart Color: Black and White

C. Chart Expert – Data –Chart Color: Black and White

D. Chart Expert – Options –Chart Color: Black and White

Q25. Within the Chart Expert, which of the following tabs will be unavailable when you select any of the following Chart Types: Pie, Doughnut, Gantt or Funnel?

A. Axes

B. Options

C. Text

D. Color Highlight

Q26. Which of the following settings can be implemented under the Axes tab? *(Multiple Answers)*

A. Show Gridlines

B. Data values

C. Number of divisions

D. Legend

Q27. You want to assign a specific colour (Blue) to your bar Chart, if the county equals 'London'. Which method applies?

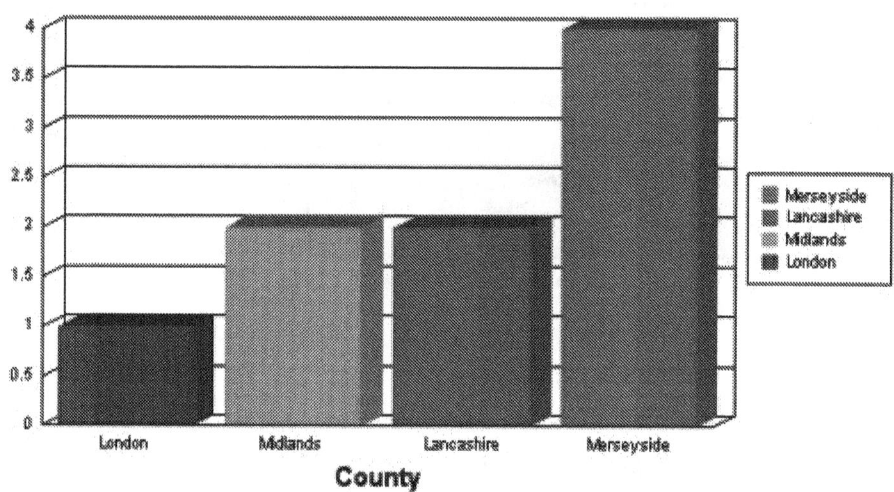

A. Within the Chart Expert, select the Options Tab and click the new button, the county field will appear, set the value to London and select the color Blue and click ok
B. Within the Chart Expert, select the Color Highlights tab and click the new button, the county field will appear, set the value to London and select the color Blue and click ok
C. Within the Chart Expert, select the Axes tab and click the new button, the county field will appear, set the value to London and select the color Blue and click ok
D. Within the Chart Expert, select the Data Tab and click the new button, the county field will appear, set the value to London and select the color Blue and click ok

Q28. You want to add a title to the Chart. Which of the following methods apply?

A. Within the Chart Expert, select the Text tab and enter your new title
B. Within the Chart Expert, select the Data Tab and enter your new title
C. Within the Chart Expert, select the Options Tab and enter your new
D. Within the Chart Expert, select the File tab and enter your new title

Q29. Which Chart is most suitable for displaying development over time?

A. Pie Chart
B. 3 –D Surface
C. Bar Chart
D. Doughnut
E. Line

Q30. Which of the following options has been applied to the Chart below?

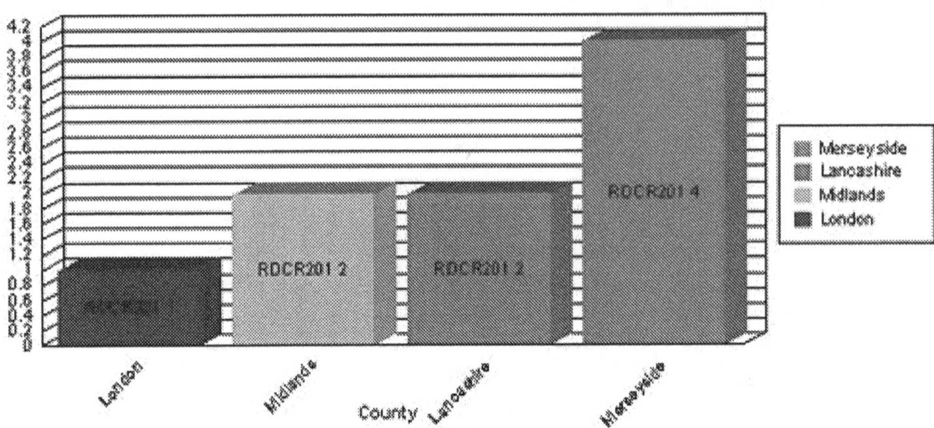

A. Chart Expert – Options – Data Points, Show Label

B. Chart Expert – Labels – Data Points, Show Label and Show Value

C. Chart Expert – Values – Data Points, Show Label and Show Value

D. Chart Expert – Text – Data Points, Show Label and Show Value

Q31. You want to remove the Chart Legend. Which of the following methods apply?

A. Within Chart Expert – Options Tab – Legend, uncheck Show Legend

B. Within Chart Expert – Legend Tab – Legend, uncheck Show Legend

C. Within Chart Expert – Text Tab – Legend, uncheck Show Legend

D. Within Chart Expert – Placement Tab – Legend, uncheck Show Legend

Q32. You have right-clicked your Chart in Preview Mode. Which of the following options will be available? *(Multiple Answers)*

A. Auto-Arrange Chart

B. Zoom in

C. Load Template

D. Save as Template

E. Select Mode

F. Format Background

G. Format Foreground

Q33. Which of the following three options allow the user to choose when the Advanced Chart starts a new block? *(Multiple Answers)*

A. On change of

B. For each record

C. For all records

D. For group

Q34. Which of the following settings are available within the Option Tab of the Chart Expert? *(Multiple Answers)*

A. Background settings

B. Chart Color

C. Legend

D. Size

E. XY displays

Q35. Which Chart represents the percentage for each item?

A. Line

B. 3-D riser

C. Pie Chart

D. 3 –D Surface

Q36. You have just opened a report, which has a doughnut Chart placed in the Report Header section. There is a figure in the middle of the Chart. What does this figure represent?

A. The Subtotal for the groups

B. The Grand Total for the whole report

C. The summary for the groups

D. The summary for the page headers

Q37. Which of the following is not a Chart Type in Crystal? *(Multiple Answers)*

A. Rule Chart

B. Line Chart

C. Pie Chart

D. 2-D Riser

E. Gauge

Q38. Group Charts represent data that already exists in one of the following:

A. Subtotals and summary fields in the detail section
B. Subtotals and summary fields in the Report Header
C. Subtotals and summary fields in the page header
D. Subtotals and summary fields in the Group Header or Group Footer

Q39. The Data Tab of the Chart Expert provides the functionality to do which of the following? *(Multiple Answers)*

A. Denote A Group Chart Layout
B. Denote An Advanced Chart Layout
C. Denote A Cross-Tab Chart Layout
D. Denote An OLAP Layout
E. Denote Chart Type, Pie, Bubble Etc

Q40. You right-click a Stacked Bar Chart and select Chart Options. Which of the following settings will appear? *(Multiple Answers)*

A. Appearance
B. Titles
C. Data Labels
D. Gridlines
E. Axes
F. Legend

Q41. You right-click the bar within your Chart. Which of the following options will be available? *(Multiple Answers)*

A. Format series riser
B. Chart options
C. Series option
D. Trend lines
E. Lines

Q42. You want to change your Bar Chart to a Funnel Chart Type; the data is not compatible with this Chart Type. What will happen?

A. The ok button will be greyed out
B. The Chart Data and Type dialog box will appear indicating the data does not fit the Chart Type selected
C. The Chart will be presented as a blank section
D. All Chart Types are compatible will all data
E. The Chart Selection Expert will appear providing an alternative option

Q43. Which options will appear when an incorrect Chart Type is selected for data in your report? *(Multiple Answers)*

A. Continue
B. Return to Chart Expert
C. Automatically choose the most appropriate Chart Type
D. None of the above

Q44. Each Chart Type within the Chart Expert provides a Chart functional description.

A. True
B. False

Chapter 10 - Creating Cross-Tab

Chapter 10 covers questions on the creation of Cross-Tabs.

Key areas

- **Cross-Tabs**
- **Cross-Tab Pivot**

Q1. Which of the following defines a Cross-Tab? *(Multiple Answers)*

A. Cross-Tabs consist of rows and columns and are used to present data in a logical format

B. Cross-Tabs can only be created when groups exist within the report

C. Cross-Tabs are Excel based sheets imported into a report

D. Fields within the Cross-Tab can be summarized based on sums, counts, distinct counts and all other summaries applicable to a field type

Q2. You have created a report and inserted a Cross-Tab in the Group Header. You want to ensure objects in the Cross-Tab are not being printed over each other. What should you do?

A. Select Field Expert, highlight the Group Header where the Cross-Tab is placed and place a tick in the check box or Relative Position

B. Select Selection Expert, highlight the Group Header where the Cross-Tab is placed and place a tick in the check box or Relative Position

C. Select Group Expert, select the Common Tab and highlight the Group Header where the Cross-Tab is placed and place a tick in the check box or Relative Position

D. From the Section Expert, select the Common Tab and highlight the Group Header where the Cross-Tab is placed and place a tick in the Relative Position check box

Q3. You are presented with the following data as illustrated below which you have used to create a Cross-Tab. Which of the following fields have been used within the section of the Cross-Tab?

DATA

	Quantity Ordered
Product Name: Alice Mutton	978
Country: Austria	191
Belgium	40
Brazil	27
Canada	126
France	67
Germany	15
Italy	20
Mexico	36
Spain	60
Sweden	10
UK	25
USA	361
Product Name: Aniseed Syrup	328
Country: Austria	45
Canada	20
Denmark	14
Germany	115
Sweden	30
UK	30
USA	4
Venezuela	70

Fig 1

CROSS-TAB

	Total	Alice Mutton	Aniseed Syrup
Total	1306	978	328
Austria	236	191	45
Belgium	40	40	0
Brazil	27	27	0
Canada	146	126	20
Denmark	14	0	14
France	67	67	0
Germany	130	15	115
Italy	20	20	0
Mexico	36	36	0
Spain	60	60	0
Sweden	40	10	30
UK	55	25	30
USA	365	361	4
Venezuela	70	0	70

Fig 2

A. Row = Product Name, Column = Country and Summarized Fields = Quantity Ordered

B. Row = Country, Column = Product Name and Summarized Fields = Quantity Ordered

C. Column = Product Name and Country and Summarized Fields = Quantity Ordered

D. Row = Country and Product Name and Summarized Fields = Quantity Ordered

Q4. You want to replace your Cross-Tab with a Chart. Which of the following apply?

A. Right-click the Cross-Tab and select Insert Chart

B. From the menu – select insert Chart

C. Right-click the Cross-Tab and select Convert Cross-Tab to Chart

D. From the menu – select Convert Cross-Tab to Chart

Q5. Which of the following explains the totals represented in the Cross-Tab illustrated in fig 2? *(Multiple Answers)*

A. Grand Totals Only
B. Sub Totals Only
C. Grand Total for products
D. Total for products per country

Q6. You Right-click the Cross-Tab illustrated in fig 2 and select Pivot Cross-Tab. Which of the following will happen?

A. Results will be displayed in a Vertical Format, Product Names will appear as a column and countries will appear in the row
B. Results will be displayed upside down
C. Columns will be displayed as Rows and Rows as Columns
D. None of the above

Q7. You have presented your Cross-Tab to the sales team and the following suggestions have been made. Users will like to see the name of the summarized field. Which of the following apply?

A. Right-click the Cross-Tab and select Cross-Tab Expert and select Grid Options and Show Summarized Field Labels
B. Right-click the Cross-Tab field and select Show Summarized Field Labels
C. Right-click the Cross-Tab and select Format Cross-Tab and select Summarized Field Labels and Show Summarized Field Labels
D. Right-click the Cross-Tab and select Cross-Tab Expert and select Group Sort Expert and Show Summarized Field Labels

Q8. Totals appear on the top left section of the Cross-Tab. You want to change the location to the bottom of the Cross-Tab. Which of the following apply?

A. Right-click the Total text within the Cross-Tab and select Row Grand Totals and select Totals On Top

B. Right-click the Total text within the Cross-Tab and select Grand Totals and select Totals on Top

C. Right-click the Total text within the Cross-Tab and select Totals and select Totals on Top

D. Right-click the Total text within the Cross-Tab and select move Grand Totals to Top

	Total	Alice Mutton	Aniseed Syrup
Total	1306	978	328
Austria	236	191	45
Belgium	40	40	0

Fig 3.0: Cross-Tab 1

	Alice Mutton	Aniseed Syrup	Total
Austria	191	45	236
Belgium	40	0	40
Brazil	27	0	27
Canada	126	20	146
Denmark	0	14	14
France	67	0	67
Germany	15	115	130
Italy	20	0	20
Mexico	36	0	36
Spain	60	0	60
Sweden	10	30	40
UK	25	30	55
USA	361	4	365
Venezuela	0	70	70
Total	978	328	1306

Fig 3.1: Cross-Tab 2

Q9. You are presented with data as illustrated in Fig 1 and you want to create a Cross-Tab based on this data, which of the following procedures should be implemented?

A. From the menu select View – Cross-Tab, a Cross-Tab object will appear, place the box in the Report Header, Right-click the Cross-Tab box and select Cross-Tab Expert, the Cross-Tab dialog box will appear, from the available fields section – select Product Name for your columns using the arrow, Country for your Rows and quantity for your summarized fields and click Ok
B. From the menu select Insert – Cross-Tab, a Cross-Tab object will appear, place the box in the Report Header, Right-click the Cross-Tab box and select Cross-Tab Expert, the Cross-Tab dialog box will appear, from the available fields section – select Product Name for your columns using the arrow, Country for your Rows and quantity for your summarized fields and click Ok
C. From the menu select Report - Insert – Cross-Tab, a Cross-Tab object will appear, place the box in the Report Header, Right-click the Cross-Tab box and select Cross-Tab Expert, the Cross-Tab dialog box will appear, from the available fields section – select Product Name for your columns using the arrow, Country for your Rows and quantity for your summarized fields and click Ok
D. From the menu select Insert – Chart- Chart type- Cross-Tab, a Cross-Tab box will appear, place the box in the Report Header, Right-click the Cross-Tab box and select Cross-Tab Expert, the Cross-Tab dialog box will appear, from the available fields section – select Product Name for your columns using the arrow, Country for your Rows and quantity for your summarized fields and click Ok

Q10. Which of the following apply when creating a new Cross-Tab report?

A. Select File – New – Cross-Tab Chart – Create a New Data Connection – Select the required tables from the available Data source – Assign fields to the Column. Rows and summarized sections of the Cross-Tab and click next, No chart, apply filter if applicable – choose Cross-Tab style and click finish
B. Select File – New – Cross-Tab Report – Create a New Data Connection using the Cross-Tab Report Creation Wizard – Select the required tables from the available Data source – Assign fields to the Column. Rows and summarized sections of the Cross-Tab and click next, No chart, apply filter if applicable – choose Cross-Tab style and click finish
C. Select File – New – Cross-Tab Dialog – Create a New Data Connection – Select the required tables from the available Data source – Assign fields to the Column. Rows and summarized sections of the Cross-Tab and click next, No chart, apply filter if applicable – choose Cross-Tab style and click finish
D. Select File – New – Cross-Tab Expert Report – the Cross-Tab Report Creation Wizard dialog box will appear - Create a New Data Connection – Select the required tables from the available Data source – Assign fields to the Column. Rows and summarized sections of the Cross-Tab and click next, No chart, apply filter if applicable – choose Cross-Tab style and click finish

Q11. You have summary sales totals based on the Country group and a Cross-Tab, you want to display the top five sales per country based in your existing Cross-Tab. Which of the following apply? *(Multiple Answers)*

A. Right-click the Cross-Tab and select Group Sort Expert, for Top N based on the quantity where N is 5 and click ok
B. Select Report - Group Sort Expert, select Top N based on salesamount where N is 5 and uncheck include others and click ok
C. Select Report – Cross-Tab, Group Sort Expert, for Top N based on the quantity where N is 5 and uncheck include others and click ok
D. The Group Sort Expert cannot be applied to a Cross-Tab

Q12. You want to display the total discount awarded to each country and the name of the customer within the country.

A. Right-click the Cross-Tab and select Cross-Tab Expert, add the discount field to the summarized section and add the Customer Name to the Row and click ok
B. Right-click the Cross-Tab and select Format Cross-Tab Expert, add the discount field to the summarized section and add the Customer Name to the Row and click ok
C. Right-click the Cross-Tab and select Edit Cross-Tab, add the discount field to the summarized section and add the Customer Name to the Row and click ok
D. Right-click the Cross-Tab and select Format Expert, add the discount field to the summarized section and add the Customer Name to the Row and click ok

Q13. Which of the following sections can you place a Cross-Tab? *(Multiple Answers)*

A. Report Header
B. Group Header
C. Details section
D. Group Footer
E. Report Footer

Q14. Which one of the following statements is true?

A. Charts and Cross-Tab objects placed in the Page Header area print at the beginning of each page
B. Charts or Cross-Tabs cannot be placed in the page header section
C. Charts and Cross-Tabs cannot be placed in the Group Header section
D. Charts or Cross-Tabs can be placed in the page header section
E. Charts and Cross-Tabs can be placed in the detail section

Q15. The Cross-Tab chart is only available when Cross-Tab objects already exist in your report.

A. True
B. False

Q16. Which one of the following is true?

A. A Cross-Tab is not based on an existing group or its summarized fields
B. A Cross-Tab requires a group or summary fields
C. A Cross-Tab requires a group
D. A Cross-Tab requires summary fields with the main report

Q17. You want to highlight the background of all orders less than or equal to 50 with red and sales of 51 and over with blue. This will enable the Sales Team to identify customers who will be awarded a discount on their next orders. Which of the following apply?

A. Right-click the summarized filed within the Cross-Tab and select Format Field, select the Border Tab and click the formula button beside the background and enter the following formula: if CurrentFieldValue <= 50 then Crred else CrBlue
B. Right-click the summarized filed within the Cross-Tab and select Format Field, select the Font tab and click the formula button beside the background and enter the following formula: if CurrentFieldValue <= 50 then Crred else CrBlue
C. Right-click the summarized filed within the Cross-Tab and select Format Field, select the Number tab and click the formula button beside the background and enter the following formula: if CurrentFieldValue <= 50 then Crred else CrBlue
D. Right-click the summarized filed within the Cross-Tab and select Format Field, select the Common Tab and click the formula button beside the background and enter the following formula: if CurrentFieldValue <= 50 then Crred else CrBlue

Q18. You want to display the text discount awarded for all sales equal to 51 and over and no discount for 50 and less. Which of the following apply?

A. Right-click the summarized filed within the Cross-Tab and select Format Field, select the Border Tab and click the formula button beside the background and enter the following formula: if CurrentFieldValue <= 50 then No Discount else Discount Awarded
B. Right-click the summarized filed within the Cross-Tab and select Format Field, select the Font tab and click the formula button beside the background and enter the following formula: if CurrentFieldValue <= 50 then No Discount else Discount Awarded
C. Right-click the summarized filed within the Cross-Tab and select Format Field, select the Number tab and click the formula button beside the background and enter the following formula: if CurrentFieldValue <= 50 then No Discount else Discount Awarded

D. Right-click the summarized filed within the Cross-Tab and select Format Field, select the Common Tab and click the formula button beside the Display String and enter the following formula: if CurrentFieldValue <= 50 then 'No Discount' else 'Discount Awarded'

Q19. You want to change the current style of the Cross-Tab. Which of the following methods apply?

A. Right-click the Cross-Tab and select Cross-Tab Expert, click the Style Tab and select the style required
B. Highlight the Cross-Tab and select format from the Menu Bar and select Cross-Tab Expert, click the Style Tab and select the style required
C. Select Cross-Tab from the Menu Bar and select Cross-Tab Expert, click the Style Tab and select the style required
D. Select view Cross-Tab from the Menu Bar and select Cross-Tab Expert, click the Style Tab and select the style required

Q20. You have checked the style gallery of the Cross-Tab Expert, but you are unable to find a suitable style. What can you do to create your own style? *(Multiple Answers)*

A. Highlight the Cross-Tab, select format from the Menu Bar and select Cross-Tab Expert, click the Customize Style Tab and create the style required
B. Select Cross-Tab from the Menu Bar and select Cross-Tab Expert, click the Style Tab and select the style required
C. Select view Cross-Tab from the Menu Bar and select Cross-Tab Expert, click the Style Tab and select the style required

Q21. By Highlighting the field and dragging the arrows across a Cross-Tab field can be resized

A. True
B. False

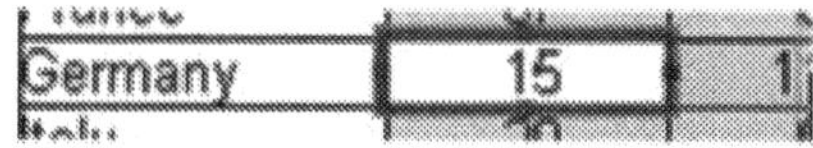

Q22. There are several empty columns in your Cross-Tab. Which of the following methods will enable you to remove these columns? *(Multiple Answers)*

A. Select Cross-Tab from the Menu Bar and select Cross-Tab Expert, click the Style Tab and select the style required
B. Select View Cross-Tab from the Menu Bar and select Cross-Tab Expert, click the Style Tab and select the style required
C. Select format from the Menu Bar and select Cross-Tab Expert, click the Customize Style Tab and check the Suppress Empty Columns
D. Right-click the Cross-Tab and select Cross-Tab Expert, click the Customize Style Tab and check the Suppress Empty Columns

Q23. Formulas can be added to Cross-Tabs

A. True
B. False

Q24. You want to remove all cell margins within the Cross-Tab. Which of the following apply?

A. Right-click the Cross-Tab and select Grid options and click remove cell margins, the tick will disappear
B. Right-click the Cross-Tab and select Grid options and click Show Cell Margins the tick will disappear
C. Right-click the Cross-Tab and select Grid options and click edit cell margins and remove cell margins the tick will disappear
D. Right-click the Cross-Tab and select Cross-Tab Grid options and click remove cell margins the tick will disappear

Q25. Which of the following can you perform within the Customize Style Tab? *(Multiple Answers)*

A. Suppress Empty Columns
B. Suppress Empty Rows
C. Suppress Columns Grand Total
D. Suppress Row Grand Total
E. Format Grid lines
F. Repeat Row Labels
G. Display String Value

Q26. You are presented with a Cross-Tab. You want to show the Grid lines which of the following apply?

A. Right-click the Cross-Tab and select Cross-Tab Expert, select the Customize Style Tab and click the Format Gridlines button and uncheck the Show Grid Lines checkbox
B. Right-click the Cross-Tab and select Cross-Tab Expert, select the Grid Options Tab and click the Format Gridlines button and uncheck the Show Grid Lines checkbox
C. Right-click the Cross-Tab and select Cross-Tab Expert, select the Customize Style Tab and check the Show Grid Lines checkbox
D. Right-click the Cross-Tab and select Cross-Tab Expert, select the Style Tab and click the Format Gridlines button and uncheck the Show Grid Lines checkbox

Chapter 11 – Creating Custom Functions

This chapter covers questions on Custom Functions; knowledge of Custom Functions is fundamental as it is a central function for creating and sharing customized formulas for present and future use hence reducing the processing time used to recreate formula. This chapter provides questions on the various functionalities of Custom Functions, their uses and limitations.

Key areas

- **Custom Functions**
- **Convert Formulas to Custom Functions**
- **Advantages of Custom Functions**
- **Repository**

Q1. You want to share your formula with other users. Which of the following will allow you to do this?

A. Operation Functions

B. Report Functions

C. Report Editor

D. File Editor

E. Custom Functions saved to the Repository

Q2. Where are default Custom Functions located?

A. Function Tree - Repository Custom Functions

B. Formula Workshop - Repository Custom Functions

C. Operations Tree - Repository Custom Functions

D. Report Editor - Repository Custom Functions

Q3. You want to launch the Formula Workshop to create a Custom Function. What must you do?

A. From the Menu Bar select Report | Formula Workshop Or click the Formula Workshop icon

B. From the Menu Bar select File | Formula Workshop

C. From the Menu Bar select insert Formula Workshop

D. From the Menu Bar select Database Formula Workshop

Q4. You have created a formula, which prefixes all London candidates with 001. You have also converted the formula into a Custom Function, and the formula is as follows:

If {Student.ExamCenter} startswith 'Lon' then "001" + "\" + {Student.StudentID} else {Student.StudentID}

Which of the following Custom Functions represents this formula?

A. Function (StringVar e1, StringVar e2) If e1 startswith 'Lon' then "001" + "\" + Mv2 else Mv2
B. Func (StringVar v1, StringVar v2) if v1 startswith 'London' then "001" + "\" + v2 else v2
C. Function (StringVar v1, StringVar v2) if v1 startswith 'London' then "001" + "\" + v2 else v2
D. Function (stVar v1, stVar v2) if v1 startswith 'London' then "001" + "\" + v2 else v2

Q5. How can you covert an existing formula to a Custom Function?

A. Use Extractor
B. Use Editor

Q6. You have moved an existing formula with 3 arguments to a Custom Function. What will the arguments be replaced with?

A. B1,B2,B3
B. V1,V2.V3
C. Aa,Bb,Cc
D. Z1,Z2,Z3

Q7. You have created the following formula, which you want to convert into a Custom Function using the Extractor. Which of the following statements apply? *(Multiple Answers)*

A. Custom Functions cannot use WhilePrintingRecords
B. Custom Functions cannot use any evaluation time functions
C. Custom Functions cannot use any summary functions
D. Custom Functions can only use local variable scope

```
WhilePrintingRecords;
NumberVar ExamFee;
if {Exam.ExamName} in ["RDCR200","RDCR300"] then
ExamFee:= ExamFee + {ExamCost.FEE};
```

Q8. You want to check the syntax options in your Custom Function. What can you do?

A. Press Ctrl + A

B. Press Ctrl + C

C. Press Alt + C

Q9. You have assigned a name, which contains spaces to a Custom Function, this will not be allowed

'Course Fees'

A. False

B. True

Q10. Which one of the following is true?

A. Custom Function names can contain spaces

B. Custom Function can start with numbers

C. The Custom Function name CBool is permissible

D. Names used by Crystal Report functions, cannot be used as Custom Function names

Q11. You want to create a new Custom Function from the start. Which of the following should you use?

A. Use Extractor

B. Use Editor

Q12. Which of the following languages are applicable to Custom Functions? *(Multiple Answers)*

A. Crystal Syntax

B. Basic Syntax

C. Basic Syntax only

D. Crystal Syntax only

Q13. Which of the following formulae can be converted into a Custom Function? *(Multiple Answers)*

A. NUMBERVAR ArrayCounter;

STRINGVAR ARRAY Alphabet;

Alphabet:=MAKEArray("RDCR201", "RDCR301", "RDCR401, "RDCR501");

ArrayCounter := ArrayCounter + 1;

Alphabet[ArrayCounter]

B.

Global Variable NumberVar ArrayCounter;

Global Variable StringVar array Alphabet;

Alphabet:=MAKEArray("RDCR201", "RDCR301", "RDCR401, "RDCR501");

ArrayCounter := ArrayCounter + 1;

Alphabet[ArrayCounter]

C.

Local NumberVar ArrayCounter;

Local StringVar array Alphabet;

Alphabet:=MAKEArray("RDCR201", "RDCR301", "RDCR401, "RDCR501");

ArrayCounter := ArrayCounter + 1;

Alphabet[ArrayCounter]

D.

Shared NumberVar ArrayCounter;

Shared StringVar array Alphabet;

Alphabet:=MAKEArray("RDCR201", "RDCR301", "RDCR401, "RDCR501");

ArrayCounter := ArrayCounter + 1;

Alphabet[ArrayCounter]

E. if {?Enter Product Name} = "Ball Point Pen" then 'Exclusive Pens'

Q14. You have made changes to an existing Repository based Custom Function. Which of the following will apply to other users of the Custom Function?

A. The changes made to the Custom Function will be automatically replicated in all other formulas that use this function.

B. You must change this Custom Function and all individual formulas that use this function

C. You must cut and past the Custom Function into all applicable reports

D. By using the Extractor, all changes will be replicated across all reports automatically

Q15. You want to modify the Custom Function. What should you do?

A. Choose Report | Formula Workshop | select Custom Function Editor and make the required changes, save changes
B. Choose Report Options | Formula Workshop | select Custom Function Editor and make the required changes, save changes
C. Choose Options | Formula Workshop | select Custom Function Editor and make the required changes, save changes
D. Choose View |Report | Formula Workshop | select Custom Function Editor and make the required changes, save changes

Q16. You want to view the Custom Function Properties, i.e. Category, Author... What should you do?

A. Right-click Custom File and select Toggle Properties Display
B. Right-click View\Custom Function and select Toggle Properties Display
C. Right-click Custom Function and select Toggle Properties Display
D. Right-click File\Custom Function and select Toggle Properties Display

Q17. You want users to have access to a descriptive help section which will enable then to obtain help with your Custom Function. Where can this be located?

A. Right-click the Custom Function, and click Help Text
B. From the Field Explorer, Right-click the Custom Function, Toggle Property Display and click Help Text
C. Select Edit from the Menu Bar and select Help Text
D. Right-click the Custom Function, Toggle Property Display and click Help Text

Q18. Based on the following Custom Function, identify the replaceable arguments?

```
Function  (StringVar v1)
If v1 startswith 'Examhints-RDCR201' then right (v1, 7) else
v1
```

A. v1
B. startswith
C. Right
D. Function

Q19. Which of the following reflects the field type used to create a Custom Function?

A. Name
B. Summary
C. Category
D. Repository
E. Author
F. Return Type
G. Help Text

Q20. Which of the following are Custom Function Properties? *(Multiple Answers)*

A. Name
B. Summary
C. Category
D. Repository
E. Author
F. Return Type
G. Help Text

Q21. Which of the following make up the Custom Function Arguments? *(Multiple Answers)*

A. Name
B. Type
C. Description
D. Default Values

Q22. Which of the following statements are true? *(Multiple Answers)*

A. When the Display In Experts checkbox is unchecked the Custom Function will appear in the Formula Editor and Not in the Formula Expert
B. When the Display In Experts checkbox is checked the Custom Function will not appear in the Formula Editor but will appear in the Formula Expert
C. When the Display In Experts checkbox is checked the Custom Function will only appear if the Formula Expert is clicked

Q23. The text section of the Custom Function is disabled when you try to make changes. What is this attributed to?

A. The Custom Function has been deleted
B. You do not have rights to change the Custom Function
C. The Custom Function has not been refreshed
D. You have not disconnected the Custom Function from the Repository to make the necessary changes

Q24. You want to group all code related Custom Function under the heading ExamhintsCodes. In which section should this title be placed within the Custom Function properties?

A. Repository
B. Category
C. Return Type
D. Author

Q25. You try to add a Custom Function to the Repository but it fails. What could the problem be?

A. You have not installed crystal Reports properly
B. You need patch SDECRY11
C. You do not have rights to update the Repository database
D. None of the above

Q26. You are using the Formula Expert to create a formula, and you notice only one (Student Code), of the three Custom Functions you created appears under Report Custom Functions –Formula Expert. Which of the following reasons apply?

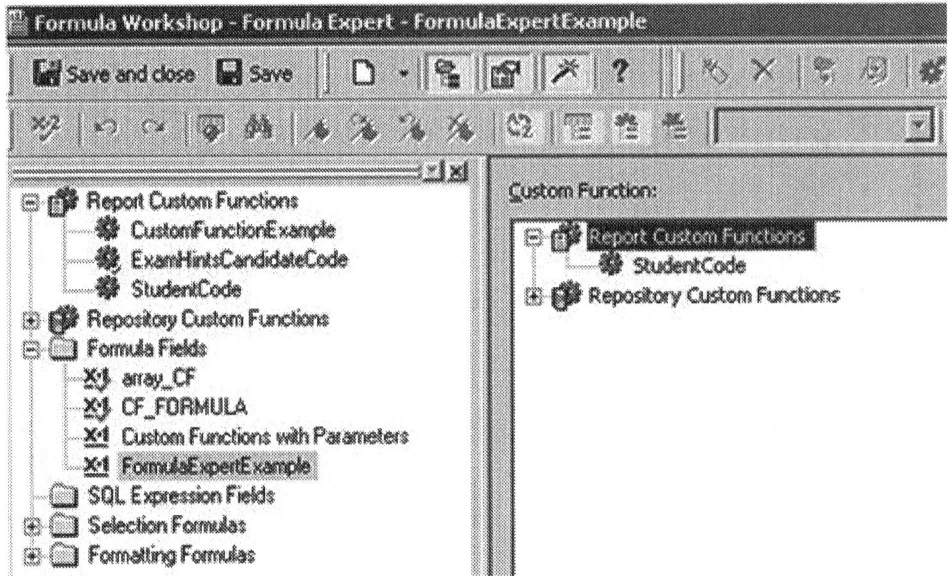

A. The Display In Experts checkbox is checked in the Custom Function area, Right-click the Custom Function- Toggle Property Display -Display In Experts uncheck box
B. The Display In Experts checkbox is unchecked in the Custom Function area, Right-click the Custom Function- Toggle Property Display and click the Display In Experts check box
C. A Custom Function will never appear in within the Formula Expert
D. The Display In Experts checkbox is unchecked in the Custom Function area, Right-click the Custom Function- Toggle Property Display, and check the Display In Experts checkbox

Q27. You want to create a Custom Function. What should you do?

A. From the toolbar, choose Report | Formula Workshop| right-click report Custom Functions, select new, enter name of the new Custom Function and click the Use Editor button
B. From the toolbar, choose Formula Workshop| right-click report Custom Functions, select new, enter name of the new Custom Function and click the Use Editor button
C. From the toolbar, choose Database | Formula Workshop| right-click report Custom Functions, select new, enter name of the new Custom Function and click the Use Editor button

D. From the toolbar, choose View | Formula Workshop| right-click report Custom Functions, select new, enter name of the new Custom Function and click the Use Editor button

Q28. The Custom Functions dialogue box enables the Designer to apply a description to the Custom Function. Which of the following also applies?

A. The grey sections of the dialogue box cannot be changed within the dialogue box
B. The grey sections of the dialogue box can be changed within the dialogue box
C. The grey sections of the dialogue box cannot be changed within the format dialogue box

Q29. You want to use Crystal Reports Financial custom formulas. Where can this be located?

A. Formula Workshop - Formula Editor| Operators Tree
B. Formula Workshop - Formula Editor| Functions Tree
C. Formula Workshop - Formula Editor| Formula Tree
D. Repository Explorer

Q30. You have created a Custom Function and would like to add it to the Repository. Which of the following methods apply?

A. Highlight the Custom Function code and select Add to Repository from the Operators window, the Business Objects logon dialog box will appear, enter your login details and click ok
B. Right-click the Repository within the Formula Workshop and select Add to Repository, the Business Objects logon dialog box will appear, enter your login details and click ok
C. Highlight the Custom Function code and select Add to Repository from the Functions window, the Business Objects logon dialog box will appear, enter your login details and click ok
D. Highlight the Custom Function code and select Add to Repository from the Basic Syntax window, the Business Objects logon dialog box will appear, enter your login details and click ok

Q31. You try to edit a Custom Function but the Formula Text Window is greyed out and you cannot edit the Custom Function. Which reason applies? *(Multiple Answers)*

A. All Custom Function functions cannot be edited once created and saved

B. The Custom Function has been saved to the Repository

C. The Custom Functions has not been disconnected from the Repository

D. The Custom Function must be refreshed

Q32. Within the Formula Workshop, a Custom Function which has been saved to the Repository will appear under one of the following sections. Which one is applicable?

A. Repository Functions

B. Repository Operators

C. Custom Functions

D. Repository Custom Function

Q33. Within the Formula Workshop, a Custom Function which has NOT been saved to the Repository will appear under one of the following sections. Which one is applicable?

A. Report Functions

B. Report Operators

C. Report Custom Functions

D. Custom Function

Q34. How can you determine if a Custom Function has been saved to the Repository? *(Multiple Answers)*

A. The Custom Function will appear under Repository Custom Function if it is saved to the Repository

B. There will be a vertical line beside the Custom Function

C. The Formula Text Window will be greyed out

D. The Custom Function will be editable within the Formula Text Window

Chapter 12 - Previewing, Saving and Exporting A Report

There are several export options available to the Report Designer and the end-user when creating a report. Questions in this chapter cover the export, preview and saving options available within the Crystal Reports environment.

Key Areas

- **Exporting Reports**
- **Export Type**
- **Export Destinations**
- **Saving Reports with Data**

Q1. Which of the following options will activate the preview tab? *(Multiple Answers)*

A. Refresh 

B. HTML Preview 

C. Print Preview 

D. F5

E. Preview Sample

Q2. Which of the following can be used to refresh a report? *(Multiple Answers)*

A. From the Menu Bar select report and select refresh report data

B. Click the Refresh Icon 

C. Choose File | select refresh 

D. Press F5

Q3. How can you access the preview options?

A. From the Menubar select File - Preview

B. From the Menubar select Report - Preview

C. From the Menubar select View - Preview

D. From the Menubar select Database - Preview

Q4. You want to preview the first 10 records of your report. Which of the following methods apply?

A. From the Menu Bar, select file, Preview, from the Preview Sample dialog box select the First button and enter 10.
B. From the Menu Bar, select View, Preview Sample, from the Preview Sample dialog box select the First button and enter 10.
C. From the Menu Bar, select Report, Preview, from the Preview Sample dialog box select the First button and enter 10.
D. From the Menu Bar, select refresh and Preview, from the Preview Sample dialog box select the First button and enter 10.

Q5. You will like to see a web view format of your report. Which of the following apply?

A. From the Menu Bar, select View, XML Preview
B. From the Menu Bar, select View, SXML Preview
C. From the Menu Bar, select View, DHTML Preview
D. From the Menu Bar, select View, HTML Preview

Q6. The Preview Icon is greyed out. What does this indicate?

A. The requires refreshing
B. The Report has failed to preview
C. The Report is not connected to the database
D. The Report is already in preview mode

Q7. Your report is in preview mode but you cannot read the text. What can you do to make the report more readable? *(Multiple Answers)*

A. Select windows from the Menu Bar and select zoom, select the magnification factor and enter the required percentage
B. Select report from the Menu Bar and select zoom, select the magnification factor and enter the required percentage
C. From the tool bar select the zoom control box and select the appropriate zoom percentage
D. Select view from the Menu Bar and select zoom, select the magnification factor and enter the required percentage

Q8. Which of the following icons represent the Print Preview?

A. 

B. 

C. 

D. 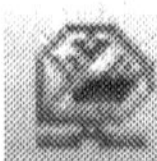

Q9. Which of the following icons represent the HTML Preview?

A. 

B. 

C. 

D. 

Q10. The preview icon is greyed out . You want to reactivate the preview button. Which one of the following apply?

A. From the Menu Bar, select View, Delete Current View
B. From the Menu Bar, select View, Current View Shut
C. From the Menu Bar, select View, Close Current View
D. From the Menu Bar, select View, Close View
E. Click the cross beside the Design Icon

Q11. You have clicked the Print Preview button. Which of the following sections will be visible? *(Multiple Answers)*

A. The Group Tree
B. The Report in preview mode
C. The Field Explorer
D. The Repository Explorer

Q12. Where can you view recent reports?

A. Front Page
B. Last Page
C. View Page
D. Start Page

Q13. Which of the following are available from the Start Page? *(Multiple Answers)*

A. Resources
B. Files
C. New Reports
D. Recent Reports

Q14. You want to check for current updates to Crystal Reports. Which of the following apply?

A. Front Page\Check for updates
B. Last Page\Check for updates
C. View Page\Check for updates
D. Start Page\Check for updates

Q15. You want to save a new report. Which of the following apply? *(Multiple Answers)*

A. Select Report and Save, the Save As dialog box will appear, select the folder you want to save the report into and give the report a name and click the save button
B. Select View and Save, the Save As dialog box will appear, select the folder you want to save the report into and give the report a name and click the save button
C. Select File and Save, the Save As dialog box will appear, select the folder you want to save the report into (Save in) and give the report a name (File Name) and click the save button
D. Select the Save icon, the Save As dialog box will appear, select the folder you want to save the report into and give the report a name and click the save button

Q16. You want other users to see the last data you saved with your report. Which of the following apply?

A. Select Report and Save Data with Report when saving the report
B. Select Database and Save Data with Report when saving the report
C. Select File and Save Data with Report when saving the report
D. Select View and Save Data with Report when saving the report

Q17. You want to save an existing report into a different folder. Which of the following apply?

A. Select File and Save As, the Save As dialog box will appear, select the folder you want to save the report into and give the report a name and click the save button
B. Select the Save icon, the Save As dialog box will appear, select the folder you want to save the report into and give the report a name and click the save button
C. Select Report and Save As, the Save As dialog box will appear, select the folder you want to save the report into and give the report a name and click the save button
D. Select View and Save As, the Save As dialog box will appear, select the folder you want to save the report into and give the report a name and click the save button

Q18. You have opened several reports and all reports appear with their own tabs. You want to close the Cross-Tab report without closing all other opened reports. How would you do this? *(Multiple Answers)*

A. Select the Cross-Tab report tab and close
B. Select the Cross-Tab report tab and click the cross, a dialog box will appear prompting you to save, (Yes, No or Cancel)
C. From the Menu Bar, select View, Report and close Report
D. Select the Cross-Tab report tab , from the Menu Bar, select File and close, a dialog box will appear prompting you to save, (Yes, No or Cancel)

Q19. You want to save a Subreport. Which of the following apply?

A. Highlight the Subreport and select File - Save Subreport As, the Save As dialog box will appear, select the folder you want to save the report into and give the report a name and click the save button
B. Highlight the Subreport and select Report, Save Subreport As, the Save As dialog box will appear, select the folder you want to save the report into and give the report a name and click the save button
C. Highlight the Subreport and select View, Save Subreport As, the Save As dialog box will appear, select the folder you want to save the report into and give the report a name and click the save button
D. Select File save as the Save As dialog box will appear, select the folder you want to save the report into and give the report a name and click the save button

Q20. You have moved a field to a different section within your report and you click print preview. Which of the following will take place?

A. Crystal Reports will refresh the report from the Database
B. Crystal Reports will use the data saved with report when you preview the report
C. Crystal Reports will prompt you with a refresh option
D. Crystal Reports will inform you of the recent change

Q21. You have changed the Record Selection of your report. What will happen?

A. Crystal Reports will use the data saved with report when you preview the report
B. Crystal Reports will prompt you with a refresh option
C. Crystal Reports will inform you of the recent change
D. Crystal Reports will re-query the database and it will do so without prompting you
E. Crystal Reports will give you an option to refresh the report by using saved data or refresh the report by re-querying the database

Q22. You have created a report and saved the data with the report. Which of the following apply?

A. Saved Data is the current data in the database based on the time the report has been opened
B. Saved Data is the Crystal Administrators last data run
C. Saved Data is data based on the last time the report was run
D. None of the above

Q23. A report is refreshed. Which of the following occurs?

A. Saved data with the report is showed
B. The report will fail if saved data is not ticked
C. The report queries the database
D. None of the above

Q24. You open an existing report and it opens in preview mode. Which of the following apply?

A. The report is invalid
B. Report was saved with data
C. The database no longer exist
D. None of the above

Q25. Which of the following formats are available when exporting a report? *(Multiple Answers)*

A. Acrobat Reader, Microsoft Excel
B. Crystal Reports, Text, ODBC
C. HTML, Report Definition, XML
D. Report Style, Text

Q26. Which one of the following is not an Export Destination available in Crystal Reports?

A. Application
B. Disk File
C. Lotus Domino Mail
D. Exchange Folder
E. Lotus Domino
F. MAPI
G. Folder

Q27. You are exporting a report to Microsoft Excel Data Only format. Which of the following are Microsoft Excel format export options? *(Multiple Answers)*

A. Set Column Width
B. Constant Column width
C. Export object formatting
D. Export Images
E. Main Column alignments

Q28. What does the Use Worksheet Functions For Summaries option indicate?

A. All calculations within the crystal report will be reflected in the exported Excel file
B. All calculations within the report will NOT be reflected in Excel format
C. All objects within the report can be formatted within Excel
D. None of the above

Q29. You are exporting your report to Microsoft Excel format and you check the Export Object Formatting checkbox. What will happen?

A. All calculations within the report will be reflected in Excel
B. All calculations within the report will NOT be reflected in Excel
C. All objects within the report can be formatted within Excel
D. None of the above

Q30. You have selected Microsoft Excel Data Only as the export format. Which of the following three options will appear? *(Multiple Answers)*

A. Maximum: Data is exported with no formatting applied
B. Typical: Data is exported with default options applied
C. Minimal: Data is exported with no formatting applied
D. Custom: Data is exported according to selected options

Q31. What is the export limit per sheet when exporting to Microsoft Excel format?

A. 65537
B. 65534
C. 65577
D. 65536

Q32. Which of the following export formats will include the reports complete design and formatting details?

A. Definition
B. Report Formula
C. Design
D. Report Definition

Q33. Which of one the following export application gives the user the option to export the report using the Group Tree as a bookmark?

A. Acrobat Reader
B. Microsoft Excel
C. Crystal Reports,
D. Text, ODBC
E. HTML,
F. Report Definition,
G. XML
H. Report Style,
I. Text

Q34. You want to export the results from your report into a table which other users can connect to. Which of the following apply?

A. Click the export button and select Microsoft Word – Editable (RTF) as your format and Application as your destination and click ok

B. Click the export button and select Record Style – Columns with space as your format and Application as your destination and click ok

C. Click the export button and select ODBC as your format, select the ODBC format option, (E.g. Microsoft Access, Microsoft Excel) and click ok, select the database to export the reporting data to and click OK, assign a table name and click OK, data can be accessed via the database selected

D. Click the export button and select OLEDB as your format, select the OLEDB format option, (E.g. Microsoft Access, Microsoft Excel) and click ok, select the database to export the reporting data to and click OK, assign a table name and click OK, data can be accessed via the database selected

Q35. Your current report returns all candidates who have taken all exams, you now only want to see candidates who have taken RDCR201, you add a filter within the Select Expert of your existing report and select use saved data. Which of the following apply?

A. The report will filter down the existing records within the report and return only data applicable to the current record selection

B. The report query the database and return only data applicable to the current record selection

C. The report will return an error message reading' use Refresh data only'

D. None of the above

Chapter 13 – Using Subreport

The following chapter covers questions on Subreports and how they can be integrated into an existing report or created from scratch, it also presents questions relating to the types of Subreports and their functionality. At the end of this chapter knowledge gained should be in the following sections, creating a Subreport, linking a Subreport, using Subreport parameters and formatting Subreports to display data from different data sources.

Key Areas:

- **Definition Of A Subreport**
- **Unlinked Subreports**
- **Linked Subreports**
- **On-Demand Reports**
- **Using Shared Variables Within Subreports**
- **Using Shared Array Values Within Subreports**
- **Link Un-linkable Data**

Q1. What is a Subreport?

A. Two reports created separately but saved in the same folder

B. A main report and an embedded report

C. Two main reports created from different data sources

D. None of the above

E. All of the above

Q2. A report request has been made to create a report from two different data sources, which have no referential integrity links. Which of the following apply?

A. This cannot be done

B. Force a link between the two databases

C. Use a Global Variable

D. Create a Subreport with a shared variable

E. Create an Unlinked Subreport

Q3. Based on the information in the two reports below, you have embedded a Subreport in the Main report; you create a link based on the Client name. Which of the following records within the Subreport will NOT be retrieved?

MAIN REPORT

Record No	Merchandise Name	Price	Product Class	Client Name
1	Bronze Plated Pen	£539.85	Collectable Pens	Books and Books
2	Silver Rim Pen	£1000	Collectable Pens	Books and Books
3	Blue Pen	£10	Pens	Books and Books
4	Blue Pen	£10	Pens	Books and Books
5	Bronze Plated Pen	£764.85	Collectable Pens	Examhints
6	Bronze Plated Pen	£764.85	Collectable Pens	Examhints
7	Yellow Pen	£5.9	Pens	Folks Books
8	Ball Point Pen	£500.00	Collectable Pens	Great Stone
9	Ball Point Pen	£500.00	Collectable Pens	Great Stone
10	Silver Plated Pen	£329.85	Collectable Pens	Great Stone
11	Green Pen	£14.50	Pens	Great Stone
12	Green Pen	£14.50	Pens	Ink Onk
13	Fountain Pen	£33.90	Pens	Mobile Books
14	Bronze Plated Pen	£539.85	Collectable Pens	Pens Gallery
15	Ball Point Pen	£500.00	Collectable Pens	Stationary Gallore
16	Fountain Pen	£33.90	Pens	Writers n Pens

SUBREPORT

Record No	Merchandise Name	Price	Product Class	Client Name
1	Gold Plated Pen	£539.85	Collectable Pens	Books and Books
2	Ball Point Pen	£1000	Collectable Pens	Mobile Books
3	Bronze Rim Pen	£10	Collectable Pens	Iroko Books
4	Ball Point Pen	£10	Collectable Pens	Folks Books
5	Ball Point Pen	£764.85	Collectable Pens	Books and Books
6	Silver Rim Pen	£764.85	Collectable Pens	Stationary Gallore
7	Red Pen	£5.9	Pens	Examhints
8	Red Pen	£500.00	Pens	Folks Books
9	Fountain Pen	£500.00	Pens	Mobile Books
10	Blue Pen	£329.85	Pens	Stationary Gallore
11	Blue Pen	£14.50	Pens	Mobile Books

A. Record 3

B. Record 8

C. Record 1

D. Record 6

Q4. What impact will a filter applied to the main report have on a linked the Subreport?

A. The Subreport will return the same record
B. The Subreport will not return any record
C. The Subreport will return records based on the filter applied.
D. The Subreport will produce an error message

Q5. Which of the following are the two types of Subreports?

A. Linked and Delinked Subreports
B. Linked and Unlinked Subreports
C. Equal and unequal Subreports
D. Main and Subreports
E. Main and unlinked Subreports

Q6. You double click your Subreports, what will appear.

A. Nothing will appear
B. Another Subreport
C. The Subreport design section will appear
D. A preview tab for the Subreport will appear

Q7. Several tabs have appeared after you have double-clicked your Subreport you want to close some tabs. Which of the following apply?

A. Refresh the report
B. Preview the report
C. Close the report and open again
D. Click the red arrow which is situated next to the page navigation controls

Q8. You preview a main report on its own preview tab; this will also result in the preview of the Subreport at the same time.

A. True
B. False

Q9. You want to pass data from the main report to the Subreport, what should you use?

A. Shared variables
B. Variable
C. NumberVar
D. StringVar
E. Global Variable

Q10. To activate a Subreport's Design Tab. Which of the following apply?

A. Preview Subreport
B. Right-click the Subreport and select edit Subreport
C. Double-click Subreport
D. Refresh main report

Q11. How would you deal with a Subreport, which returns no data?

A. Format Subreport
B. Delete Subreport
C. Suppress conditionally or Suppress Blank Subreport
D. Re-import Subreport

Q12. You have opened the Book Sales Report and the following appears,

MAIN REPORT

	Mechandise Name	Price	Product Class	Order Date	Client Name
Books and Books					
1	Bronze Rim Pen	$ 539.85	Collectable Pens	05/06/2006	Books and Books
2	Silver Rim Pen	$ 1,000.00	Collectable Pens	25/06/2006	Books and Books
3	Blue Pen	$ 10.00	Pen	21/06/2006	Books and Books
4	Blue Pen	$ 10.00	Pen	25/06/2006	Books and Books

Double Click to view Books and Books Client records for 2005

When you double click the link the records below appear

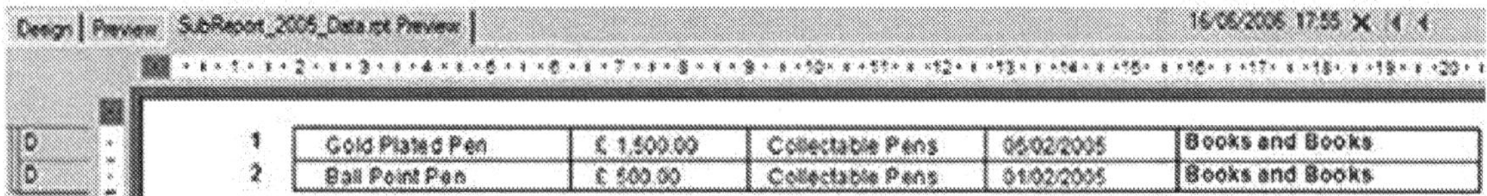

Design | Preview SubReport_2005_Data.rpt Preview | 16/06/2006 17:55

1	Gold Plated Pen	£ 1,500.00	Collectable Pens	06/02/2005	Books and Books
2	Ball Point Pen	£ 500.00	Collectable Pens	01/02/2005	Books and Books

Which of the following has been applied to the Subreport and where?

A. Right click the Subreport and select Format Subreport from the drop-down menu, select the Common Tab and check the on-demand Subreport checkbox, click the x+2 button and paste the formula "Double Click to view " + GroupName ({Client.Client Name}) + " Client records for 2005 " into this section
B. Right click the Subreport and select Format Subreport from the drop-down menu, select the Subreport tab and check the Re-Import When Opening checkbox and click the x+2 button and paste the formula "Double Click to view " + GroupName ({Client.Client Name}) + " Client records for 2005 " into this section
C. Right click the Subreport and select Format Subreport from the drop-down menu, select the File tab and check the on-demand Subreport checkbox, click the x+2 button

and paste the formula "Double Click to view " + GroupName ({Client.Client Name}) + " Client records for 2005 " into this section

D. Right click the Subreport and select Format Subreport from the drop-down menu, select the Subreport tab and check the On-Demand Subreport checkbox, click the x+2 formula button beside On-Demand Subreport Caption and paste the following formula into this section "Double Click to view " + GroupName ({Client.Client Name}) + " Client records for 2005 "

Q13. You have created a Subreport; you click the preview button and notice the Subreport has a box around it. What can you do to remove this box?

A. This box cannot be removed
B. If the box is removed the Subreport data will not show.
C. Right click the box and press delete
D. Right-click the Subreport and select Format Subreport, select the Border Tab and set all borders (left, right, top and bottom) to none

Q14. When you pass a parameter from the main report to the Subreport, the Subreport will use the parameter in the Record Selection.

A. False
B. True

Q15. When previewing a Subreport on its own Preview Tab, the main report can also be viewed.

A. True
B. False

Q16. Which of the following will improve report processing of the main report when a Subreport is included? *(Multiple Answers)*

A. Run both reports separately
B. Separate both reports
C. Create an On-Demand Subreport which allows the user click the caption place holder when required
D. Debug the Subreport
E. Use indexed fields for linking the main report to the Subreport.

Q17. You want to save your Subreport as its own separate report. What should you do?

A. From the Menu Bar, select report and save as
B. From the Menu Bar select report, options, Save Subreport As
C. Right click the Subreport and select Save Subreport As
D. A Subreport cannot be saved as a separate report

Q18. Which of the following statements are true? *(Multiple Answers)*

A. You cannot Drill-Down into Subreports
B. You can Drill-Down into Subreports
C. A Subreport can be saved as a separate report
D. A Subreport can be created within a Subreport

Q19. When your mouse rolls over an on-demand Subreport from the main report, what happens?

A. The cursor disappears
B. The Subreport is refreshed
C. The cursor changes to the Standard Windows Hand and the name of the Subreport is displayed
D. The Subreport database path is shown

Q20. You have two Subreports in your main report, you Right-click the first Subreport and the Re-Import option exist, however, the Re-Import option does not exist when a Right-click on the second Subreport is performed. Which of the following could explain this missing option?

A. The main report should be refreshed
B. A link has not been established between the main report and the second Subreport
C. The first Subreport was imported in the main report and the second Subreport was created from scratch via the report wizard
D. None of the above

Q21. You have created a Shared Variable for the Client.City sales amount for 2005, which you will like to add to the 2006 data in your main report. Where should you place the reset formula within your main report?

A. City Group Header
B. Details Section
C. Report Header
D. Page Header
E. Page Footer

Q22. You want to create a link based on the customer_id between your main report and Subreport, although the data held in both fields are the same, the customer id in the main report is a numeric field and the customer id in the Subreport is a text field. Which of the following methods should you use to create the link?

A. Create a formula to convert the customer_id to a number in the main report and use this formula as a link between the Subreport and main report
B. Create a formula to convert the customer_id to a number in the Subreport report and use this formula as a link between the Subreport and main report
C. Use the Field Explorer to create the following formula:- tovalue({client_id}) and use this formula as a link
D. Use the Field Explorer to create the following formula:- Value({client_id}) and use this formula as a link

Q23. Which of the following statements is true about Subreports? *(Multiple Answers)*

A. A formula can be used as a link between a Subreport and a main report
B. A Subreport cannot be linked to a main report via a formula
C. A parameter can be used as a link between the main report and the Subreport
D. Shared variables can be passed from a Subreport to a main report
E. Shared variables can be passed from main reports to Subreports

Q24. Which of the following statements is true? *(Multiple Answers)*

A. A Subreport includes its own layout
B. A Subreport Includes its own database connection
C. A Subreport Includes its own selection criteria
D. A Subreport Is always controlled by the main report
E. The unlinked Subreport does not communicate with the main report.
F. The unlinked Subreport communicates only at runtime
G. A linked Subreport is controlled by the main report

Q25. You want to change an existing link between the Subreport and the main report. What should you do?

A. Choose Subreport, View, reports, Subreport links, or right click the Subreport and choose Change Subreport Links
B. Choose file, edit, Subreport links, or right click the Subreport and choose Change Subreport Links
C. Choose edit, Subreport links, or right click the Subreport and choose Change Subreport Links
D. Choose Format, Subreport links, or right click the Subreport and choose Change Subreport Links

Q26. Where can the Object Name of the Subreport be changed?

A. You cannot change the name of the Subreport, once it has been created

B. Right-click the Subreport and select change name

C. Right-click the Subreport and select Format Subreport, select the Common Tab and enter the name of the Subreport

D. Right-click the Subreport and select Format Subreport or select format and Format Subreport from the Menu Bar, click the Common Tab and type in the name of the Subreport object in the Object Name section of the tab.

Q27. You have created a report and will now like to include an unlinked Subreport. What should you do?

A. From the Menu Bar select File, Subreport, choose or create the Subreport, click OK and insert the Subreport in your main report.

B. From the Menu Bar select, insert Subreport, choose an existing report or create the Subreport, click OK and insert the Subreport into the main report.

C. From the Menu Bar select view, Subreport, choose an existing report or create the Subreport, click OK and insert the Subreport in your main report.

D. From the Menu Bar select File, Report, Subreport, choose an existing report or create the Subreport, click OK and insert the Subreport in your main report.

Q28. You Drill-Down into the clients' name of the Subreport and the preview tab appears as follows with the client name details. How can you apply this format to your Subreport?

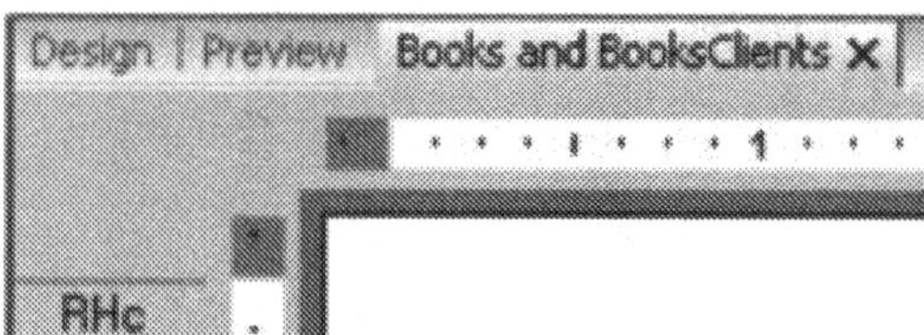

GroupName ({Client.Client Name}) + " " + "Clients"

A. Right click the Subreport and select Format Subreport from the drop-down menu, select the Common Tab and check the on-demand Subreport checkbox, click the x+2 button and paste the formula into this section

B. Right click the Subreport and select Format Subreport from the drop-down menu, select the Border Tab and check the on-demand Subreport checkbox, click the x+2 button and paste the formula into this section

C. Right click the Subreport and select Format Subreport from the drop-down menu, select the Subreport tab and click the x+2 button beside the Subreport Preview Tab Caption and paste the formula into this section

D. Right click the Subreport and select Format Subreport from the drop-down menu, select the File tab and check the on-demand Subreport checkbox, click the x+2 button and paste the formula into this section

Q29. Which of the following variables are available to the Subreport from the main report?

A. Global
B. Shared Variable
C. Local
D. Shared Local

Q30. You have created an On-Demand Subreport within your main report, you have also used a shared variable to pass information from the Subreport to the main report and nothing happens. What could be the cause of the problem?

A. The shared variable is not functional because you failed to include a variable name
B. The shared variable is not functional because you failed to include an evaluation time
C. The shared variable is not functional because you failed to include it in the Subreport
D. An on-demand Subreport cannot share information with the main report as it does not process at the same time as the main report

Q31. You have created a Shared Variable in the main report, which you would like to pass to the Subreport; which of the following should be placed in the Subreport to display the results?

```
WhilePrintingRecords;
Shared NumberVar ClientTotal:= Sum({Purchase.Amount});
```

A. WhilePrintingRecords; Shared NumberVar ClientTotal:= Sum({Purchase.Amount});
B. WhilePrintingRecords; Shared ClientTotal:= Sum({Purchase.Amount});
C. WhilePrintingRecords; NumberVar ClientTotal:= Sum({Purchase.Amount});
D. WhilePrintingRecords; Shared NumberVar ClientTotal

Q32. A shared variable can be used to create a chart or a summary within the main report

A. True
B. False

Q33. A shared variable can be passed from an Unlinked Subreport to a main report

A. True
B. False

Q34. You want to create a link between the main report and the Subreport; however you do not want the Subreport to use the link in its Record Selection. What should you do?

A. This is not possible, the link must be used
B. Delete the Subreport and recreate the link
C. Un-check the select data in Subreport based on the field checkbox when creating the link between the main report and the Subreport

Q35. You want to create a linked Subreport. What should you do?

A. Choose, insert Subreport from the Menu Bar, choose an existing report or create one from scratch, click the link tab and select the field to be linked and click arrow > to select the field, choose the field from the main report to be linked to the field in the Subreport and click ok, places the Subreport within the main report as required
B. Choose, view, insert Subreport from the Menu Bar, choose an existing report or create one from scratch, click the link tab and select the field to be linked and click arrow > to select the field, choose the parameter field on the main report to be linked to the Subreport and choose the Subreport field, you can limit the size to records that match the main report linked field only.
C. Choose, report, insert Subreport from the Menu Bar, choose an existing report or create one from scratch, click the link tab and select the field to be linked and click arrow > to select the field, choose the parameter field on the main report to be linked to the Subreport and choose the Subreport field, you can limit the size to records that match the main report linked field only.
D. Choose, edit, insert Subreport from the Menu Bar, choose an existing report or create one from scratch, click the link tab and select the field to be linked and click arrow > to select the field, choose the parameter field on the main report to be linked to the Subreport and choose the Subreport field, you can limit the size to records that match the main report linked field only.

Q36. You have created a Subreport, you place your cursor over the Subreport. What will appear?

A. Nothing will appear
B. Only the name of the Subreport will appear
C. The name of the Subreport and a magnifying glass will appear indicating the Drill-Down propensity of the report
D. The cursor will disappear

Q37. You have drilled down into a Subreport. What will happen?

A. Additional tabs will appear for each section drilled into
B. The Subreport will freeze and an error message will appear
C. The Subreport will request a parameter input.

Q38. You have performed several Drill-Downs on your Subreport, and you notice several tabs now appear after the Design and Preview Tabs; there is no more space to display all tabs at once. What will happen?

A. Two small left to right scroll arrows will appear on the right hand side of the group of tabs, enabling the user to scroll back and forward
B. You will be prompted with a limitation record message
C. None of the above

Q39. You have created a Subreport and would like to re-import the Subreport each time it is opened. What should you do?

A. Right-click the Subreport and select Format Subreport tab, select the Subreport tab and check the Re-Import When Opening checkbox
B. Right-click the Subreport and select Format Subreport tab, select the Common Tab and check the Re-Import When Opening checkbox
C. Right-click the Subreport and select Format Subreport tab, select the Border Tab and check the Re-Import When Opening checkbox
D. Right-click the Subreport and select Format Subreport tab, select the font tab and check the Re-Import When Opening checkbox

Q40. You want to create a link between the main report and the Subreport, the field data type in the main report is a string and the field data type in the Subreport is a number. How can you achieve this link?

A. You cannot link the main report to the Subreport
B. Create a formula in the main report to change the field datatype to a number and create a link from the main report to the Subreport based on this formula
C. Change the datatype in the database
D. None of the above

Q41. You have created a Subreport, you notice only one line of data appears when the main report is refreshed; you know there is more data applicable to that Group. Which of the following should be implemented?

A. Right-click the Subreport and select the Subreport check the Can Grow Checkbox
B. Right-click the Subreport and select the Border Tab and check the Can Grow Checkbox
C. Right-click the Subreport and select the Report Tab and check the Can Grow Checkbox
D. Right-click the Subreport and select the Common Tab and check the Can Grow Checkbox

Q42. You are creating a Subreport using the Report Wizard. Which of the following sections will appear? *(Multiple Answers)*

A. Data, Fields
B. Grouping, Summaries
C. Formulas, Functions
D. Group Sorting, Record Selection
E. Charts, Template

Q43. Which of the following enhances the performance of Subreports? *(Multiple Answers)*

A. Use On-Demand Placeholder, processing only takes place when the user clicks the placeholder
B. Use indexed fields to link the main report to the Subreport
C. Always refresh the Subreport

Chapter 14 - Working with the Repository

This chapter covers questions on the utilization of the Repository.

Key Areas

- **Repository Explorer**
- **SQL Command**
- **Custom Funvtions**

Q1. Which of the following is the definition of a Repository?

A. The administrative console for report filing

B. Crystal Management Server

C. Central database for storing and sharing codes, Custom Functions, Text Objects, logos, SQL Commands, and Business Views

D. Central Management Server

Q2. Which of the following enable the user to view the contents of the Repository?

A. Field Explorer

B. Custom Function Explorer

C. Report Explorer

D. Enterprise Explorer

E. Repository Explorer

F. Repository Expert Explorer

Q3. Which of the following methods allows you to access the Repository Explorer within a report? *(Multiple Answers)*

A. Choose view | Field Explorer | Repository Explorer

B. Choose view | Repository Explorer

C. Section Expert | Repository Explorer

D. Select Expert| Repository Explorer

E. Database Explorer | Repository Explorer

F. Click the Repository icon 

G. Click the Repository icon 

Q4. Which of the following applies to folder creation within the Repository?

A. Repository Folders are limited to single folders.
B. A maximum of 7 folders apply to the Repository folder.
C. Repository sub-folders cannot be created within the Repository Explorer
D. A set of Folders and Subfolders can be created within the Repository for logical information storage

Q5. You want to rename a folder that already exists in the Repository Explorer, which of the following three describes the best procedure to follow? *(Multiple Answers)*

A. Select the folder, hold the mouse button down on the folder for a few seconds and rename Commands
B. Select folder and click F2 Commands
C. Right-click the folder and choose rename from the pop-up menu Commands
D. Select the folder from the Report Expert and rename

Q6. Which of the following are Repository Explorer position options? *(Multiple Answers)*

A. Undock
B. Autohide
C. Close
D. Open

Q7. You place your cursor over the Repository Explorer. What will happen?

A. The mouse icon will disappear
B. The mouse icon will turn to an hour glass icon
C. The Tool Tips will appear
D. None of the above

Q8. Which of the following cannot be seen through the Repository Explorer?

A. Text Objects
B. Bitmap (pictures)
C. Custom Functions
D. SQL Commands/Queries

Q9. You want to see all objects within the Repository that were created by Antonia Iroko. Which of the following options should be selected?

A. Change View settings
B. Change Filter settings
C. Advanced Filtering
D. Change Repository settings

Q10. Which of the following applies to Repositories? *(Multiple Answers)*

A. Changes and updates can be made and saved to the Repository for shared use
B. The Repository can only be accessed by logging on to Business Objects Enterprise
C. User authentication is not required
D. Code sharing is one of the advantages of the Repository
E. Reduces design time due to its sharing capability

Q11. You want to add a sub-folder to the Examhints Repository folder within the Repository. Which of the following apply? *(Multiple Answers)*

A. Right-click the Examhints folder and select new folder from the drop-down menu
B. Highlight the Examhints folder and click the  insert a new folder icon
C. Highlight the Examhints folder and click the  insert a new folder icon
D. Highlight the Examhints folder and click the  insert a new folder icon

Q12. Which of the following options allows the users to determine which objects within the Repository are shown and how they are arranged?

A. Change Repository Settings
B. Change File Settings
C. Change View Settings
D. Change Filter Settings

Q13. You want to ensure that objects within your report which are connected to the Repository will be updated automatically when a report is initially opened. What should you do? *(Multiple Answers)*

A. Select File from the toolbar – click on Repository options – select the Repository Tab – check the update connected Repository objects when loading reports
B. Select File from the toolbar – click on Report options – select the Repository Tab – check the update connected Repository objects when loading reports
C. Select File from the toolbar – click on Summary info – select the Repository Tab – check the update connected Repository objects when loading reports Select File from the toolbar – click on options – select the Repository Tab – check the update connected Repository objects when loading reports
D. Select File from the Menu Bar – click on options – select the reporting Tab – check Update Connected Repository Objects on Open
E. Select File – Save As, select the Enterprise Folder, within Enterprise select the required folder and tick the Enable Repository Refresh checkbox

Q14. You want to view all subfolders within folders in the Repository which of the following should you select?

A. Expand All
B. Refresh Folders
C. Open All
D. Refresh All

Q15. Although a Repository Object has been deleted from the Repository, it still remains in the report.

A. True
B. False

Q16. You want to log off the Repository Explorer. Which of the following methods apply?

A. Right-click the Repository and select Log Off Server
B. Right-click the top folder within the Repository and select Log Off Server
C. Press the F4 key
D. Press the F12 key

Q17. You want to delete folders in a Repository. Which of the following applies? *(Multiple Answers)*

A. You must delete all objects and subfolders within the folder, before you delete the folder

B. Right-click the empty folder and select delete

C. Right-click the folder, select save as, this will save the folder and it's contents to the C:\ drive then right click again and delete

Q18. You have selected the option to view the Repository Explorer, but you are not logged on. Which of the following should be applied to enable this process?

A. Press the F5 and the Repository will automatically be activated

B. Click the logon icon and enter your authentication details

C. Click the Repository icon, this should log the user on automatically

D. Select database Repository Explorer and log on

Q19. A Repository object must be disconnected before it can be modified?

A. True

B. False

Q20. You want to add a Custom Function to the Repository. Which of the following methods apply? *(Multiple Answers)*

A. Drag and Drop the Custom Function from the Field Explorer into the Repository

B. Right-Click the Custom Function within the Formula Workshop and 'Add to Repository'

C. Drag and Drop the Custom Function from the Report Explorer into the Repository

D. Drag and Drop the Custom Function from the File Explorer into the Repository

E. Drag the Custom Function from the Report Custom Functions node within the Formula Workshop Tree and drop into a Repository Custom Functions node.

Q21. You want to amend the company logo which is saved to the Repository. Which of the following actions must you do?

A. Right-click the object on the report in the Formula Explorer, choose disconnect from the Repository, amend object, then right-click object again and add to Repository with the same name.

B. Right-click the object on the report in the Repository Explorer, choose disconnect from the Repository, amend object, then right-click object again and add to Repository with the same name.

C. Right-click the object on the report in the Database Explorer, choose disconnect from the Repository, amend object, then right-click object again and add to Repository with the same name.

D. Right-click the object on the report in the Report Explorer, choose disconnect from the Repository, amend object, then right-click object again and add to Repository with the same name.

E. Right-click the object, choose disconnect from the Repository, amend object, then right-click object again and add to Repository with the same name.

Q22. You have added an object (Bitmap) to your report through the shared Repository and you have been granted all the necessary permissions to update the Repository, you have been asked by your department Manager to resize and format this bitmap object, but you cannot modify it. What is the likely cause of this problem?

A. The object cannot be modified as it has been created with PaintshopPro and must be resized within the PaintShopPro environment

B. The object cannot be modified as it is still connected to the shared Repository and therefore needs to be disconnected before the amendment can be made.

C. Right-click the object and tick modification allowed

Q23. Folders within the Repository cannot be renamed.

A. True

B. False

Q24. Which of the following apply to the Repository? *(Multiple Answers)*

A. Drag and drop object images into the Repository

B. Custom Functions can be added via the Formula Workshop

C. SQL Commands can be added through the Database Expert.

D. Reports can be dragged into the Repository

Q25. You want to add a Text Object within your report to the Repository. Which of the following apply?

A. Right-click the Text Object and click edit Repository
B. Right-click the Text Object and select add to Repository from the drop-down menu, enter the authentication details and enter the required descriptions and save to the appropriate folder
C. Right-click the Text Object and click save to Repository
D. Right-click the Text Object and click Format Graphic and Save to Repository

Q26. You place the mouse over a SQL Command in the Repository. Which of the following will appear?

A. Repository Name
B. Script creation date
C. File Name
D. Description and Script

Q27. You want to add a SQL Command to the Repository. Which of the following apply?

A. SQL Commands can be added through the Explorer Expert, by clicking the 'Add to Repository' Checkbox from the ADD COMMAND section
B. SQL Commands can be added through the Report Expert, by clicking the 'Add to Repository' Checkbox from the ADD COMMAND section
C. SQL Commands can be added through the Database Expert, by selecting 'Add Command with the database connection and entering the SQL script within the Add Command to Report dialog section, clicking ok and selecting Add to Repository'
D. SQL Commands can be added through the Section Expert, by clicking the 'Add to Repository' Checkbox from the ADD COMMAND section

Q28. Which of the following scripts will produce an error message when entered within the Add Command?

A. SELECT Merchandise.* FROM Merchandise;
B. SELECT Merchandise FROM Merchandise
C. select * from Merchandise
D. None of the above

Q29. Given the query below in the SQL Command, you want to add a parameter to replace the EXAM_ID. Which of the following apply?

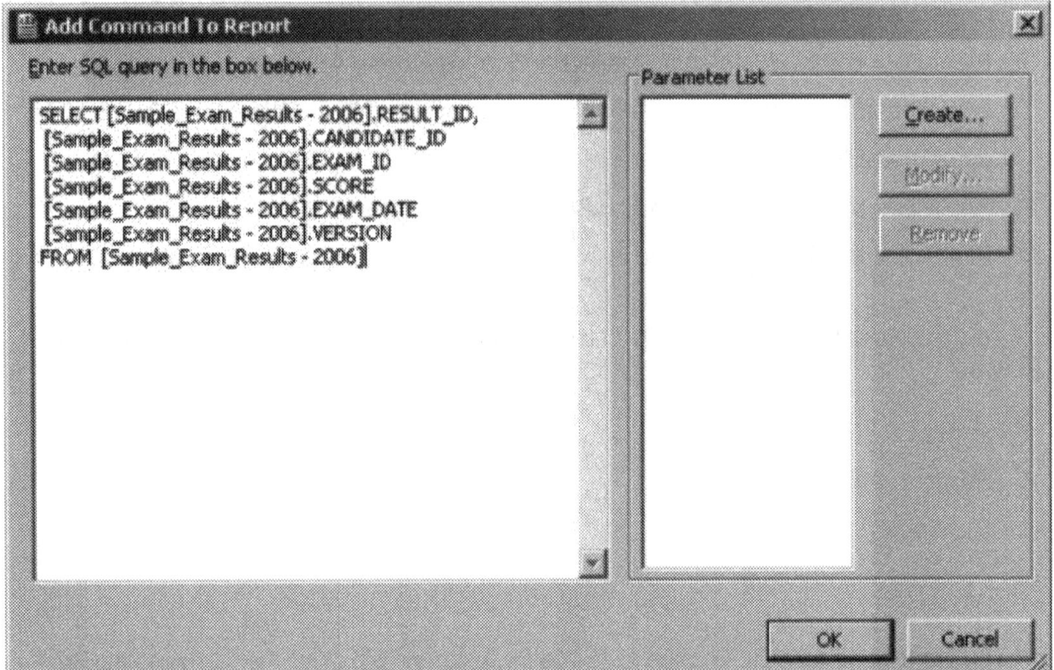

A. Click the parameter button within the SQL Command dialog box and enter the parameter details as follows: parameter name: Exam ID, prompting text: Enter Exam ID, value type: String and default value: RDCR201, highlight the exam_id within the parameter list and replace the exam_id with the parameter created, users will be prompted for an Exam ID when using the SQL Command created.

B. Click the modify button within the SQL Command dialog box and enter the parameter details as follows: parameter name: Exam ID, prompting text: Enter Exam ID, value type: String and default value: RDCR201, highlight the exam_id within the parameter list and replace the exam_id with the parameter created, users will be prompted for an Exam ID when using the SQL Command created.

C. Click the Command button within the SQL Command dialog box and enter the parameter details as follows: parameter name: Exam ID, prompting text: Enter Exam ID, value type: String and default value: RDCR201, highlight the exam_id within the parameter list and replace the exam_id with the parameter created, users will be prompted for an Exam ID when using the SQL Command created.

D. Click the create button within the SQL Command dialog box and enter the parameter details as follows: parameter name: Exam ID, prompting text: Enter Exam ID, value type: String and default value: RDCR201, highlight the exam_id within the parameter list and replace the exam_id with the parameter created, users will be prompted for an Exam ID when using the SQL Command created

Chapter 15 - Business Views

This chapter covers questions on Business Views the objects within the Business Views and the utilization of the functionality which each object provides.

Key Areas

- ❑ **Data Foundation**
- ❑ **Data Connection**
- ❑ **Business Views**
- ❑ **Business Elements**
- ❑ **SQL Commands**
- ❑ **SQL Expressions**
- ❑ **Assigning Rights**

Q1. Which one of the following controls access to objects in the Business Views?

A. Business View

B. Business View Manager

C. View Manger

D. Crystal Developer

Q2. You want to give 'User A' View and Edit rights to the Finance Data Connection. Which of the following methods apply?

A. Right-click the Finance Data Connection and select Edit Rights, select the Add User Icon and highlight User A and click Add, set View and Edit to Granted and click OK

B. Right-click the Finance Data Connection and select Rights, select the Add User Icon and highlight User A and click Add and close, assign the required rights

C. Right-click the Finance Data Connection and select security, select the Add User Icon and highlight User A and click Add and close, assign the required rights

D. Right-click the Finance Data Connection and select Administrator, select the Add User Icon and highlight User A and click Add and close, assign the required rights

Q3. Which of the following are rights, which can be assigned to a filter? *(Multiple Answers)*

A. Applied

B. Not Applied

C. Edit

D. View

E. Set Security

F. Data Access

Q4. Which of the following are properties which can be set within the Property Browser for a Data Connection? *(Multiple Answers)*

A. Name, Description, Author
B. User Name, Password
C. Use Single Sign On when viewing
D. Connection, Runtime Run Mode
E. Use Owner, Use Catalog
F. Rights

Q5. You want to change the Database of your current Data Connection without using the Dynamic Data Connection. Which of the following apply?

A. Right-click the Data Connection within the Object Browser and select Edit Connection from the drop-down menu, from the Choose a Data Source dialog box select the connection type and replace database as required
B. Right-click the Data Connection within the Field Browser and select Edit Connection from the drop-down menu, from the Choose a Data Source dialog box select the connection type and replace database as required
C. Right-click the Data Connection within the Data Connection Browser and select Edit Connection from the drop-down menu, from the Choose a Data Source dialog box select the connection type and replace database as required
D. Right-click the Data Connection within the Object Explorer and select Edit Connection from the drop-down menu, from the Choose a Data Source dialog box select the connection type and replace database as required

Q6. You have selected the FS Dynamic Data Connection to create a Data Foundation. Which of the following will occur?

A. You will be prompted to enter a Parameter value indicating the Data Connection required
B. You will be prompted to type in the name of the Data Connection required
C. You will receive an error message as the Data Foundation must be connected directly to the Data Connection required without going via the Dynamic Data Connection required

Q7. What does this icon represent? 

A. Business View
B. Business Elements
C. Data Foundation
D. Dynamic Data Connection
E. Data Connection

Q8. You have created a formula in the Data Foundation, this formula has been selected as part of the Business Elements and has now been incorporated into the Business View, which is available to all users, however all users have complained they cannot see the formula. What should you do?

A. Refresh the Business View
B. Assign Rights to the Formula via the Data Foundation
C. Refresh the Business Element
D. Refresh the Data Foundation

Q9. You want to add a Custom Function to your Data Foundation. Which of the following methods apply? *(Multiple Answers)*

A. From the Menu Bar select Insert – Import Custom Function and select the Custom Function required and Click Add
B. From the Menu Bar select Insert – Import Custom Function and select the Custom Function required and Click Add
C. From the Menu Bar select View– Custom Function – Import Custom Function and select the Custom Function required and Click Add
D. Click the Import Custom Function icon – and select the Custom Function required and Click Add

Q10. You want to Show The Dependent Objects of the Data Foundation. Which of the following apply?

A. Tools – Show Dependent objects 

B. Tools – Show Dependent objects 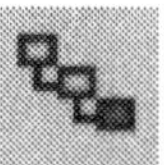

C. Tools – Show Dependent objects 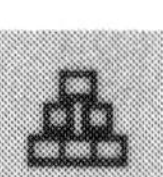

D. Tools – Show Dependent objects 

Q11. You want to see the Reference Objects which your Data Foundation is affiliated with. Which of the following apply?

A. Tools – Show Referenced Objects 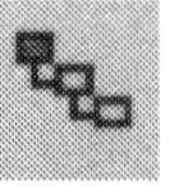

B. Tools – Show Referenced Objects 

C. Tools – Show Referenced Objects 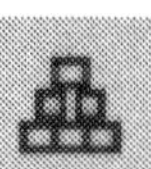

D. Tools – Show Referenced Objects 

Q12. Which of the following objects must be created to complete a Business View? *(Multiple Answers)*

A. Data Connection
B. Dynamic Data Connection
C. Business Element
D. Business Connection
E. Business View

Q13. Which of the following best describes a Business View? *(Multiple Answers)*

A. Logical collation of data
B. Flexible method of data access
C. Security enhanced data access

Q14. Business Views can report from multiple dissimilar sources?

A. True
B. False

Q15. The Business View Manager runs within which of the following environments?

A. Unix
B. Sysbase
C. Windows
D. Linux

Q16. Field Level Security can be set within which of the following? *(Multiple Answers)*

A. Business Element
B. Data Connection
C. Business View
D. Data Foundation

Q17. Which of the following are Business View Objects? *(Multiple Answers)*

A. Data Connections
B. Dynamic Data Connection
C. Data Foundations
D. Business Elements
E. Repository

Q18. You want to restrict Access to the Salary Field of the Payment Table. Where can this restriction be applied?

A. Within the Business View, Expand the Tables section and right-click the field within the Object Explorer and Edit Rights, Set Denied to the Everyone group under View Field Data
B. Within the Data Connection, Expand the Tables section and right-click the field within the Object Explorer and Edit Rights, Set Denied to the Everyone group under View Field Data
C. Within the Data Foundation, Expand the Tables section and right-click the field within the Object Explorer and Edit Rights, Set Denied to the Everyone group under View Field Data

Q19. Which of the following can be performed against database tables within the Data Foundation?

A. Select Display path
B. Select Path
C. Fetch Table Indexes
D. Display Legend

Q20. You are applying a filter to a Business Element. Which of the following properties can be set in the Property Browser? *(Multiple Answers)*

A. Name
B. File
C. Data source
D. Description
E. Rights
F. Parent Folder
G. Data Foundation
H. Author
I. Filter

Q21. Which of the following apply to the Business View Manager? *(Multiple Answers)*

A. Dynamic movement from one connection to the other is allowed
B. Switching from one view to the other is not allowed
C. All Business View must come from one data source
D. A Business View's data must come from one Data Foundation
E. Business Views reside on the Repository
F. Rights are assigned to Business Views via the Business View Manager
G. A single Business View's data can come from more than one Data Foundation

Q22. You want to test the Data Connection connectivity. Which of the following methods apply? *(Multiple Answers)*

A. Tools – Test Connectivity
B. Click the Connectivity icon 
C. Click the Connectivity icon 
D. Right-click the Data Connection within the Object Explorer and select Test Connectivity

Q23. Which of the following are the two tabs available in the Business Element Window? *(Multiple Answers)*

A. Structure
B. Fields List
C. Field Structure
D. Lists

Q24. Which one of the following fall within the Data Tier of Business View Architecture?

A. Report Application Server
B. Data Sources
C. Business Views
D. Business Elements
E. Data Foundation
F. Data Elements
G. Data Connection
H. Dynamic Data Connection
I. Crystal Reports

Q25. What type of system is a Business View?

A. Single-Tier System
B. Multi-Tier System
C. Multiple Tier System
D. Discrete- Tier System

Q26. How many Tiers do Business Views consist of?

A. 1
B. 2
C. 4
D. 5
E. 3

Q27. Which of the following are the Business View Tiers? *(Multiple Answers)*

A. Client Tier
B. Business Tier
C. Data Tier
D. File Tier

Q28. You have opened the Business Element and would like to view the Field Source. Which of the following tabs should you select?

A. Structure
B. Fields List
C. Field Structure
D. Lists

Q29. What are the two filter Edit Rights options? *(Multiple Answers)*

A. Data Access
B. No Access
C. Full Data Access
D. No Data Access

Q30. You have opened the Sales Data Connection and right-clicked the Data Connection within the Repository to Edit Rights previously assigned. Which of the following will occur?

A. The Edit Rights dialog box will appear
B. The Business View Manager dialog box will appear
C. An error message will appear as rights to the Data Connection cannot be assigned through the Repository Explorer while it is open
D. None of the above

Q31. You want to view all objects in your Repository Explorer within the Business View Manager that are owned by the user:FinanceDesigner. Which of the following methods apply?

A. Right-click the root folder within the Repository Explorer and select Advanced Filtering and type FinanceDesigner in the Show items by this Author
B. Right-click the root folder within the Repository Explorer and select Advanced Filtering and type FinanceDesigner in the Show Author
C. Right-click the root folder within the Repository Explorer and select Users and type FinanceDesigner in the Show items by this Author
D. Right-click the root folder within the Repository Explorer and select Author and type FinanceDesigner in the Show items by this Author

Q32. You have denied 'User A' access to the salary field within your Business Element which has been used in your Business View. Which of the following will take place when User A uses the Business View?

A. User A will be unable to see the salary field in the Business View
B. User A will be notified of this restriction when the view is opened
C. The Salary field will produce null
D. Restriction cannot be placed on individual fields

Q33. Which of the following Objects can you apply security to via the Business View Manager? *(Multiple Answers)*

A. Bitmaps
B. Microsoft Word Document
C. Text Objects
D. Custom Functions
E. Commands

Q34. View Field Data rights can be set against which of the following? *(Multiple Answers)*

A. Formula
B. SQL Expressions
C. Business Fields
D. Database Fields

Q35. Business Views consist of which of the following?

A. Files
B. Reports
C. Objects
D. Marts

Q36. Which of the following Repository Objects can you apply security rights to? *(Multiple Answers)*

A. Text Objects
B. Bitmaps
C. Custom Functions
D. Commands

Q37. Which Business View Objects is being described? Provides log on information to the Data Source

A. Data Foundations
B. Business Elements
C. Business Views
D. Data Connections
E. Business Files
F. Business Reports

Q39. Which Business View Objects is being described below?
Consist of the tables and fields which are used to create Business Elements

A. Data Foundations
B. Dynamic Data Connection
C. Business Elements
D. Business Views
E. Data Connections
F. Business Files
G. Business Report

Q38. Which Business View Object is being described? Enables a switch between data sources

A. Dynamic Data Connection
B. Data Foundations
C. Business Elements
D. Business Views

E. Data Connections
F. Business Files
G. Business Reports

Q39. Which Business View Object is being described? Consist of the tables and fields, which are then used to create Business Elements

A. Data Foundations
B. Dynamic Data Connection
C. Business Elements
D. Business Views
E. Data Connections
F. Business Files
G. Business Reports

Q40. Which Business View Object is being described? Can be used to create a logical assemble of field for further Business reference.

A. Data Foundations
B. Dynamic Data Connection
C. Business Elements
D. Data Connections
E. Business Files
F. Business Views
G. Business Reports

Q41. Which Business View Object is being described? It is a collation of Business Elements

A. Data Foundations
B. Dynamic Data Connection
C. Business Elements
D. Data Connections
E. Business Files
F. Business Views
G. Business Reports

Q42. Your Organization has multiple databases, you would like to create a Business View to encompass all databases giving the user the option to run Business Views based on any database required. Which of the following connections should be used?

A. Data Connection
B. Dynamic Data Connection
C. Data Foundation
D. Dynamic

Q43. You want to import a Custom Function which you have created and saved to the Repository. Which of the following methods will enable you to achieve this?

A. File – Import Custom Function, select Custom Function from the Custom Function dialog box and click Add.
B. Edit – Import Custom Function, select Custom Function from the Custom Function dialog box and click Add.
C. Insert – Import Custom Function, select Custom Function from the Custom Function dialog box and click Add.

Q44. You right-click the Data Connection and select Edit Rights. Which of the following rights can be assigned? *(Multiple Answers)*

A. View
B. Edit
C. Set Security
D. Data Access
E. View Field Data

Q45. A Business View requires the following objects: Data Foundation, Dynamic Data Connection, Business Elements, Data Connections. Which one is optional?

A. Data Foundations
B. Dynamic Data Connection
C. Business Elements
D. Data Connections

Q46. You want to create a Business View, in what order do the objects have to be created?
(Multiple Answers)

A. Create the Data Foundations - Dynamic Data Connection - Business Elements – Business View
B. Create the Business View- Data Foundations - Dynamic Data Connection - Business Elements
C. Create the Data Connection - Data Foundation - Business Element – Business View
D. Create the Data Connections - Create the Dynamic Data Connection - Data Foundations - Business Elements – Business View

Q47. You want users to have access to the Finance and Sales Database which are in two different Schemas. How many Business Views would you have to create?

A. One Business View would be required
B. Four Business Views would be required
C. Two Business Views would be required
D. Three Business Views would be required

Q48. You want to access a Business View within Crystal Reports. Where are Business Views located?

A. File Repository
B. Business Element
C. Data Element
D. Database Expert - Repository

Q49. Users who have access to Business Views are created within Business Objects Enterprise?

A. True
B. False

Q50. You want to add an existing Business Element to a new Business View. Which of the following should you do?

A. File – Edit -New – Business View – Select Business Element from the insert Business Elements dialog box and click Add – close and Save, enter name of Business View in Property Browser
B. File – New – Business View – Select Business Element from the insert Business Elements dialog box and click Add – close and Save, enter name of Business View in Property Browser

C. File – Report -New – Business View – Select Business Element from the insert Business Elements dialog box and click Add – close and Save, enter name of Business View in Property Browser

D. Open the Business View and select Insert – Insert Business Elements, select the Business View from the insert Business Elements dialog box and click Add

Q51. Which of the following actions will activate the prompt for user logon authentication when reporting off a Business View?

A. Set runtime prompt mode to do not store the login information in the Crystal Repository

B. Set runtime prompt mode to 'Always Prompt' and save the login information in the Crystal Repository

C. Set runtime prompt mode to 'Always Prompt'

D. Set runtime prompt mode to 'Prompt Only' do not store the login information in the Crystal Repository

Q52. You have exported your Business View. What file format will it be exported as?

A. DHTML

B. HTML

C. XML

D. JAVA

E. .NET

Q53. Which of the following groups has automatic full rights to all objects in the Business View?

A. Guest

B. Enterprise Manager

C. Reports Administer

D. Administrators

Q54. The Property Browser for Business Views contains which of the following? *(Multiple Answers)*

A. Name

B. Description

C. Author

D. Parent Folder

E. Business Element Filter Combination

F. Rights

Q55. You click the Preview Button within the Edit Rights dialog box. What will happen?

A. The final rights allocated will be displayed
B. All rights will be refreshed and left blank
C. All Rights assigned will be set to the systems default
D. None of the above

Q56. You want to view the rights which have been granted to particular folder. What should you do?

A. Right-click the folder in the Business View and select View Rights from the drop-down menu
B. Right-click the folder and select Edit Rights from the drop-down menu
C. Right-click the folder in the Business View and select Change Rights from the drop-down menu
D. From the menu select view – Edit Rights

Q57. Which of the following have automatic inherited rights to Business View objects? *(Multiple Answers)*

A. Everyone
B. Guest
C. Administrators
D. Reporter

Q58. You do not want users to be prompted for login details when using your Data Connection. Which of the following should be implemented to ensure users are not prompted for logon information?

A. Set runtime prompt mode to Prompt Only
B. Set runtime prompt mode to Never Prompt
C. Set runtime prompt mode to Prompt do not store the login information in the Crystal Repository
D. Set runtime prompt mode to Never

Q59. You want to add a Command to the Data Foundation. Which of the following methods will you use?

A. View - Data Connection Window and click the Add Command and enter the SQL query
B. View - Dynamic Data Connection Window and click the Add Command and enter the SQL query

C. View - Referenced Data Connection Window and click the Add Command and enter the SQL query

D. View - Data Connection and click the Add Command and enter the SQL query

Q60. A Business Objects Enterprise group can be assigned access to Business View Objects

A. True

B. False

Q61. Which of the following options will allow the user to establish the rights associated with each Business Element field in the Business View?

A. Edit Rights

B. Rights

C. Business View Rights

D. Rights Test View

Q62. You have just installed Business View Manager. What is the default name of a new Data Connection?

A. DataConnect1

B. Data Connection1

C. Data1 Connection

D. Data Con

Q63. The SQL Expression Formula can be changed within which of the following windows?

A. From the Object Browser right-click the SQL expression and Edit SQL Expression

B. From the Report Browser right-click the SQL expression and Edit SQL Expression

C. From the Property Browser right-click the SQL expression and Edit SQL Expression

D. From the Object Explorer right-click the SQL expression and Edit SQL Expression

Q64. You have created a formula in the Data Foundation, this formula has been selected as part of the Business Element which has been incorporated into the Business View, User A has complained that he cannot see the formula. Which of the following will resolve the problem?

A. Assign View Rights to 'User A' within the Data Foundation to the formula

B. User A must refresh the report

C. User A must verify the Database to pick up the changes

D. User A must reset the location of the Business View

Q65. Which one of the following statements is true?

A. Data sources and Dynamic Data Connections must have similar schemas

B. Data sources and Dynamic Data Connections must have dissimilar schemas

C. Data sources have similar schemas to Business Views

D. Data sources have similar schemas to Business Elements

Q66. You have based a Dynamic Data Connection on a Data Connection which always prompts the users for login information. Which of the following will happen?

A. User must enter login information

B. An error message will appear

C. The login information box will be greyed out

D. User must click OK to bypass logo information requirements

Q67. Your Dynamic Data Connection is composed of client information from various countries. Which of the following will be the logical name to assign to the Dynamic Data Connection?

A. Dynamic
B. Dynamic Data
C. Dynamic Connect
D. DynamicConnectionClients

Q68. You inherit the same rights as assigned to an Object Parent Folder. What type of rights have you inherited?

A. Row rights

B. Group Rights

C. Column-level rights

D. Folder Inheritance

E. Parent Inheritance

Q69. You inherit the same rights as assigned to other members of the group. What type of rights have you inherited?

A. Row rights

B. Group Rights

C. Column-level rights

D. Folder Rights

E. Section Rights

Q70. You open a Dynamic Data Connection. Which of the following will happen?

A. A prompt to specify the Business connection will appear
B. A prompt to specify the Business Element connection will appear
C. A prompt to specify the Business View connection will appear
D. A prompt to specify the Data Connection required will appear

Q71. Which object within the Business View Manager requires the users to select the data fields from the tables in the Data Foundation?

A. Data Foundations
B. Dynamic Data Connection
C. Business Elements
D. Data Connections
E. Business Files
F. Business Views
G. Business Reports

Q72. Parameters can be applied to some Business View Objects. Which of the following apply? *(Multiple Answers)*

A. Data Foundation
B. Data Connection
C. Business View
D. Business Element

Q73. You want to see the tables which have been used to create the Business View. Which Business View Object requires investigation?

A. Data Connection
B. Data Foundation
C. Business Element
D. Business View

Q74. Which of the following procedures will enable you to add Business Elements to a Business View?

A. Select File – New – Business View; from the 'Insert Business Elements dialog box' select the Business Element you would like to add to the Business View and select Add and Close, assign a logical name.
B. Select File – New – Business Element; from the 'Insert Business Elements dialog box' select the Business View you would like to add to the Business View and select Add and Close, assign a logical name.
C. Select File – New – Data Foundation; from the 'Insert Business Elements dialog box' select the Business Element you would like to add to the Business View and select Add and Close, assign a logical name.

Q75. Which of the following procedures will enable you to assign a name to an existing Business View?

A. From the Object Browser, highlight the Business View and allocated a name in the Property Browser associated with the Business View and save.
B. From the Object Inspector, highlight the Business View and allocated a name in the Property Browser associated with the Business View and save.
C. From the Object Explorer, highlight the Business View and allocated a name in the Property Browser name section and save.
D. From the Object Finder, highlight the Business View and allocated a name in the Property Browser associated with the Business View and save.

Q76. Which of the following can be added to the Data Foundation? *(Multiple Answers)*

A. Data Tables
B. SQL Command
C. Formulas
D. SQL Expressions
E. Filters
F. Parameters
G. Custom Functions

Q77. Which of the following best describes a Business View?

A. A logical collation of tables
B. A logical collation of views
C. A logical collation of Business Views
D. A logical collation of Business Elements

Q78. You want to apply a filter to a Business Element. Which of the following apply? *(Multiple Answers)*

A. Select Insert – Insert filter from the Menu Bar, select the field required and apply the filter from the add filters dialog box and enter your selection criteria and check filter validity and click apply
B. From the Object Explorer of the Business Element, right-click filters and select insert filters from the drop down menu, select the field to apply the filter from the add filters dialog box and enter your selection criteria and check filter validity and click apply
C. Select the icon and select the field used to apply the filter from the add filters dialog box and enter your selection criteria and check filter validity and click apply

Q79. You have added a stored procedure to the Data Foundation. What will the Stored Procedure appear as in the Data Foundation?

A. A Stored Procedure
B. An SQL expression
C. A file
D. A Table

Q80. Which object is created before the Business View?

A. Business Element
B. Business File
C. Business Foundation
D. Data Connection

Q81. To activate the Repository Explorer Window you must apply one of the following methods?

A. From the Menu Bar select edit and Repository Explorer
B. From the Menu Bar select file and Repository Explorer
C. From the Menu Bar select tools and Repository Explorer
D. From the Menu Bar select view and Repository Explorer

Q82. You want to add more fields to your opened Business Element. Which of the following apply?

A. From the Menu select insert Business Fields and select the additional fields from the insert Business Fields dialog box.

B. From the File Menu select insert Business Fields and select the additional fields required from the insert Business Fields dialog box.

C. From the menu, select Insert Business Fields, the Business Fields dialog box will appear, expand the tables and select the additional Business Fields required and click Add

D. From the menu, select view Business Fields, the Business Fields dialog box will appear, expand the tables and select the additional Business Fields required and click Add

Q83. You want to make formulas available to all Business View Designers, preventing the need for the repetition of generic formulas. Which of the following should you implement?

A. Custom Functions

B. Formulas

C. Parameters

D. Stored Procedure

Q84. You want to apply a Formula to the Data Foundation. Which of the following methods apply? *(Multiple Answers)*

A. From the Repository Explorer, right-click the Data Foundation and select insert formula enter the formula in the Add fields, formulas and operators window and check then apply

B. Open the Data Foundation from the Repository Explorer and select Insert – Insert Formula – enter the formula in the Add fields, formulas and operators window and check then apply

C. Open the Data Foundation, within the Object Explorer window, right- click the formula and select insert formula – enter the formula in the Add fields, formulas and operators window and check then apply

D. Open the Data Foundation from the Repository Explorer, within the Property Browser window, right- click the formula and select insert formula – enter the formula in the Add fields, formulas and operators window and check then apply

Q85. You want to apply a parameter to the Data Foundation which you have opened. Which of the following will achieve this?

A. From the Menu select parameter – Insert Parameter– enter parameter details: - Name, Prompting Text, Value Type and Set Default Values and select OK
B. From the Menu select file – Insert Parameter– enter parameter details: - Name, Prompting Text, Value Type and Set Default Values and select OK
C. From the Menu select view – Insert Parameter– enter parameter details: - Name, Prompting Text, Value Type and Set Default Values, List of values and select OK
D. From the Menu select insert – Insert Parameter– enter parameter details: - Name, Prompting Text, Value Type and Set Default Values, List of values and select OK

Q86. Which of the following will enable you to change the name of a Business Field via the Business Element?

A. Within the object browser expand the Business Element and select the field, from the Property Browser change the name of the field and save.
B. Within the Object Explorer expand the Business Element and select the Business Field, from the Property Browser change the name of the field in the Name section
C. Within the object browser expand the Business Element and select the field the alias would be applied to, from the Property Browser change the name to the alias as required and save.
D. Within the Property Browser expand the Business Element and select the field the alias would be applied to, from the Property Browser change the name to the alias as required and save

Q87. What is a Business View?

A. Collection of Formulas
B. Collection of Parameters
C. Collection of Logical Business Elements
D. Collection of Files

Q88. Which of the following are types of rights which can be assigned to a user of a Business View? *(Multiple Answers)*

A. Granted
B. Denied
C. Inherited
D. Yes
E. No

Q89. Rights can be assigned at the following levels? *(Multiple Answers)*

A. Repository Business View Level
B. Repository Root
C. Folder Level
D. Object Level

Q90. You want to swap between three Data Connections. Which of the following apply?

A. Create 3 Dynamic Connection and 3 Data Connections
B. Create 1 Data Connection and 3 Dynamic Connections
C. Create 1 Data Connection and 3 Dynamic Connections
D. Create 3 Data Connections and One Dynamic Connection

Q91. What does the icon below represent? 

A. Business View
B. Business Elements
C. Data Foundation
D. Data Connection

Q92. What does the icon below represent? 

A. Business View
B. Business Elements
C. Data Foundation
D. Data Connection

Q93. What does the icon below represent? 

A. Business View

B. Business Elements

C. Data Foundation

D. Data Connection

Q94. What does the icon below represent? 

A. Business View

B. Business Elements

C. Data Foundation

D. Data Connection

Q95. A Business View can only include Business Elements created from one Data Foundation only

A. True

B. False

Q96. A Business View can contain Business Elements from more than one Data Foundations

A. True

B. False

Q97. What is the definition of CMC?

A. Crystal Management Server

B. Connection Management Server

C. Connect Management Server

D. Central Management Console

Q98. The Data Connection Name can be changed within which of the following? *(Multiple Answers)*

A. File Browser

B. Data Browser

C. Property Browser

D. Report Browser

E. Repository Explorer (F2)

Q99. Which of the following can be modified from the Data Connection Property Browser?
(Multiple Answers)

A. Name
B. Description
C. Password
D. User Name
E. Author
F. Connection
G. Run Time Prompt Mode
H. Use Owner
I. Use Catalog
J. Rights

Q100. Your Property Browser does not appear within the Business View Manager. What should you do to activate it?

A. From the Menu Bar select edit and Property Browser
B. From the Menu Bar select view and Property Browser
C. From the Menu Bar select file and Property Browser
D. From the Menu Bar select tools and Property Browser

Q101. You have created 2 Data Connections using your ClientBank and ClientHospital database, you now want to create a Dynamic Data Connection. What should you do?

A. Select File – Database -Dynamic Data Connection from the 'choose Data Connection dialog box' and select the ClientBank Data Connection and click add, repeat the same process for the ClientHospital Data Connection
B. Select Edit – New - Dynamic Data Connection from the 'choose Data Connection dialog box' and select the ClientBank Data Connection and click add, repeat the same process for the ClientHospital Data Connection
C. Select File – New - Dynamic Data Connection from the 'choose Data Connection dialog box' and select the ClientBank Data Connection and click add, repeat the same process for the ClientHospital Data Connection

Q102. You want to add additional Data Connections to your Dynamic Data Connection. What should you do?

A. Select file from the Menu Bar and select add Data Connection or select the add data connect icon Dynamic Data Connection
B. Select report from the Menu Bar and select add Data Connection or select the add data connect icon Dynamic Data Connection
C. From the Repository Explorer, double-click the Dynamic Data Connections and click the Add button, or Select edit from the Menu Bar and select add Data Connection or click the Add Data Connection icon
D. Select report from the Menu Bar and select add Dynamic Data Connection

Q103. What are the 3 sort options available in the Dynamic Data Connection window? *(Multiple Answers)*

A. Alphabetical ascending
B. Alphabetical descending
C. No Sort
D. Sort

Q104. The Data Foundation is a collation of tables, which the Business Element extracts data from to create logical Business Fields for Business Views

A. True
B. False

Q105. All Business Views are saved to the Repository

A. True
B. False

Q106. Where do you set the access rights for the Business View objects?

A. File Explorer
B. Report Explorer
C. Repository Explorer
D. Object Explorer

Q107. Which of the following rights can be assigned within a Business View? *(Multiple Answers)*

A. View
B. Edit
C. Set security
D. Read

Q108. Security can be applied to which of the following via the Business View Manager? *(Multiple Answers)*

A. Data Connection

B. Dynamic Data Connection

C. Data Foundation

D. Business Elements

E. Business Views

Chapter 16 – Report Management

This chapter covers questions on the following areas: The Field Explorer, Report Explorer, Workbench, Dependency Checker and Publishing a Report to Business Objects Enterprise

Key Areas

- **Field Explorer**
- **Report Explorer**
- **Workbench**
- **Dependency Checker**
- **Publishing a Report to Business Objects Enterprise**

Q1. Which of the following reside under the Field Explorer? *(Multiple Answers)*

A. Formula Fields

B. Parameter Fields

C. Record Selection Fields
D. Parameter Special Fields
E. Running Total Fields
F. Group Name Fields
G. Special Fields
H. Database Fields

Q2. What role does the Dependency Checker perform?

A. Error Checking

B. Repository setting

C. Workbench Add-on

D. Data Type validation

Q3. Which of the following cannot be extracted from the Special Field category of the Field Explorer? *(Multiple Answers)*

A. PrintDate

B. PrintTime

C. DataDate

D. DateDate

E. DateTime

F. Filename

G. File Author

H. File Creation Date

I. Tools

J. Report Comments

Q4. You want to check the Property Report within the Workbench. To establish its dependencies. Which of the following will you select?

A. Checker

B. Check Dependencies

C. Dependency

D. Dependencies

Q5. You click the Dependency Checker icon and receive a message with the following icon

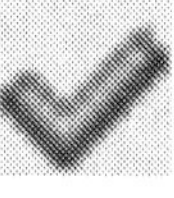. What does this icon represent?

A. Failed

B. Error Established

C. Unidentified fault

D. Success

Q6. Which one of the following icons will activate the Workbench?

A. Workbench 

B. Workbench

C. Workbench 

D. Workbench 

Q7. You want to see the field data type when viewing database tables within the Field Explorer. Which of the following apply?

A. Right-Click Database Field within the Field Explorer and Select Show Field Type from the list

B. Right-Click Database Field within the Field Explorer Reports Tab and Select Show Field Type from the list

C. Right-Click Database Field within the Field Explorer Fields Tab and Select Display Field Type

D. Right-Click Database Field within the Field Explorer Reports Tab and Select Display Field Type

Q8. Which of the following can be accessed within the Field Explorer? *(Multiple Answers)*

A. The Database Expert

B. Set Datasource Location

C. Log On or Off Server

D. Show Field Type

E. Refresh

F. Sort Tables Alphabetically

Q9. The number of groups present within a report can be located within which of the following sections of the Field Explorer?

A. Group

B. Group Name Fields

C. Group Field

D. Field Groups

Group Name Fields
Group #1 Name: EXAMRECORDS.Exam_No
Group #2 Name: EXAMRECORDS.County

Q10. You want to add an existing report to the Exam Details Project folder, within the Workbench. Which of the following methods will apply? *(Multiple Answers)*

A. Select View from the menu – Workbench - Right-click the Exam Details Project folder and select Add – Add Existing Report, browse the drive and select the required report and click open

B. Click the Workbench icon - Right-click the Exam Details Project folder and select Add – Add Existing Report, browse the drive and select the required report and click open

C. Select Project from the menu – Workbench - Right-click the Exam Details Project folder and select Add – Add Existing Report, browse the drive and select the required report and click open 

D. Click the Workbench icon - Right-click the Exam Details Project folder and select Add – Add Existing Report, browse the drive and select the required report and click open

Q11. You have placed a formula within a section of your report which you are now trying to locate. How can you locate the formula?

A. Use the Report Finder 

B. Use the Report Explorer 

C. Use the File Explorer 

D. Use the Section Expert 

Q12. You click the Dependency Checker icon and receive a message with the following icon . What does this icon represent?

A. Failed
B. Error Identified
C. Warning
D. Success

Q13. You click the Dependency Checker icon and receive a message with the following icon . What does this icon represent?

A. Failed
B. Error Identified
C. Warning
D. Success

Q14. You have a graph placed in the Report Header, however you cannot locate it within your report. What must you do to activate its visibility?

A. Click the Show/Hide Data Fields icon
B. Click the Show/Hide Grids and Subreports 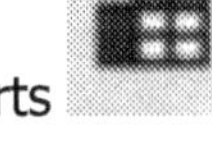
C. Click the Show/Hide Graphical Objects
D. Graphical Objects cannot be accessed within the Report Explorer

Q15. A report field can be formatted within the Report Explorer.

A. True
B. False

Q16. What impact will the button  have on the Report Explorer, when clicked?

A. Close sections if open

B. Locate Field

C. Hide or Show fields within sections in the Report Explorer

D. Close Report Explorer

E. Expand sections if closed

Q17. The Field Explorer and Report Explorer can be embedded into one dialog box

A. True

B. False

Q18. You are creating reports for several projects. Which of the following can be used to organize your projects?

A. Work File

B. Project Workbench

C. Workbench

D. Project File

Q19. Multiple report fields can be formatted from the Report Explorer.

A. False

B. True

Q20. You activate the Dependency Checker against a set of reports within the Workbench. Some of the reports produce error messages, and you want to investigate the error further. Which of the following apply?

Dependency Checker

	Description	Location
1	Cannot find this file. Please verify that the correct path and file name are given.	date formulas.rpt
3	Cannot find this file. Please verify that the correct path and file name are given.	boolean.rpt
2	Failed to open document.	date formulas.rpt
4	Failed to open document.	boolean.rpt
5	Success: no errors were detected in this file.	Series_Chart_7.rpt
6	Success: no errors were detected in this file.	Series_Chart_5.rpt

A. Right-click the error within the Dependency Checker dialog box and select Options and query report

B. Right-click the error within the Dependency Checker dialog box and select Go To enter.... and query report

C. Right-click the error within the Dependency Checker dialog box and select Find Error and query report

Q21. You want to add a new project to the Workbench. What should you do?

A. Right-click the Workbench and select Add New Workbench Project, a project folder entitled Untitled Project will appear, assign an appropriate name
B. Right-click the Workbench and select Add New Project, a project folder entitled Untitled Project will appear, assign an appropriate name
C. Right-click the Workbench and select Add New Folder, a project folder entitled Untitled Project will appear, assign an appropriate name
D. Right-click the Workbench and select Add New File, a project folder entitled Untitled Project will appear, assign an appropriate name

Q22. A Workbench Project can be published to Business Objects Enterprise

A. True
B. False

Q23. Within the Field Explorer what do the icons in the diagram below represent?

A. The icons apply to Database Fields, Formulas, Running Totals, Parameters and SQL Expression Fields created, they represent New, Edit, Rename and Delete
B. The icons apply to Formulas and Parameters only, they represent New, Edit, Rename and Delete
C. The icons apply to Group Name Fields and Special Fields and they represent New, Edit, Rename and Delete
D. The Icons are for Insert To Report, Browse, New, Edit, Duplicate, Rename And Delete

Q24. You want to publish a project to Business Objects Enterprise via the workbench. Which of the following apply?

A. Right-click the project and select Publish to Business Objects Enterprise
B. Select File and Save Project to Business Objects Enterprise
C. All of the above
D. None of the above

Q25. You want your users to view reports via Business Objects Enterprise. What is the process of transferring reports to Business Objects Enterprise?

A. Publishing
B. Transfer
C. Report Expert
D. Report Pass

Q26. You have just created a report and you want to publish it to Business Objects Enterprise. Which one of the following methods applies?

A. Choose Format | Save As | enter the name of the file, select the Enterprise Folder, Enter the Crystal Management Server name - User Name and Password and authentication and click ok, select the folder required and click ok
B. Choose Report | Save As | enter the name of the file, select the Enterprise Folder, Enter the Crystal Management Server name - User Name and Password and authentication and click ok, select the folder required and click ok
C. Choose File | Save As | select the Enterprise Folder, Enter the Crystal Management Server name - User Name and Password and authentication and click ok, select the folder required and click ok
D. Choose Database | Save As | enter the name of the file, select the Enterprise Folder, enter the Crystal Management Server name - User Name and Password and authentication and click ok, select the folder required and click ok

Q27. You want to publish a Workbench Project to Business Objects Enterprise. Which method applies?

A. Choose Format | Save As | enter the Project name, select the Enterprise Folder, Enter the Crystal Management Server name - User Name and Password and authentication and click ok, select the folder required and click ok
B. Right-click the Project Folder within the Workbench and select Publish to Business Objects Enterprise, enter the Crystal Management Server name - User Name, Password and authentication and click ok, select the folder required and click ok
C. Choose Report | Save As | enter the Project Name, select the Enterprise Folder, Enter the Crystal Management Server name - User Name and Password and authentication and click ok, select the folder required and click ok
D. Choose Database | Save As | enter the Project Name, select the Enterprise Folder, enter the Crystal Management Server name - User Name and Password and authentication and click ok, select the folder required and click ok

Q28. You want to find out where a particular formula has been referenced within other formulas. Which of the following apply?

A. Right-click the formula in the Field Explorer and select Find Formulas

B. Right-click the formula in the Field Explorer and select Formulas

C. Right-click the formula in the Field Explorer and select Find

D. Right-click the formula in the Field Explorer and select Find in Formulas

Q29. You want to create a duplicate copy of an existing formula and modify the code. Which of the following apply?

A. Right-click the formula in the Field Explorer and select New, enter the name of the existing formula, a dialog box will appear with a message requesting an overwrite or a duplicate, select duplicate

B. Right-click the formula in the Field Explorer and select Duplicate

C. Right-click the formula in the Field Explorer and select Save As

D. Right-click the formula in the Field Explorer and select Copy

Chapter 17 - Building And Planning A Report

Chapter 17 presents a combination of questions and practice lessons which the reader can undertake. The questions cover the area of planning a report building process. The sample reports are based on sample data provided by the author; the reader may use alternative data to practice the report creation process.

Key Areas

- **Planning a report and building reports**
- **Report Definition**
- **Alerts**
- **Lessons**

Q1. You are in the process of planning a report. Which of the following should be taken into consideration? *(Multiple Answers)*

A. Report specification and content

B. Develop a prototype

C. Report Users

D. Database structure and tables

E. End format of report (.rpt, .csv,.doc,.txt)

F. Method of deployment

G. Understanding of the business process

Q2. Which of the following does a Report Definition File comprise of? *(Multiple Answers)*

A. Sections (including formatting)

B. Fields (including formatting)

C. Formulas (including formula syntax and formatting)

D. Record Selection Formula

E. Grand Total of data retrieved

F. Group Selection Formula

G. Record Sort Fields

H. Group Sort Fields

Q3. Which of the following are important in the decision making process of designing a report? *(Multiple Answers)*

A. Purpose of the report

B. Layout requirements

C. Data

D. Database software used

Q4. You are designing a template for a financial report. What should you take into consideration? *(Multiple Answers)*

A. Paper size
B. Headings
C. Description information
D. Layout
E. Connection

Q5. Which of the following should be included in the end users documentation? *(Multiple Answers)*

A. Description of report
B. Explanation of formulas and how they have been derived
C. Tables used and description of their links
D. Report Location
E. Support contact
F. Date Created
G. Software version
H. Owner

Q6. Which of the following are significant when creating a data source? *(Multiple Answers)*

A. Database type
B. Database connectivity – ODBC or Native
C. Server Name?
D. Performance and speed of the database connectivity?
E. Availability of database drivers

Q7. Which of the following are significant to the deployment and distribution of a report? *(Multiple Answers)*

A. How many users will be requiring the report
B. Scheduling Times
C. Assignment of rights to users or groups and viewing restrictions
D. Type of report
E. Report scheduling format
F. Archiving requirements for instance threshold

Q8. Which aspects of end user training need to be taken into consideration? *(Multiple Answers)*

A. How to access the system
B. How to schedule reports
C. How to export reports
D. Provision of a report description enabling user to schedule the appropriate report to meet their requirements
E. How to save scheduled instances locally
F. How to design a report
G. Support contacts

Q9. Which of the following are important elements of report testing? *(Multiple Answers)*

A. Maximum report runtime
B. Report export quality
C. Error determination
D. Limitations
E. Effects of database data types changes on report
F. Test data source connectivity
G. How effective is data source relocation
H. Does retrieved data meet the report specification

Bonus Practice Section

Lesson 1:

Sample Report 1

Create a draft certificate, which will be sent out to candidates detailing their exam results, the reader can create their own design scenario or use the one illustrated in Fig 1.1. Given the sample data in Figure 1.0 (on page 290) create the certificate report illustrated in fig 1.1 below. You can create your own watermark using an image of your choice.

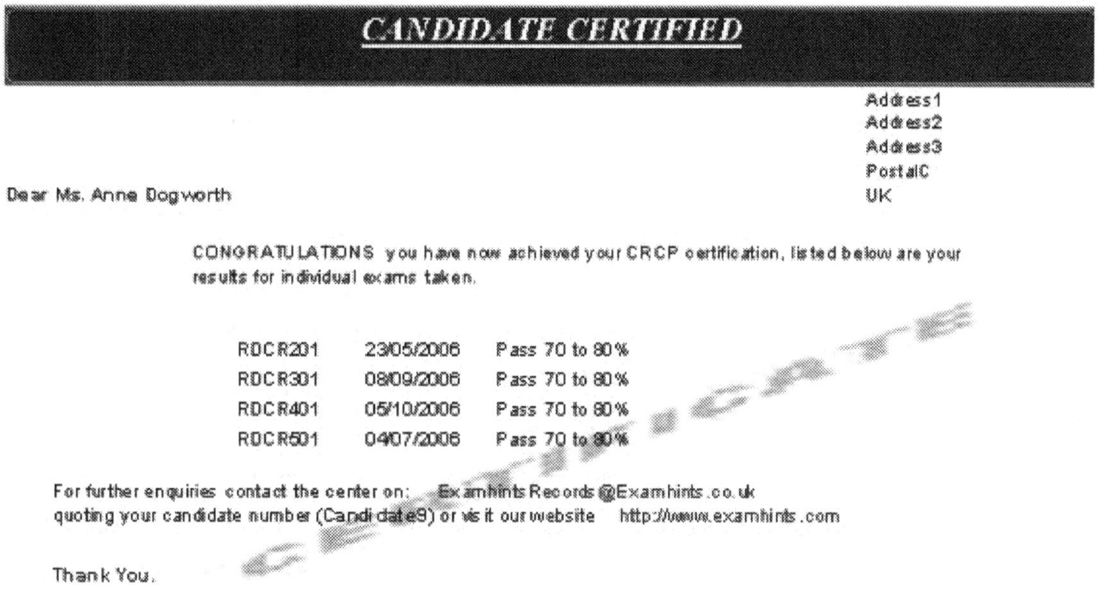

CANDIDATE CERTIFIED

Address1
Address2
Address3
PostalC
UK

Dear Ms. Anne Dogworth

CONGRATULATIONS you have now achieved your CRCP certification, listed below are your results for individual exams taken.

RDCR201	23/05/2006	Pass 70 to 80%
RDCR301	08/09/2006	Pass 70 to 80%
RDCR401	05/10/2006	Pass 70 to 80%
RDCR501	04/07/2006	Pass 70 to 80%

For further enquiries contact the center on: ExamhintsRecords@Examhints.co.uk
quoting your candidate number (Candidate9) or visit our website http://www.examhints.com

Thank You.

CERTIFICATE

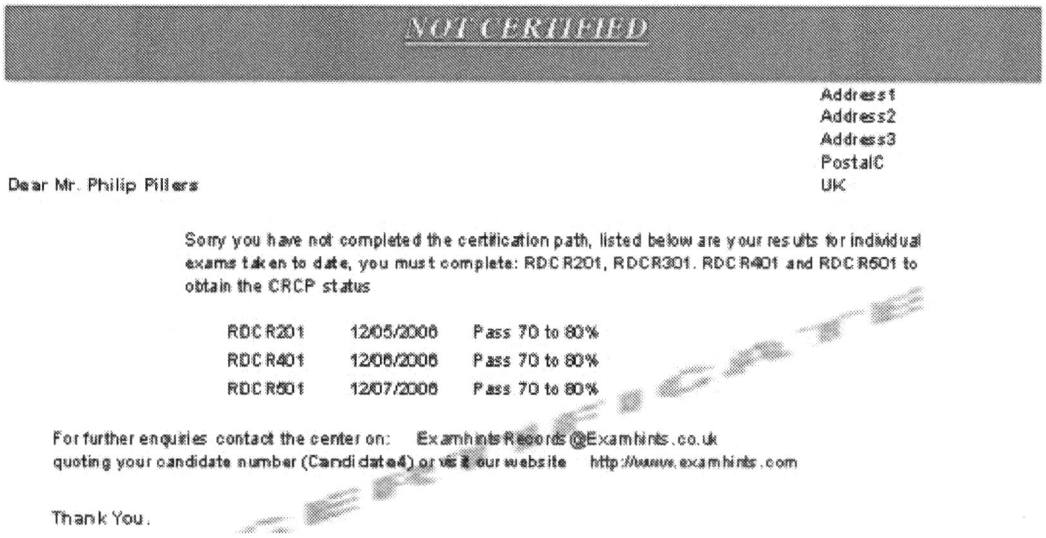

NOT CERTIFIED

Address1
Address2
Address3
PostalC
UK

Dear Mr. Philip Pillers

Sorry you have not completed the certification path, listed below are your results for individual exams taken to date, you must complete: RDCR201, RDCR301. RDCR401 and RDCR501 to obtain the CRCP status

RDCR201	12/05/2006	Pass 70 to 80%
RDCR401	12/06/2006	Pass 70 to 80%
RDCR501	12/07/2006	Pass 70 to 80%

For further enquiries contact the center on: ExamhintsRecords@Examhints.co.uk
quoting your candidate number (Candidate4) or visit our website http://www.examhints.com

Thank You.

CERTIFICATE

Reporting Requirement for Sample Report 1

- When a candidate passes the following modules: RDCR201, RDCR301, RDCR401 and RDCR501, the candidate will be issued a certified professional status
- Candidates with incomplete modules are issued a report, which also outlines their current exam status.
- The title of the certificate changes depending on the candidate status: CERTIFIED/NOT CERTIFIED
- Letters to candidates with a certified status will read: 'Congratulations you have now achieved your CRCP certification, listed below are your results for individual exams taken.'
- Letters to candidates with a 'Not certified' status will read: 'Sorry you have not completed the certification path, listed below are your results for individual exams taken to date, you must complete: RDCR201, RDCR301. RDCR401 and RDCR501 to obtain the BOCP status'
- The report must be flexible, allowing users to use the same report for 'certified' candidates or 'non-certified' candidates only or both.
- The date of the exam should also be displayed as illustrated in fig 1.0, you will notice the dates are held in different columns Day, Month and Year, convert the columns to date format taking into account non-date data, i.e. 'unknown'.
- One page should be assigned to each candidate
- Insert a watermark using an image of your choice as illustrated in fig 1.1
- Create a hyperlink to the centers website and email address
- Highlight the "Fail - Retake Required" field as red

Candidate No	Exam No	Day	Month	Year	Result	Surname	First Name	Title
Candidate1	RDCR501	1	April	2006	Pass 70 to 80%	Richards	Antonia	Ms
Candidate2	RDCR501	1	May	2006	Pass 70 to 80%	Manning	Andrew	Mr
Candidate4	RDCR501	12	July	2006	Pass 70 to 80%	Pilers	Philip	Mr
Candidate4	RDCR201	12	May	2006	Pass 70 to 80%	Pilers	Philip	Mr
Candidate4	RDCR301	UNKNOWN	February	2006	Pass 70 to 80%	Pilers	Philip	Mr
Candidate4	RDCR401	12	June	2006	Pass 70 to 80%	Pilers	Philip	Mr
Candidate5	RDCR201	10	August	2006	Pass 70 to 80%	Boston	Charles	Mr
Candidate5	RDCR301	19	August	2006	Pass 70 to 80%	Boston	Charles	Mr
Candidate6	RDCR501	31	August	2006	Pass 70 to 80%	Boston	Charles	Mr
Candidate6	RDCR501	30	April	2006	Pass 70 to 80%	Stuart	Linda	Mr
Candidate6	RDCR201	13	June	2006	Pass 70 to 80%	Stuart	Linda	Mr
Candidate6	RDCR301	3	October	2006	Pass 70 to 80%	Stuart	Linda	Mr
Candidate6	RDCR401	21	June	2006	Pass 70 to 80%	Stuart	Linda	Mr
Candidate9	RDCR401	8	July	2006	Pass 70 to 80%	Stuart	Linda	Mr
Candidate9	RDCR401	5	October	2006	Pass 70 to 80%	Dogworth	Anne	Ms
Candidate9	RDCR401	22	July	2006	Pass 70 to 80%	Dogworth	Anne	Ms
Candidate9	RDCR401	1	June	2006	Pass 70 to 80%	Dogworth	Anne	Ms
Candidate9	RDCR401	3	February	2006	Pass 70 to 80%	Dogworth	Anne	Ms
Candidate9	RDCR301	8	September	2006	Pass 70 to 80%	Dogworth	Anne	Ms
Candidate9	RDCR201	11	January	2006	Pass 70 to 80%	Dogworth	Anne	Ms
Candidate9	RDCR201	23	May	2006	Pass 70 to 80%	Dogworth	Anne	Ms
Candidate9	RDCR501	3	June	2006	Pass 70 to 80%	Dogworth	Anne	Ms
Candidate9	RDCR501	4	July	2006	Pass 70 to 80%	Dogworth	Anne	Ms

Fig. 1.0

Lesson 2:

Reporting Requirements For Sample Report 2

Using the data in Fig 2.0 implement the following reporting requirements, the output report should look like the report in Fig.2.1, however the user can create a report format of their choice.

- You will notice the buyer's order date contains data which is inconsistent with a date format, extract dates only
- The quantity ordered is non-numeric, multiple the unit price by the quantity ordered to obtained the total amount due
- The background for total amount due should be set to red for total amounts less then 200 and yellow for amounts over 200

SAMPLE REPORT 2

Merchandise Name	Buyer Order No	Unit Price	Quantity Ordered	Total Amount Due	Buyer Amount Date	Convert To Date
Ball Point Pen	101151	$55.00	Four	$0	300506	
Ball Point Pen	101152	$55.00	1	$55	2308006	
Ball Point Pen	101171	$55.00	3	$165	300506	
Ball Point Pen	101172	$55.00	3	$165	300506	
Ball Point Pen	101181	$55.00	4	$220	300506	
Ball Point Pen	101182	$55.00	66	$3630	1706006	
Ball Point Pen	101201	$55.00	2	$110	21/01/2006	21/01/2006
Ball Point Pen	101202	$55.00	12	$660	21/01/2006	21/01/2006
Ball Point Pen	101221	$55.00	9	$495	21/01/2006	21/01/2006
Ball Point Pen	101222	$55.00	Seventy Six	$0		

$5500

Pentrell Clay Plates	2201	$5900	5	$29500	17/06/2006	17/06/2006
Pentrell Clay Plates	2202	$5900	1	$5900	23/08/2006	23/08/2006
Pentrell Clay Plates	2203	$5900	1	$5900	Not Recorded	
Pentrell Clay Plates	2204	$5900	1	$5900	23/08/2006	23/08/2006
Pentrell Clay Plates	2205	$5900	14	$82600	080806	
Pentrell Clay Plates	2206	$5900	56	$330400	080806	

$460,200.00

Buyer Order No	Merchandise Name	Unit Price	Quantity Ordered	Merchandise Class	Buyer Order Date
101151	Ball Point Pen	55.00	Four	Pen	300506
101152	Ball Point Pen	55.00	1	Pen	2308006
101171	Ball Point Pen	55.00	3	Pen	300506
101172	Ball Point Pen	55.00	3	Pen	300506
101181	Ball Point Pen	55.00	4	Pen	300506
101182	Ball Point Pen	55.00	66	Pen	1706006
101201	Ball Point Pen	55.00	1	Pen	21/06/2006
101202	Ball Point Pen	55.00	12	Pen	21/06/2006
101221	Ball Point Pen	55.00	9	Pen	21/06/2006
101222	Ball Point Pen	55.00	Seventy Six	Pen	NULL
2201	Pentrell Clay Plates	5900	5	Plates	17/06/2006
2202	Pentrell Clay Plates	5900	1	Plates	23/08/2006
2203	Pentrell Clay Plates	5900	1	Plates	Not Recorded
2204	Pentrell Clay Plates	5900	1	Plates	23/08/2006
2205	Pentrell Clay Plates	5900	14	Plates	080806
2206	Pentrell Clay Plates	5900	56	Plates	080806

Lesson 3:

Sample Report 3

Estate Agent Scenario

The following section presents a case scenario based on an Estate Agent's database. Using the Entity Relationship illustrated in this section and the sample data the following requirements can be completed

Reporting Requirements for Sample Report 3: Create Property Alert Report

Using the fictional data in the tables provided, create a report which alerts Agents to properties within a buyers price range when buyers make enquiries about new properties; the report will prompt the Agent for the buyers name\buyers ID and an alert will appear which will display properties which meets the Buyer's criteria.

Below is a report created by the Author, the reader can follow the same style format or create one of their own choice using their preferred logo and images.

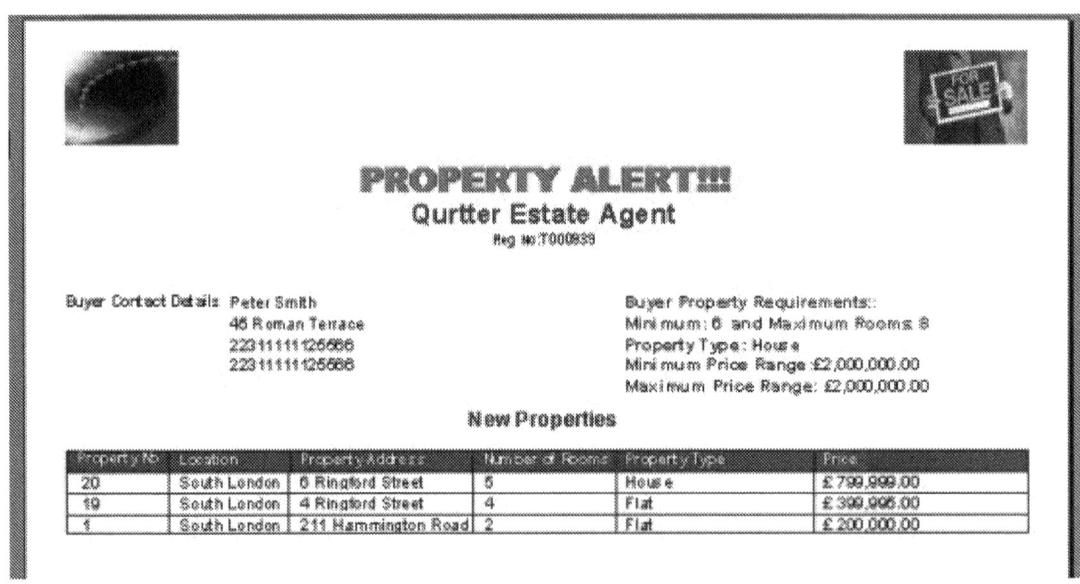

PROPERTY ALERT!!!
Qurtter Estate Agent
Reg no:T000839

Buyer Contact Details: Peter Smith
46 Roman Terrace
223111111125686
223111111125686

Buyer Property Requirements::
Minimum: 6 and Maximum Rooms: 8
Property Type: House
Minimum Price Range :£2,000,000.00
Maximum Price Range: £2,000,000.00

New Properties

Property No	Location	Property Address	Number of Rooms	Property Type	Price
20	South London	6 Ringford Street	5	House	£ 799,999.00
19	South London	4 Ringford Street	4	Flat	£ 399,995.00
1	South London	211 Hammington Road	2	Flat	£ 200,000.00

Q10. What condition will create an alert for all the buyer's requirements and where should it be placed?

Q11. You have created a report which alerts the Agent to properties within a Buyer's criteria, which properties will appear when the report is run for Buyer BRY009?

Q12. Which properties must be set for the Property Alert to work?

Q13. Your Property Alert does not work when you run the report, what could be the cause?

Estate Agents Case Scenario

- Agents can work with more than one Estate Agents Branch
- Properties for Sale can be registered with more than one Branch
- Buyers can be registered with more than one Estate Agents Branch
- One Vender can have more than one property up for sale
- Buyers can view a property more than once

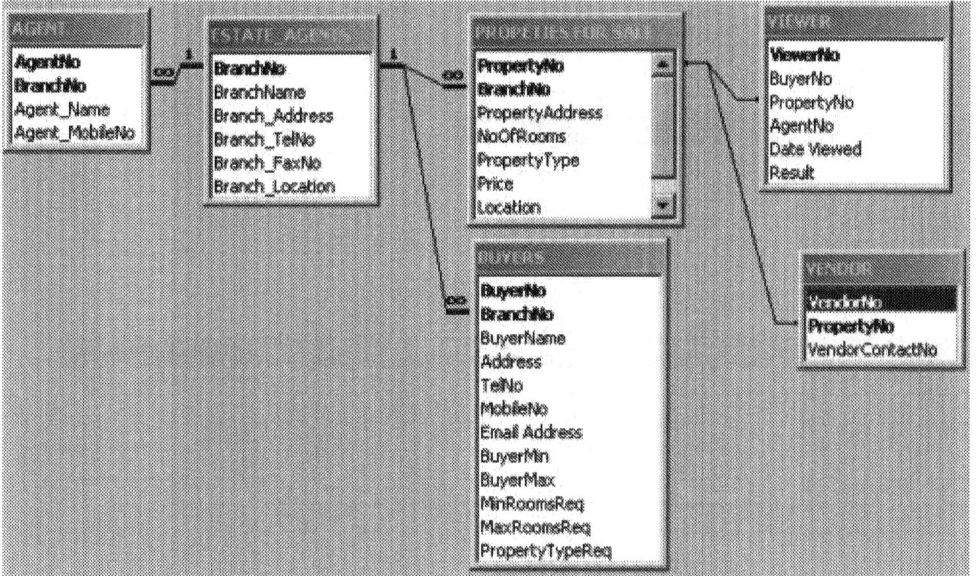

Tables

Listed below are the tables and data for the Estate Agents scenario

AgentNo	BranchNo	AgentName
A005	T000939	Shelly King
AI005	T882219	Shelly King
CR001	T009622	Coleman Rinder
EL002	T442334	Elizabeth Lyngham
JR	T631123	John Richards
MJ004	T882219	Martin Johnson
UI003	T993811	Unice Iga

BranchNo	BranchName	BranchLocation
T000939	Qurtter Estate Agents	South London
T009622	Hendson Estate Agents	North London
T442334	Rubbin Estate Agents	West London
T631123	Volyer Estate Agents	West London
T882219	Greensom Estate Agents	South London
T993811	Rubbin Estate Agents	East London

ViewerNo	BuyerNo	PropertyNo	AgentNo	Date Viewed	Result
VR001	BRY002	1	AI005	01/01/2006	Second Viewing Required
VR002	BRY002	1	AI005	01/01/2006	Sold
VR004	BRY003	6	CR001	07/03/2006	Not Suitable
VR005	BRY003	11	MJ004	23/02/2006	Not Suitable
VR566	BRY600	19	UI003		Sold
VR600	BRY711	23	CR001		Sold
VR601	BRY711	23	CR001		Second Viewing Required

Properties for Sale

PROPETIES FOR SALE : Table

PropertyNo	BranchNo	PropertyAddress	NoOfRooms	PropertyType	MaximumPrice	Location
1	T000939	211 Hammington Road	2	Flat	£200,000.00	South London
19	T000939	4 Ringford Street	4	Flat	£399,995.00	South London
20	T000939	6 Ringford Street	5	House	£799,999.00	South London
3	T009622	18 Lockford Avenue	6	House	£159,000.00	North London
9	T009622	78 Ashley Road	1	Flat	£890,000.00	North London
12	T009622	3 Westrind Road	3	Flat	£225,255.00	North London
13	T009622	8 Grove Terrac	2	Flat	£223,300.00	North London
14	T009622	778 Millfoot Road	3	House	£500,000.00	South London
23	T009622	4 Lower Road	1	Studio	£50,000.00	North London
7	T442334	77 Westtin Ryley	8	House	£6,500,000.00	West London
15	T442334	55 Goodge Road	1	Studio	£99,000.00	West London
22	T442334	5 2 Goodge Road	6	House	£1,900,000.00	West London
5	T631123	2 Goodge Road	4	Flat	£700,000.00	West London
11	T631123	22 Gillingham Road	3	House	£899,995.00	West London
17	T631123	34 Gillingham Road	1	Studio	£70,000.00	West London
18	T631123	4 Gillingham Road	1	Studio	£60,000.00	West London
2	T882219	90 Ringford Street	3	House	£456,667.00	South London
21	T882219	32a Ringford Street	6	House	£234,567.00	South London
4	T993811	88 Pennington Road	2	House	£240,000.00	East London
6	T993811	4 Hamilford Avenue	6	House	£1,000,000.00	East London
8	T993811	45 Romgon Road	4	Flat	£776,665.00	East London
10	T993811	555 Fullingham Terrace	2	Flat	£105,995.00	East London
16	T993811	8 Hamilford Avenue	1	Studio	£89,995.00	East London
AutoNumber)					£0.00	

BUYERS : Table

BuyerNo	BranchNo	Address	BuyerMin	BuyerMax	MinRoom	MaxRoom	PropertyType
BRY002	T000939	1 Windsor Aver	£200,000.00	£200,000.00	2	2	Flat
BRY002	T882219	1 Windsor Aver	£200,000.00	£200,000.00	2	2	Flat
BRY003	T000939	45 Roman Terr	£2,000,000.00	£2,000,000.00	6	8	House
BRY005	T442334	89 Glengold Ro	£150,000.00	£199,999.00	2	2	Flat
BRY007	T631123	90 Yardley Roa	£200,000.00	£250,000.00	2	2	Any
BRY008	T442334	34 Finchley Str	£300,000.00	£378,900.00	4	4	House
BRY009	T631123	7 Vandover Ro	£1,000,000.00	£1,995,555.00	4	7	House
BRY600	T442334	9 Goodgeford A	£400,000.00	£499,995.00	2	5	Any
BRY711	T009622	2 Ludgate Cour	£70,000.00	£80,000.00	1	1	Any
BRY777	T442334	44 Collier Road	£8,990,000.00	£8,990,000.00	7	4	House
BRY825	T993811	6 Robin Street	£5,000,000.00	£7,000,000.00	8	8	House
BRY989	T631123	6 Fulhampton F	£99,000.00	£100,000.00	2	2	Any
BRY990	T442334	13 Hamilton Ro	£450,000.00	£600,000.00	5	6	House

VENDOR : Table

VendorNo	PropertyNo	VendorContactNo
VEN1	1	00011145582274
VEN10	16	00011475599554
VEN11	17	44447800014441
VEN12	22	00127956520001
VEN13	15	44478892000001
VEN14	19	12348522697744
VEN2	2	11585788852522
VEN20	20	77747888844477
VEN211	8	00012477895555
VEN22	14	44522228777471
VEN278	12	11257774778551
VEN3	3	75652441455554
VEN32	9	44487447755444
VEN4	5	77754444441155
VEN5	4	75555887777777
VEN55	11	77784444112300
VEN6	6	44400001444444
VEN66	10	11440000147441
VEN7	7	11111777777000
VEN8	21	03300012210000
VEN89	13	00258852229555
VEN9	18	01122100220100

Lesson 4:

Reports Developer's can use the Add command section within the Database Expert to create a SQL Command, in this lesson the reader will utilize this functionality to meet the requirements outlined below.

Properties for Sale

PROPETIES FOR SALE : Table

PropertyNo	BranchNo	PropertyAddress	NoOfRooms	PropertyType	MaximumPrice	Location
1	T000939	211 Hammington Road	2	Flat	£200,000.00	South London
19	T000939	4 Ringford Street	4	Flat	£399,995.00	South London
20	T000939	6 Ringford Street	5	House	£799,999.00	South London
3	T009622	18 Lockford Avenue	6	House	£159,000.00	North London
9	T009622	78 Ashley Road	1	Flat	£890,000.00	North London
12	T009622	3 Westrind Road	3	Flat	£225,255.00	North London
13	T009622	8 Grove Terrac	2	Flat	£223,300.00	North London
14	T009622	778 Millfoot Road	3	House	£500,000.00	South London
23	T009622	4 Lower Road	1	Studio	£50,000.00	North London
7	T442334	77 Westtin Ryley	8	House	£6,500,000.00	West London
15	T442334	55 Goodge Road	1	Studio	£99,000.00	West London
22	T442334	5 2 Goodge Road	6	House	£1,900,000.00	West London
5	T631123	2 Goodge Road	4	Flat	£700,000.00	West London
11	T631123	22 Gillingham Road	3	House	£899,995.00	West London
17	T631123	34 Gillingham Road	1	Studio	£70,000.00	West London
18	T631123	4 Gillingham Road	1	Studio	£60,000.00	West London
2	T882219	90 Ringford Street	3	House	£456,667.00	South London
21	T882219	32a Ringford Street	6	House	£234,567.00	South London
4	T993811	88 Pennington Road	2	House	£240,000.00	East London
6	T993811	4 Hamilford Avenue	6	House	£1,000,000.00	East London
8	T993811	45 Romgon Road	4	Flat	£776,665.00	East London
10	T993811	555 Fullingham Terrace	2	Flat	£105,995.00	East London
16	T993811	8 Hamilford Avenue	1	Studio	£89,995.00	East London
AutoNumber)					£0.00	

ViewerNo	BuyerNo	PropertyNo	AgentNo	Date Viewed	Result
VR001	BRY002	1	AI005	01/01/2006	Second Viewing Required
VR002	BRY002	1	AI005	01/01/2006	Sold
VR004	BRY003	6	CR001	07/03/2006	Not Suitable
VR005	BRY003	11	MJ004	23/02/2006	Not Suitable
VR566	BRY600	19	UI003		Sold
VR600	BRY711	23	CR001		Sold
VR601	BRY711	23	CR001		Second Viewing Required

Reporting Requirements for SQL Command

Q14. Using a SQL Command create a query to extract Sold and Unsold Properties, add a field to the query named 'property status' this field should be populated with 'Sold Subject to Contract' if the result in the Viewers table is 'Sold' and 'Property For Sale' if the result in the viewer table is 'Unsold'. How would you apply this requirement?

Q15. How can you edit the SQL Command to include a parameter, which prompts the user for a property location?

Q16. How can you assign a logical name to a SQL Command within the Database Expert?

Q17. How can you add more values to the SQL Command Default Values parameter?

Q18. How can you add a SQL Command to the Repository?

Q19. When adding fields to a report, which section should be your main work area?

A. Design Section

B. Preview Section

Answers: Chapter 1: Report Settings and Options

Q1 Answer: D
Q2 Answer: E
Q3. Answer: ABCDE

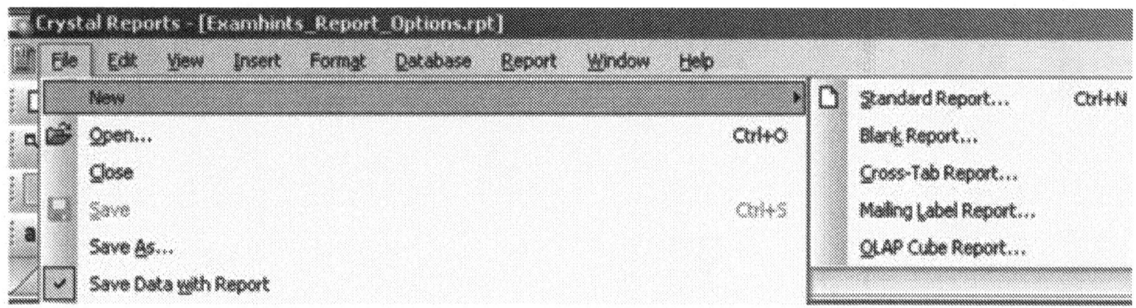

Q4: Answer: A
Q5 Answer: E
Q6 Answer: E
Q7 Answer: ABCDE

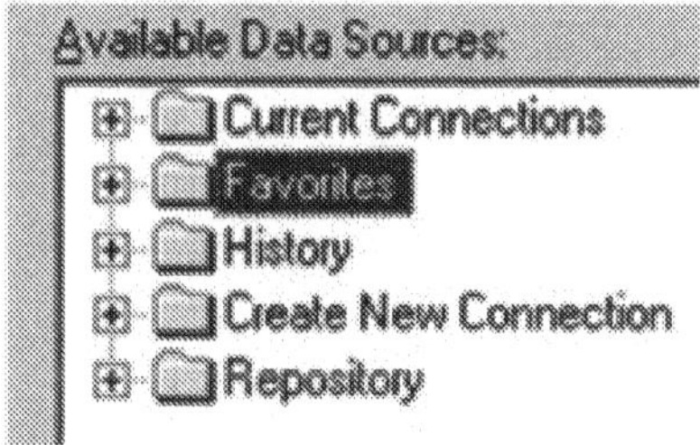

Q8 Answer: D

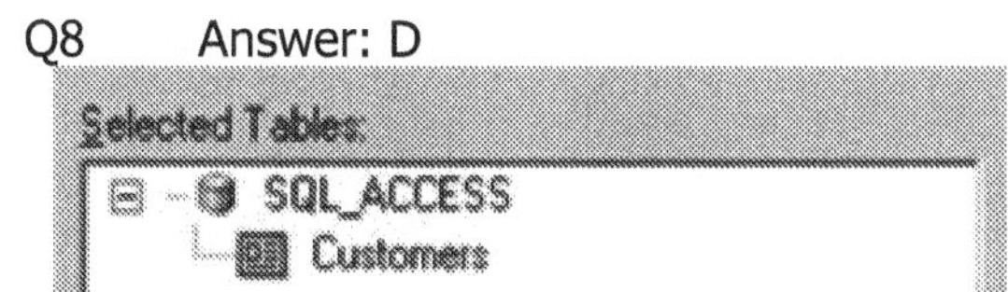

Q9 Answer: B

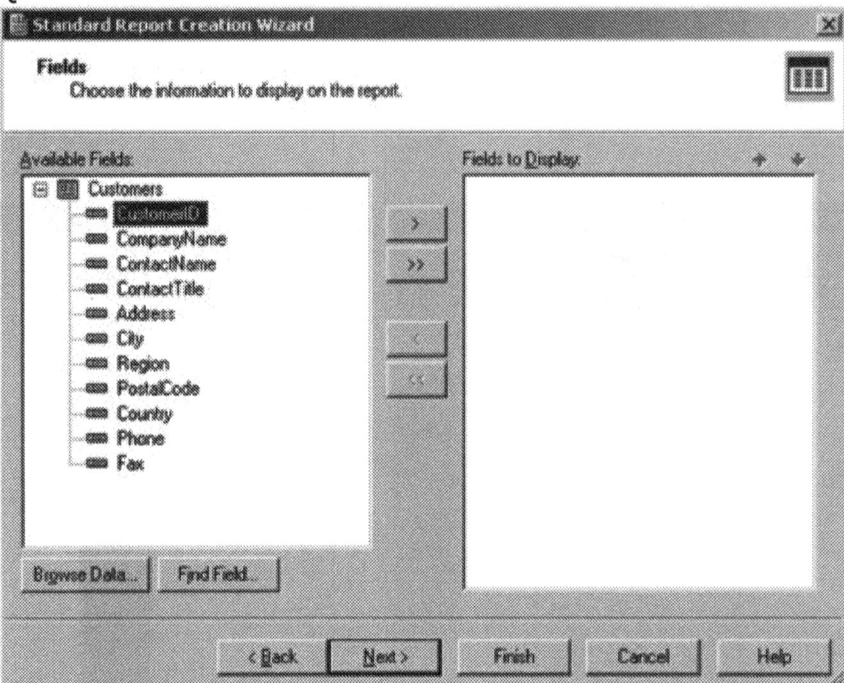

Q10 Answer: E

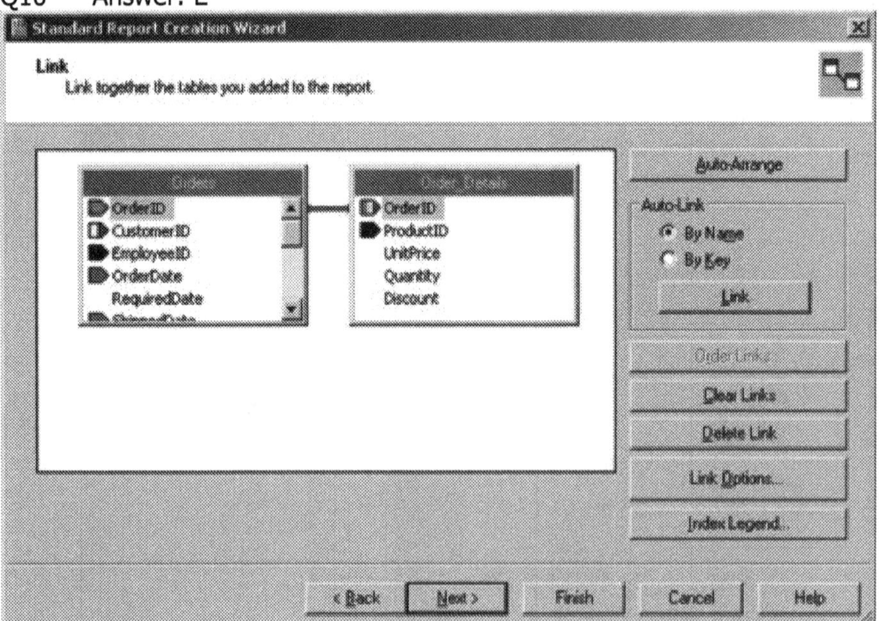

Q11 Answer: E
Q12 Answer: ABCDE
Q13 Answer: ABCDE

Q14 Answer: ACDE

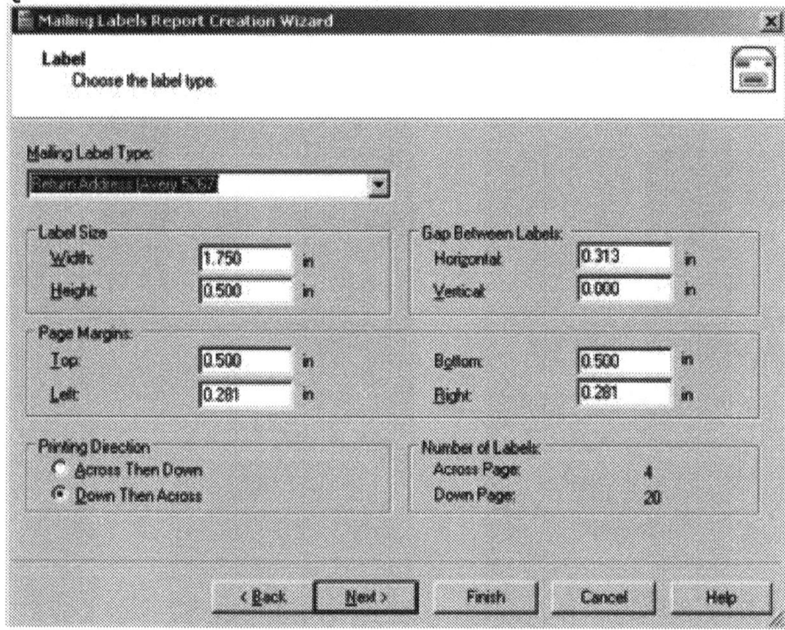

Q15: Answer: AD

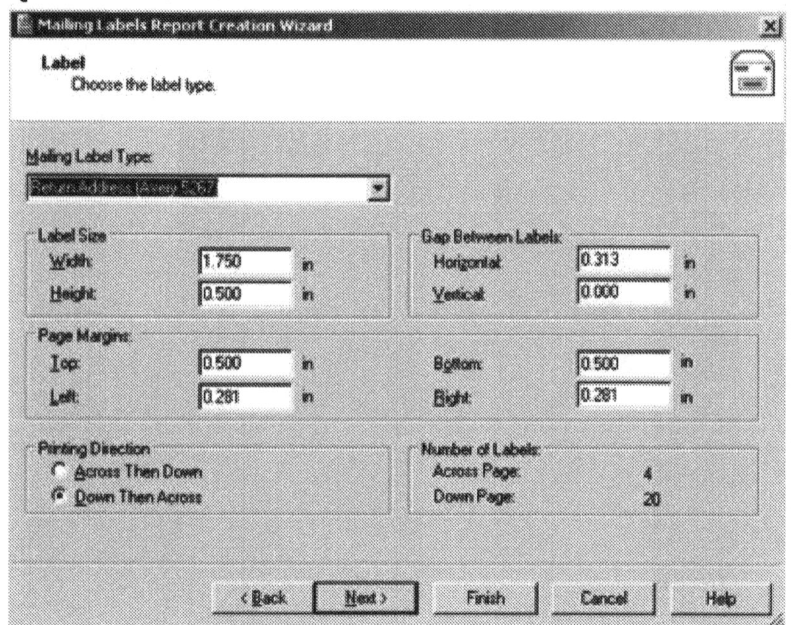

Q16: Answer: ABCD

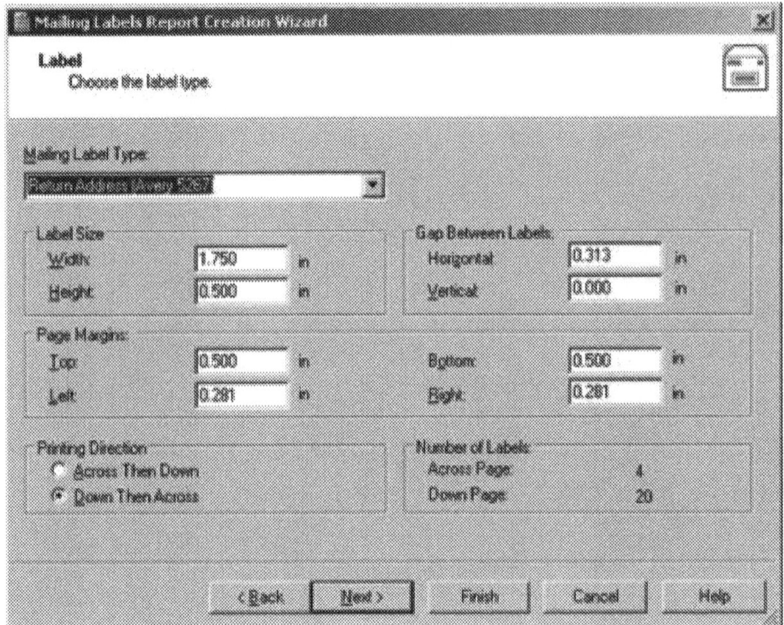

Q17: Answer: AB
Q18: Answer: A
Q19: Answer: D
Q20: Answer: EF
Q21: Answer: ABCDFGHIJ
Q22: Answer: B
Q23: Answer: ABDE
Q24: Answer: E
Q25: Answer: BE
Q26: Answer: AC
Q27: Answer: B
Q28: Answer: D
Q29: Answer: B
Q30: Answer:C
Q31: Answer: D
Q32: Answer: EG
Q33: Answer: A
Q34: Answer: B
Q35: Answer: B
Q36: Answer: B
Q37: Answer: B
Q38: Answer: AB
Q39: Answer: BC
Q40: Answer: D
Q41: Answer: BC
Q42: Answer: D
Q43: Answer: A

Q44: Answer: C

Database Explorer Options

Show:
Tables
Views
System Tables
Synonyms
Stored Procedures

Table name LIKE: (%,_)
Owner LIKE: (%,_)
Maximum Number of Tables: 8000

List Tables and Fields by:
Name
Description
Both

Sorting:
Sort Tables Alphabetically

OK
Cancel

Q45: Answer: ABEFGHI

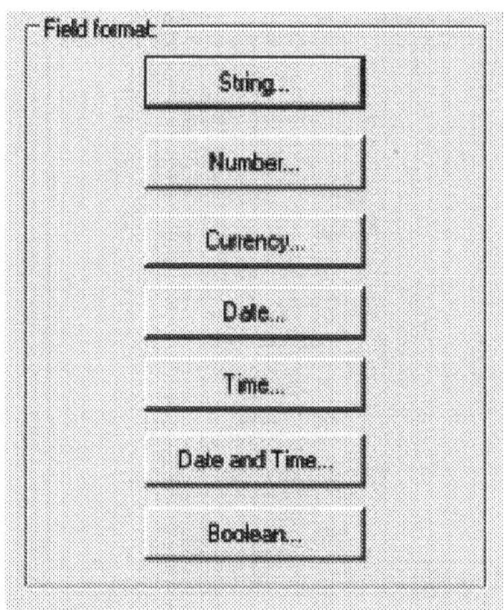

Q46: Answer: BCFGH
Q47: Answer: BCDF
Q48: Answer: C
Q49: Answer: D
Q50: Answer: AD
Q51: Answer: A
Q52: Answer: C
Q53: Answer: B
Q54: Answer: ABFG
Q55: Answer: B
Q56: Answer: B
Q57: Answer: ABC
Q58: Answer: D

Q59: Answer: D

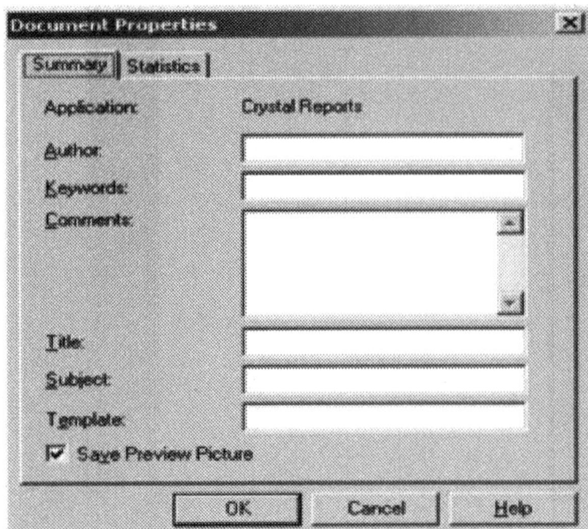

Q60: Answer: D
Q61: Answer: C

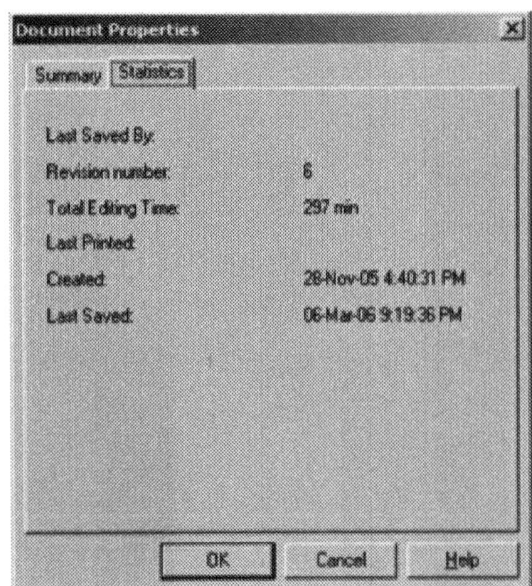

Q62: Answer: B
Q63: Answer: C
Q64: Answer: BC
Q65: Answer: B
Q66: Answer: A
Q67: Answer: C
Q68: Answer: D
Q69: Answers: B
Q70: Answer: C
Q71: Answer: D

Answers: Chapter 2 **Creating a Datasource**

Q1. Answer: A
Q2. Answer: B

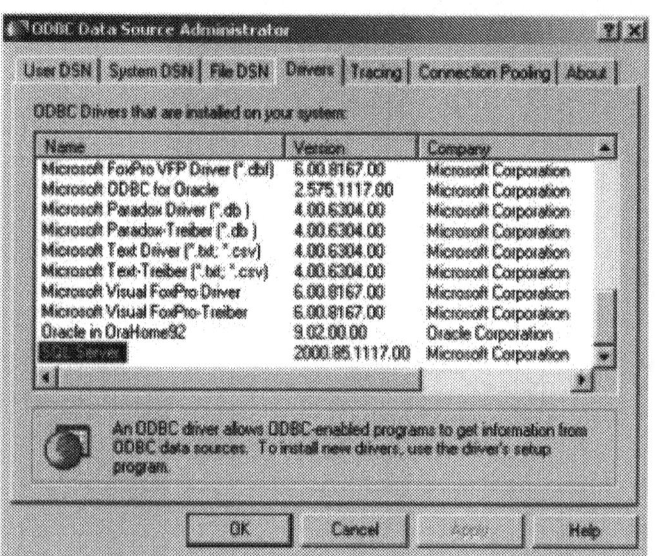

Q3. Answer: C

Q4. Answer: A

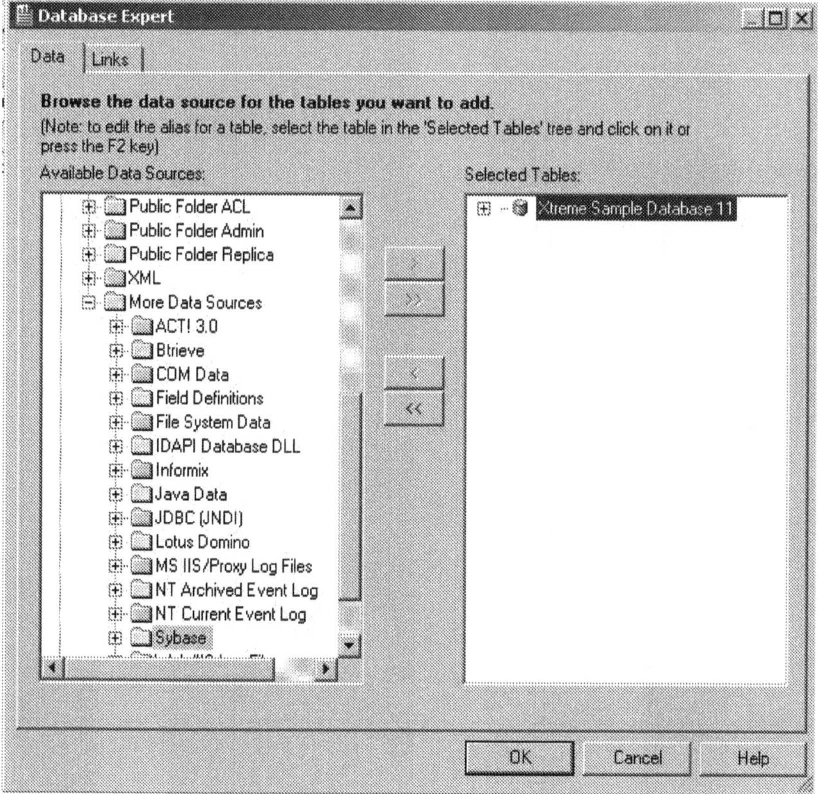

Q5. Answer: ABCDEFG
Q6. Answer: ABCD
Q7. Answer: ABCDEG

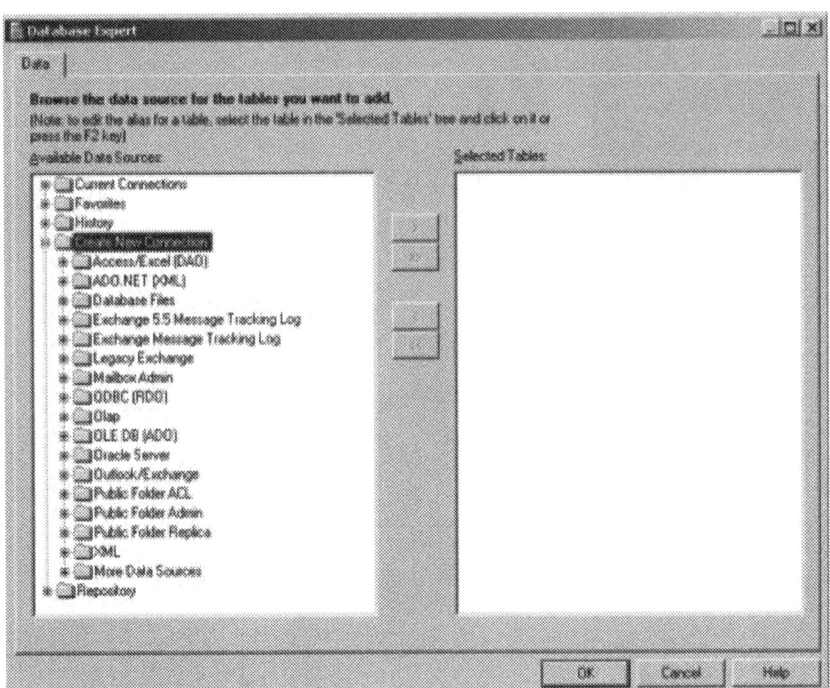

Q8. Answer: C

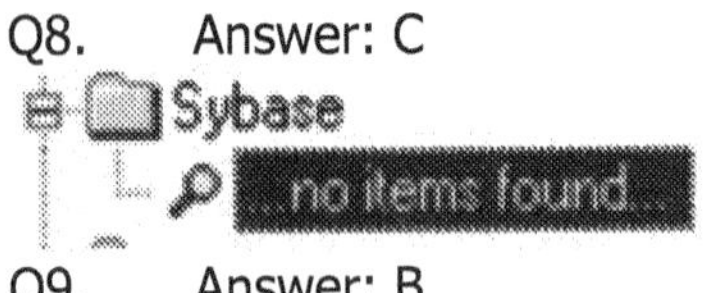

Q9. Answer: B
Q10. Answer: ABCDF

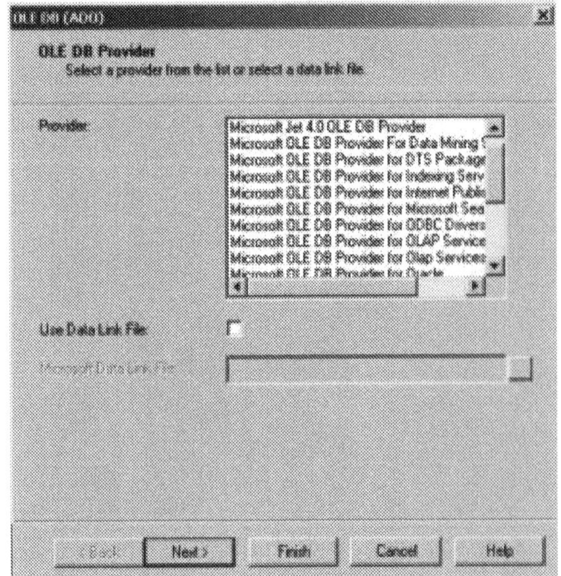

Q11. Answer: D
Q12. Answer: A

Q13. Answer: C
Q14. Answer: D
Q15. Answer: A
Q16. Answer: ABC
Q17. Answer: A

Answers: Chapter 3 Database Expert

Q1: Answer: A
Q2: Answer: B
Q3: Answer: ABCDE
Q4: Answer: C
Q5: Answer: C
Q6: Answer: ACDEF
Q7: Answer: B

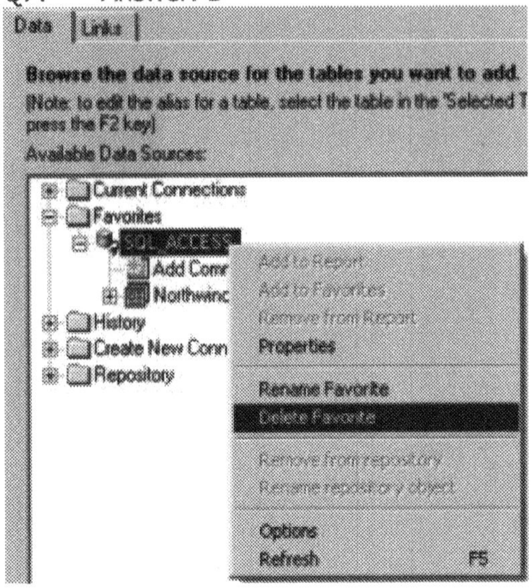

Q8: Answer: B
Q9: Answer:AC
Q10: Answer: E
Q11: Answer: A
Q12: Answer: D
Q13: Answer: A

Q14: Answer: ABC

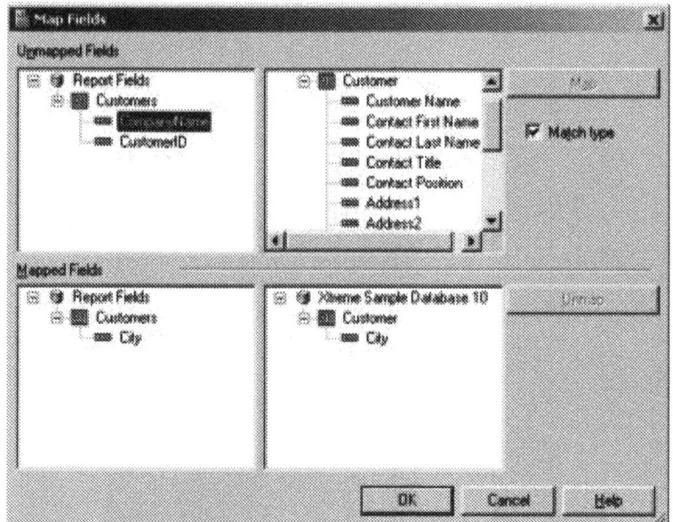

Q15: Answer: D
Q16: Answer: D
Q17: Answer: B
Q18: Answer: DE

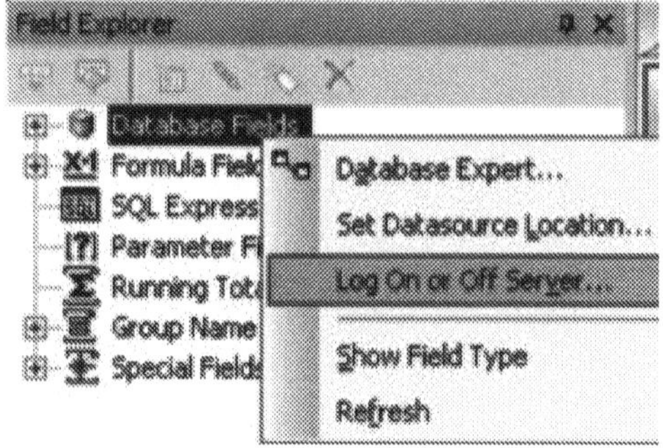

Q19: Answer: D
Q20: Answer: AB
Q21: Answer: A
Q22: Answer: ABC
Q23: Answer: ACD
Q24: Answer: C
Q25: Answer: D
Q26: Answer: B
Q27: Answer: AD
Q28: Answer: B
Q29: Answer: ABCDGH
Q30: Answer: A
Q31: Answer: E
Q32: Answer: F
Q33: Answer: C
Q34: Answer: B
Q35: Answer: D
Q36: Answer: C
Q37: Answer: C
Q38: Answer: C
Q39: Answer: D
Q40: Answer: B
Q41: Answer: B

Q42: Answer: B
Q43: Answer: A
Q44: Answer: B
Q45: Answer: BCDE
Q46: Answer: B
Q47: Answer: E
Q48: Answer: C
Q49: Answer: D
Q50: Answer: ACEF
Q51: Answer: AD
Q52: Answer: ABCD
Q53: Answer: ABCDE
Q54: Answer: BEFG
Q55: Answer: AB
Q56: Answer: A
Q57: Answer: A
Q58: Answer: D
Q59: Answer: AC
Q60: Answer: D
Q61: Answer: A
Q62: Answer: D
Q63: Answer: B
Q64: Answer: B
Q65: Answer: C
Q66: Answer: A
Q67: Answer:B

Answers: Chapter 4 Creating and Working with Formulas

Q1. Answer: AC

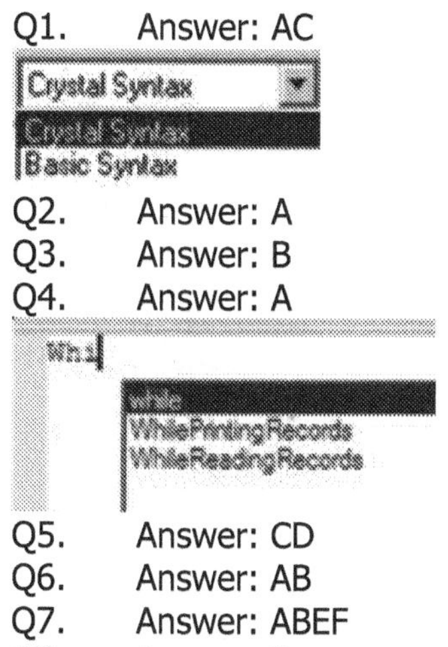

Q2. Answer: A
Q3. Answer: B
Q4. Answer: A
Q5. Answer: CD
Q6. Answer: AB
Q7. Answer: ABEF
Q8. Answer: B

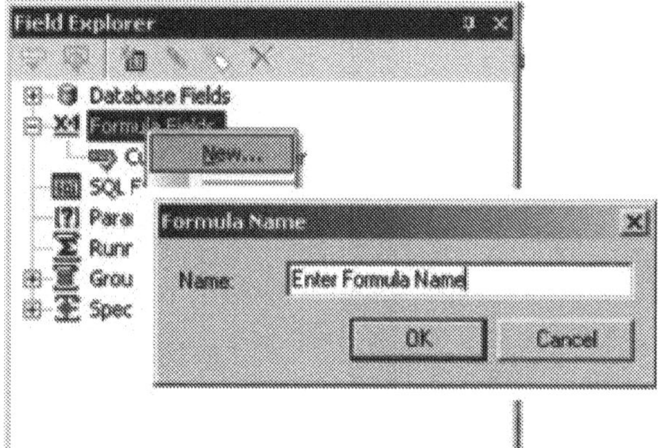

Q9. Answer: E
Q10. Answer: B

Report Area:Sum of Orders.Order Amount

Q11. Answer: C
Q12. Answer: E
Q13. Answer: F
Q14. Answer: ABE
Q15. Answer: BEFGHI
Q16. Answer: B
Q17. Answer: ABDEFGH
Q18. Answer: B

Apply Date Calculations

Q1. Answer: AE
Q2. Answer: D
Q3. Answer: CDE
Q4. Answer: ADE
Q5. Answer: B
Q6. Answer: C
Q7. Answer: C
Q8. Answer: A

Q9. Answer: B
Q10. Answer: D

Order Number 1,317 is required in 9days
Order Number 1,319 is required in 14days
Order Number 1,322 is required in 11days
Order Number 1,323 is required in 10days
Order Number 1,325 is required in 11days

Q11. Answer: B
Q12. Answer: DE
Q13. Answer: C
Q14. Answer: ABCDEFGHIJ
Q15. Answer: ADE
Q16. Answer: D

Working With Numbers

Q1. Answer: E
Q2. Answer: B
Q3. Answer: C
Q4. Answer: D

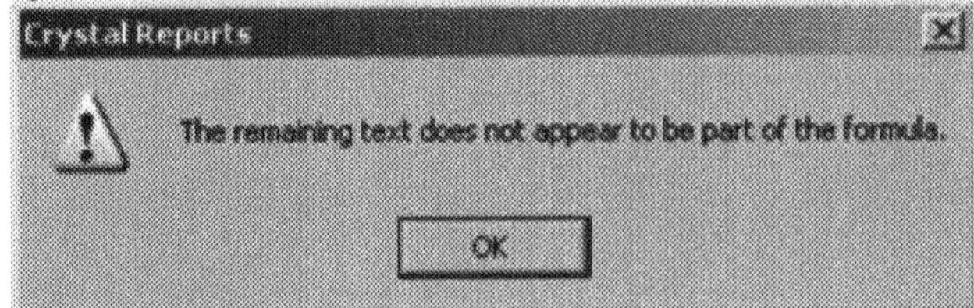

Q5. Answer: A
Q6. Answer: A
Q7. Answer: C
Q8. Answer: C
Q9. Answer: C
Q10. Answer: C
Q11. Answer: C
Q12. Answer: AB
Q13. Answer: C
Q14. Answer: D
Q15. Answer: A
Q16. Answer: D
Q17. Answer: C
Q18. Answer: D
Q19. Answer: C

Apply String Formulas

Q1. Answer: B
Q2. Answer: E
Q3. Answer: A
Q4. Answer: B
Q5. Answer: A
Q6. Answer: C

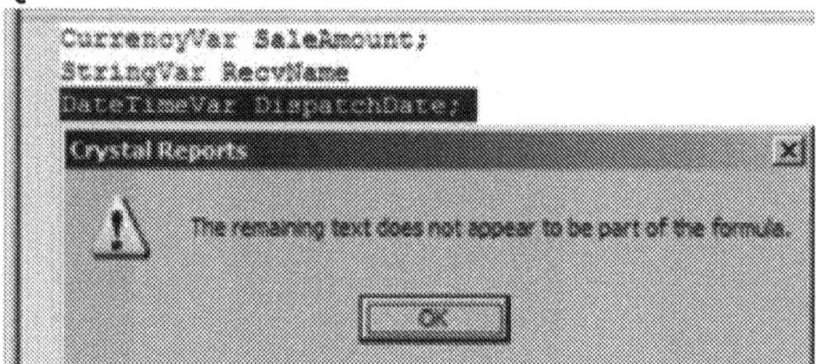

Q7. Answer: D
Q8. Answer: E

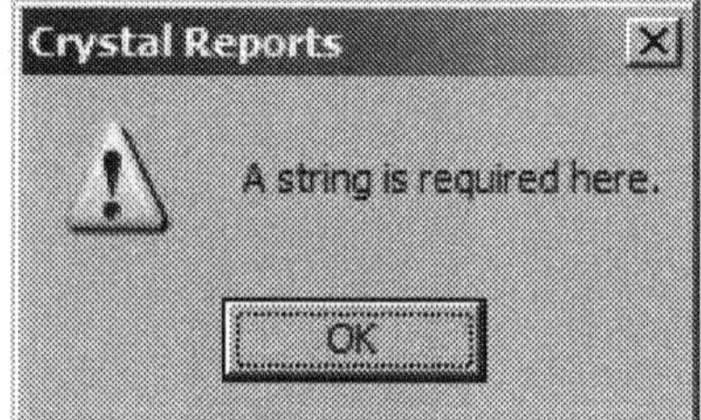

Q9. Answer: AEF
Q10. Answer: ADE
Q11. Answer: A
Q12. Answer: AB
Q13. Answer: C
Q14. Answer: C
Q15. Answer: A
Q16. Answer: ABCD

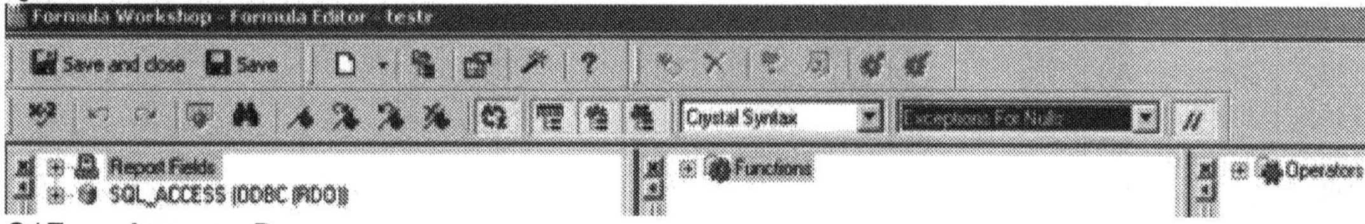

Q17. Answer: B
Q18. Answer: C
Q19. Answer: C
Q20. Answer: BEF
Q21. Answer: D
Q22. Answer: B
Q23. Answer: AB

Using Functions – Crystal Financial Functions

Q1. Answer: B
Q2. Answer: B
Q3. Answer: B
Q4. Answer: A
Q5. Answer: D
Q6. Answer: E
Q7. Answer: A
Q8. Answer: AC
Q9. Answer: C
Q10. Answer: A
Q11. Answer: B
Q12. Answer: B
Q13. Answer: B
Q14. Answer: B
Q15. Answer: E
Q16. Answer: F
Q17. Answer: A
Q18. Answer: D
Q19. Answer: C
Q20. Answer: A
Q21. Answer: A
Q22. Answer: B
Q23. Answer: F
Q24. Answer: A
Q25. Answer: A
Q26. Answer: G
Q27. Answer: B
Q28. Answer: B
Q29. Answer: A
Q30. Answer: B
Q31. Answer: D
Q32. Answer: E
Q33. Answer: D
Q34. Answer: C
Q35. Answer: A
Q36. Answer: B
Q37. Answer: A
Q38. Answer: C
Q39. Answer: A
Q40. Answer: A
Q41. Answer: E
Q42. Answer: CDF
Q43. Answer: ABC

Working With Null Values

Q1. Answer: A
Q2. Answer: ABC
Q3. Answer: C
Q4. Answer: B

Q5. Answer: D
Q6. Answer: A
Q7. Answer: BC
Q8. Answer: B

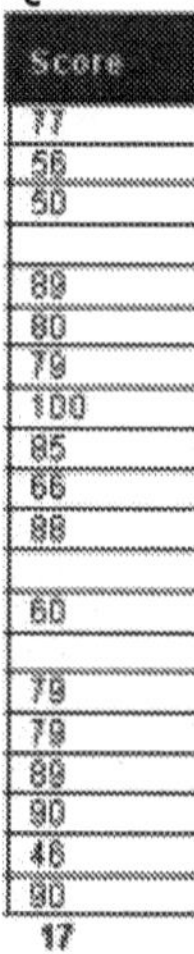

Score
77
56
50
89
80
79
100
85
66
88
60
79
79
89
90
46
90
17

Arrays

Q1. Answer: B
Q2. Answer: B
Q3. Answer: A
Q4. Answer: B
Q5. Answer: E

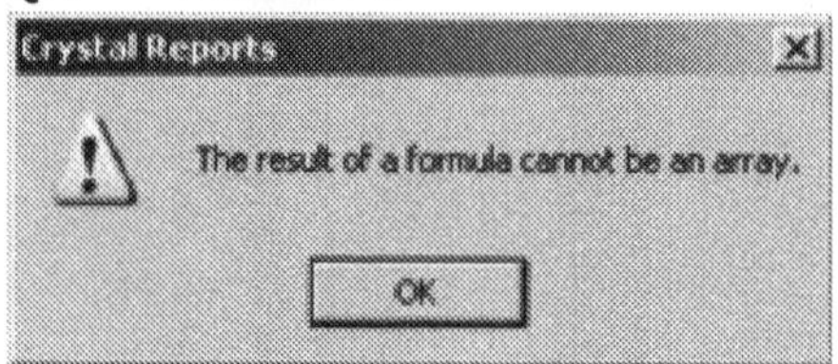

Q6. Answer: A
Q7. Answer: AB
Q8. Answer: EF
Q9. Answer: D
Q10. Answer: A
Q11. Answer: A
Q12. Answer: A
Q13. Answer: A
Q14. Answer: A
Q15. Answer: A
Q16. Answer: A
Q17. Answer: A
Q18. Answer: D
Q19. Answer: A
Q20. Answer: ABCDG
Q21. Answer: B
Q22. Answer: B
Q23. Answer: A
Q24. Answer:A

Sql Expressions

Q1. Answer: A
Q2. Answer: B
Q3. Answer: A
Q4. Answer: ABCDE
Q5. Answer: E
Q6. Answer: A
Q7. Answer: B
Q8. Answer: B
Q9. Answer: A
Q10. Answer: AB

Control Structures

Q1. Answer: DE
Q2. Answer: ABD
Q3. Answer: D
Q4. Answer: C
Q5. Answer: AB
Q6. Answer: ABCDEFGH
Q7. Answer: D
Q8. Answer: C
Q9. Answer: A

Processing A Report

Q1. Answer: ABCDG
Q2. Answer: C
Q3. Answer: B
Q4. Answer: D
Q5. Answer: A
Q6. Answer: A
Q7. Answer: C
Q8. Answer: B
Q9. Answer: D
Q10. Answer: A
Q11. Answer: A
Q12. Answer: G
Q13. Answer: E
Q14. Answer: ABCDEFHIJ
Q15. Answer: ABCD
Q16. Answer: C

Creating Report Alerts

Q1. Answer: B
Q2. Answer: AB
Q3. Answer: C
Q4. Answer: C
Q5. Answer: D

Answers: Chapter 5 Report Formatting

Q1. Answer: CE
Q2. Answer: BCD
Q3. Answer: Fixed = B. Floating =A
Q4. Answer: BC
Q5. Answer: A
Q6. Answer: A

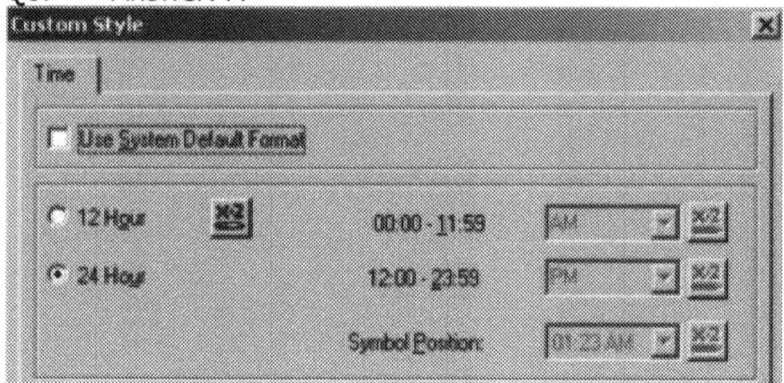

Q7. Answer: B
Q8. Answer: B
Q9. Answer: B
Q10. Answer: C
Q11. Answer: A

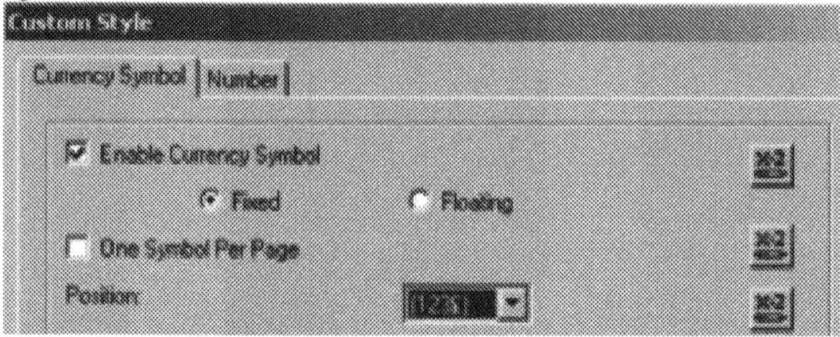

Q12. Answer: C 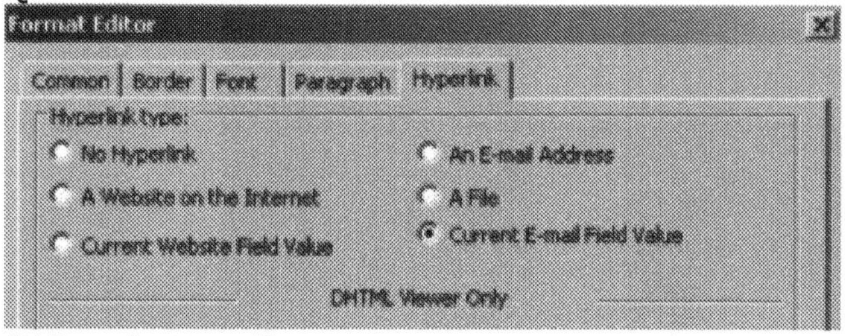
Q13. Answer: E
Q14. Answer: AF
Q15. Answer: B
Q16. Answer: B
Q17. Answer: D

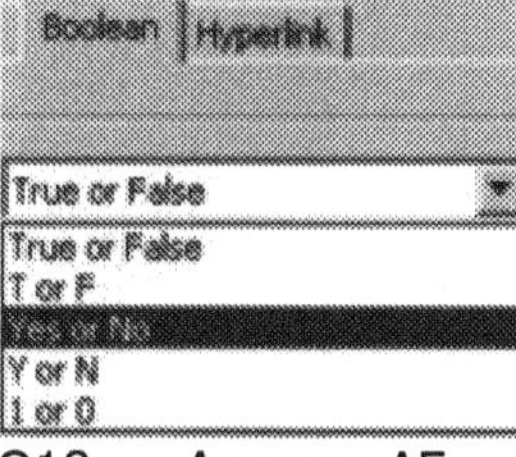

Q18. Answer: AE

Q19.Answer: A
Q20. Answer: E
Q21. Answer: C
Q22. Answer: B
Q23. Answer: A
Q24. Answer: D
Q25. Answer: C
Q26. Answer: BC
Q27. Answer: D
Q28. Answer: B
Q29. Answer: ABCDE
Q30. Answer: AB
Q31. Answer: ABCDE
Q32. Answer: A
Q33. Answer: ACD
Q34. Answer: AB
Q35. Answer: AE
Q36. Answer: A
Q37. Answer: B
Q38. Answer: C
Q39. Answer: B
Q40. Answer: E
Q41. Answer: C
Q42. Answer: E
Q43. Answer: C
Q44. Answer: A
Q45. Answer: A
Q46. Answer: C
Q47. Answer: D
Q48. Answer: A
Q49. Answer: ABC
Q50. Answer: ABCD

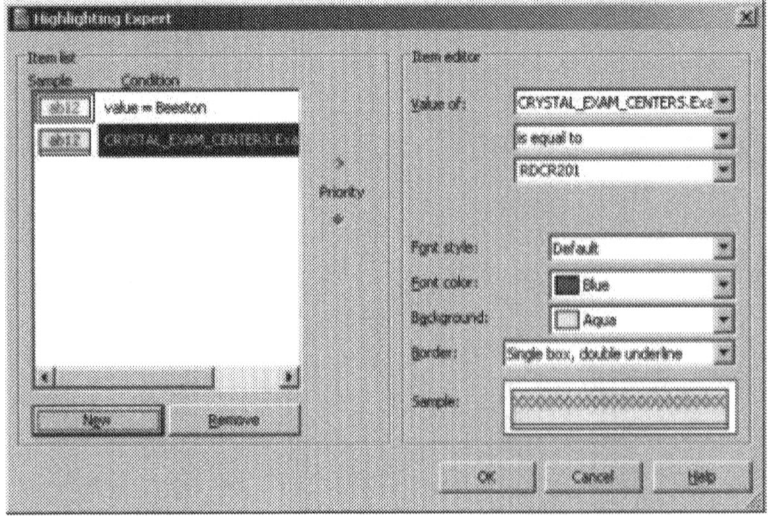

Q51. Answer: A
Q52. Answer: A

Q53. Answer: C
Q54. Answer: B
Q55. Answer: A

Creating Report Templates

Q56. Answer: B
Q57. Answer: A
Q58. Answer: AB
Q59. Answer: C

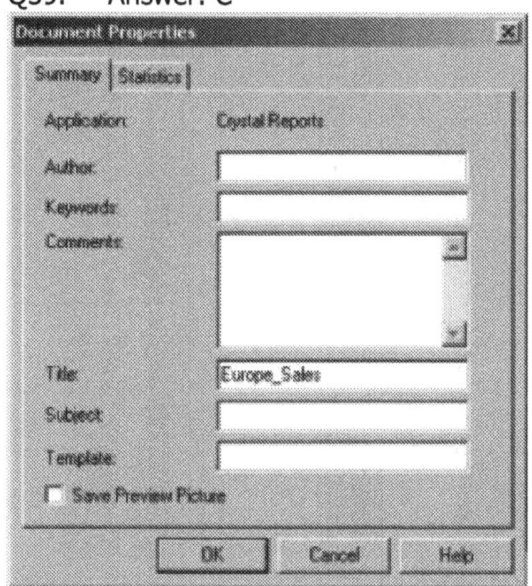

Q60. Answer: D

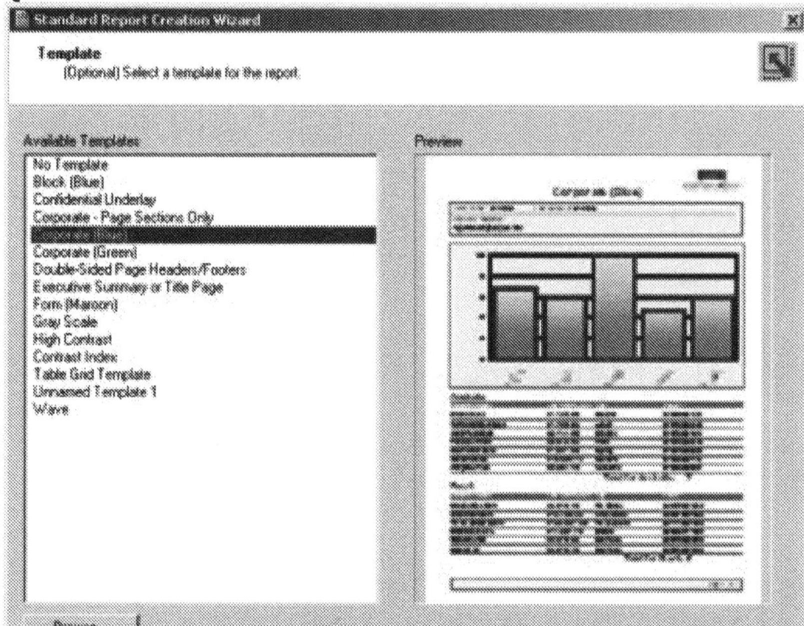

Q61. Answer: C

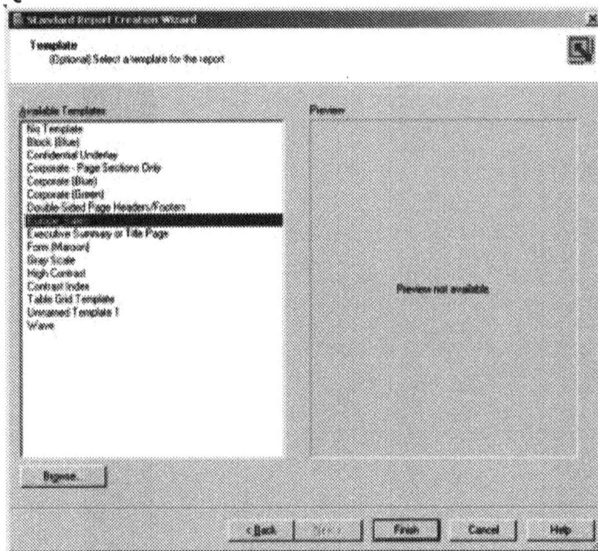

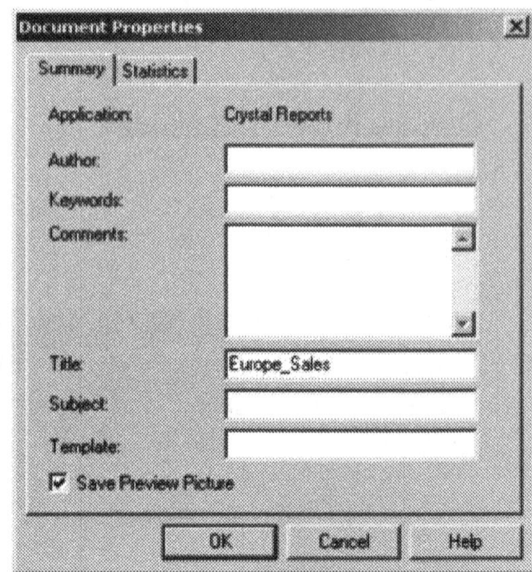

Q62. Answer: D

Q63. Answer: B

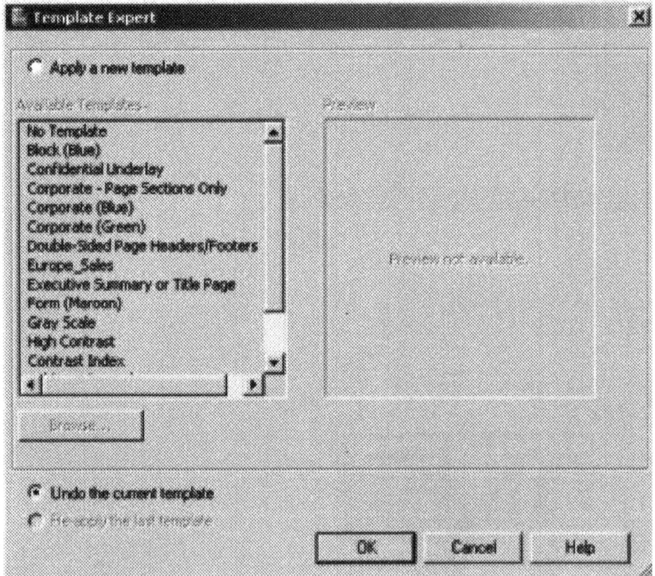

Q64. Answer: AB

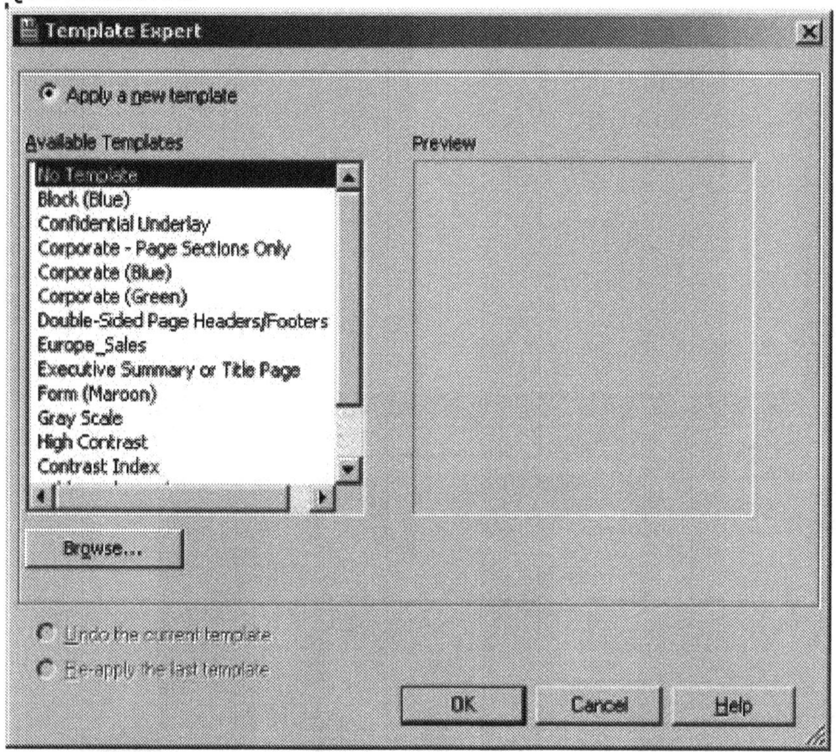

Q65. Answer: D

//Crystal Report Template Field
WhileReadingRecords;Space(10)

//Crystal Report Template Field
WhileReadingRecords;{Sample_Exam_Results___2006.EXAM_DATE}

Q66. Answer: B

Q67. Answer: D

Q68. Answer: A

Q69. Answer: B

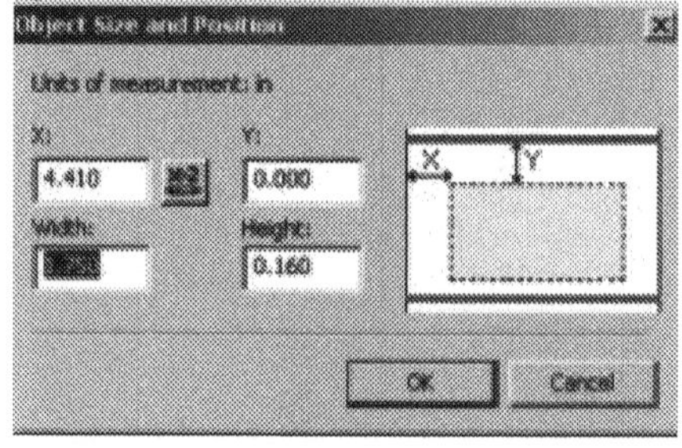

Q70. Answer: D

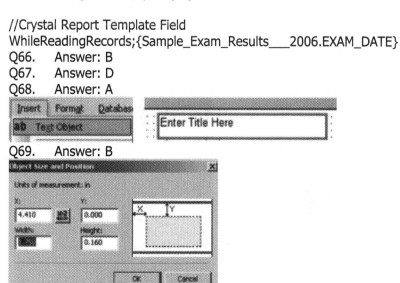

Q71. Answer: ABDEFG

Q72. Answer: A

Q73. Answer: ABCDE

Q74. Answer: A

Q75. Answer: C

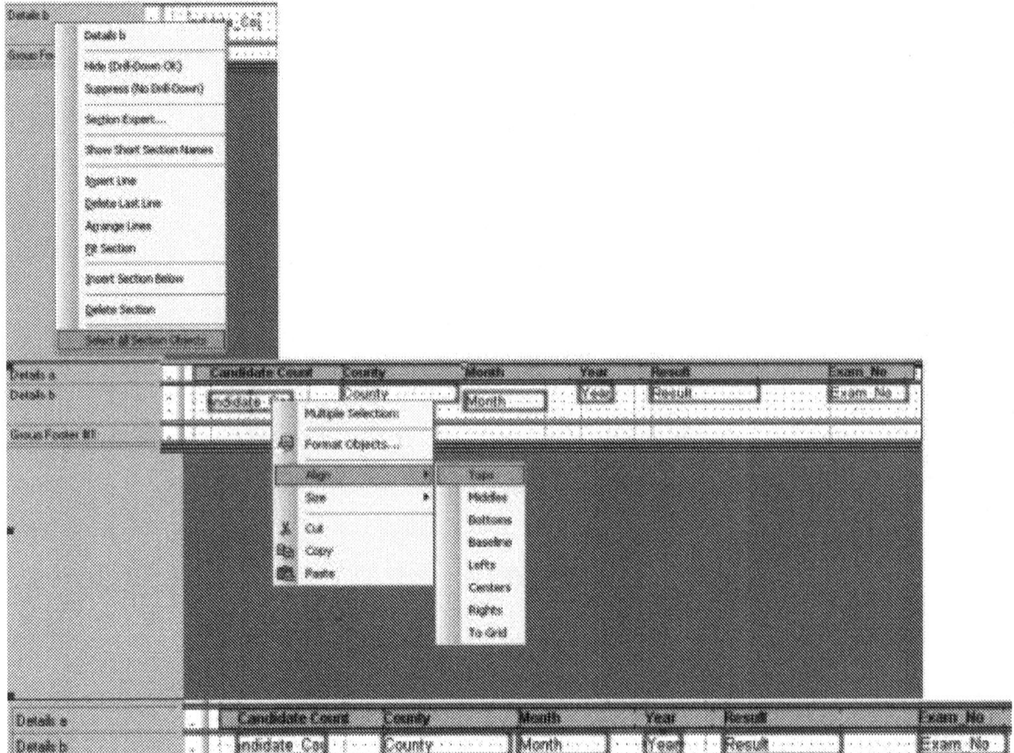

Q76. Answer: D

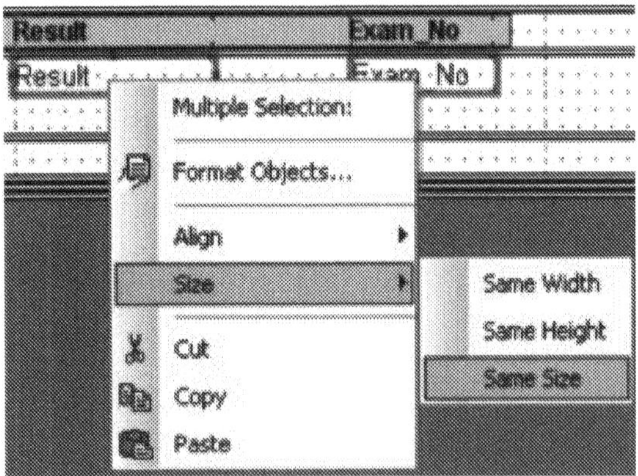

Q77.Answer: A

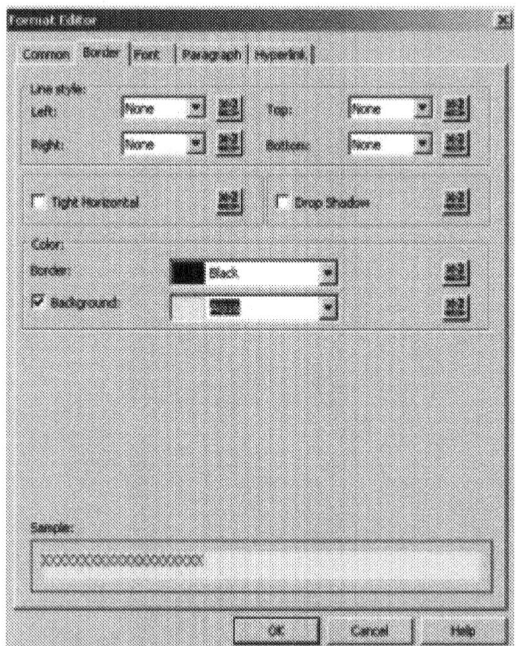

Q78: Answer: CD

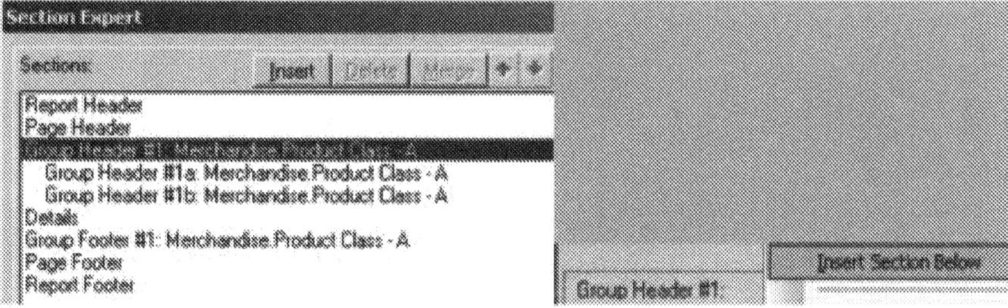

Q79: Answer: AB
Q80. Answer: C
Q81. Answer: A
Q82. Answer: B
Q83. Answer: B

Answers: Chapter 6 Using the Select Expert

Q1: Answer: C
Q2: Answer: A
Q3: Answer: C
Q4: Answer: A
Q5: Answer: D
Q6: Answer: BC
Q7: Answer: C
Q8: Answer: AC
Q9: Answer: A
Q10: Answer: C
Q11: Answer: B
Q12: Answer: CD
Q13: Answer: B
Q14: Answer: ABD
Q15: Answer: G
Q16: Answer: B
Q17: Answer: DF
Q18: Answer: D
Q19: Answer: B
Q20: Answer: A
Q21: Answer: ABC
Q22: Answer: AE

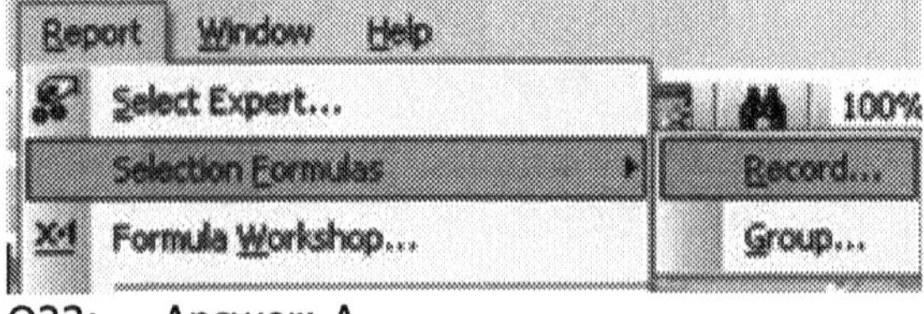

Q23: Answer: A

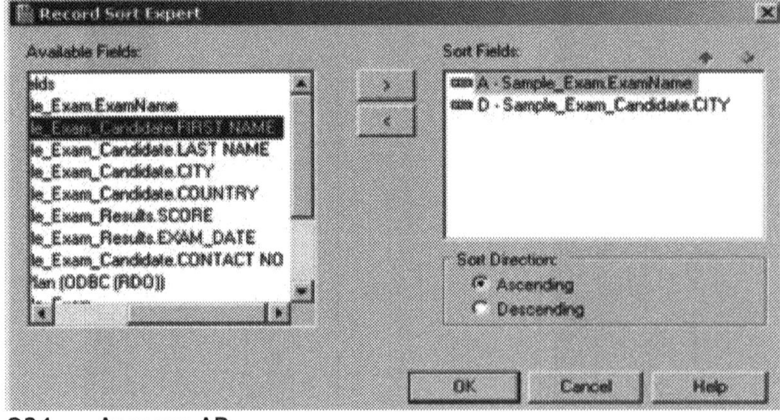

Q24: Answer: AB

Q25: Answer: D

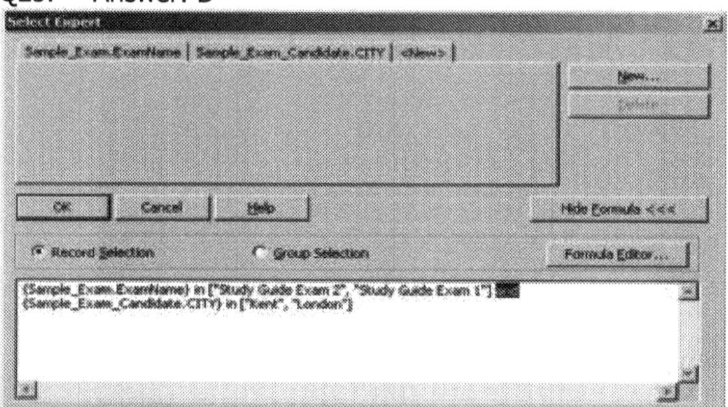

Q26. Answer: C
Q27. Answer: A
Q28. Answer: E
Q29. Answer: B
Q30. Answer: A
Q31. Answer: A

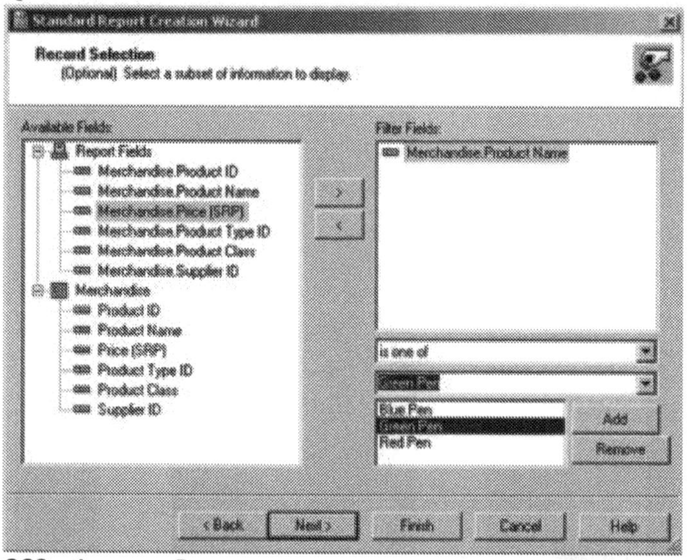

Q32. Answer: B

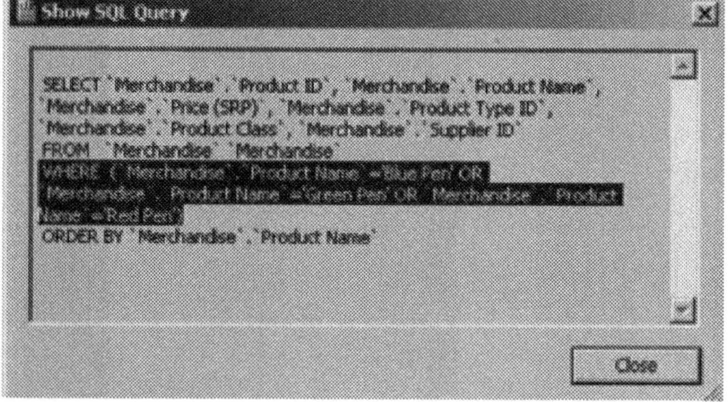

Q33. Answer: ABCE
Q34. Answer: D
Q35. Answer: AB
Q36. Answer: C

Answers: Chapter 7 Parameters

Q1: Answer: ABC
Q2: Answer: D
Q3: Answer: B
Q4: Answer: AB
Q5: Answer: D
Q6: Answer: ABCDE
Q7: Answer: D
Q8: Answer: D
Q9: Answer: D
Q10: Answer: ABC
Q11: Answer: B
Q12: Answer: D
Q13: Answer: D
Q14: Answer: C
Q15: Answer: ABDE
Q16: Answer: B
Q17: Answer: B
Q18: Answer: C
Q19: Answer: ABC
Q20: Answer: A
Q21: Answer: B
Q22: Answer: C
Q23: Answer: A
Q24: Answer: B
Q25: Answer: B
Q26: Answer: ABCE
Q27: Answer: A
Q28: Answer: C
Q29: Answer: B
Q30: Answer: A
Q31: Answer: D
Q32: Answer: ABCD
Q33: Answer: C
Q34: Answer B

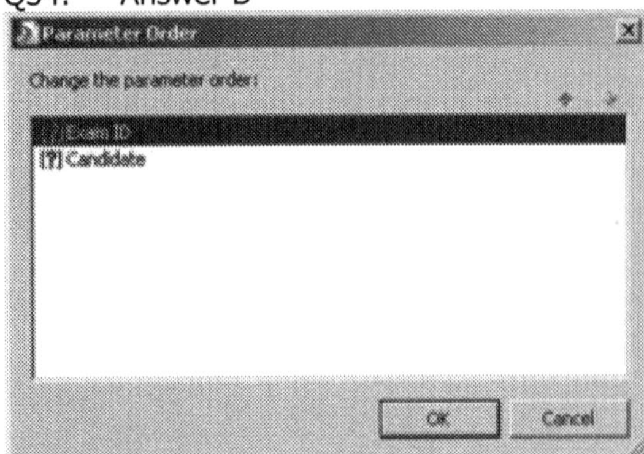

Q35 Answer ABC

Q36. Answer: A

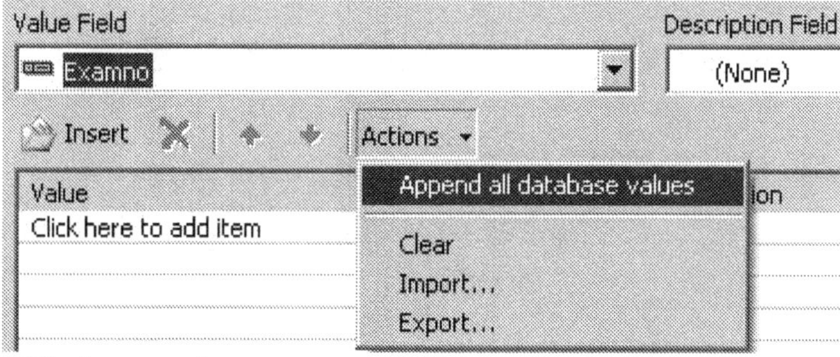

Q37. Answer: A

Q38. Answer: A

Answers: Chapter 8 Creating Groups

Q1: Answer: A

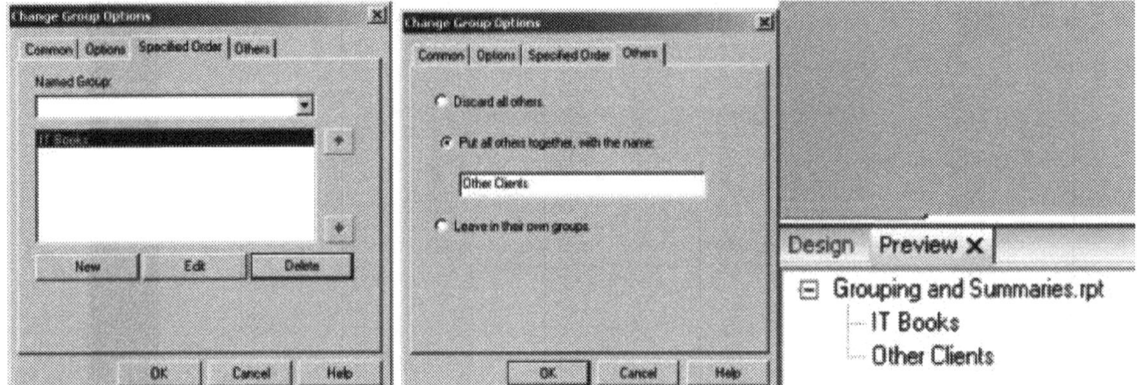

Q2: Answer: A
Q3: Answer: D
Q4: Answer: ABDEH

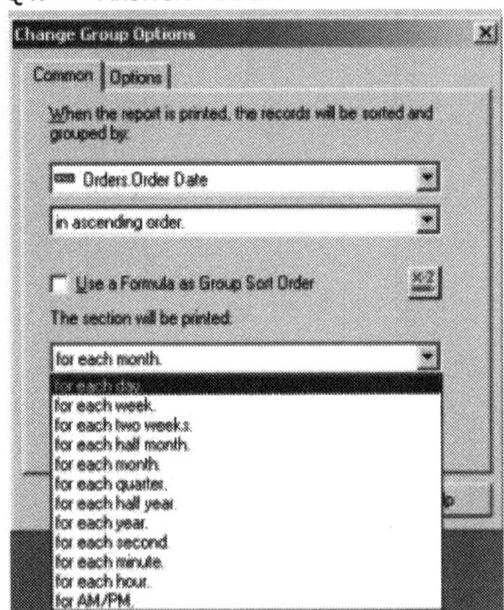

Q5: Answer: A
Q6: Answer: C

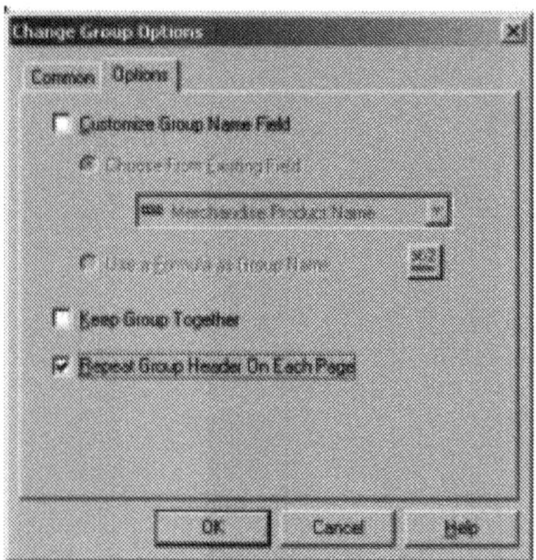

Q7: Answer: AD
Q8: Answer: B
Q9: Answer: A

Q10: Answer: A

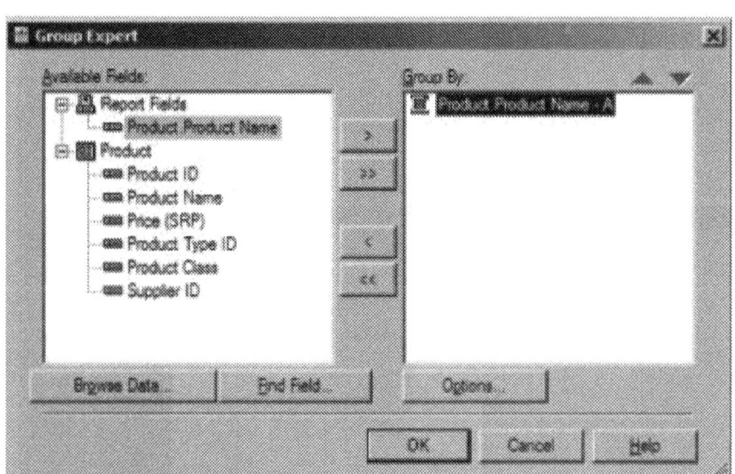

Q11: Answer: B

Details a	-
Details b	-
Details c	-

Q12: Answer: D

Product Name	Sales for Month July
Silver Rim Pen	£ 8,000.00
Gold Plated Pen	£ 7,500.00
Diamomd Pen	£ 6,000.00

Q13: Answer: B

Product Name	Sales for Month July
Silver Rim Pen	£ 8,000.00
Gold Plated Pen	£ 7,500.00
Diamomd Pen	£ 6,000.00
Others Sales for this period	£ [illegible]

Q14: Answer: C
Q15: Answer: AD
Q16: Answer: D
Q17: Answer: BH
Q18: Answer: D
Q19: Answer: A
Q20: Answer: FG
Q21: Answer: ABD

Q22: Answer: C

Product Name	Sales for Month July	
Silver Rim Pen	£ 8,000.00	
Gold Plated Pen	£ 7,500.00	
Diamomd Pen	£ 6,000.00	
Ball Point Pen	£ 5,000.00	
Bronze Plated Pen	£ 3,824.25	
Grand Total:	£ 30,324.25	£ 36,831.15

Q23: Answer: A
Q24: Answer: B
Q25: Answer: BF
Q26: Answer: C
Q27: Answer: B
Q28: Answer: C
Q29: Answer: A

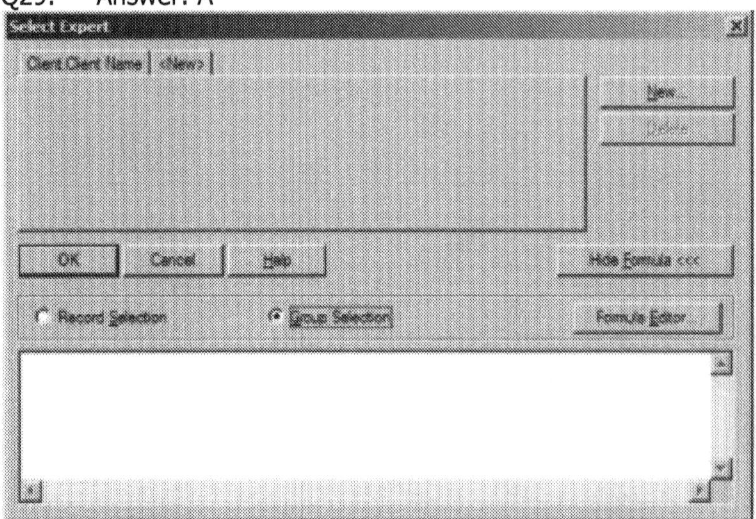

Q30: Answer: C

Q31: Answer: CD

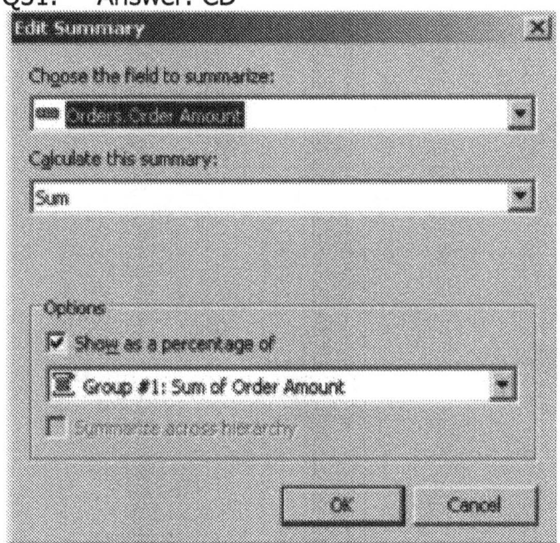

Q32: Answer: AD
Q33: Answer: A
Q34: Answer: A
Q35. Answer: AC
Q36. Answer: D

Suppress (No Drill-Down)

Q37. Answer: AB
Q38. Answer: A

Answers: Chapter 9 Charts

Q1. Answer: ABCEFG
Q2. Answer: ABCD
Q3. Answer: A
Q4. Answer: C

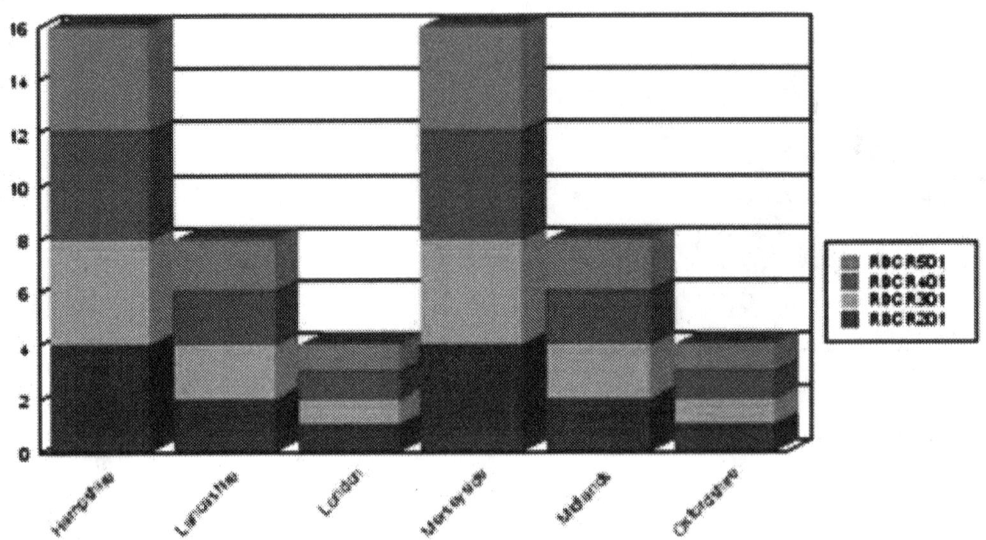

Q5. Answer: B
Q6. Answer: ABCEG
Q7. Answer: A
Q8. Answer: B
Q9. Answer: AE
Q10. Answer: A

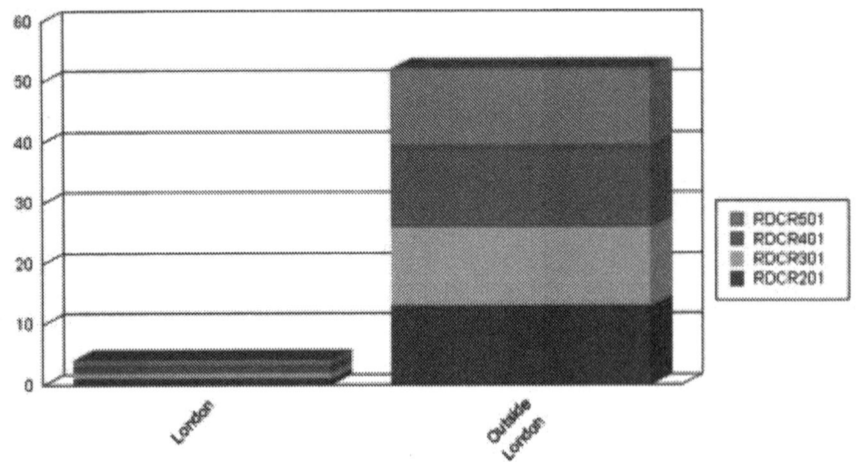

Q11. Answer: A
Q12. Answer: C

Q13. Answer: ABCD

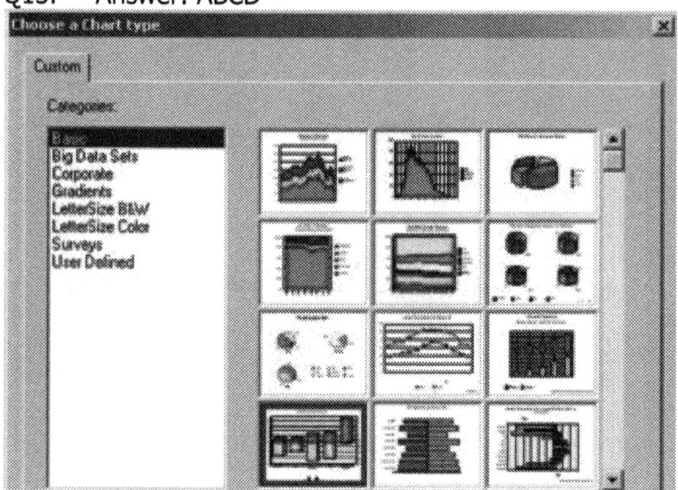

Q14. Answer: B
Q15. Answer: D
Q16. Answer: B

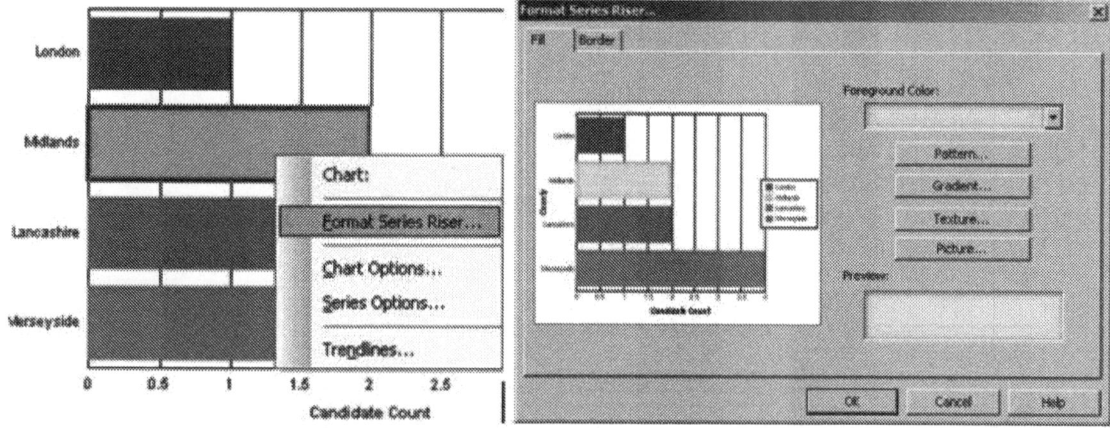

Q17. Answer: D
Q18. Answer: E
Q19. Answer: B
Q20. Answer: B

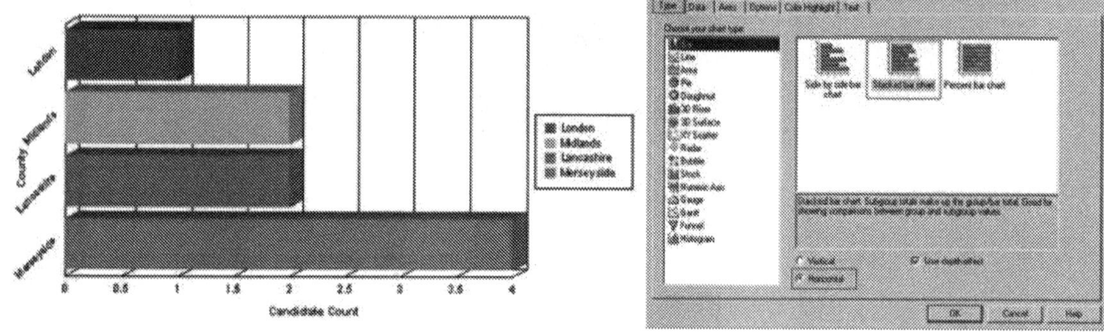

Q21. Answer: A

Q22. Answer: C

Candidate Count per County

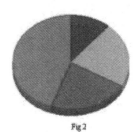

Candidate Count per County

Fig 2

Q23. Answer: A

Q24. Answer: D

Candidate Count per County

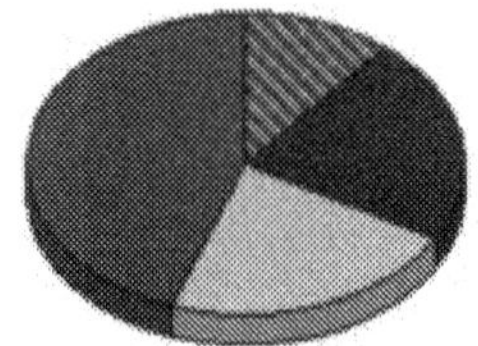

London	11.1%
Midlands	22.2%
Lancashire	22.2%
Merseyside	44.4%
Total	100.0%

Q25. Answer: A

Q26. Answer: ABC

Q27. Answer: B

Q28. Answer: A

Q29. Answer: E

Q30. Answer: A

Candidate Count per County

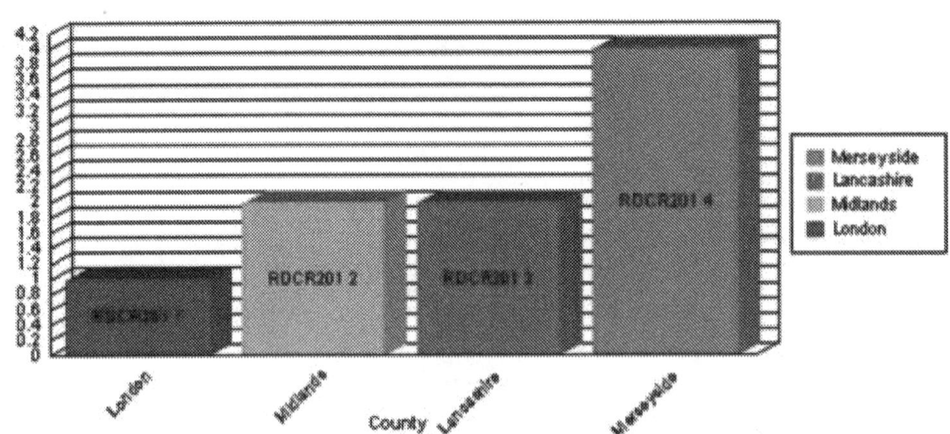

Q31. Answer: A

Q32. Answer: ACDF

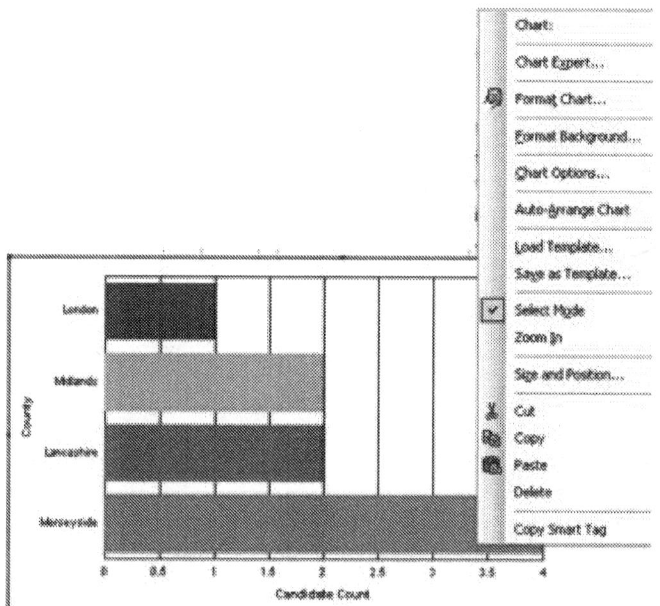

Q33. Answer: ABC
Q34. Answer: ABCD
Q35. Answer: C
Q36. Answer: B
Q37. Answer: AD
Q38. Answer: D
Q39. Answer: ABCD
Q40. Answer: ABCDEF

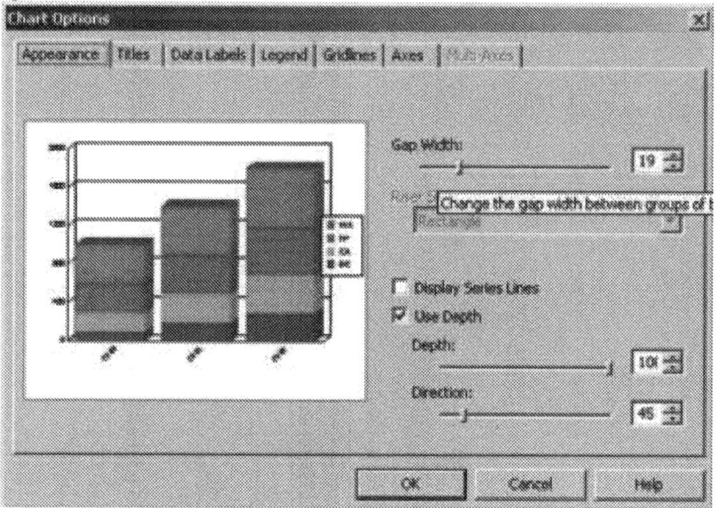

Q41. Answer: ABCD

Q42. Anwers: A

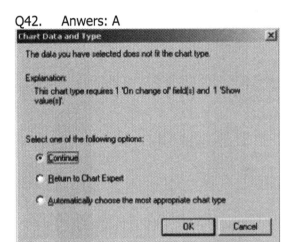

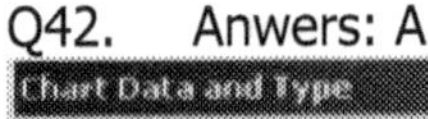

Q43. Answer. D

Q44. Answer. A

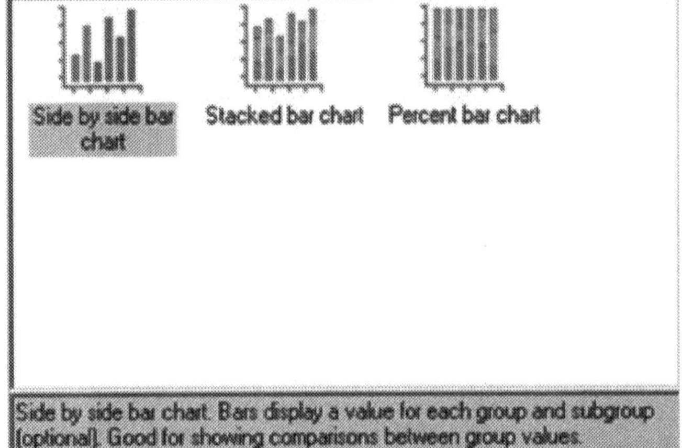

Answers: Chapter 10 Cross-Tabs

Q1. Answer: AD
Q2. Answer: D
Q3. Answer: B
Q4. Answer: A

Sum of Quantity / ProductName & Country

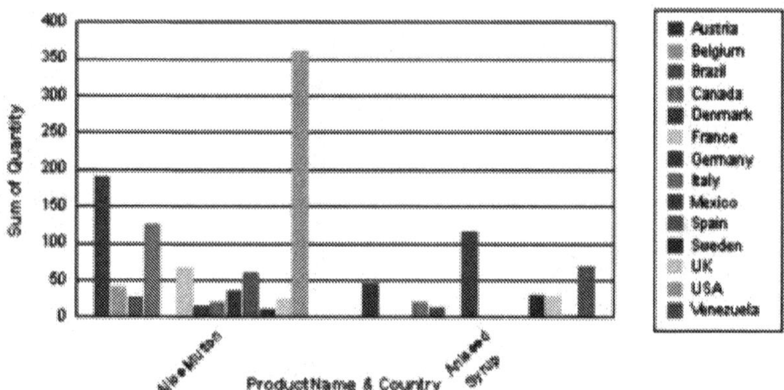

Q5. Answer: CD
Q6. Answer: C

	Total	Austria	Belgium
Total	1306	236	40
Alice Mutton	978	191	40
Aniseed Syrup	328	45	0

Q7. Answer: B

	Total	Alice Mutton	Anis
		Quantity	
Total			328
Austria			45
Belgium			0
Brazil			0
Canada			20
Denmark			14
France			0
Germany			

Cross-Tab:
Cross-Tab Expert...
Format Cross-Tab...
Format Painter
Group Sort Expert...
Insert Chart...
Insert Map...
Pivot Cross-Tab
Grid Options
Summarized Field Labels
Summarize Horizont
Summarize Vertically

Q8. Answer: A

Q9. Answer: B

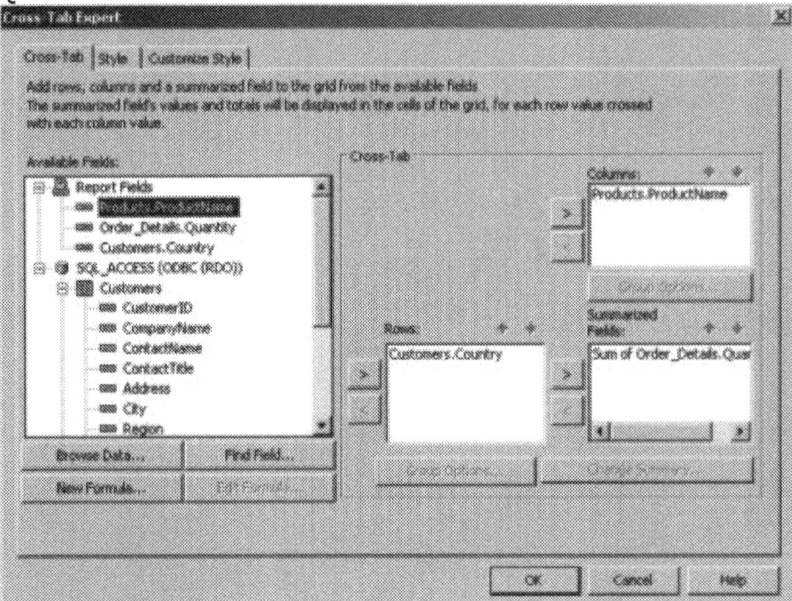

Q10. Answer: B

Q11. Answer: AB

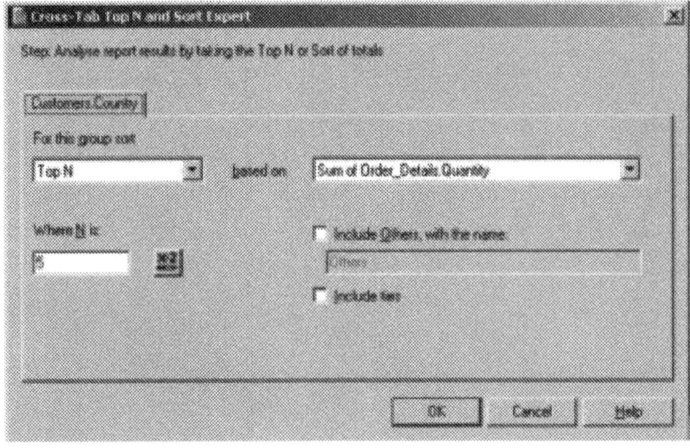

Q12. Answer: A

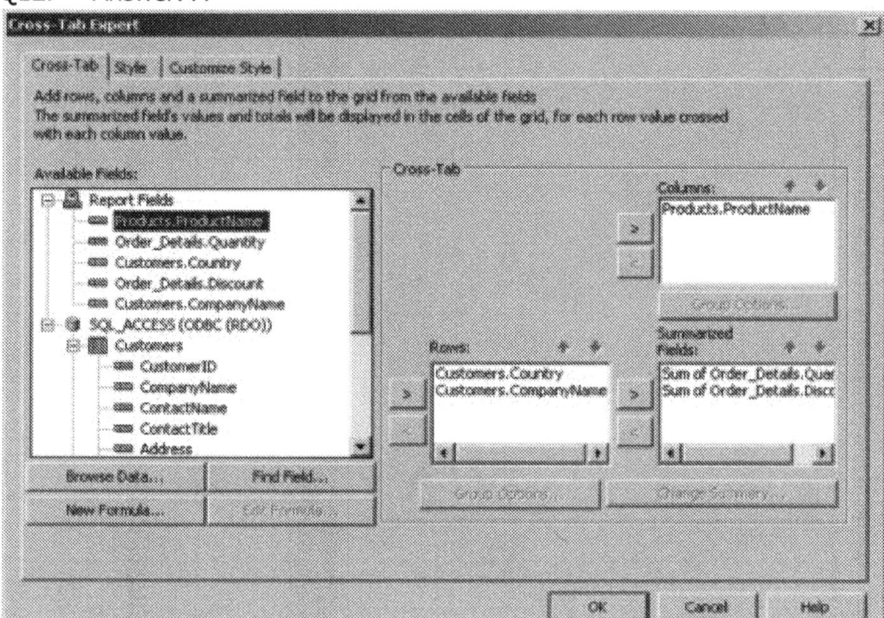

Q13. Answer: ABDE

Q14. Answer: B

Q15. Answer: A

Q16. Answer: A

Q17. Answer: A

	Alice Mutton	Aniseed Syrup	Total
Austria	191	45	**236**
Belgium	40	0	**40**
Brazil	27	0	**27**
Canada	126	20	**146**
Denmark	0	14	**14**
France	67	0	**67**
Germany	15	115	**130**
Italy	20	0	**20**
Mexico	36	0	**36**
Spain	60	0	**60**
Sweden	10	30	**40**
UK	25	30	**55**
USA	361	4	**365**
Venezuela	0	70	**70**
Total	978	328	1306

Q18. Answer: D

	Alice Mutton	Aniseed Syrup	Total
Austria	Discount Awarded	No Discount	236
Belgium	No Discount	No Discount	40
Brazil	No Discount	No Discount	27
Canada	Discount Awarded	No Discount	146
Denmark	No Discount	No Discount	14
France	No Discount	No Discount	67
Germany	No Discount	Discount Awarded	130
Italy	No Discount	No Discount	20
Mexico	No Discount	No Discount	36
Spain	No Discount	No Discount	60
Sweden	No Discount	No Discount	40
UK	No Discount	No Discount	55
USA	Discount Awarded	No Discount	365
Venezuela	No Discount	No Discount	70
Total	978	328	1306

Q19. Answer: A

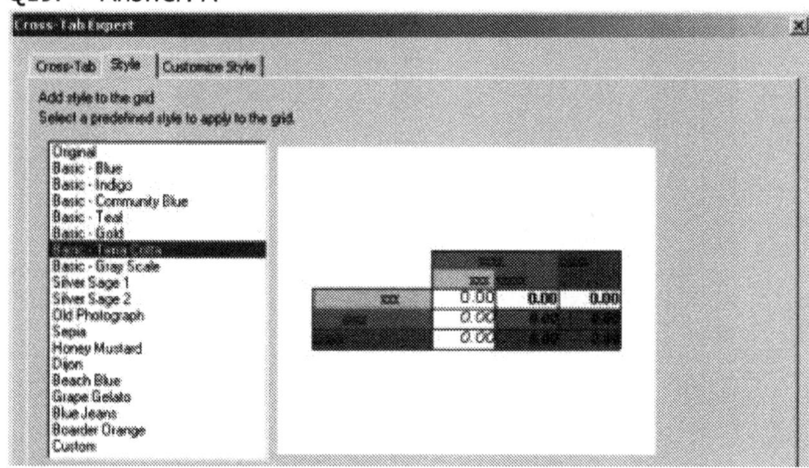

Q20. Answer: A

Q21. Answer: A

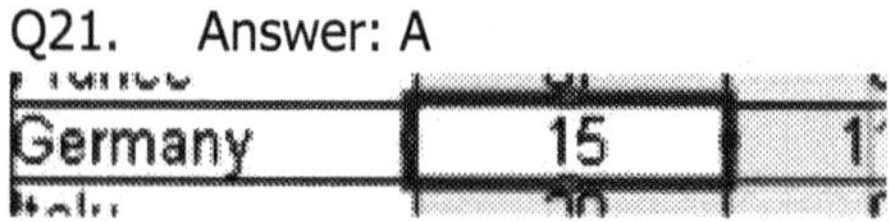

Q22. Answer: CD

Q23. Answer: A

Q24. Answer: B

	Alice Mutton	Aniseed Syrup	Total
Austria	191	45	236
Belgium	40	0	40
Brazil	27	0	27
Canada	126	20	146
Denmark	0	14	14
France	67	0	67
Germany	15	115	130
Italy	20	0	20
Mexico	36	0	36
Spain	60	0	60
Sweden	10	30	40
UK	25	30	55
USA	361	4	365
Venezuela	0	70	70
Total	978	328	1306

Grid Options ▸ ✓ Show Cell Margins

Grid Options ▸ Show Cell Margins

Q25. Answer: ABCDEF

Q26. Answer: C

Answers: Chapter 11 Custom Function

Q1. Answer: E
Q2. Answer: B
Q3. Answer: A

Q4. Answer: C
Q5. Answer: A
Q6. Answer: B
Q7. Answer: ABCD

```
WhilePrintingRecords;
numbervar ExamFee;

if {Exam.ExamName} in ["RDCR200","RDCR300"] then
ExamFee:= ExamFee + {ExamCost.FEE};
```

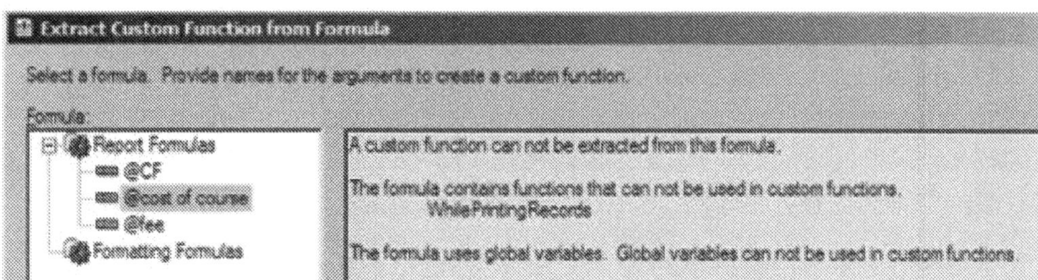

Q8. Answer: C

Q9. Answer: B

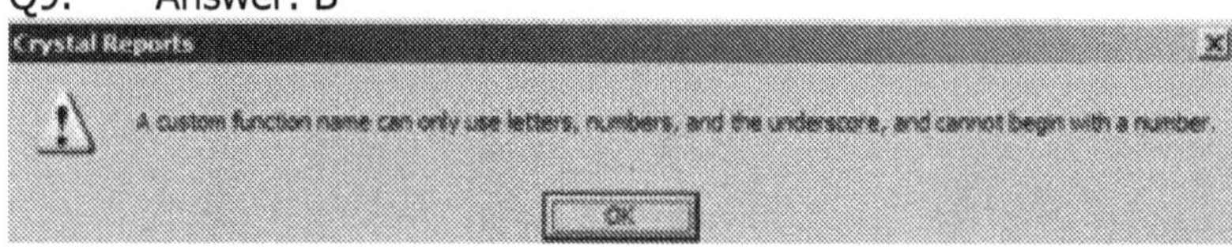

Q10. Answer: D

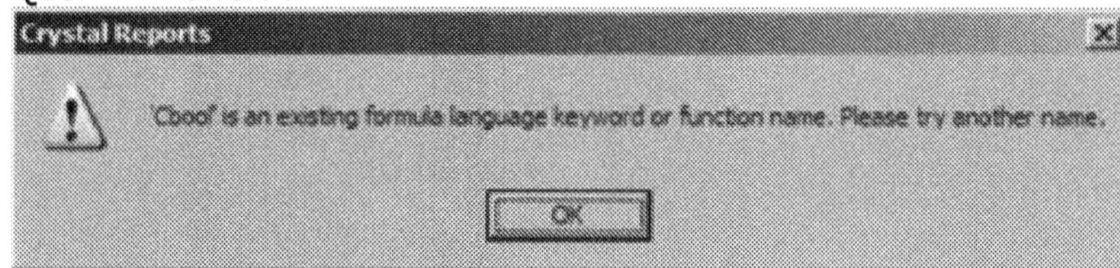

Q11. Answer: B

Q12. Answer: AB
Q13. Answer: CE
Q14. Answer: A
Q15. Answer: A
Q16. Answer: C

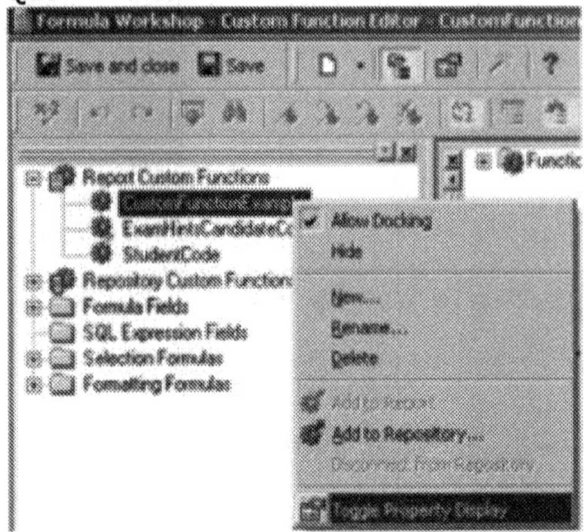

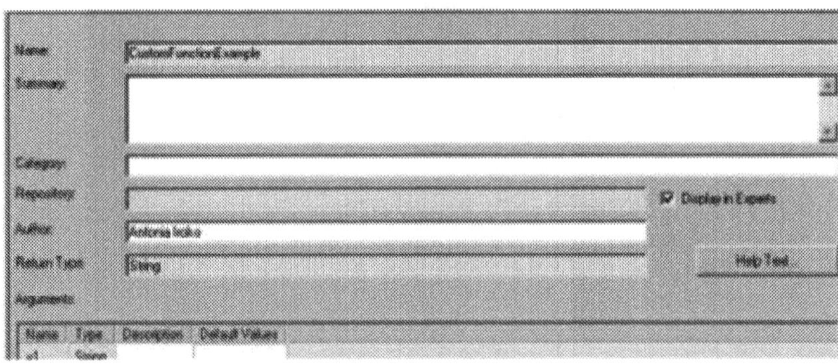

Q17. Answer: D

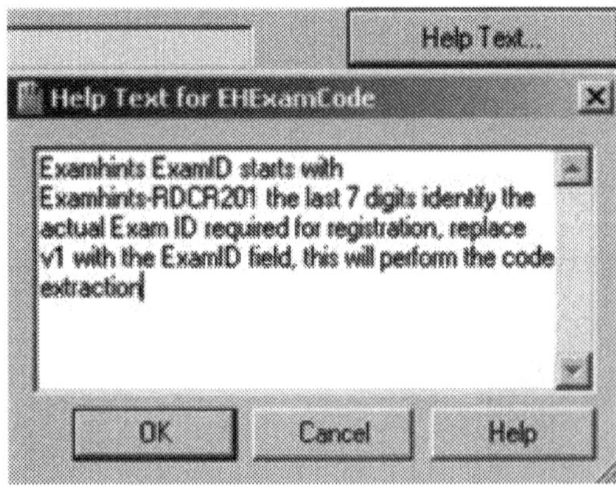

Q18. Answer: A
Q19. Answer: F

Q20. Answer: ABCDEFG

Q21. Answer: ABCD

Q22. Answer : A

Q23. Answer: D

Q24. Answer: B

Q25. Answer: C

Q26. Answer: D

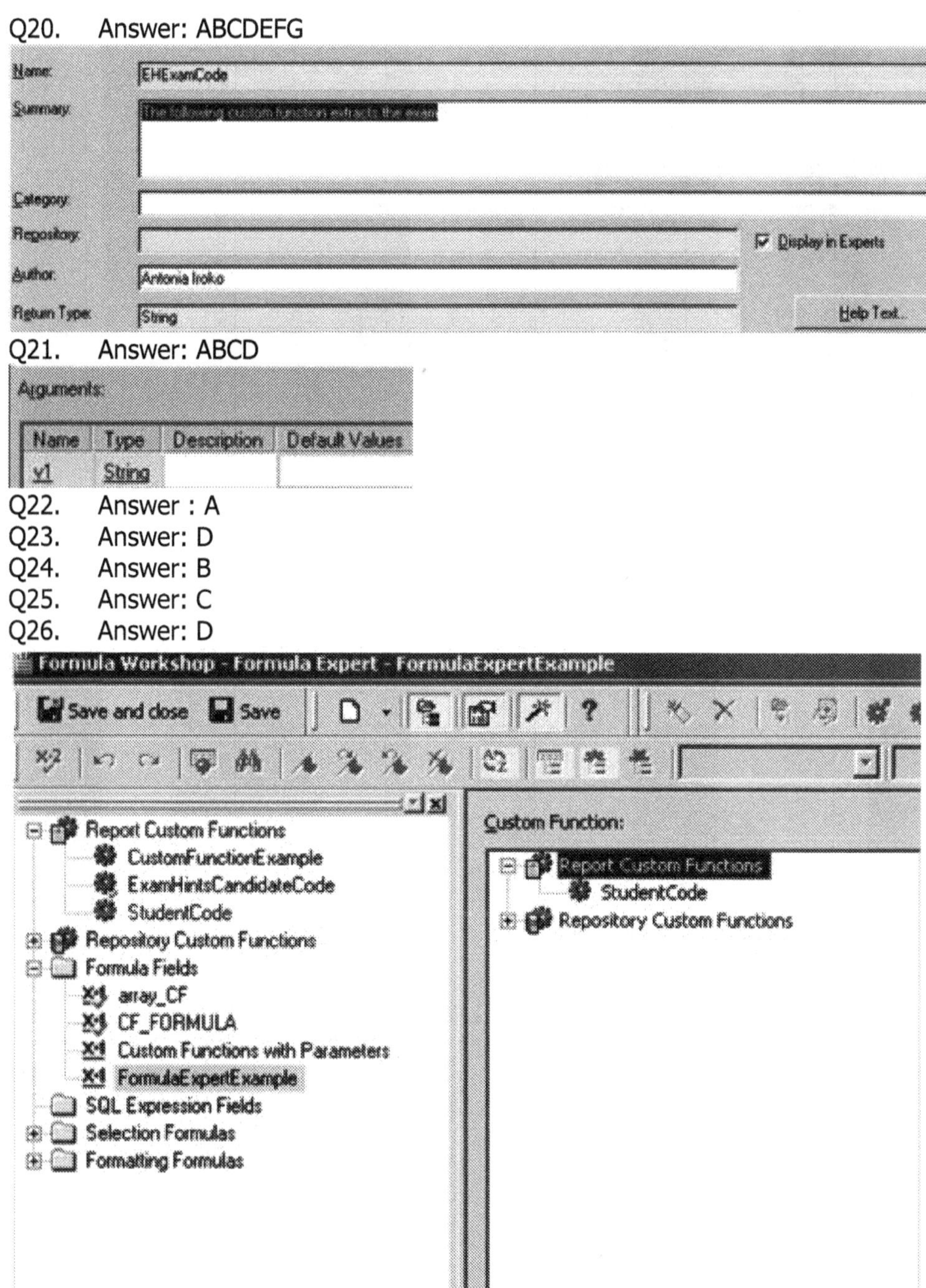

Q27. Answer: A

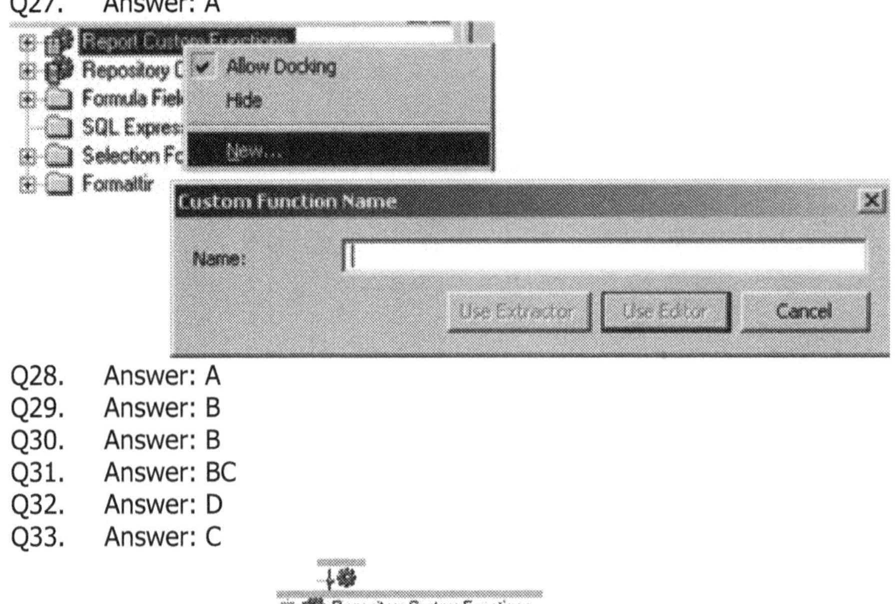

Q28. Answer: A
Q29. Answer: B
Q30. Answer: B
Q31. Answer: BC
Q32. Answer: D
Q33. Answer: C
Q34. Answer: ABC

Repository Custom Functions

Answers: Chapter 12 Previewing and Exporting Reports

Q1. Answer: ABCDE
Q2. Answer: ABD
Q3. Answer: C

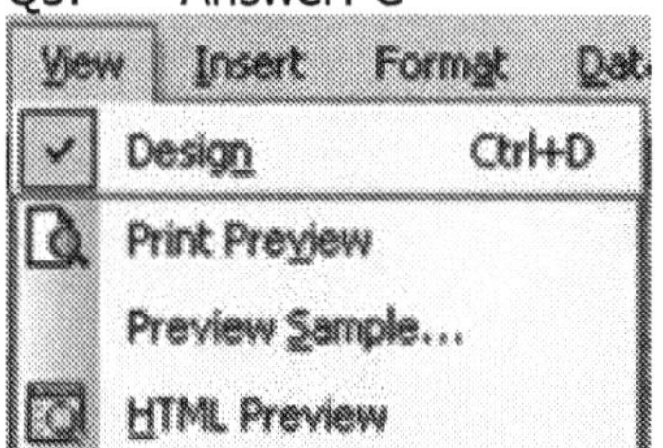

Q4. Answer: B

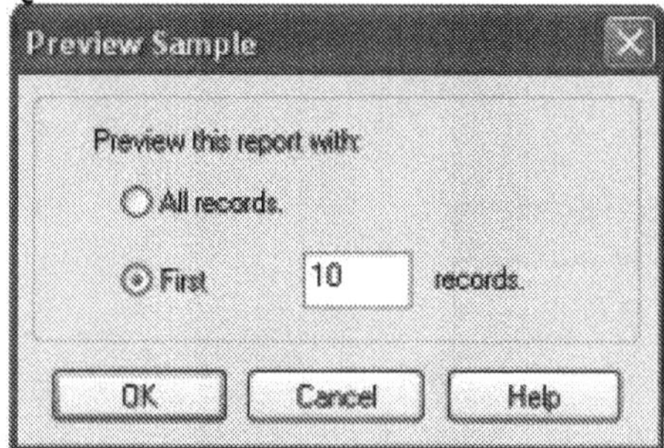

Q5. Answer: D
Q6. Answer: D
Q7. Answer: CD

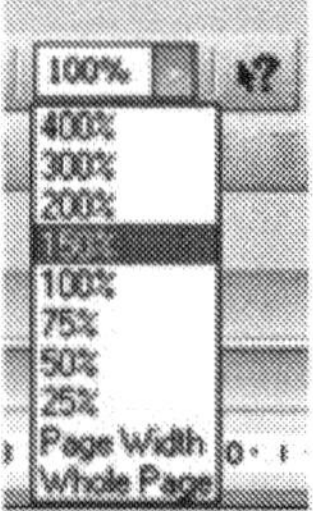

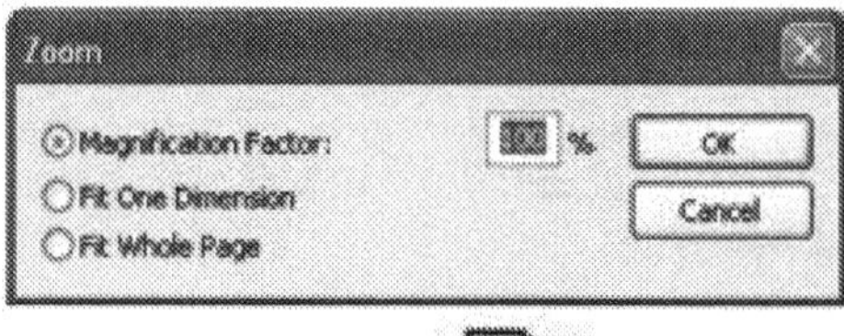

Q8. Answer: A

Q9. Answer: B

Q10. Answer: C
Q11. Answer: AB
Q12. Answer: D

Q13. Answer: ACD

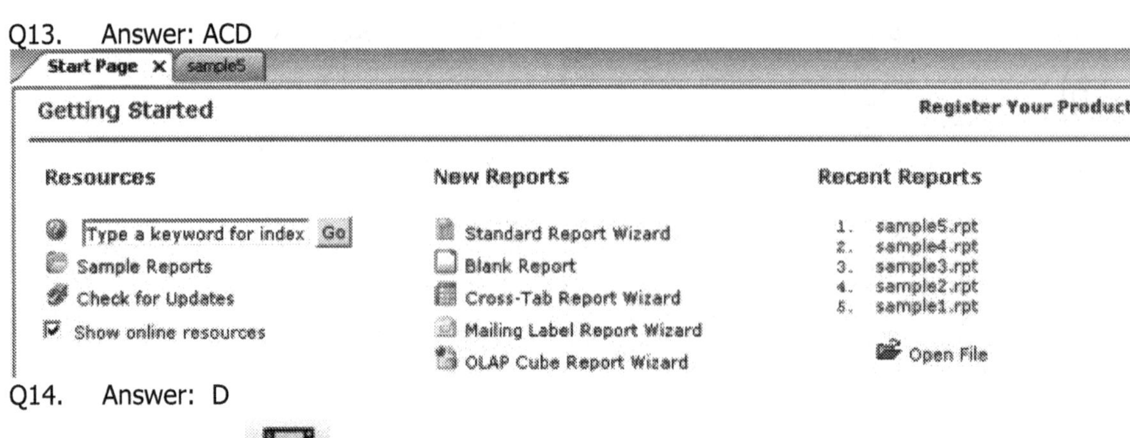

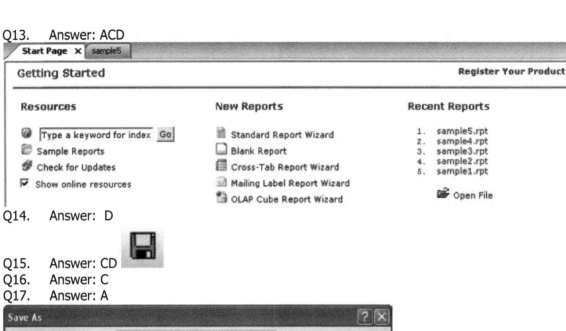

Q14. Answer: D

Q15. Answer: CD

Q16. Answer: C

Q17. Answer: A

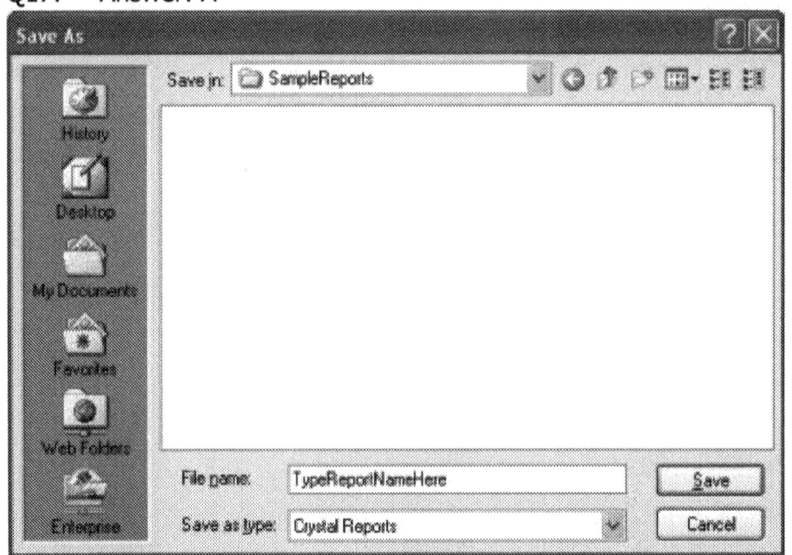

Q18. Answer: BD

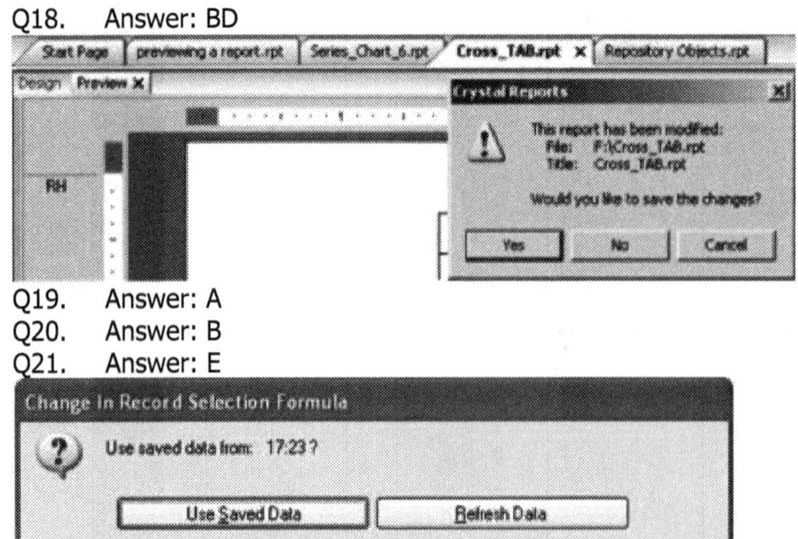

Q19. Answer: A

Q20. Answer: B

Q21. Answer: E

Q22:. Answer: C
Q23. Answer: C
Q24. Answer: B
Q25. Answer: ABCD
Q26. Answer: G
Q27. Answer: ABCDE

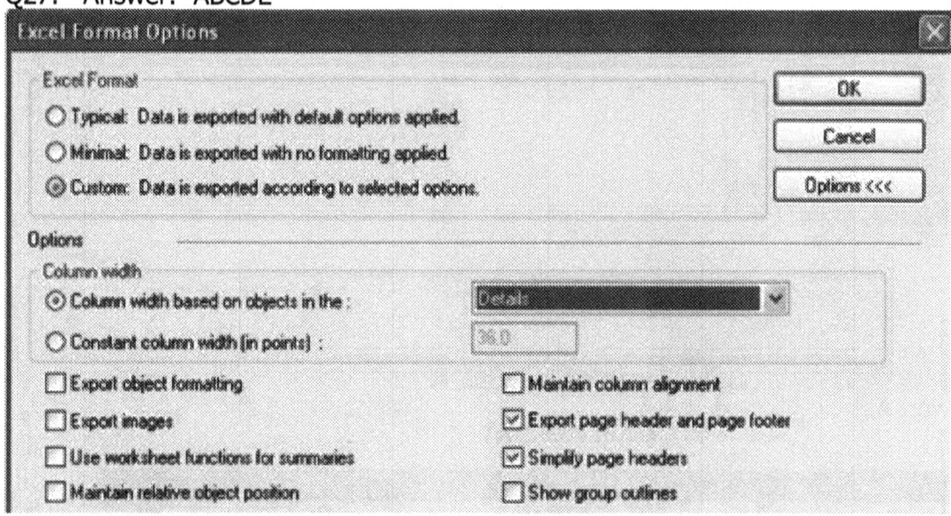

Q28. Answer: A
Q29. Answer: C
Q30. Answer: BCD

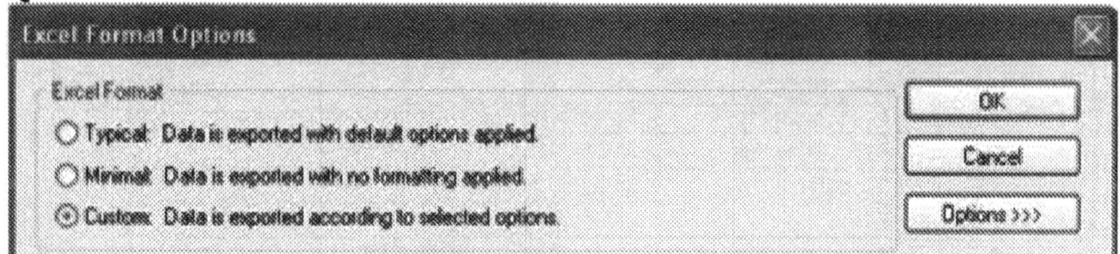

Q31. Answer: D
Q32. Answer: D
Q33. Answer: A
Q34. Answer: C

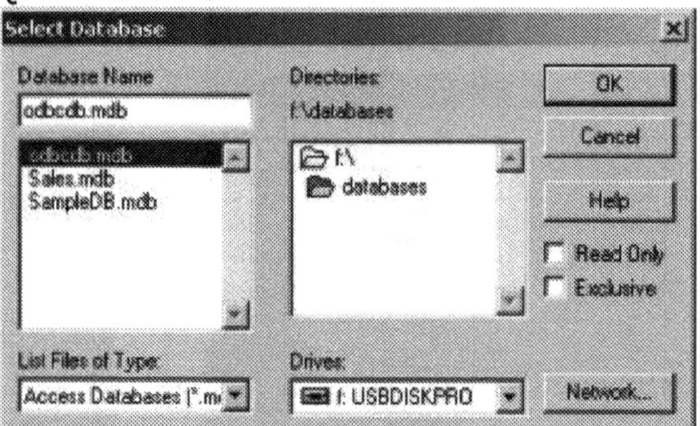

Q35. Answer: A

Answers: Chapter 13 Subreports

Q1. Answer: B
Q2. Answer: E

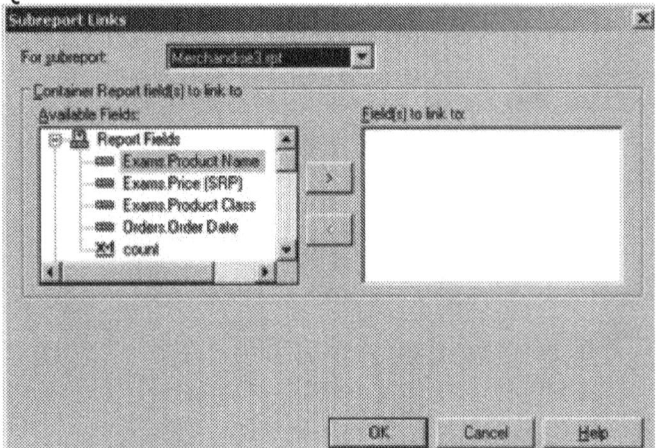

Q3. Answer: A

MAIN REPORT

	Mechandise Name	Price	Product Class	Order Date	Client Name
1	Bronze Rim Pen	$ 539.95	Collectable Pens	05/06/2006	Books and Books
2	Silver Rim Pen	$ 1,000.00	Collectable Pens	25/06/2006	Books and Books
3	Blue Pen	$ 10.00	Pen	21/06/2006	Books and Books
4	Blue Pen	$ 10.00	Pen	25/06/2006	Books and Books
5	Bronze Plated Pen	$ 764.95	Collectable Pens	06/06/2006	Examhints
6	Bronze Plated Pen	$ 764.95	Collectable Pens	06/06/2006	Examhints
7	Yellow Pen	$ 5.90	Pen	26/06/2006	Folks Books
8	Ball Point Pen	$ 500.00	Collectable Pens	01/06/2006	Great Stone
9	Ball Point Pen	$ 500.00	Collectable Pens	24/06/2006	Great Stone
10	Silver Plated Pen	$ 329.95	Collectable Pens	24/06/2006	Great Stone
11	Green Pen	$ 14.50	Pen	01/06/2006	Great Stone
12	Green Pen	$ 14.50	Pen	25/06/2006	Ink Only
13	Fountain Pen	$ 33.90	Pen	02/06/2006	Mobile Books
14	Bronze Rim Pen	$ 539.95	Collectable Pens	24/06/2006	Pens Gallery
15	Ball Point Pen	$ 500.00	Collectable Pens	22/06/2006	Stationary Gallore
16	Fountain Pen	$ 33.90	Pen	20/06/2006	Writers and Pens

SUBREPORT

	Mechandise Name	Price	Product Class	Order Date	Client Name
1	Gold Plated Pen	$ 1,500.00	Collectable Pens	08/02/2005	Books and Books
2	Ball Point Pen	$ 500.00	Collectable Pens	13/02/2005	Mobile Books
3	Bronze Rim Pen	$ 539.95	Collectable Pens	25/02/2005	Iroko Books
4	Ball Point Pen	$ 500.00	Collectable Pens	06/02/2005	Folks Books
5	Ball Point Pen	$ 500.00	Collectable Pens	01/02/2005	Books and Books
6	Silver Rim Pen	$ 1,000.00	Collectable Pens	15/02/2005	Stationary Gallore
7	Red Pen	$ 16.50	Pen	13/02/2005	Examhints
8	Red Pen	$ 16.50	Pen	06/02/2005	Folks Books
9	Fountain Pen	$ 33.90	Pen	28/02/2005	Mobile Books
10	Blue Pen	$ 10.00	Pen	15/02/2005	Stationary Gallore
11	Blue Pen	$ 10.00	Pen	28/02/2005	Mobile Books

Q4. Answer: C
Q5. Answer: B

Q6. Answer: D

Design | Preview | SubReport_2005_Data.rpt Preview |

Q7. Answer: D

Q8. Answer: A

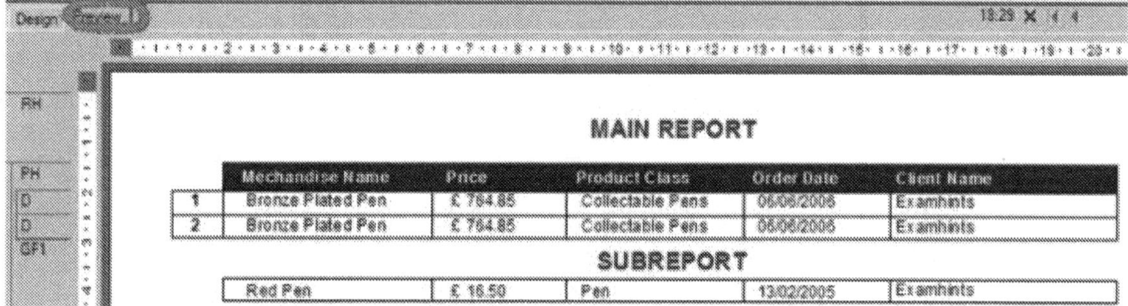

MAIN REPORT

	Mechandise Name	Price	Product Class	Order Date	Client Name
1	Bronze Plated Pen	£ 764.85	Collectable Pens	06/06/2006	Examhints
2	Bronze Plated Pen	£ 764.85	Collectable Pens	06/06/2006	Examhints

SUBREPORT

Red Pen	£ 16.50	Pen	13/02/2005	Examhints

Q9. Answer: A

Q10. Answer: B

Q11. Answer: C

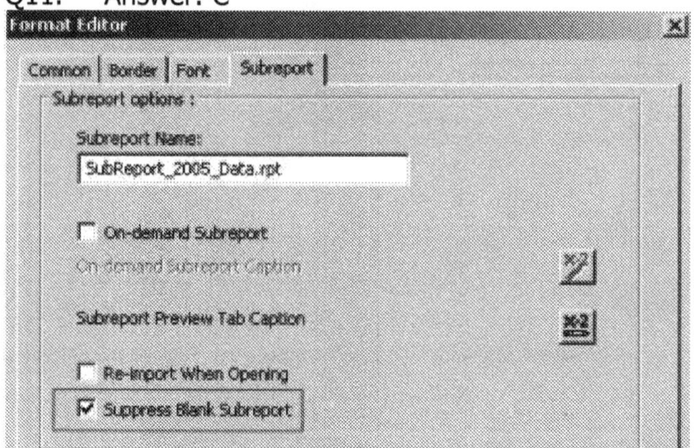

Unsuppressed Blank Subreport

MAIN REPORT

	Mechandise Name	Price	Product Class	Order Date	Client Name
1	Bronze Plated Pen	£ 764.85	Collectable Pens	06/06/2006	Examhints
2	Bronze Plated Pen	£ 764.85	Collectable Pens	06/06/2006	Examhints

SUBREPORT

Suppressed Blank Subreport

MAIN REPORT

	Mechandise Name	Price	Product Class	Order Date	Client Name
1	Bronze Plated Pen	£ 764.85	Collectable Pens	06/06/2006	Examhints
2	Bronze Plated Pen	£ 764.85	Collectable Pens	06/06/2006	Examhints

Q12. Answer: D

Q13. Answer: D

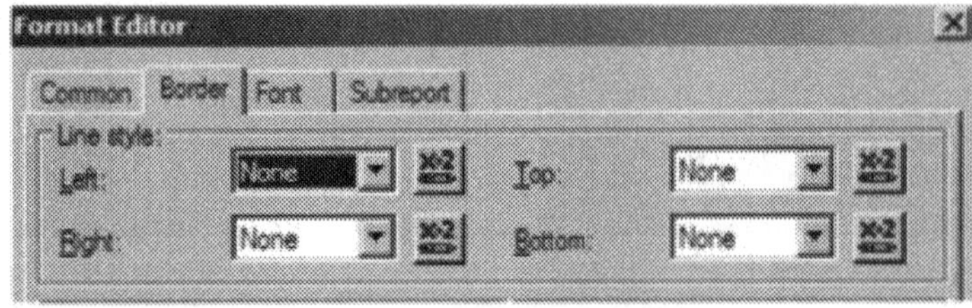

Q14 Answer: B

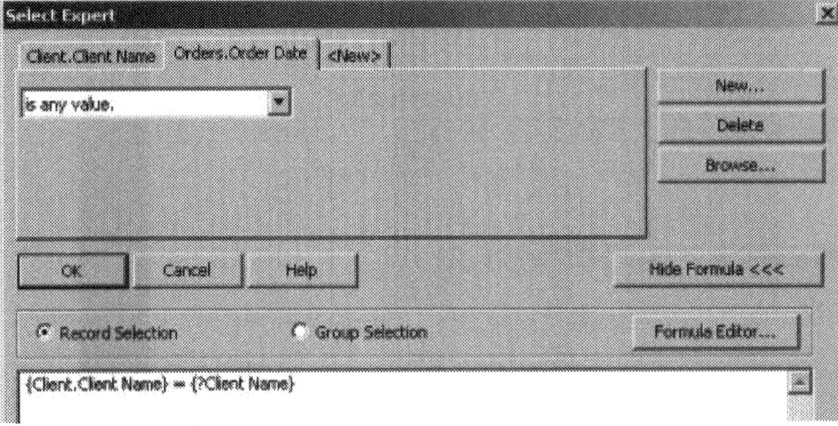

Q15. Answer: B

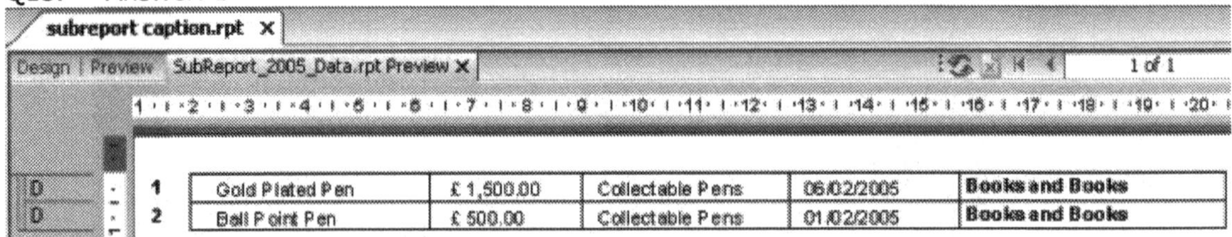

Q16. Answer: CE

Q17. Answer: C

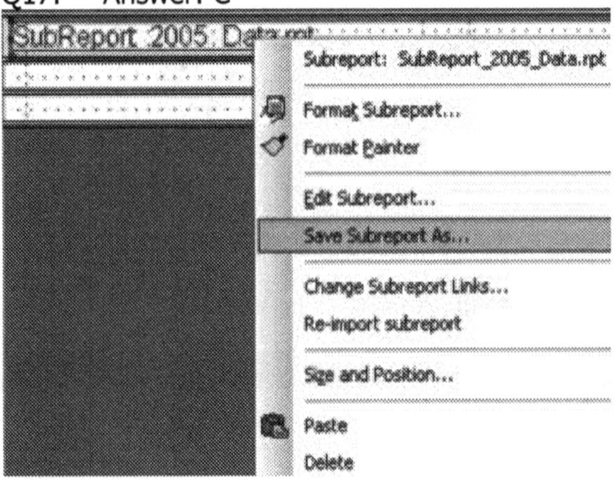

Q18. Answer: BC

Q19. Answer: C

Q20. Answer: C

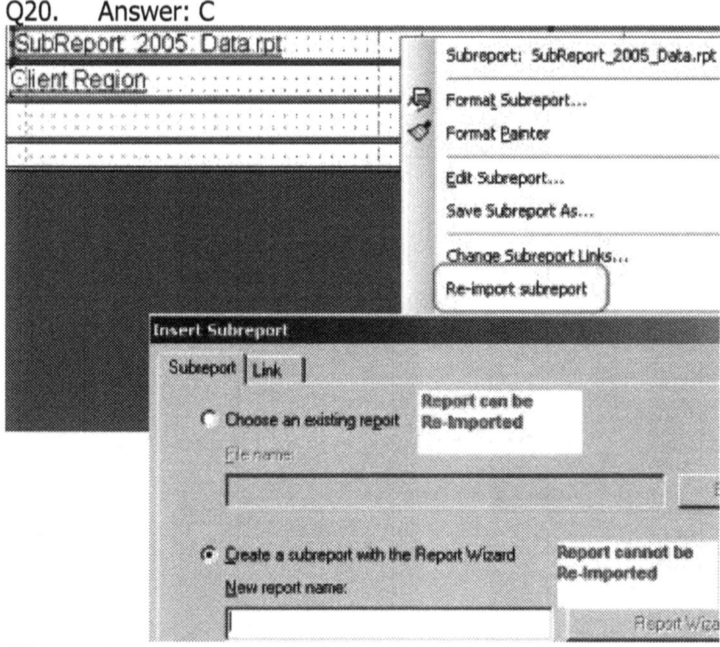

Q21. Answer: A
Q22. Answer: B
Q23. Answer: ACDE
Q24. Answer: ABCEG
Q25. Answer: C
Q26. Answer: D

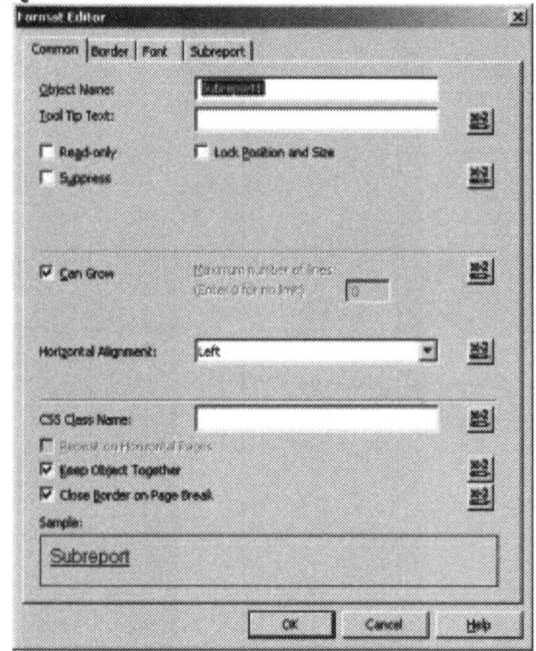

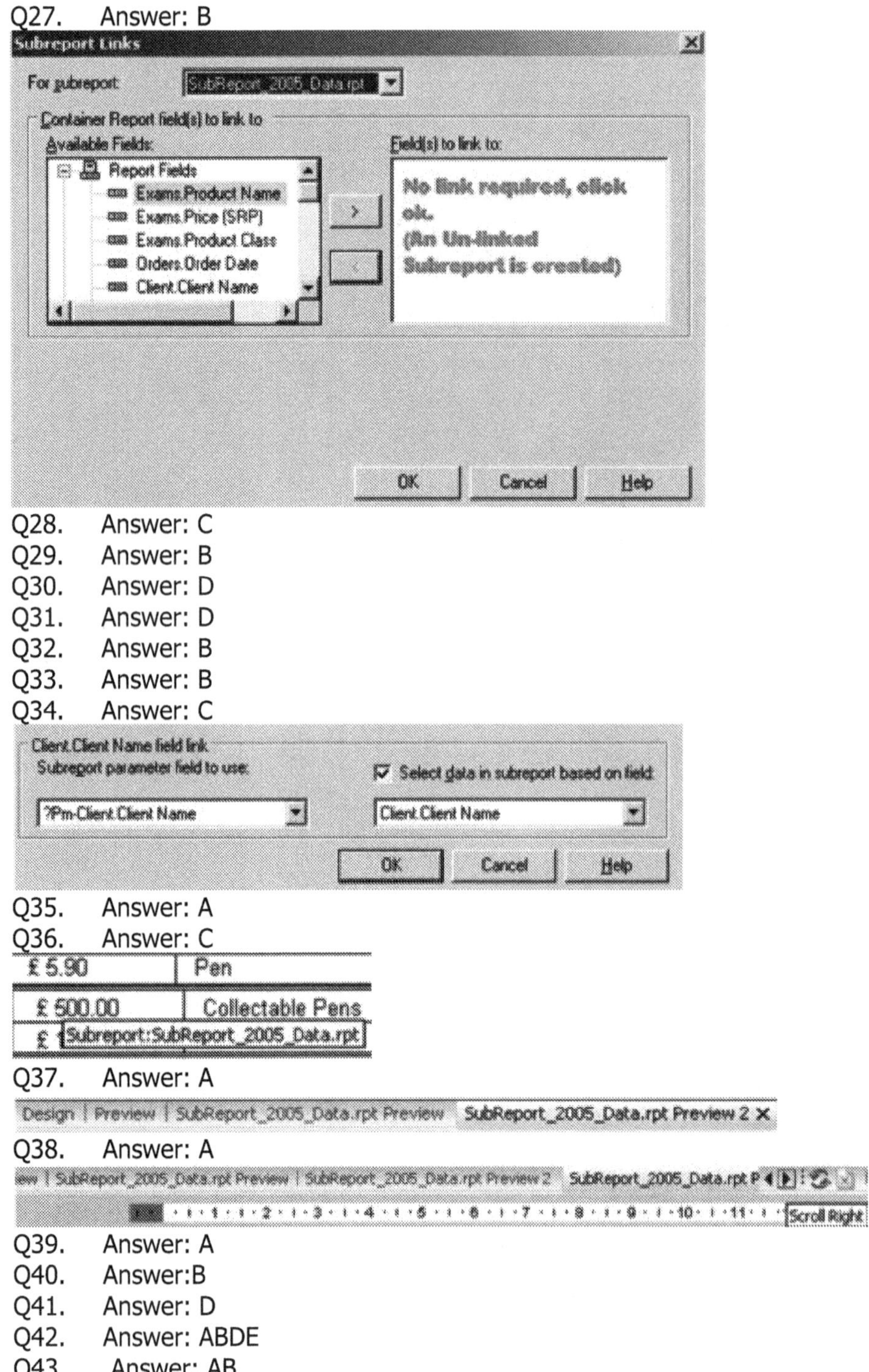

Q27. Answer: B

Q28. Answer: C
Q29. Answer: B
Q30. Answer: D
Q31. Answer: D
Q32. Answer: B
Q33. Answer: B
Q34. Answer: C

Q35. Answer: A
Q36. Answer: C

Q37. Answer: A

Q38. Answer: A

Q39. Answer: A
Q40. Answer:B
Q41. Answer: D
Q42. Answer: ABDE
Q43 Answer: AB

Answers: Chapter 14 Repository

Q1. Answer: C
Q2. Answer: E
Q3. Answer: BF

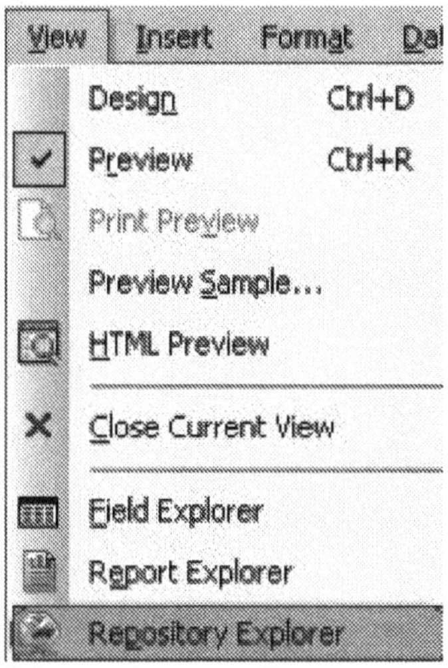

Q4. Answer: D
Q5. Answer: ABC
Q6. Answer: ABC

Q7. Answer:C

Q8. Answer: C
Q9. Answer: C

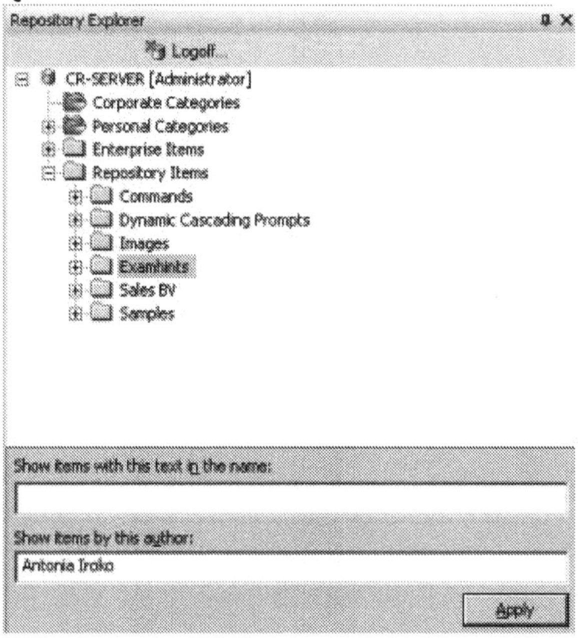

Q10. Answer:ABDE

Q11. Answer: AB

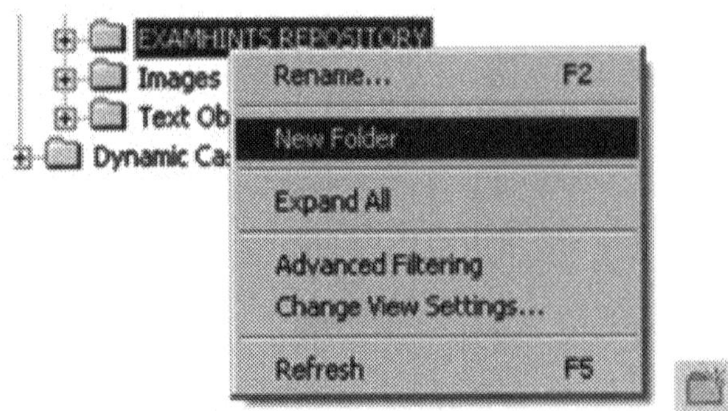

Q12. Answer: C

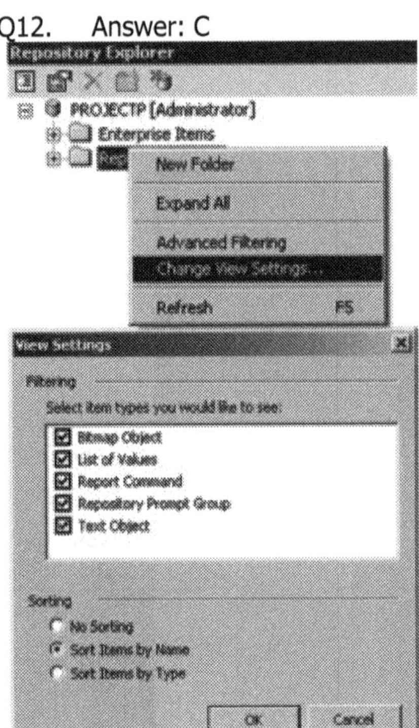

Q13. Answer: DE

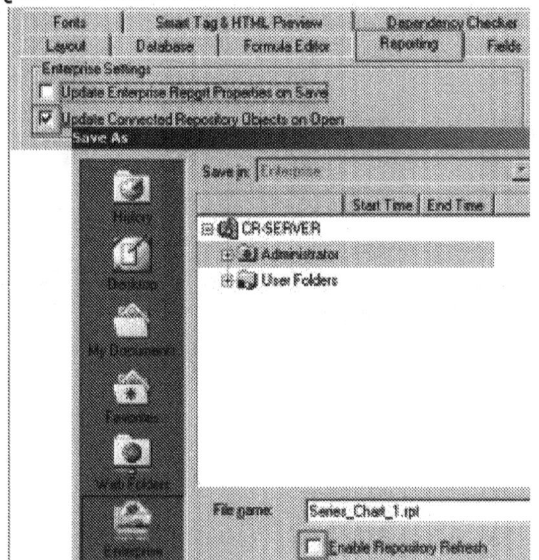

Q14. Answer: A
Q15. Answer: A
Q16. Answer: A

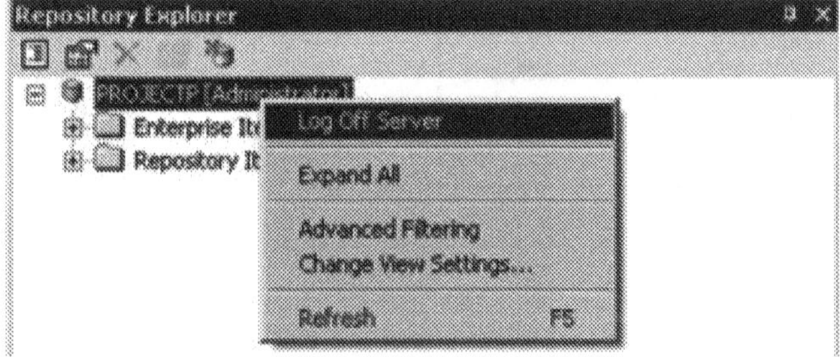

Q17. Answer: AB
Q18. Answer: B

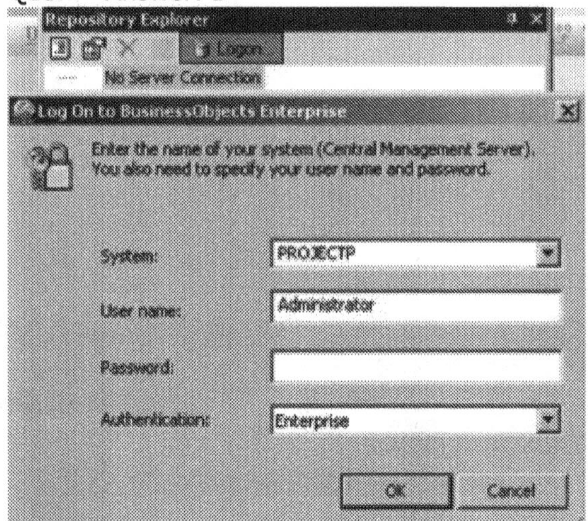

Q19. Answer:A
Q20. Answer: BE
Q21. Answer: E
Q22. Answer: B
Q23. Answer:B
Q24. Answer:ABC

Q25. Answer: B

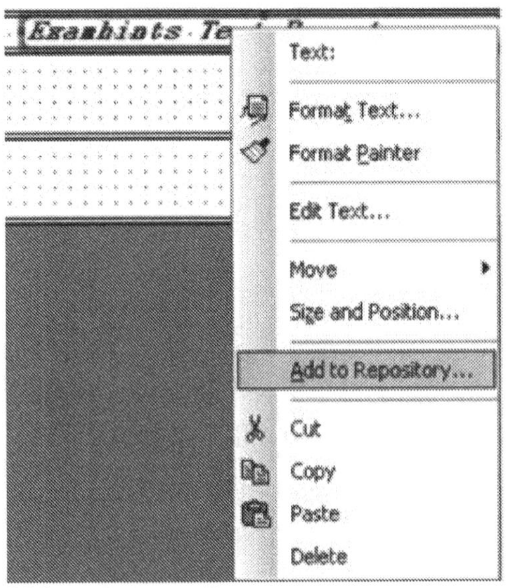

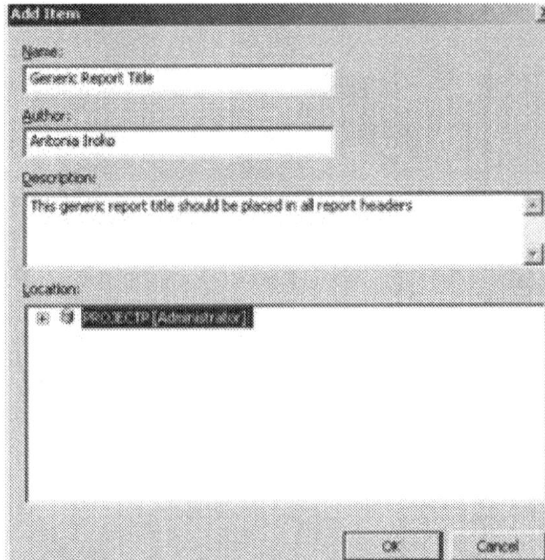

Q26. Answer: D

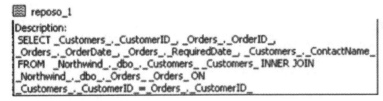

reposo_1

Description:
SELECT _Customers_._CustomerID_, _Orders_._OrderID_, _Orders_._OrderDate_, _Orders_._RequiredDate_, _Customers_._ContactName_ FROM _Northwind_._dbo_._Customers_ _Customers_ INNER JOIN _Northwind_._dbo_._Orders_ _Orders_ ON _Customers_._CustomerID_ = _Orders_._CustomerID_

Q27. Answer:C

Q28. Answer: B

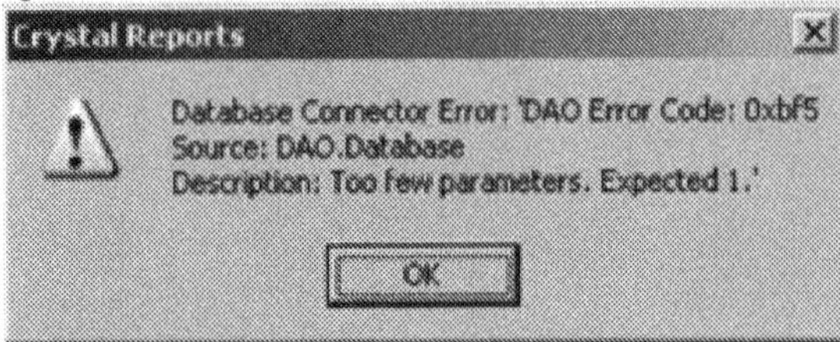

Q29. Answer: D

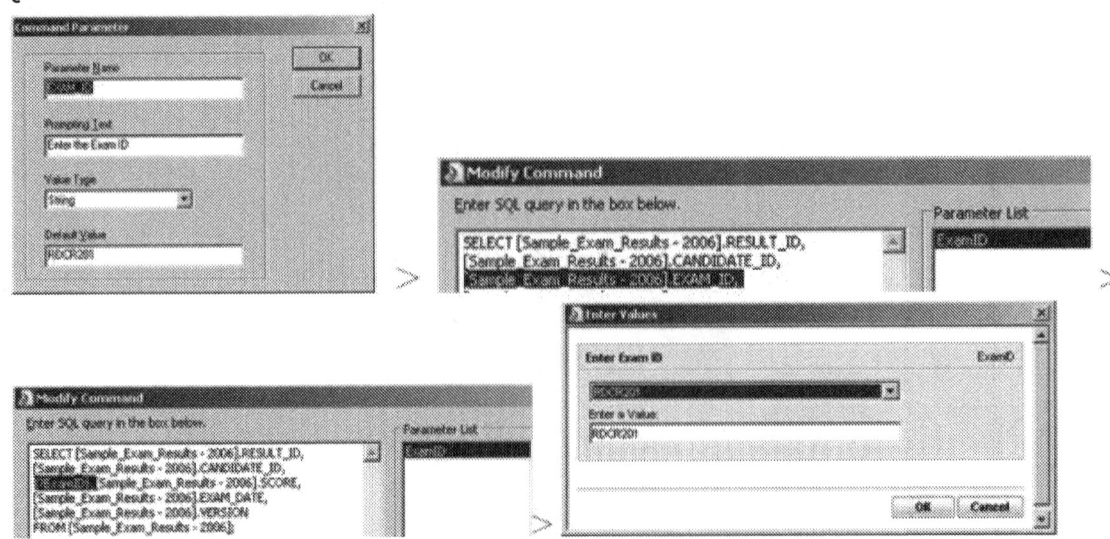

Answers: Chapter 15 Business Views

Q1. Answer: B
Q2. Answer: A
Q3. Answer: AB

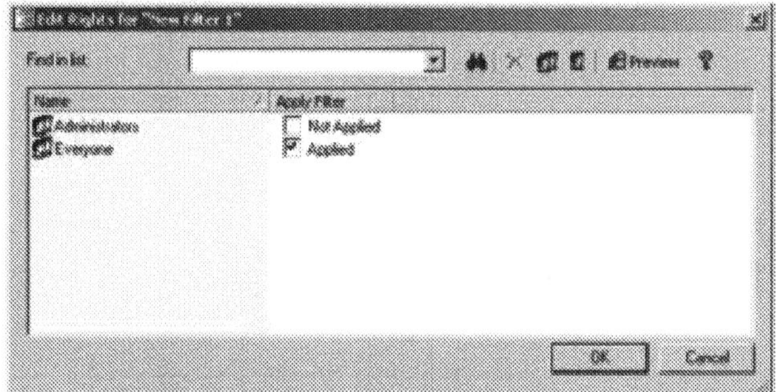

Q4. Answer: ABCDEF

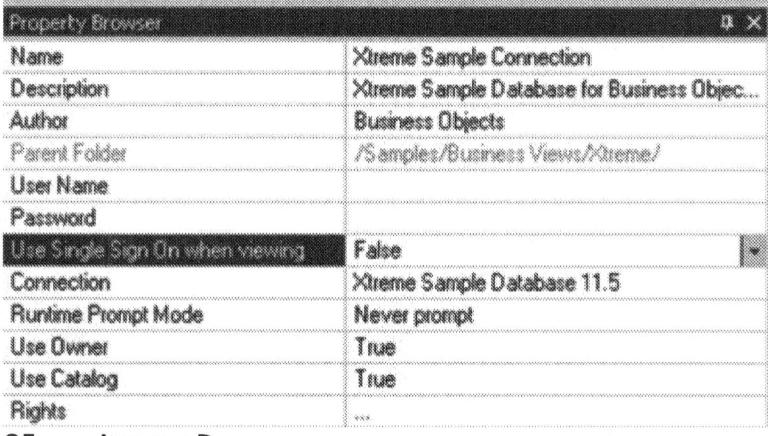

Q5. Answer: D

Object Explorer
Finance Data Connection
Edit Connection...
Edit Password...
Edit Rights...

Q6. Answer: A

Enter Parameter Value
Enter prompt values.
FS Dynamic Data Connection Parameter
FS Dynamic Data Connection Parameter
Sales Data Connection
Finance Data Connection
OK

Q7. Answer: D

Q8. Answer:B

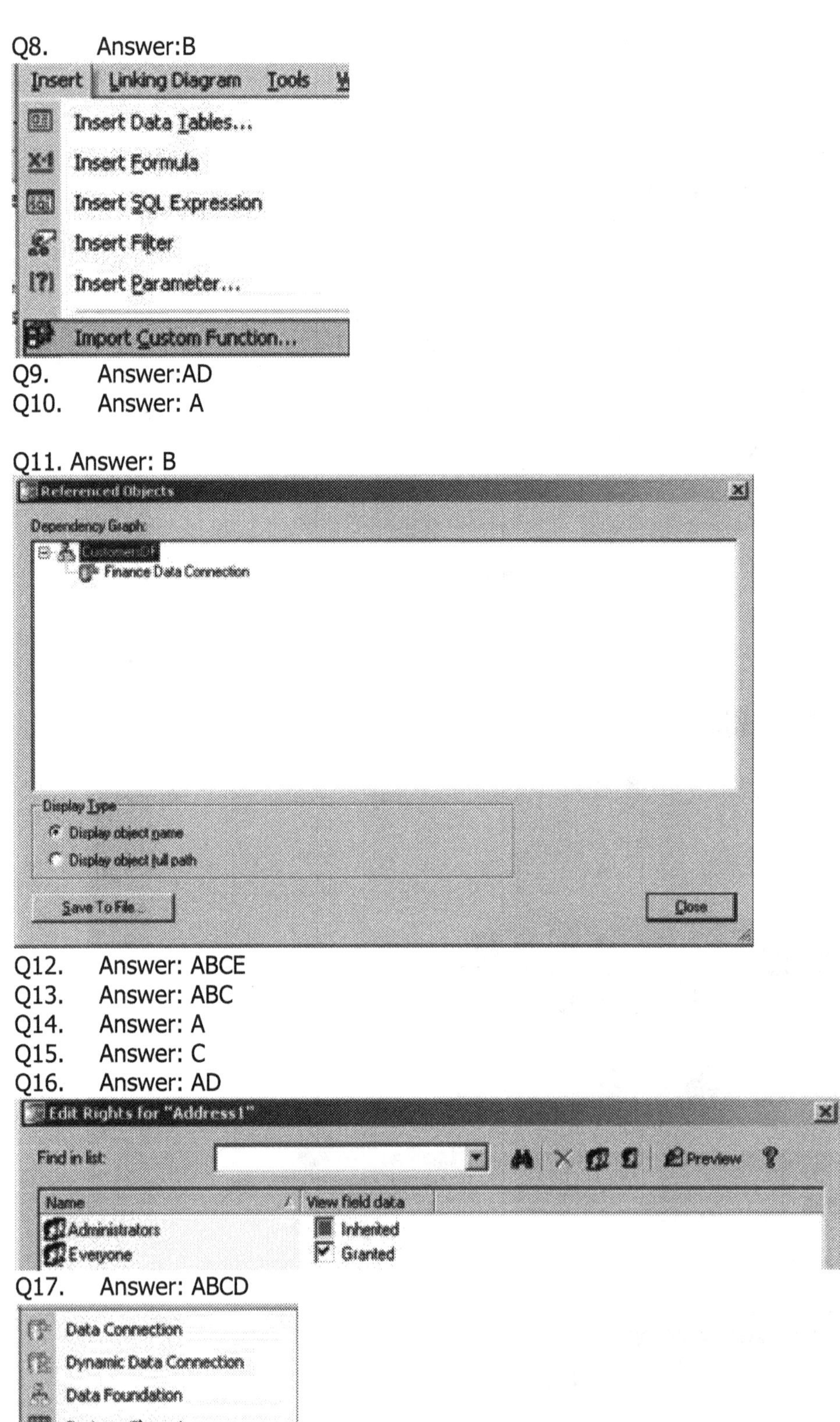

Q9. Answer:AD

Q10. Answer: A

Q11. Answer: B

Q12. Answer: ABCE

Q13. Answer: ABC

Q14. Answer: A

Q15. Answer: C

Q16. Answer: AD

Q17. Answer: ABCD

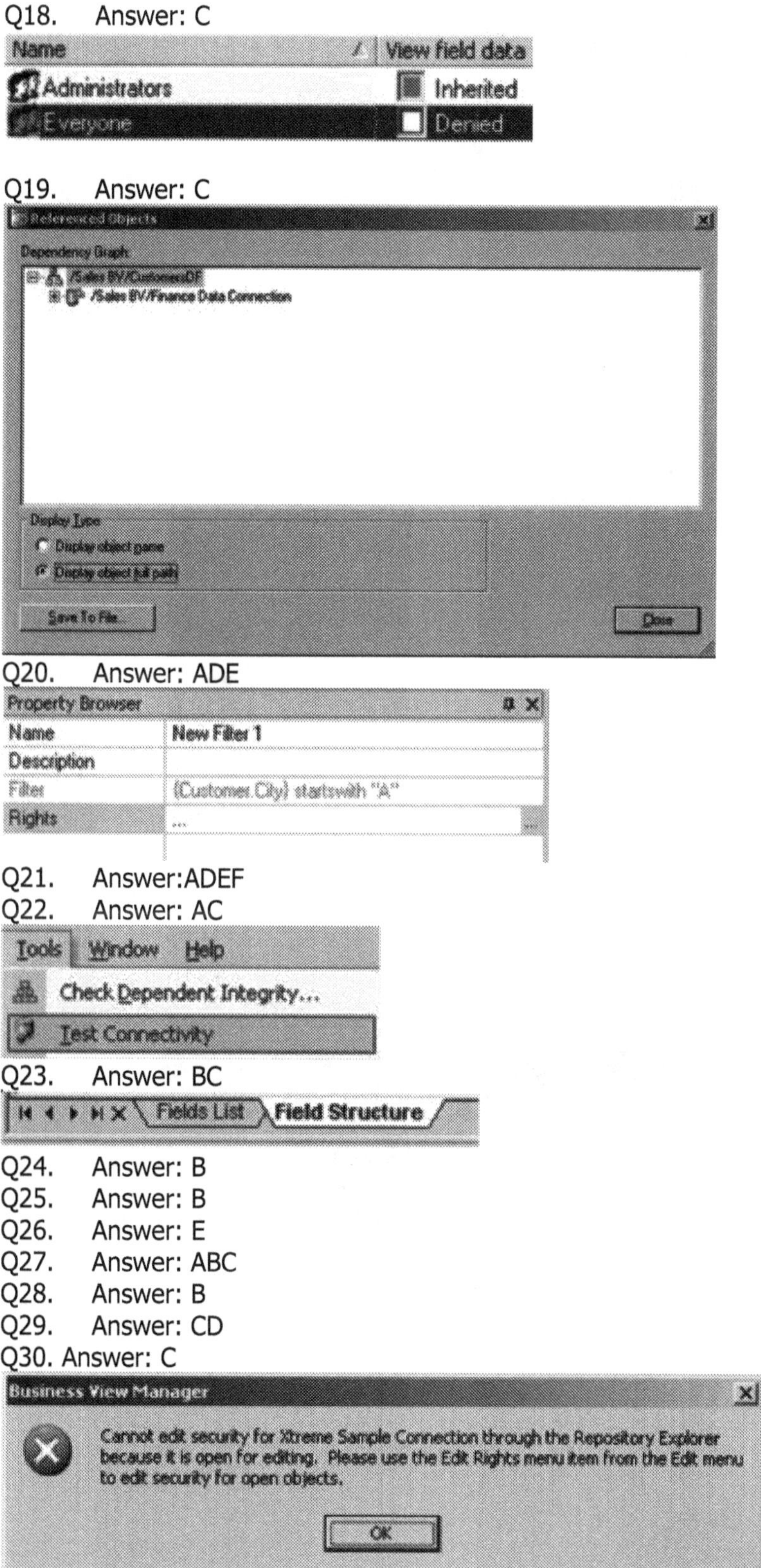

Q18. Answer: C

Q19. Answer: C

Q20. Answer: ADE

Q21. Answer:ADEF
Q22. Answer: AC

Q23. Answer: BC

Q24. Answer: B
Q25. Answer: B
Q26. Answer: E
Q27. Answer: ABC
Q28. Answer: B
Q29. Answer: CD
Q30. Answer: C

Q31. Answer: A

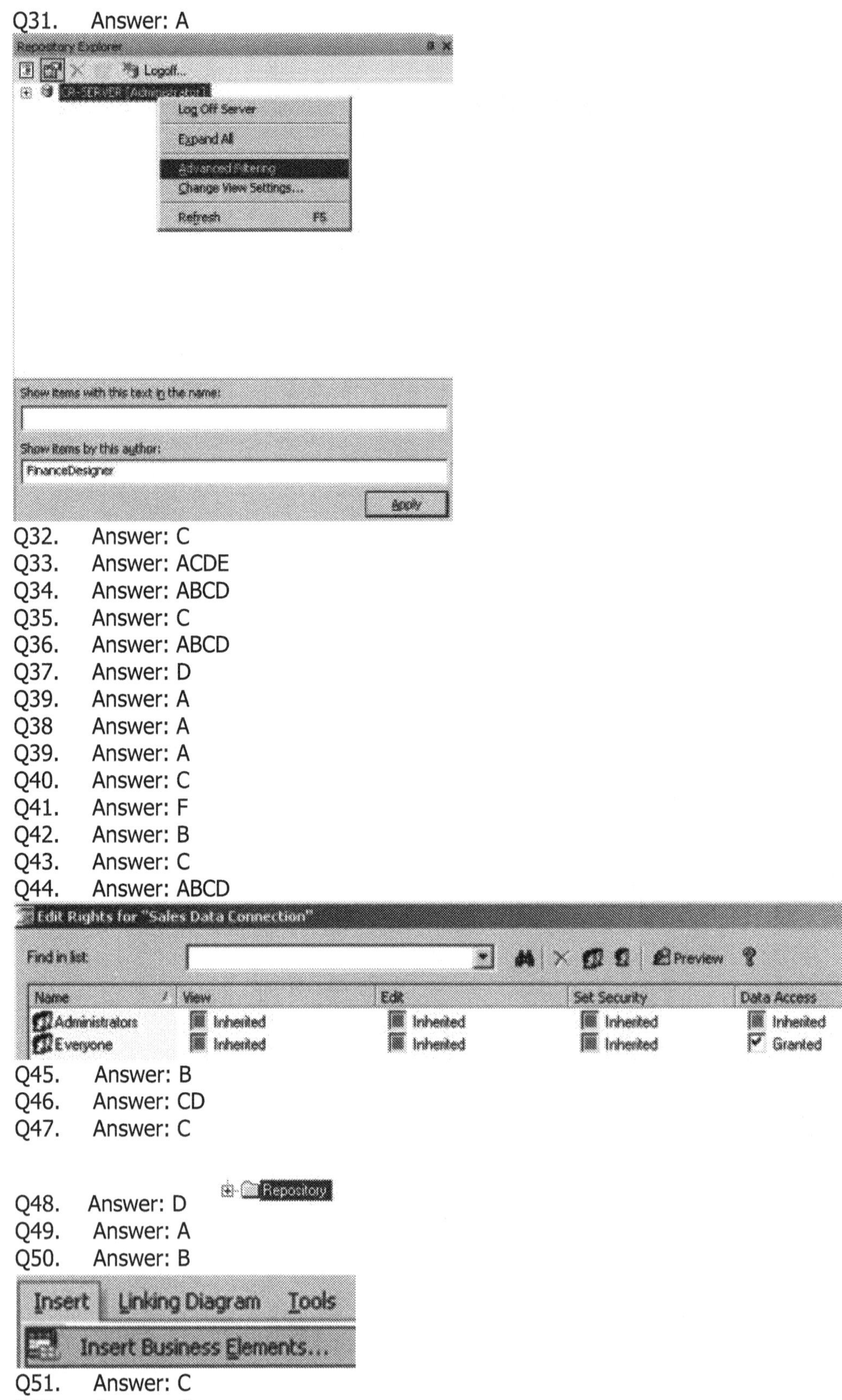

Q32. Answer: C
Q33. Answer: ACDE
Q34. Answer: ABCD
Q35. Answer: C
Q36. Answer: ABCD
Q37. Answer: D
Q39. Answer: A
Q38 Answer: A
Q39. Answer: A
Q40. Answer: C
Q41. Answer: F
Q42. Answer: B
Q43. Answer: C
Q44. Answer: ABCD

Q45. Answer: B
Q46. Answer: CD
Q47. Answer: C

Q48. Answer: D
Q49. Answer: A
Q50. Answer: B

Q51. Answer: C
Q52. Answer: C

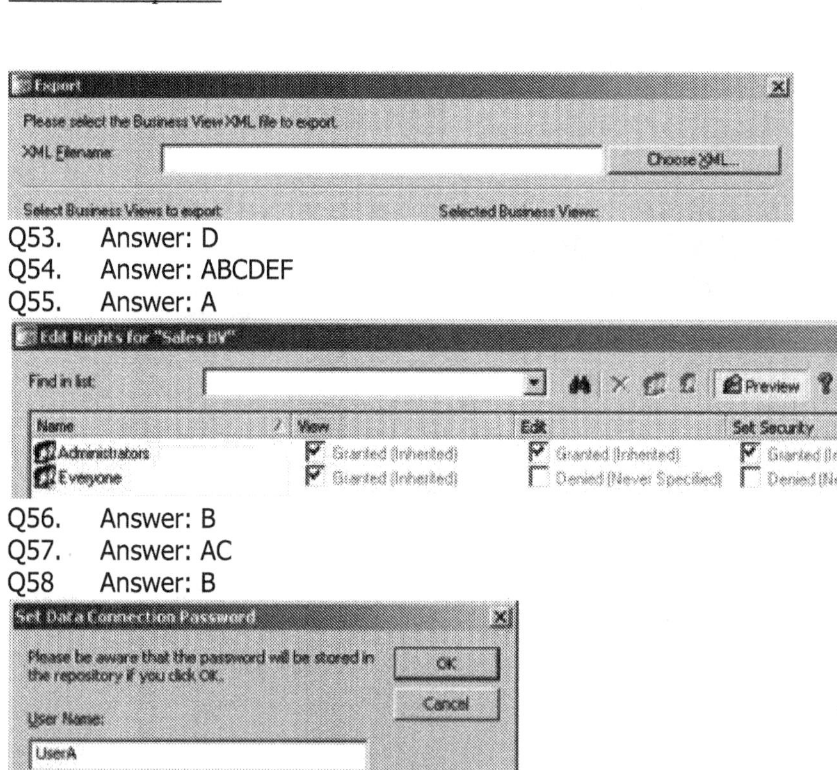

Q53. Answer: D
Q54. Answer: ABCDEF
Q55. Answer: A
Q56. Answer: B
Q57. Answer: AC
Q58 Answer: B

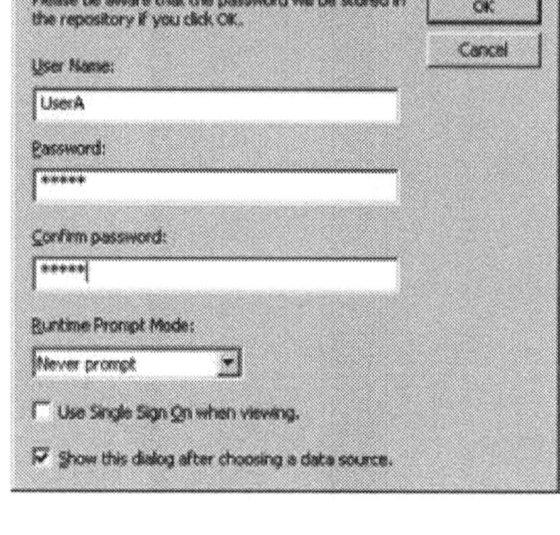

Q59. Answer: C

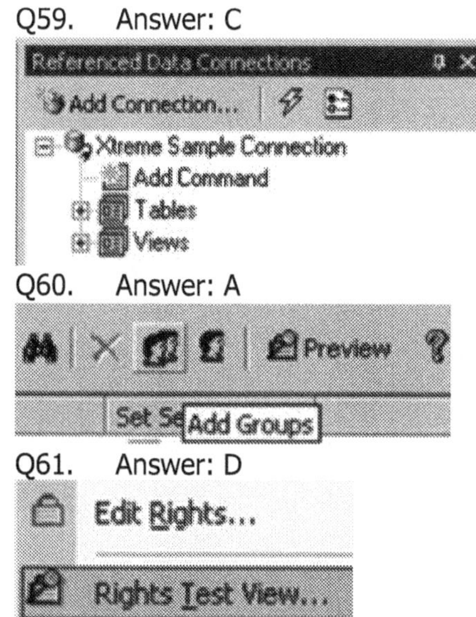

Q60. Answer: A
Q61. Answer: D

Q62. Answer: B
Q63. Answer: D
Q64. Answer: A
Q65. Answer: A
Q66. Answer: B 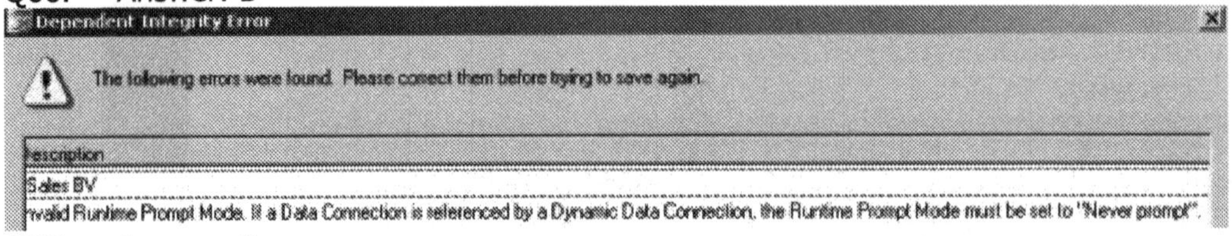
Q67. Answer: D
Q68. Answer: D
Q69. Answer: B
Q70. Answer: D 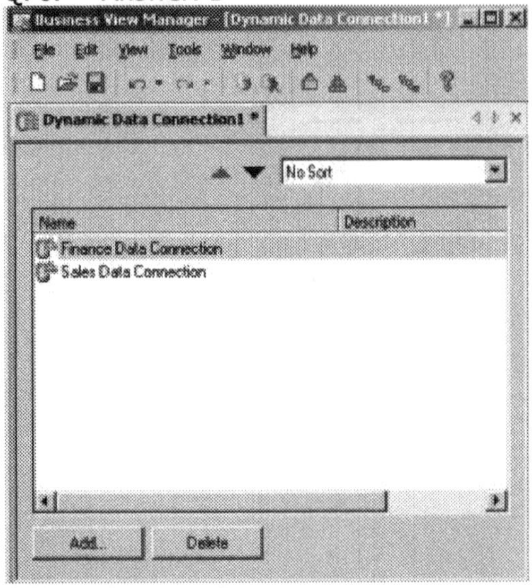
Q71. Answer: C
Q72. Answer: AD
Q73. Answer: B
Q74. Answer: A
Q75. Answer: C
Q76. Answer: ABCDEFG 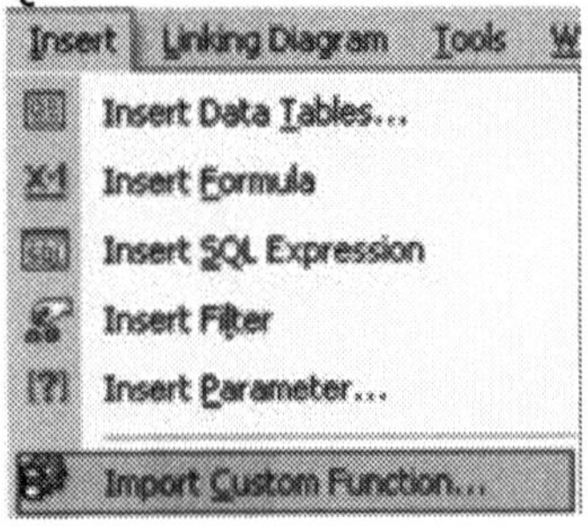
Q77. Answer: D

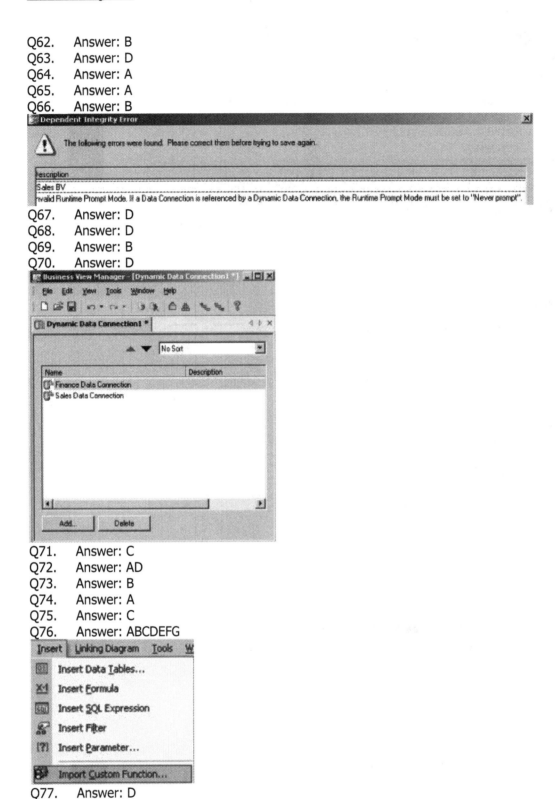

Q78. Answer: ABC

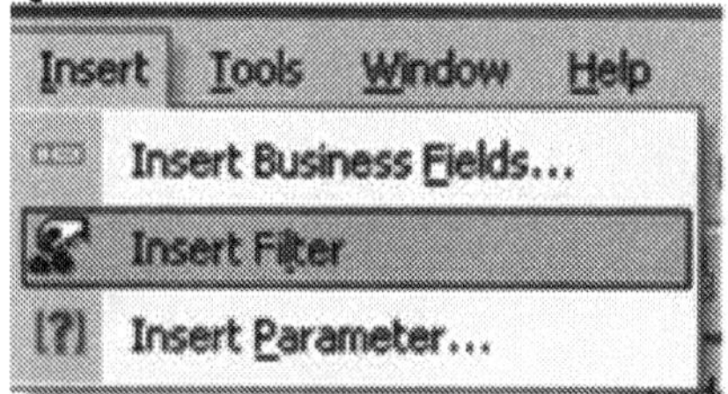

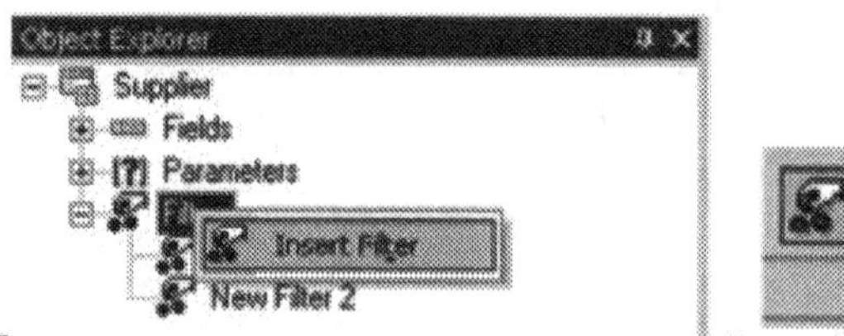

Q79. Answer: D
Q80. Answer: A
Q81. Answer: D

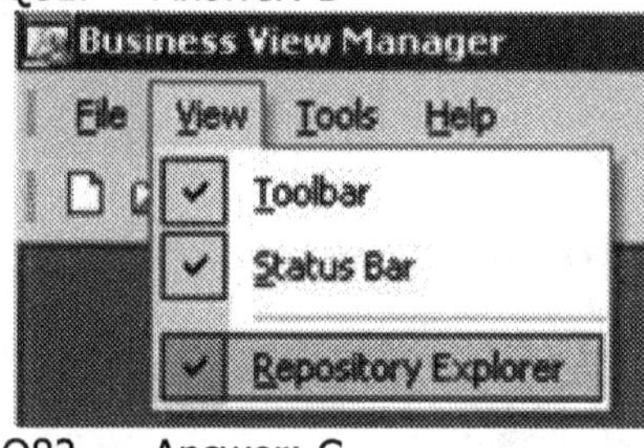

Q82. Answer: C

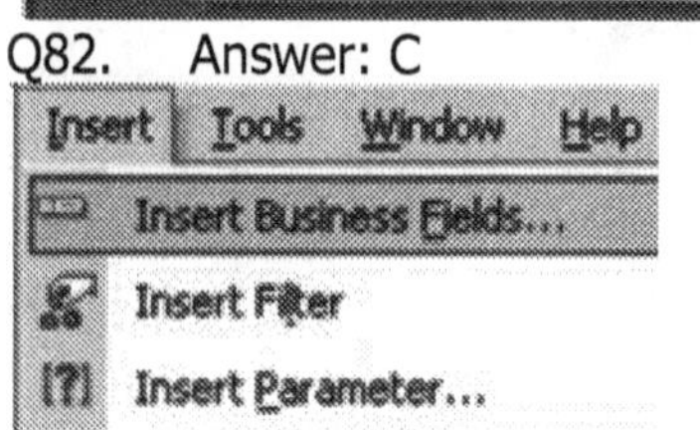

Q83. Answer: A
Q84. Answer: BC

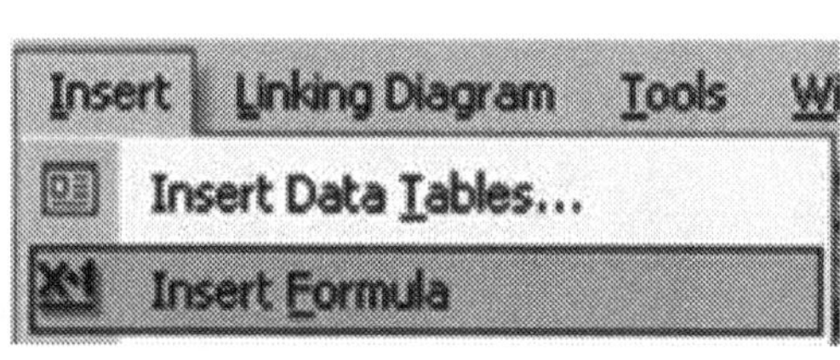

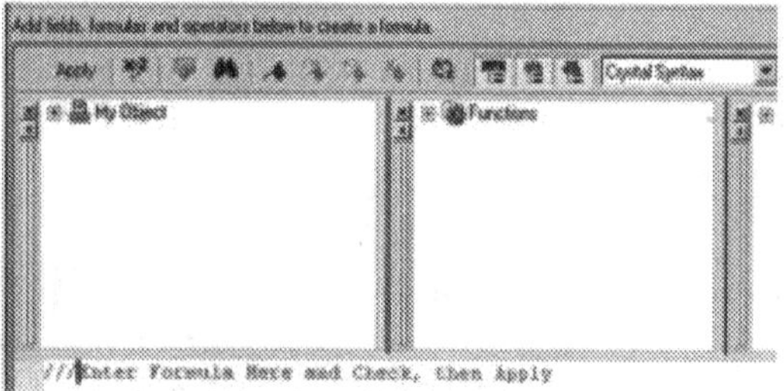

Q85. Answer: D
Q86. Answer: B

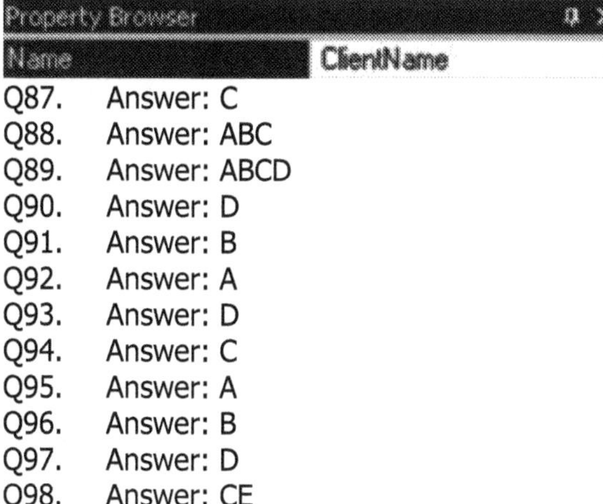

Q87. Answer: C
Q88. Answer: ABC
Q89. Answer: ABCD
Q90. Answer: D
Q91. Answer: B
Q92. Answer: A
Q93. Answer: D
Q94. Answer: C
Q95. Answer: A
Q96. Answer: B
Q97. Answer: D
Q98. Answer: CE

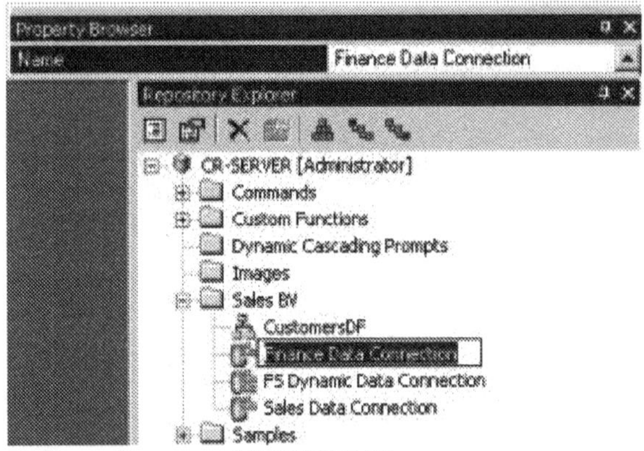

Q99. Answer: ABCDEFGHIJ

Q100. Answer: B

Q101. Answer: C

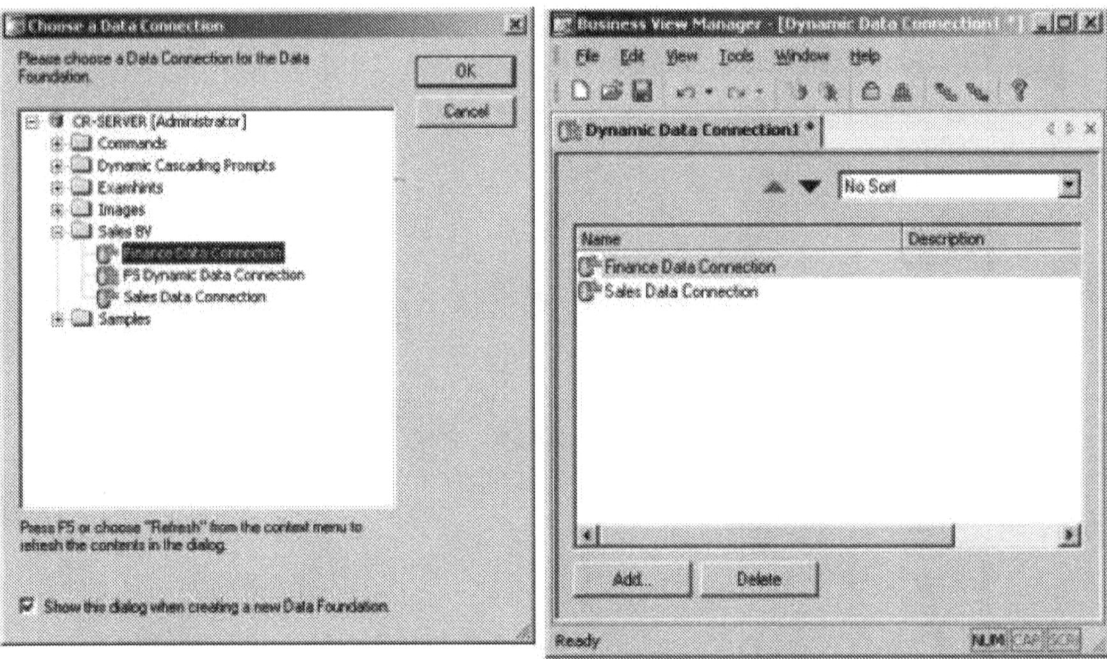

Q102. Answer: C

Q103. Answer: ABC

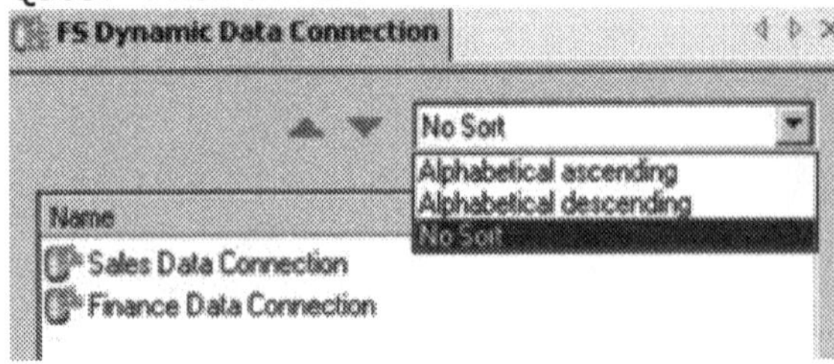

Q104. Answer: A

Q105. Answer: A

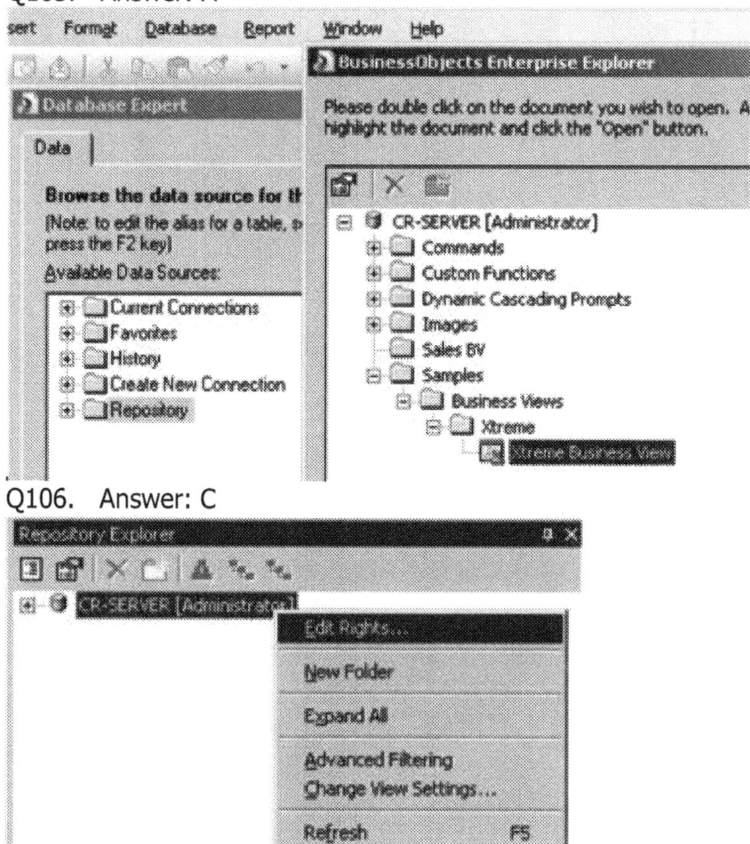

Q106. Answer: C

Q107. Answer: ABC

Q108 Answer: ABCDE

Answers: Chapter 16 Report Management

Q1. Answer: ABEFGH

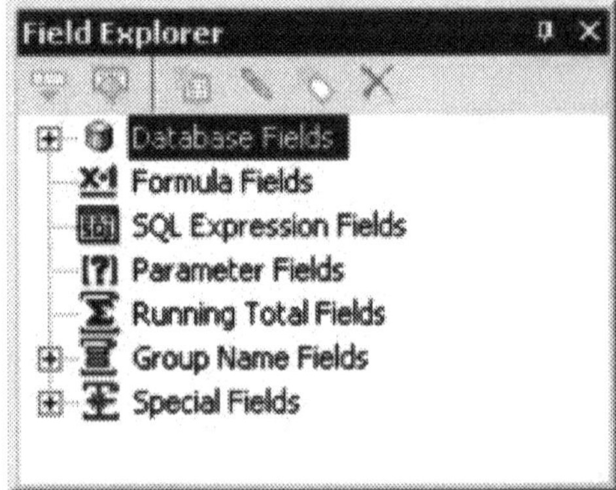

Q2. Answer: A

Q3. Answer: DI

Special Fields
- Content Locale
- Current CE User ID
- Current CE User Name
- Current CE User Time Zone
- Data Date
- Data Time
- Data Time Zone
- File Author
- File Creation Date
- File Path and Name
- Group Number
- Group Selection Formula
- Horizontal Page Number
- Modification Date
- Modification Time
- Page N of M
- Page Number
- Print Date
- Print Time
- Print Time Zone
- Record Number
- Record Selection Formula
- Report Comments
- Report Title
- Total Page Count

Q4. Answer: B

Q5. Answer: D

Q6. Answer: C

Q7. Answer: A

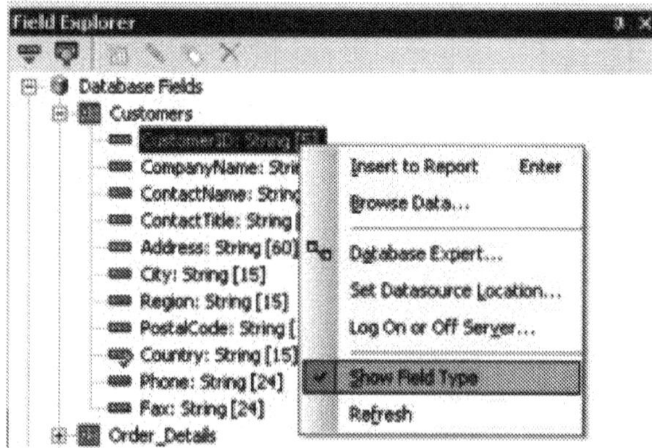

Q8. Answer: ABCDEF

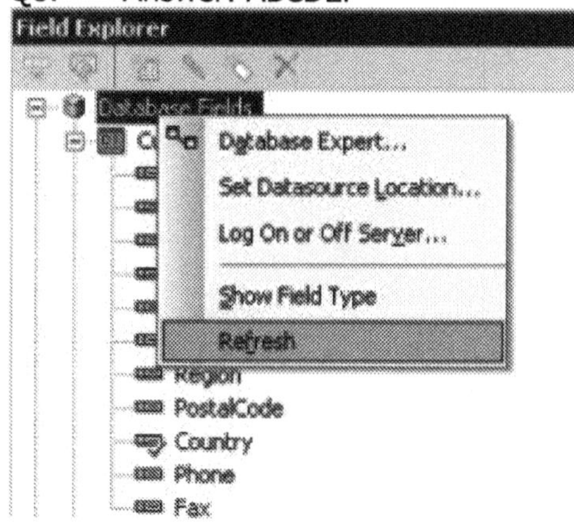

Q9. Answer: B

Group Name Fields
Group #1 Name: EXAMRECORDS.Exam_No
Group #2 Name: EXAMRECORDS.County

Q10. Answer: AB

Q11. Answer: B

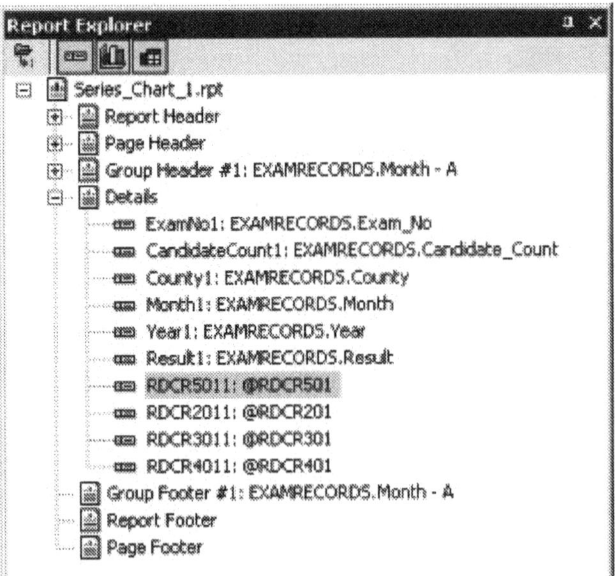

Q12. Answer: C

Q13. Answer: B

Q14. Answer: C

Q15. Answer: A

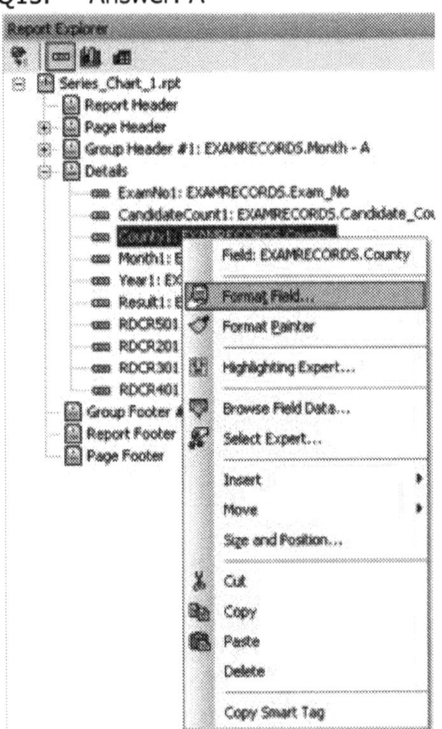

Q16. Answer: E

Q17. Answer: A

Q18. Answer: C

Q19. Answer: B

Q20. Answer: B

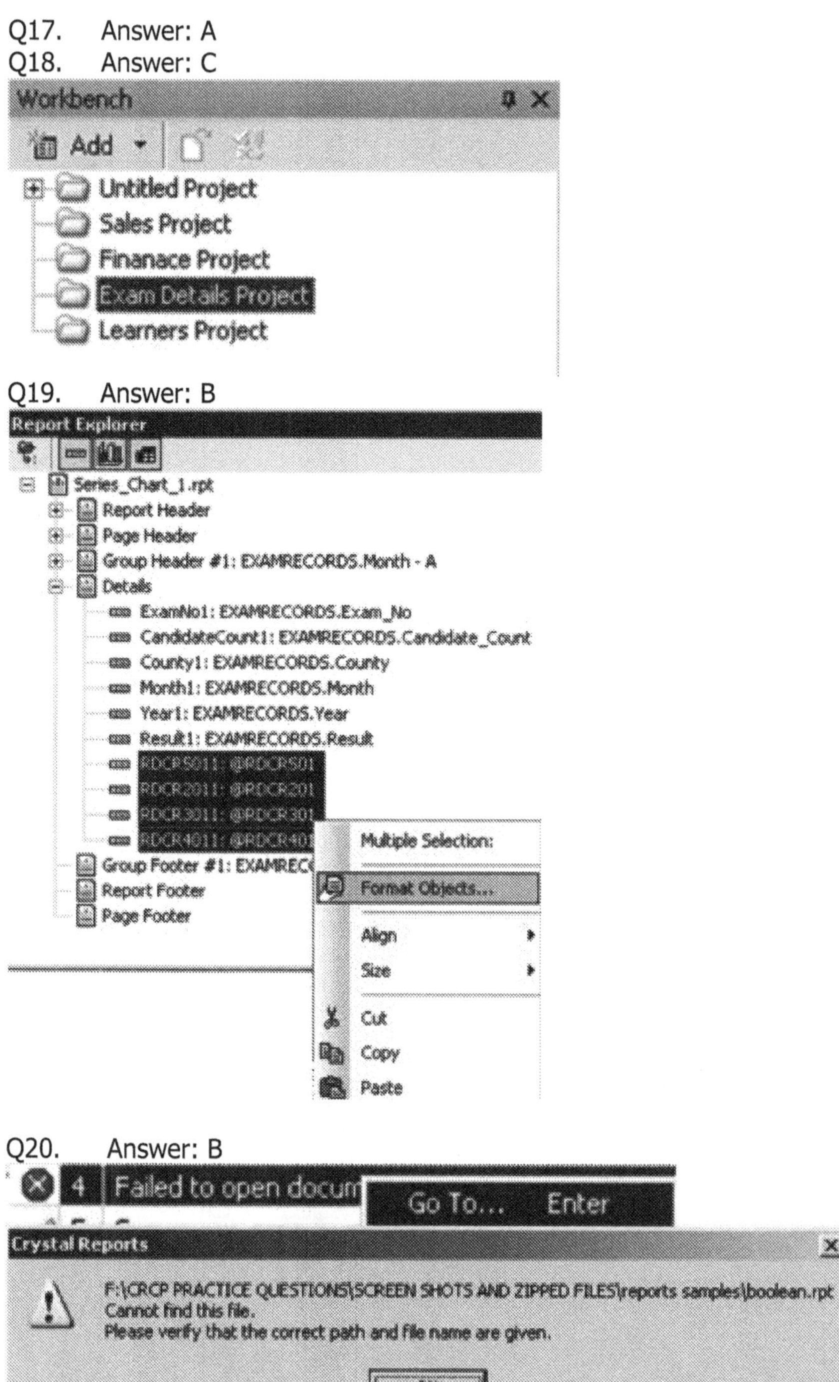

Q21. Answer: B

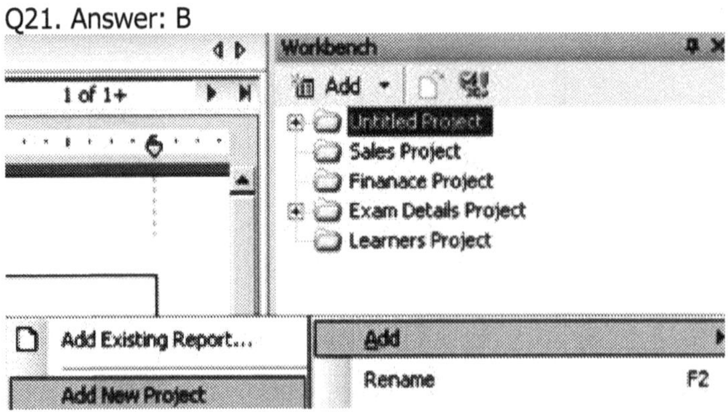

Q22. Answer: A

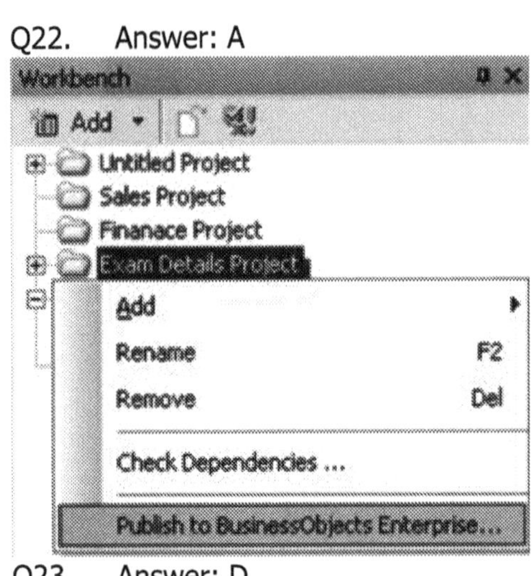

Q23. Answer: D
Q24. Answer: A
Q25. Answer: A
Q26. Answer: C
Q27. Answer B
Q28. Answer: D
Q29. Answer: B

Answers: Chapter 17 Building Reports – Lessons and Questions

Q1. Answer: ABCDEFG
Q2. Answer: ABCDFGH
Q3. Answer: ABCD
Q4. Answer: ABD
Q5. Answer: ADE
Q6. Answer: ABCDE
Q7. Answers: ABCEF
Q8. Answer: ABCDEG
Q9. Answer: ABCDEF

Creating An Alert - Reporting Requirements For Sample Report 3: Create Property Alert Report

Select Report from the menu, click Alerts - Create or Modify Alerts,
select New
Enter the name of the Alert e.g. 'Property Alert!!!'
In the Message section enter' There are properties which meet the buyers requirements'
Click the Condition Button and enter the following formula:
(tonumber({PROPETIES_FOR_SALE.NoOfRooms})in
{BUYERS.MinRoomsReq} to {BUYERS.MaxRoomsReq} and
{BUYERS.PropertyTypeReq} ={PROPETIES_FOR_SALE.PropertyType}
and {PROPETIES_FOR_SALE.Price} in {BUYERS.BuyerMin} to {BUYERS.BuyerMax})

Q10. What condition will create an alert for all the buyer's requirements and where should it be placed?

Q11. You have created a report, which alerts the Agent to properties within a Buyer's criteria, which properties will appear when the report is run for Buyer BRY009?

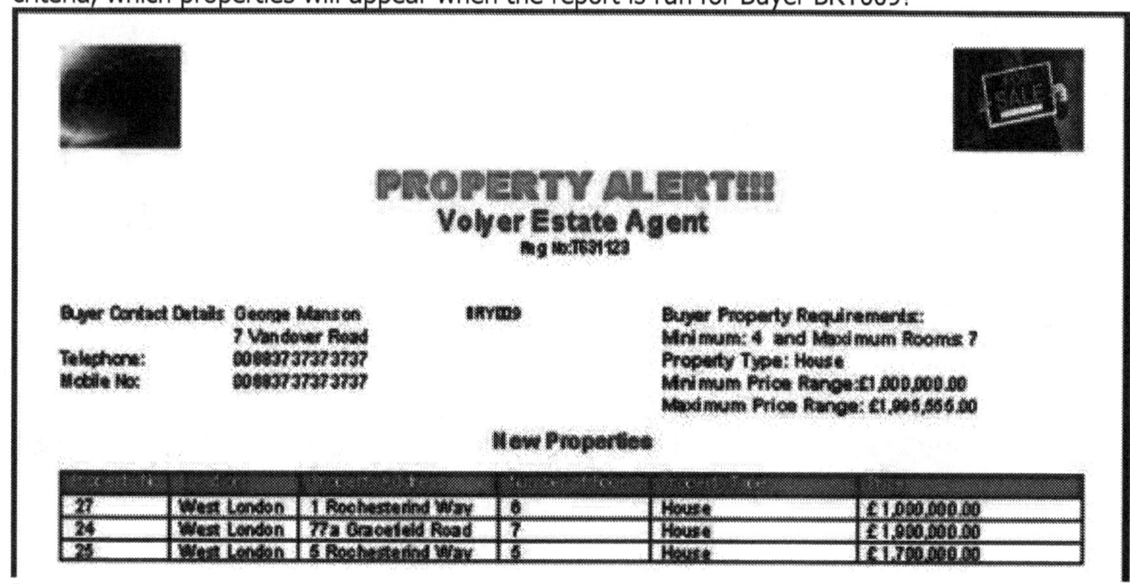

PROPERTY ALERT!!!
Volyer Estate Agent
Reg No:T631123

Buyer Contact Details George Manson
7 Vandover Road
Telephone: 00883737373737
Mobile No: 00883737373737

BRY009

Buyer Property Requirements:
Minimum: 4 and Maximum Rooms: 7
Property Type: House
Minimum Price Range:£1,000,000.00
Maximum Price Range: £1,995,555.00

New Properties

[illegible]	[illegible]	[illegible]	[illegible]	[illegible]	[illegible]
27	West London	1 Rochesterind Way	6	House	£ 1,000,000.00
24	West London	77a Gracefeld Road	7	House	£ 1,900,000.00
25	West London	5 Rochesterind Way	5	House	£ 1,700,000.00

Property 24, 25 and 27 as illustrated above

Q12. Which property must be set for the Property Alert to work?
A condition must be set

Q13. Your Property Alert does not work when you run the report, what could be the cause?
You have not enabled the condition

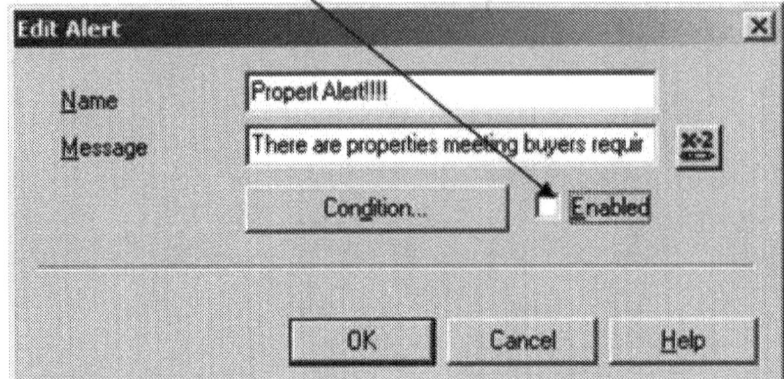

Q14. Using the SQL Command you want to create a query to extract Sold and Unsold Properties, add a field to the query named property status which will be populated with 'Sold Subject to Contract' if the result in the Viewers table is 'Sold' and 'Property For Sale' if the property is 'Unsold', which SQL Code is applicable?

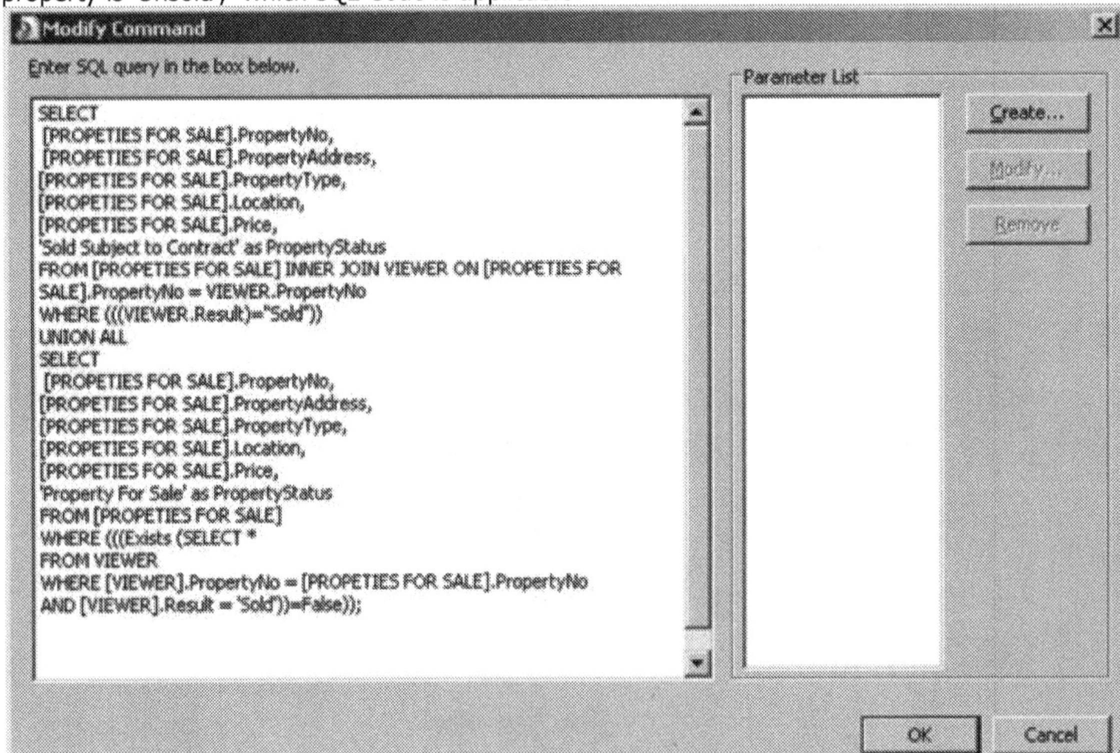

Q15. How can you edit the SQL Command to include a parameter, which prompts the user for a property location.

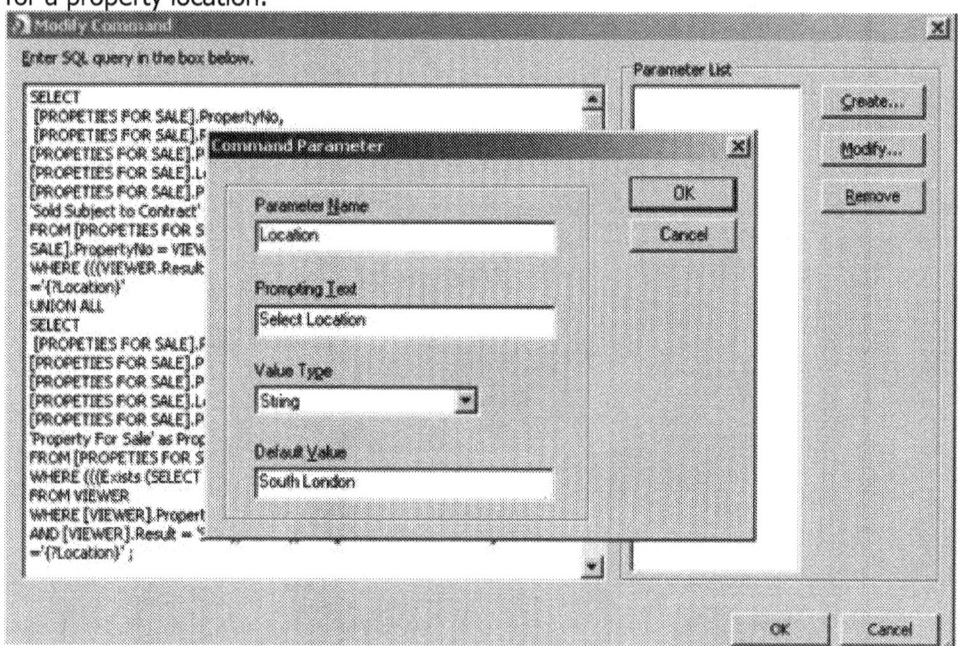

Click the create button and enter the parameter details, add the parameter within the where clause as follows, where location = {?Location} and click ok

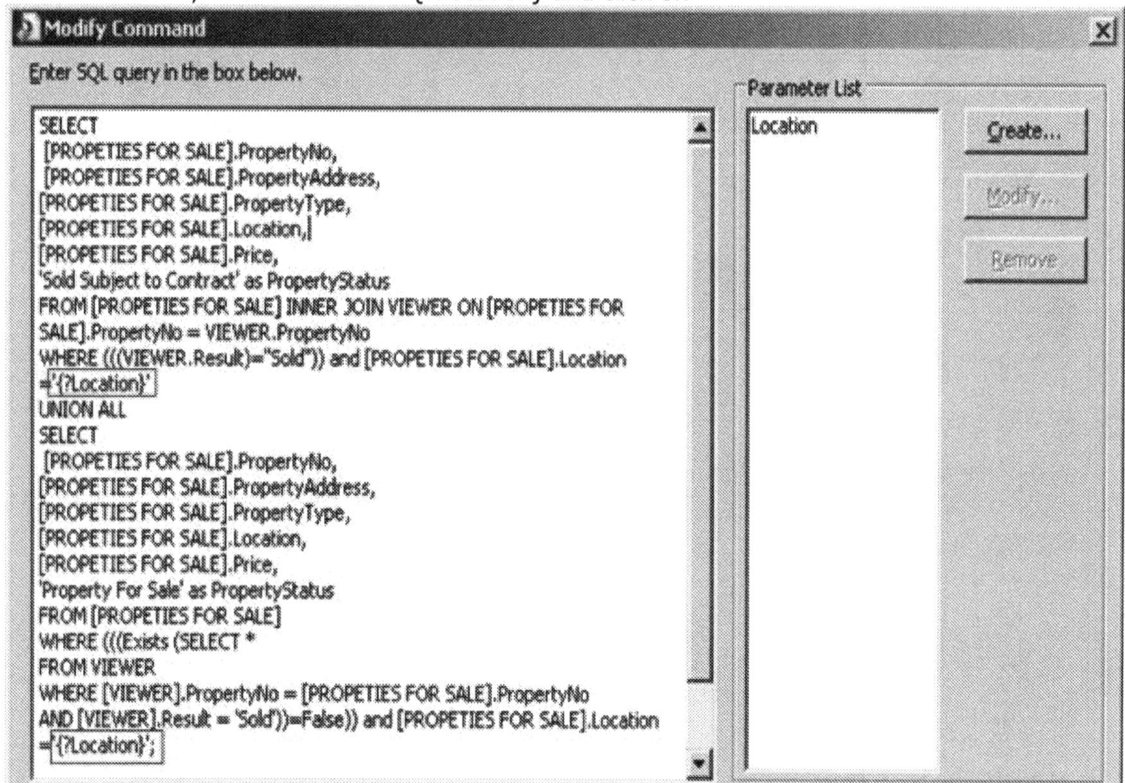

Q16. How would you assign a logical name to a SQL Command within the Database Expert?

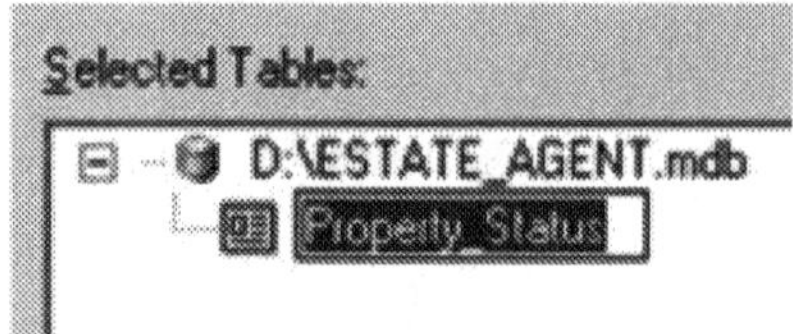

Q17. How would you add more values to the location parameter Default Values list

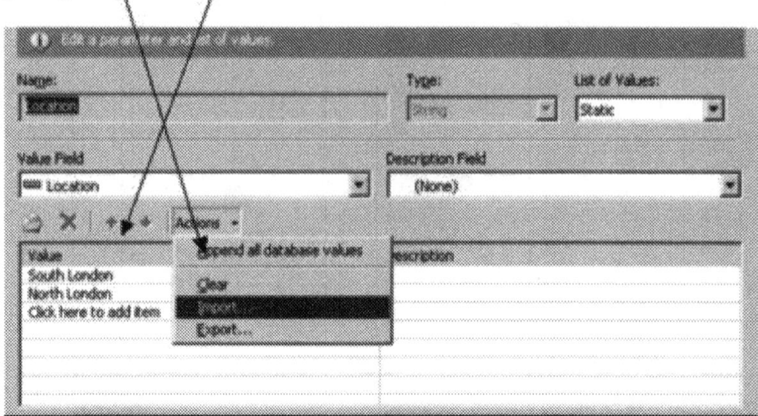

Q18. How would you add your SQL Command to the repository
Right-click and select Add to Repository from dropdown list, log into the Business Objects Enterprise Server and located the Folder required to save the SQL Command

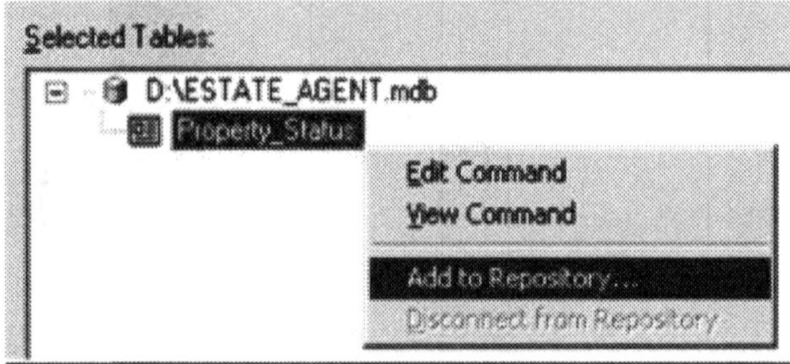

Q19. When designing a report which section should be our main work area when adding fields to the report?
Answer: A

Index

A

B

C

Index

D

E

Index

Index

Index

Index

About the Author

Antonia Iroko is the CEO of Projection Programmers Ltd - a Crystal Reports Consulting Company which over the years had provided consulting and training services to financial, banking, manufacturing, pharmaceutical fortune 500 companies both nationally and Internationally.

Antonia is the editor of the Examhints.com (http://www.examhints.com) which is one of the first websites to provide study guides for the Crystal Reports Certified Professional exams. Antonia has authored many customized training manuals for various companies, which are currently being used for user training.

Antonia graduated from the university of Nottingham with a BEng in Manufacturing Engineering and Operations Management and then went on to Study for an MSc in Computer Science. Antonia now provides business intelligence reporting consulting services to many financial companies. For consulting services visit http://www.projectionpro.com

www.ingramcontent.com/pod-product-compliance
Lightning Source LLC
Chambersburg PA
CBHW080146060326
40689CB00018B/3874
* 9 7 8 1 4 3 4 3 2 0 5 9 9 *